BEATRICE OJAKANGAS'
GREAT HOLIDAY BAKING BOOK

ALSO BY BEATRICE OJAKANGAS

Pot Pies

Scandinavian Feasts

Quick Breads

Light Desserts

The Great Scandinavian Baking Book

Country Tastes

Great Old-Fashioned American Desserts

New Ideas for Casseroles

Great Whole Grain Breads

Scandinavian Cooking

The Convection Oven Cookbook

The Best of the Liberated Cook

The Food Processor Bread Book

The Complete Fondue Menu and Party Book

Gourmet Cooking for Two

The Finnish Cookbook

BEATRICE OJAKANGAS'

Great Holiday Baking Book

CLARKSON POTTER/PUBLISHERS

NEW YORK

Published by Clarkson N. Potter, Inc., 201 East 50th Street, New York, New York 10022.
Member of the Crown Publishing Group.

Random House, Inc. New York, Toronto, London, Sydney, Auckland

CLARKSON N. POTTER, POTTER, and colophon
are trademarks of Clarkson N. Potter, Inc.

Manufactured in the United States of America
Design by Beth Tondreau Design

Library of Congress Cataloging-in-Publication Data
Ojakangas, Beatrice A.
    [Great Holiday Baking Book]
    Beatrice Ojakangas' Great Holiday Baking Book.—1st ed.
    Includes index.
    1. Baking. 2. Holiday Cookery   I. Title. II. Title: Great holiday baking book.
    TX763.O33   1994
    641.8´15—dc20   94-31425
                                                              CIP

ISBN 0-517-59330-0

10 9 8 7 6 5 4 3 2 1

First Edition

Dedicated to my family and extended family
with whom holidays come alive

Contents

Acknowledgments

Writing a book such as this is a journey. You start at one point and end at another. As I leapt from season to season and holiday to holiday, innumerable people contributed in various ways—from conversation to ideas, to recipes, to stories—at various turns along the way. Friends, family, extended family, and colleagues were incredibly generous and important to this book. I mention only a few.

Special thanks are due my husband, Richard, my children and their spouses, Cathy and Gerhard, Greg and Tracie, Susanna and Peter, whose constant interest and support kept me going. My son-in-law Gerhard's mom, "Hati" Friehs in Graz, Austria, collected all of her favorite baking recipes for me to review. Thanks go to my daughter Cathy for selecting a hundred of the best and to Gerhard, her husband, who faxed them all to me in a communication so long that my machine overheated and gave up until it could cool down. I wish I could have used them all! And then my daughter Susanna spent hours in an Iowa library researching holidays of the world, after which my manuscript ballooned out beyond all reason.

My son-in-law Peter lifted my spirits every time he would taste something and say, "This is the best thing I've ever eaten!" Then my son, Greg (with his analytical mind), spent hours with me trying to describe in words the complicated twists and turns in shaping various bread and cookie doughs. Thanks go to my daughter-in-law, Tracie, who helped me organize my year of holidays and who added stories, lore, and ideas from her life. This has truly been a family affair!

Thanks to my mother-in-law, Grace Wold, who loves to search cookbooks and magazines. And to my mother, Esther Luoma, who loves the challenge of locating a recipe we haven't thought of for years.

My thanks for the graciousness of my friends, from whom I "disappeared" for about half a year to work on this book and who will still take me back.

I'm grateful to a superb Duluthian and baker and cook, Marge Portella, who gen-erously volunteered her favorite Jewish recipes, along with her descriptions of special holidays. Thanks to Laurie Erickson for suggesting her. Thanks to Peg Fox, my longtime friend who teaches very popular classes in fancy cookie making, for sharing her recipes and ideas.

Thanks to my colleagues, especially Linda Funk at Wisconsin Dairies, the Twin Cities HEIBs, members of the IACP, the home economists at Pillsbury, Land O Lakes, and numerous others who share with me the newest in baking information.

Not the least of all, after all this information gathering, I owe a great debt of gratitude to my agent, Elise Simon Goodman, without whose "push" this manuscript wouldn't be done yet. I then handed it over to my able and talented editor, Katie Workman, who managed to cut and mold and rework the text and recipes so that they would actually fit between two covers as they appear here: a complete book.

BEATRICE OJAKANGAS'
GREAT HOLIDAY BAKING BOOK

Introduction

Our years are punctuated by holidays. Holidays keep us going; they give us something to look forward to and something to look back at. Holidays are memory makers. They are full of tradition, and tradition is often tied to special foods, most of the time baked treats.

When I reflect on my history of holiday baking, I feel very grateful for my simple Finnish heritage based on immigrant cuisine. Holidays didn't have to be ten thousand things on the table. One or two fine specialties were enough. Usually there was a bread, but often there were cookies, and maybe a cake, too. At Christmastime we baked Pulla, perhaps a Swedish Tea Ring or Finnish Prune Tarts, and some butter cookies. Around Easter, there was always a symbolic braided bread wreath

with eggs, and a seasonal sweet, such as a strawberry pie.

As I grew up, I met people who weren't Finnish or even Scandinavian, and found that for special occasions they baked specialties that were far more elaborate than what I had known. This was exciting! Soon I had added volumes of cakes, pastries, breads, and cookies to my repertoire. After the examples from friends came the inspiration from the world of cookbooks. I love the fact that whatever your heritage, whatever the occasion, there are a multitude of baked goods, either traditional or innovative, that make the holiday memorable and special.

So, when I began writing this book, I thought it would be a snap. My files were bulging with recipes from classes I'd taught, parties I'd had, articles I'd written, and recipes I'd invented just for the fun of it. The more I dug in, the more I found. Finally, 250 recipes later, I had to force myself to call it quits. It wasn't the gathering of recipes that was a problem; it was the cutting! There will always be just one more recipe to add, but this book had truly become a comprehensive collection of old favorites and new renditions.

Due to many factors, the way we bake has changed a lot over the years. We have many technical conveniences that didn't exist even ten or fifteen years ago. Our ovens are more consistent, and we use food processors, microwave ovens, minichoppers, and dough hooks in our heavy-duty electric mixers. We have busier schedules and less time to spend in the kitchen, although the holidays certainly give us an excuse to throw on an apron and devote a few enjoyable hours to creat-

ing a delicious treat. These technological advances have called for changes in preparation methods; I use the food processor for making pastry, kneading bread (with the dough blade), chopping, puréeing, mixing ingredients, and smoothing out batters. Whenever I can, I include food processor directions in a recipe. The microwave oven, too, is a timesaver, and cuts down on dirty pots and pans as well! Each piece of equipment has its advantages, and if we make bread more often because we have the convenience of a dough hook, then let's hear it for progress.

Our tastes and dietary concerns have changed, too, and although this is by no means a low-calorie/low-fat book, I have made adjustments in the recipes to include less fat and sugar when appropriate. Obviously, there's no substitute for fresh whipped cream or a buttercream frosting that will make you sigh with pleasure.

Another contemporary concern is how much can be done ahead of time. Holidays are a wonderful time to get busy in the kitchen, but often there are other demands on our time. Many baked goods can be prepared in advance, sometimes months ahead. Throughout the book I give instructions for storing, freezing, and thawing and serving foods. You will also find tips for wrapping cookies, cakes, and other items to freeze, to transport, and to give as gifts. In the boxes sprinkled throughout the chapters, I have tried to address the holiday baker's concerns and to offer information that will make being in the kitchen more fun and easier than ever before.

Writing this book has been a stroll down memory lane, and I have had countless hours of enjoyment going through all of the ideas and recipes that have filled my folders and drawers for years. I hope this book provides you with many ideas for ways to celebrate. And I sincerely hope that this book inspires you to take up your spoon and travel to the kitchen to create holiday memories for years to come.

ABOUT INGREDIENTS

Freshness of ingredients is perhaps the most important component of baking. Use the highest quality ingredients available; as the old saying goes, you can't make a silk purse out of a sow's ear.

Economy goes hand-in-hand with the sensible management of ingredients. There's no use buying in quantity if left-over-ingredients will get stale or rancid.

EGGS

An important ingredient in baking, eggs provide structure and volume and help to bind ingredients. The recipes in this book were tested with large eggs. Use clean, fresh eggs with no cracks. Fresh eggs have yolks that are firm and rounded and whites that are thick and clear. Store eggs in the refrigerator to preserve their freshness and to prevent the growth of bacteria.

To separate eggs: When separating eggs, first wash the eggs in your hands. Tap the egg with a knife or on the side of a bowl or cup. Pull apart the two halves and pass the yolk from one side to another, catching the egg white in a bowl or cup placed beneath the egg. Inspect the whites for any flecks of yolk, because even a small speck of yolk in the white will prevent egg whites from beating until stiff. Specks of egg yolk can be removed with the tip of a spoon or the shell.

To freeze extra separated egg whites and yolks: To freeze whites, place in a sealable container, label, date, and freeze. Thawed, egg whites that have been frozen for up to 3 months can be used in the same way as fresh whites. To freeze egg yolks, place in a sealable container. Add ½ teaspoon salt or 3 teaspoons sugar to each ½ cup of raw egg yolks and mix well. Seal the container, label, date, and freeze. Thawed egg yolks that have been frozen for up to 3 months can be used in baking.

Fat-free and cholesterol-free egg products are made with egg whites and usually contain no fat or less fat than whole, fresh eggs. When substituting these products for fresh eggs, measure ¼ cup for each egg in the recipe. Do not use these egg products when making cream puffs or popovers because they will neither puff nor pop.

FLOUR

Store all flour in airtight containers to protect the flour from moisture, which can affect the quality and performance of the flour, and insects.

All-Purpose Flour: This type of flour is most often called for in everything from delicate pastries to breads. It has eleven or twelve grams of protein per cup. Buy unbleached all-purpose flour, if possible.

Bread Flour: This has a higher protein count (thirteen to fourteen grams per cup) than all-purpose flour and creates a more elastic dough and thus a chewier texture, which is desirable in bread recipes.

Cake Flour: Having only 4 to 9 percent protein, cake flour is made from soft wheat and produces tender, flaky pastries and crusts.

Whole Wheat Flour: Wheat germ as well as the natural bran of the grain are milled into this flour, also called graham flour, and while it does not have quite as much protein as all-purpose flour, it has additional nutrients such as niacin and iron, which have to be added to white flours during the milling process.

SWEETENERS

Granulated Sugar: When sugar is called for, use granulated. Sugar is processed from either sugarcane or sugarbeets, which have no difference in quality or performance. It should be stored in an airtight container to prevent lumps, which can be removed by passing sugar through a strainer.

Brown Sugar: I keep both light and dark brown sugars on hand. Dark brown sugar has a slightly stronger flavor because it contains more molasses than light brown sugar. Keep brown sugar in a container with a tight-fitting lid, which should keep it from drying out. To soften brown sugar that has become hard, place a piece of apple in the container with the sugar; it should soften up in just a few hours.

Superfine Sugar: This fine sugar is ideal for meringues and some cakes.

Confectioners' Sugar: This powdered sugar is finely ground sugar containing cornstarch for ease in mixing and blending. It packs into lumps easily, which can be removed by sifting it through a wire strainer once.

Pearl Sugar: I often use this sugar to decorate the tops of sweet breads and cookies; it is frequently used in Scandinavian baking. Pearl sugar looks like coarsely crushed sugar cubes.

Corn Syrup: Available in light and dark forms, corn syrup is thick and sweet, but dark syrup has a stronger flavor.

Honey: Thick and sweet, honey is made by bees from flower nectar. It adds distinct flavor to baked goods. If it crystallizes, it can be returned to the liquid condition by warming it up gently over low heat.

BAKING SODA

This is the kitchen name for sodium bicarbonate, and, when combined with acid ingredients, it generates carbon dioxide bubbles, which cause dough to rise.

BAKING POWDER

This creates carbon dioxide when combined with water, and the bubbles of the carbon dioxide cause the dough to rise.

YEAST

Yeast is a living organism that leavens bread by causing the sugars that are found in flour to become little bubbles of carbon dioxide. When the bread is baked, the bubbles expand and cause the bread to get bigger and lighter. I use dry yeast, either regular or fast-acting, which can be stored at cool room temperature. Be sure to check the date on the package; yeast that's past its prime won't do anything.

SPICES

Spices can get old and tasteless very quickly. It is good to replenish your supply frequently, preferably every four to six months. Try to find a bulk supplier, so you can buy only the amount you need and cut down on waste. Smell a spice to see if it still has punch. Some spices, like cardamom and nutmeg, lose their flavor very quickly when ground, so it is best to grind them yourself as you need them.

MILK

You may use any kind of milk in these recipes, keeping in mind that the richer the milk, the richer the final product will be. Evaporated, condensed, and instant dry milk will keep indefinitely on the shelf. Evaporated milk used cup for cup in bread recipes will give the bread extra nutritional value and a very nice crumb. Evaporated milk can also be diluted to the strength of regular milk, using a mixture of half evaporated milk, half water. Follow the directions on the package for reconstituting dry milk or buttermilk.

BUTTERS, OILS, AND OTHER FATS
Fats tenderize, bind ingredients, add flavor, and produce browning in baked goods. The most important fats used in baking today are the following:

Butter: Available salted or unsalted in 1-pound cubes, quarter-pound (½ cup) sticks (which are usually marked off into tablespoons, 8 per stick), or, whipped, in tubs. Whipped butter, because it contains a large amount of air, should be measured by weight rather than volume when used in baked recipes. Recipes in this book call for unsalted butter so that the amount of salt can be controlled in each product.

Margarine: Available salted or unsalted in quarter-pound sticks and, whipped, in tubs. Margarine can be substituted for butter in many recipes, but because it is made from a variety of oils (including corn oil, vegetable oil, and soybean oil) and has been processed into varying hardnesses, it produces different results from butter. There is also a flavor difference. Whipped margarine, because it contains a large amount of air and water to soften it, should not be used for baking.

Lard: Pure pork fat that has been processed and refined, lard is most often used in pie crusts because it is softer and creates a flakier crust than do other fats.

Lowfat or Reduced-Fat Margarines: These cannot be used in baking because they have water added to them and will offset the balance of a recipe.

Vegetable Oils: Pressed from a variety of vegetables and nuts, these oils offer a special texture and flavor to baked goods. Use oils only in recipes that call specifically for them.

Vegetable Shortening: A solid shortening made from vegetable oils by hydrogenation, vegetable shortenings are flavorless, although some have butter flavor added.

Nonstick Vegetable Spray: Providing an easy and effective way to coat baking pans, this spray works on even the fanciest mold, getting into all the crevices.

Tools and Equipment

MEASURING EQUIPMENT

MEASURING CUPS

Liquid measuring cups range from 1 cup to 1 quart or larger. Liquid measures generally are see-through glass or plastic and have an allowance on top of the measure.

Dry measures are for measuring flour, sugar, and other dry ingredients. The measures are level to the top of the cup; when measuring dry ingredients, the cup should be heaped full, then leveled off using the straight edge of a knife or spatula. I like to keep a chopstick in the sugar and flour bins to use for leveling the top of each cupful. Dry measures usually come in sets that include 1 cup, ½ cup, ⅓ cup, ¼ cup, and sometimes ⅛ cup level measures.

MEASURING SPOONS

These usually come in sets that include 1 tablespoon, 1 teaspoon, ½ teaspoon, and ¼ teaspoon measures; occasionally a ½ tablespoon measure (1½ teaspoons) and a ⅛ teaspoon measure are included. The measures are level. Scoop the dry ingredient to be measured so that the spoon is heaped, then level off with a straight edge. Measuring spoons are used for both dry and liquid measures. If a recipe calls for both dry and liquid ingredients to be measured, measuring the dry before the liquid will save washing and drying the spoons in between.

COOKING SCALES

A good balance scale is the most accurate way to measure ingredients, but it is time consuming. I find my scale handiest for weighing fruits and vegetables. A smaller scale that measures ounces and grams in delicate small increments is handy, too, when you are given a weight measurement for an ingredient, particularly in foreign cookbooks. I often measure messy things like bulk shortenings on a piece of plastic wrap on a small ounce scale to save me from scraping out a measuring cup.

THERMOMETERS

An instant-reading thermometer is a great help for measuring the temperature of water for yeast breads, dough temperatures, and for measuring the doneness of a loaf of bread. A candy thermometer is necessary for measuring the temperature of sugar syrups and jellies.

MIXING TOOLS AND MACHINERY

MIXING BOWLS

I find a nest of stainless steel mixing bowls and a nest of glass mixing bowls to be very useful. The variety of sizes is necessary, and the fact that they stack makes storage easy.

WOODEN SPOONS, SPATULAS

I have a selection of assorted sizes of wooden spoons for mixing, and a bunch of different-size rubber spatulas. I keep them handy in crocks. When buying rubber spatulas, check that they are heat proof.

ELECTRIC MIXERS

A heavy-duty hand-held mixer is indispensable for mixing doughs as well as whipping and beating eggs, cream, and the like. A heavy duty standing electric mixer with a dough hook, a dough paddle, and whisk attachments is a great help to the baker. If possible, invest in a second bowl for the machine. I like KitchenAid best.

FOOD PROCESSORS

I have two on my counter and usually have both going when I'm baking full swing. The most important thing is to invest in a high-quality food processor with a good, strong motor, such as Cuisinart. I use a dough blade (the short, stubby plastic blade) for mixing a wide variety of yeast doughs. The metal blade is great for cutting shortening into flour (as for pie crust and pastries). It saves an incredible amount of time to chop nuts and other ingredients using the metal blade.

SIFTERS

I do not use an old-fashioned sifter; instead I put dry ingredients into a wire strainer and stir them through into the creamed mixture. The dry ingredients become mixed, and any hard lumps in the flour or baking powder are broken down.

Baking Pans

baking sheets

I prefer shiny, aluminum, noninsulated pans for baking cookies and freeform breads and coffee cakes. The popular insulated pans cause the tops to brown before the bottoms do, and dark-surfaced and nonstick pans brown the food on the bottom before the top is done, so either type requires adjusting the baking time. I have tested all of the recipes in this book using noninsulated pans. For easy cleanup, I line the pans with parchment paper, a trick I learned from professional bakers.

I use baking sheets that have no sides to them. Jelly roll pans have sides, but many home bakers refer to them as cookie sheets. The sides on jelly roll pans inhibit the circulation of the air around cookies as they bake, so your baking time may be a little longer than when you bake cookies on a rimless sheet, Jelly roll pans are perfect for bar cookies, and of course, rolled cakes.

Baking pans come in standard sizes. For perfect results, it is important that you use the type and size called for in the recipe. If you don't, adjust the baking time accordingly. The types and sizes of pans used most often in this book include:

8- or 9-inch square pan

8- or 9-inch round cake pan

$5\frac{3}{4} \times 3\frac{1}{2}$-inch loaf pan

$8\frac{1}{2} \times 4\frac{1}{2}$-inch loaf pan

9×5-inch loaf pan

9-inch pie pan

10-inch springform pan

10-inch tart pan with
removable sides

12-cup fancy tube pan

16-cup angel food pan

13×9-inch rectangular cake pan

$15 \times 10 \times 1$-inch jelly roll pan
or cookie sheet

17×14-inch rimless cookie sheet

Ovens

Baking times and temperatures usually vary a little from one oven to another, which is more important when baking delicate things such as hard meringues, where the difference between gas and electric ovens can affect the baking time. I use an electric oven. If you have a gas oven with a pilot light, a meringue (such as for pavlova) might brown too much if allowed to sit in the oven overnight. The baking time may need to be shortened and the baking temperature, lowered. Convection ovens are ovens that have a fan to circulate the heat in the oven, which means the baking time will be shorter. I have not used a convection oven to test recipes in this book; so if you have one, begin checking the baked good earlier than the suggested time.

MICROWAVE OVEN

While I seldom bake or cook in the microwave oven, I would be at a loss without it. I use my microwave oven to warm ingredients, to soften or melt butter, to melt chocolate, to heat liquids, to cook syrups, and a zillion other tasks, which saves me from waiting for a burner to heat up, from burned bottoms, and from washing extra pots and pans.

St. Patrick's Day

Irish Beer Bread

This is a quick bread that's great for snacking or for serving with a meal. The bread is delicious served warm from the oven or served at room temperature.

2   cups whole wheat flour
2   cups all-purpose flour
4   teaspoons baking powder
½   teaspoon baking soda
1   teaspoon salt
½   cup (1 stick) unsalted butter, cut into pieces
1   large egg, beaten
1½ cups (one 12-ounce bottle) beer

Preheat the oven to 375°F. Lightly grease two 8- or 9-inch round cake pans.

In a large bowl, combine the flours, baking powder, baking soda, and salt. Cut the butter into the dry ingredients until completely blended in. Add the egg and beer all at once and mix until a stiff dough is formed. If mixing by hand, turn out onto a floured board and knead until smooth, 1 to 2 minutes.

Divide the dough into 2 parts. Shape each into a round loaf; place each loaf into the pan. Press down to flatten until each loaf is about 7 inches in diameter. With a sharp knife, slash a deep cross in the top of each loaf, making the cuts ⅓ inch deep and about 5 inches long.

Bake for 35 to 40 minutes or until a wooden skewer inserted in the center of the loaf comes out clean and dry.

Makes 2 loaves

ST. PATRICK'S DAY (MARCH 17)

This holiday is named after St. Patrick, the British-born monk who is credited with driving the snakes out of Ireland. Patrick converted the Irish to Christianity and is said to have used the green shamrock (which means "little clover" in Gaelic) as a visual aid to illustrate the doctrine of the trinity, three holy entities in one. As a result, the shamrock and the color green have become symbols of St. Patrick's Day.

St. Joseph's Day

St. Joseph's Day Pastries

Although there are many different kinds of Italian pastries consumed on St. Joseph's Day, these are a favorite. They're basically doughnut-shaped cream puffs that are either baked or fried and filled with sweetened and flavored ricotta cheese.

Pastry

    1   cup water
    ½   cup (1 stick) unsalted butter
    ½   teaspoon salt
    1   cup all purpose flour
    4   large eggs
    1   tablespoon sugar
    1   tablespoon grated lemon zest
        Vegetable oil, for frying (optional)
        Confectioners' sugar, for sifting

Ricotta Fruit Filling

    2   cups ricotta cheese
    3   tablespoons miniature semisweet chocolate chips
    2   tablespoons chopped candied orange peel
    3   tablespoons sugar
    2   tablespoons rum

Make the pastry. In a large saucepan, combine the water, butter, and salt. Heat to boiling over medium-high heat. Add

ST. JOSEPH'S DAY (MARCH 19)

Christians believe that Joseph was the husband of Mary (who was the mother of Jesus) and the foster father of Jesus. He was a descendant of King David and was, by trade, a carpenter, which is why he has been made the patron saint of the carpenters, of the Sicilian city Palermo, of the poor, and of the home and family.

St. Joseph's Day is observed in areas where there is a prominent Italian population—such as southern California, Chicago, and Detroit—with religious plays and processions. All sorts of foods, including fruits, fresh and cooked vegetables, pasta, fish, cakes, cookies, and breads, are part of the feast of St. Joseph. A sesame seed–coated bread baked in various shapes (for example, a long, hooked staff or cane; a crown; a small cross; or little, round loaves) is part of the celebration. Desserts consist of rich Italian pastries, which may or may not be filled with whipped cream and fruit.

the flour all at once, turn the heat to low, and beat vigorously until the mixture leaves the sides of the pan and comes together in a ball. Remove from the heat; beat and cool the mixture for 5 minutes. Add the eggs one at a time, beating well after each addition until the mixture is smooth and satiny. Add the sugar and lemon zest and mix until smooth and glossy. Let the dough stand for 10 minutes before shaping.

Preheat the oven to 375°F or heat several inches of oil in a deep fryer or saucepan to 370°F. Fill a pastry bag fitted with a ½-inch tip with the dough. Press the dough into 12 doughnut-shaped rings onto a baking sheet that has been lightly greased or covered with parchment paper or, if frying, onto 12 3-inch squares of aluminum foil.

If baking, bake for 40 minutes or until golden, then cut slits in the side of each to allow the steam to escape. Dry in the oven for another 5 minutes.

If frying, let the rings stand 15 minutes on the foil. Place each ring upside down on the hot oil and when the ring drops into the fat, remove the foil with tongs. Fry 2 or 3 at a time, turning to brown both sides. Drain and cool on a wire rack covered with a paper towel.

To make the filling, beat the ricotta in a large bowl with an electric mixer until smooth. Stir in the chocolate chips, orange peel, sugar, and rum. Split the cooled pastries in half horizontally. Just before serving, spoon the filling into the cavity, then replace the top and sift confectioners' sugar over it.

Makes 12 pastries

Stuffed Italian Bread for St. Joseph's Day

Spiraled with spicy meat and cheese, this is a wonderful bread for snacks or to serve with buttered pasta, a salad, or soup.

4½ to 5 cups bread flour
   2 packages (5½ teaspoons) active dry yeast
  1½ teaspoons salt
   2 cups very warm water

Filling
   ½ pound bacon, diced and cooked crisp
   ½ pound provolone cheese, diced into ½-inch pieces
   ½ pound hard German beef salami, diced into ½-inch pieces
   ½ cup freshly grated Parmesan cheese
   2 tablespoons extra-virgin olive oil
   1 teaspoon coarsely ground black pepper

In the work bowl of a food processor fitted with the dough blade, or in a large bowl, combine 4 cups of the flour, the yeast, and salt. If using the food processor, turn the motor on. Add the water through the feed tube and process until the dough is soft. Add the remaining flour ½ cup at a time and process until the dough cleans the sides of the bowl, then process 45 seconds longer. Let the dough rise in the work bowl until doubled, about 1 hour.

If mixing by hand, make a well in the center of the dry ingredients. Pour in the warm water. Stir until the dry ingredients are moistened. Cover with plastic wrap and let stand for 15 minutes. Stir in the remaining flour until the dough is stiff but not dry. Turn the dough out onto a floured surface. Dust the top of the dough with about 1 tablespoon flour. Knead until the dough is smooth and develops small bubbles just under the surface, about 5 minutes. Place the dough in a greased bowl, turn to grease all over. Cover and let rise in a warm place until doubled, about 1 hour.

Lightly grease a baking sheet. Divide the dough into 2 parts. Flatten each into a circle about ¼ inch thick, as if you were making a pizza crust. Spread the dough with half the bacon, provolone cheese, salami, and Parmesan cheese.

Roll the dough up tightly as for cinnamon rolls. (The ends will be tapered.) Place on the prepared baking sheet. Repeat for the second half of the dough. (If desired, at this point you can place the filled, unrisen loaves on sheets of foil and freeze. When frozen, wrap well and keep up to 4 weeks before baking. To bake, remove from the freezer and thaw overnight in the refrigerator. Before baking, let the loaf come to room temperature, about 1 hour, and bake.) To bake immediately, preheat the oven to 375°F. Let the loaves rise for 30 minutes, until puffy. Brush each loaf with 1 tablespoon olive oil and sprinkle each with ½ teaspoon pepper.

Bake for 35 to 40 minutes. Remove the loaf from the baking sheet onto a wire rack to cool slightly, slice to serve. If you wish, you can wrap the baked, cooled loaves in foil and freeze. To serve, remove from the freezer, place on a baking sheet, and reheat in a 350°F oven until hot.

Makes 2 loaves

Passover

Passover is a combination of two springtime festivals based on two historical biblical events. The first is the Festival of the paschal lamb (recorded in Exodus 34), which happened in Egypt when God "passed over" the houses of the Children of Israel, sparing them the tenth plague, which was to take the oldest son in each Egyptian family. The second is an agricultural festival (recorded in Exodus 23), The Festival of Unleavened Bread, which is tied to the hasty departure of the Children of Israel from Egypt, when they "took their dough before it was leavened" and fled the country.

Passover, for Jews today, celebrates the escape of the Children of Israel from the Egyptian "house of bondage" and reminds people of the continuing battle for freedom in every generation. There are special foods connected with Passover that are unique among holidays.

When it comes to baking, no leavening (baking powder, baking soda, and yeast) is to be used in breads and desserts. Leavening (according to the Talmud) represents the "evil impulse of the heart." An unleavened bread, "matzo," is a symbol of purity.

Except for matzo (which is made with wheat), nothing is to be consumed made of wheat, barley, rye, and oats, which are prohibited during Passover. A special matzo meal may be used as well as flour made from potato. Both matzo cake meal and potato flour are commonly available in supermarkets today.

Because beaten eggs are an acceptable leavening for Passover, many of the traditional dishes, such as sponge cake and meringues, include a lot of them.

Passover Chocolate Sponge Cake

The most delicate of cakes—sponge cake—is leavened by air trapped in beaten eggs. This characteristic makes it a perfect Passover dessert. Matzo cake meal and potato starch (or flour) is substituted for cake flour or all-purpose flour, both of which are prohibited during Passover. The cake has a light texture and an eggy-citrus flavor.

>   7 large eggs, separated
> 1¼ cups sugar, divided
>   1 tablespoon fresh lemon juice
>   ½ cup potato flour (or starch)
>   ¼ cup matzo cake meal
>   ¼ cup dark unsweetened cocoa powder

Cocoa Cream Frosting

>   ½ cup sugar
>   ¼ cup dark unsweetened cocoa

>   1 cup whipping cream
>   1 teaspoon vanilla

Preheat the oven to 300°F. Line the bottom of a 10-inch tube pan with parchment paper or waxed paper.

In a large bowl, with an electric mixer, beat the egg yolks until light and lemon colored. Gradually beat in 1 cup of the sugar. Stir in the lemon juice. In a small bowl, stir together the potato flour, matzo cake meal, and cocoa. Place into a wire sieve or strainer and sift over the egg mixture. Gently fold together until all flour is incorporated.

Wash the beaters, and in another large bowl, beat the egg whites until foamy. Gradually add the remaining ¼ cup sugar, beating until stiff peaks form. Gently fold the egg whites into the chocolate mixture. Pour into the prepared pan.

Bake for 30 minutes, and without opening the oven door, increase the temperature to 325°F. Bake 15 minutes longer or until the

---

 SPONGE CAKES

The success of sponge cakes depends on beating the eggs so that they do not lose their volume when they are combined with other ingredients and when the cake is baked. The eggs should be at room temperature when they are beaten. Room-temperature eggs can hold three times as much air as chilled eggs because the protein they contain will be more elastic. Remove the eggs from the refrigerator thirty minutes before you begin mixing. Or place the eggs in a bowl of warm water for one to two minutes.

top springs back when touched lightly. Remove from the oven. Cool the cake in the pan on a wire rack for 10 minutes. Remove from the pan and cool right side up on a wire rack. Peel off the paper and place the cake on a serving plate.

To make the frosting, stir together ½ cup sugar and ¼ cup cocoa in a small bowl. Stir in the whipping cream and vanilla. With an electric mixer, beat until stiff. Spread the top and sides of the cake with the cocoa cream frosting and serve. Refrigerate any leftover cake.

Makes 12 to 16 servings

Passover Cookie Dough

This is a basic flourless dough that my friend Marge Portilla, a cateress, uses for making all kinds of cookies for Passover. The combination of matzo cake meal and potato starch makes a tender butter cookie dough. Here are directions for two very different variations, Jam-filled Thumbprints and delicate Orange Squares.

    1 cup (2 sticks) unsalted butter, at room
       temperature
    1 cup sugar
    3 large egg yolks, lightly beaten
    2 cups less 2 tablespoons matzo cake
       meal
    2 tablespoons potato starch
    ¼ teaspoon salt
    2 teaspoons orange or lemon zest

    2 tablespoons fresh orange or lemon
       juice

Jam-filled Thumbprints
    About ½ cup strawberry or seedless
    raspberry jam

Filling for Orange Squares
    4 large eggs, lightly beaten
    2 cups sugar
    2 tablespoons potato starch
    ½ cup fresh orange juice
       Confectioners' sugar, for dusting

In a large mixing bowl with an electric mixer, or in a food processor with a steel blade in place, cream the butter and sugar until smooth. Add the egg yolks and beat until light. Mix in the cake meal, potato starch, salt, orange or lemon zest, and orange or lemon juice. Mix until smooth. Chill the dough for 30 minutes, if necessary.

Preheat the oven to 375° F.

FOR JAM-FILLED THUMBPRINTS
Cover 2 baking sheets with parchment paper or lightly grease them. Shape the dough into 1-inch balls. Place on the baking sheet, about 1 inch apart. With your thumb, press an indentation into the center of each cookie. Bake for 8 to 10 minutes or until cookies are firm and very lightly browned around the edges. Spoon ¼ to ½ teaspoon of strawberry or seedless raspberry jam into the center of each cookie. Remove the cookies from the baking sheet and cool on a rack.

Makes about 60 cookies

Press the dough into an ungreased 15x10x1-inch pan. Bake for 10 minutes at 375° F., until the dough is set. Increase oven temperature to 400°F. In a small bowl, whisk together the eggs, sugar, potato starch, and orange juice. Pour over the baked crust and return to the oven. Bake for 15 to 20 minutes or until the filling is set. Remove from the oven and cool on a rack. Dust heavily with confectioners' sugar. Cut into 1½-inch squares.

Makes 60 squares

Lemon Angel Pie

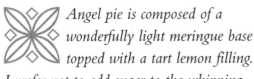 *Angel pie is composed of a wonderfully light meringue base topped with a tart lemon filling. I prefer not to add sugar to the whipping cream.*

Meringue Crust

  6 large egg whites,
    at room temperature
 ⅛ teaspoon salt
1½ cups sugar
  1 tablespoon white vinegar

Lemon Filling

  6 large egg yolks, at room temperature
 ¾ cup sugar
  1 teaspoon grated lemon zest
 ¼ cup fresh lemon juice

Topping

  1 cup whipping cream

Preheat the oven to 275°F. Lightly grease a 10-inch pie pan or a 9-inch square cake pan.

Make the crust. In a large bowl, beat the egg whites with salt until frothy. Gradually add the sugar and beat with an electric mixer at high speed until stiff and glossy, then beat in the vinegar. Turn into the prepared pan. Smooth the top and edges with a spatula.

Bake for 1½ hours until the meringue feels firm on the outside (it should be a little soft in the center).

Make the filling. Beat the egg yolks and sugar in a heavy, nonaluminum saucepan over medium-low heat until light and lemon colored. Beat in the lemon zest and juice. Cook, beating all the time, until the filling has thickened. Cover and place over a bowl of ice water to cool.

Spread the filling onto the cooled meringue. Cover and refrigerate at least 2 hours, or overnight, before serving. Before serving, beat the whipping cream until stiff and spread over the lemon filling.

Makes 8 to 9 servings

Apricot-Honey-Walnut Tart

Passover is not only a time for remembering the Children of Israel's flight from Egypt by observing the symbolic restrictions of that historic event but also a time for rejoicing and entertaining family and friends. But how can you bake a lot of goodies without using flour or baking powder? Imaginative Jewish cooks have met that challenge for centuries. This tart is a good example of a delectable dessert that passes all those tests!

Tart Shell

1 cup matzo meal
5 tablespoons unsalted butter, chilled and cut into pieces
¼ cup water
2 teaspoons honey

Filling

½ cup (1 stick) unsalted butter
⅓ cup honey
¼ cup sugar
1½ cups coarsely chopped walnuts
½ cup chopped dried apples
½ cup chopped dried apricots
1 tablespoon fresh lemon juice
½ teaspoon grated lemon zest

To make the shell, measure the matzo meal into the bowl of the food processor and process until very fine. Add the butter and process until the mixture resembles coarse meal. Combine the water and honey. Sprinkle over the matzo meal mixture and process with on/off bursts just until the dough forms a ball.

Sprinkle a work surface with matzo meal. Roll out the dough into a 10-inch round. Fit into the bottom and sides of a 9-inch tart pan with a removable bottom. Chill for 30 minutes uncovered.

Preheat the oven to 400°F.

Make the filling. In a heavy saucepan, combine the butter, honey, and sugar and heat to boiling over medium-high heat. Add the walnuts, apples, apricots, and lemon juice and zest and mix well. Boil for 1 minute, stirring, and then remove from the heat. Spoon the hot mixture into the pastry shell.

Bake for 20 minutes or until the crust is light brown and the filling is golden. Cool on a wire rack.

Makes 8 to 10 servings

Baking for the
Easter Season

Danish Carnival Buns

 The Danes take part in the European tradition celebrating the season before Lent with parties and games. Plan a coffee party on Shrove Tuesday and serve these buns. They're based on a handy refrigerator dough that can be mixed up to four days in advance of shaping and baking.

Dough

    3 cups all-purpose flour
    ¼ cup sugar
    ½ teaspoon salt
    ½ cup (1 stick) unsalted butter,
         chilled and cut into pieces
    1 package (2¾ teaspoons) active
         dry yeast (not rapid-rise)
    ½ cup warm milk (105°F to 115°F)
    1 cup whipping cream
    3 large egg yolks

Filling

    ½ cup golden raisins
    ½ cup mixed chopped candied fruits
    ½ cup almond paste
 2 to 3 tablespoons whipping cream

Glaze

    1 large egg, beaten
    2 tablespoons milk
         Pearl sugar or coarsely crushed
         sugar cubes, for sprinkling

Syrup

    ¼ cup fresh orange juice
    ¼ cup sugar

Make the dough. In a large bowl or in the food processor, combine the flour, sugar, and salt. Cut in the butter until the mixture resembles coarse crumbs. In a small mixing bowl, dissolve the yeast in the warm milk; stir in the whipping cream and egg yolks and let stand 5 minutes.

EASTER

Easter officially falls on the first Sunday after the full moon of March. It is the Christian celebration of Christ's resurrection. The word *Easter* is derived from Eostre, the Anglo-Saxon goddess of the dawn. Easter represents rebirth, or revival, after the darkness of the soul. Because of this association with rebirth, the egg has been an important Easter symbol. The egg denotes the germ from which all life comes and is a symbol of spring and fertility. It also functions for Christians as a symbol of Christ's tomb—a cold and hard casket from which new life ultimately breaks forth triumphantly.

Pour the yeast mixture over the flour mixture and stir with a fork just to moisten. Cover the bowl with plastic wrap and refrigerate overnight or up to 4 days.

To make the filling, combine the filling ingredients in the food processor and process until chopped but not puréed, or chop the mixture by hand.

Mix the egg and milk in a small bowl for the glaze.

Lightly grease a baking sheet or cover with parchment paper. Remove the dough from the refrigerator and divide into 2 parts. Working with 1 part at a time, roll out on a lightly floured surface to make a 16-inch square. Fold one third of the dough over the center third. Fold the opposite third of dough over the center one third and roll out just enough to seal the layers. This will result in a 16 × 5-inch rectangle. Fold one of the narrow ends over the center third of the dough and then fold the opposite third over the center of the dough, which will result in a 5-inch square of dough. Roll the dough out to make a 16-inch square and repeat the folding and rolling one more time until you end up with a 5-inch square of dough. Roll out again to make a 16-inch square. Fold into thirds so that the packet is about 16 by 5 inches. Roll the dough lengthwise to stretch it to 24 by 6 inches. Cut the strip down the middle lengthwise and then make 8 cuts crosswise about 3 inches apart to make 16 squares of dough. Place a teaspoon of the filling onto the center of each square. Fold the four corners of each square toward the center and press down well. Place the squares in the prepared pan, about 3 inches apart. Brush with the egg glaze and sprinkle with the sugar. Repeat the rolling-out, shaping, and filling process with the second half of the dough.

Let the filled rolls rise, covered with a cloth, about 30 minutes, until puffy. Meanwhile, preheat the oven to 350°F.

Bake the rolls for 15 minutes or until golden brown.

 ## FASHING, CARNIVAL, MARDI GRAS

New Orleans imported the frenzy of Mardi Gras from France. The wildness of Carnival evokes primitive rites of renewal. The word *carnival* comes from the Latin, meaning "farewell to meat," and *Mardi gras* is French for "fat Tuesday." Both terms refer to the period of festivity and banqueting that preceded Lent in the Medieval church calendar. Carnival, Mardi Gras, or Fashing takes place for ten days before the season of Lent.

While the rolls are baking, combine the orange juice and sugar in a small saucepan; bring to a boil over medium heat and boil just until the sugar is dissolved. Brush the hot, baked buns with the orange syrup. Serve warm.

Makes 32 buns

Almond-Filled "Semlor"

It is traditional in Sweden to serve these richly adorned and filled buns on Shrove Tuesday, the day before the fast days of Lent begin on Ash Wednesday. This is when all the fat and rich foods are to be cleaned out of the kitchen to prepare for the belt-tightening Lenten season. Semlor comes from the Latin word simila, *which means "fine wheat flour."*

These buns are usually filled with almond paste and whipped cream and sometimes served in a bowl with vanilla-flavored cream as a dessert or snack. Of course, the buns are also delicious unfilled, warm from the oven with butter and jam.

Dough
- 3¼ cups all-purpose flour
- 2 packages (5½ teaspoons) active dry yeast
- ⅓ cup sugar
- ½ teaspoon salt
- 1 cup milk
- ½ cup (1 stick) unsalted butter, cut into pieces
- 1 large egg, beaten

Glaze
- 1 large egg, beaten with 1 tablespoon milk

Filling
- 8 ounces almond paste
- ½ cup whipping cream
- 2 tablespoons confectioners' sugar

Garnish
Confectioners' sugar

Vanilla Cream Sauce (page 29)

Make the dough. In a large bowl or food processor, mix 3 cups of the flour, the yeast, sugar, and salt. Heat the milk to boiling in a small saucepan over medium-high heat. Add the butter and stir until the butter is melted and the mixture has cooled to 130°F. Pour the hot mixture into the flour mixture along with the beaten egg. Mix with a wooden spoon, an electric mixer, or the food processor until a soft, smooth, but sticky dough is formed. You will still be able to see the little particles of yeast in the mixture, but they will dissolve as the dough rises. Cover with plastic wrap and let rise until doubled, 45 minutes to 1 hour.

Lightly grease a large baking sheet or cover with parchment paper. Sprinkle a work surface with 2 tablespoons of the remaining flour. Turn the dough out onto the board.

Dust the dough with flour and knead gently to express all air bubbles. The dough will be soft. Divide into quarters. Divide each quarter into 4 equal parts. Shape each piece into a round ball and place, smooth side up, in the prepared pan. Let rise, uncovered, until almost doubled, about 45 minutes.

Preheat the oven to 400°F. Brush the tops of the buns with the egg glaze.

Bake for 10 to 12 minutes or until golden brown. Slide the parchment paper, if using, onto a countertop to cool (see Note) or remove to a wire rack.

Make the filling. Crumble the almond paste and divide into 16 equal parts. Shape each piece into a 2-inch patty. Cut off the top of each cooled bun. Place the almond paste patty into the bun. In a small bowl, whip the cream until stiff, then add the confectioners' sugar to sweeten the cream slightly. Fill a pastry bag fitted with a ½-inch tip with the cream. Just before serving, pipe the whipped cream around the edges of the almond paste. Place the top back on the bun. Garnish with a dusting of confectioners' sugar. Repeat with all the buns.

To serve with Vanilla Cream Sauce, spoon some of the sauce onto a dessert plate. Place a filled bun onto the cream. Serve immediately.

Makes 16 buns

NOTE: The unfilled buns may be frozen, well wrapped. To serve, thaw and fill.

SHROVE TUESDAY, OR FAT TUESDAY

Shrove Tuesday, or Fat Tuesday, is the last chance for pious Roman Catholics to consume meat before the forty-day fast of Lent that precedes Easter. In Scandinavia, this is the day to finish up the last of the rich foods and baked goods that may still be around from the Christmas season. Finns eat tiny buckwheat blini with sour cream and fresh caviar; Swedes consume rich yeasted buns stuffed with almond paste and whipped cream as their indulgence before the period of denial.

Vanilla Cream Sauce

There are many uses for this sauce. Serve it with apple pie, steamed pudding, rice pudding, and cake as well as with simple fresh berries and fruits.

  2 tablespoons cornstarch
  2 tablespoons sugar
  2 cups light cream or milk
  1 teaspoon vanilla extract

In a medium saucepan, combine the cornstarch, sugar, and cream. Whisk until smooth. Place over medium heat and bring to a boil, stirring all the time. Cook, stirring, until thickened, 2 to 3 minutes. Stir in the vanilla. Cover the saucepan and cool.

Makes about 2 cups

Austrian Carnival Doughnuts, or "Krapfen"

 Austrians observe the tradition of Fasching, or Carnival, for about two weeks before the beginning of the solemn Lenten season. During this time of merrymaking, they traditionally enjoy rich pastries such as these wonderful, jam-filled doughnuts, similar to bismarks. Rather than frying the doughnuts, you can bake them, which results in a different texture and crust (see Note).

  4 cups all-purpose flour
  1 package (2¾ teaspoons) active
    dry yeast
  3 tablespoons sugar
  1 teaspoon salt
  1 cup milk
  3 tablespoons unsalted butter or
    vegetable oil
  2 large eggs
    About 6 tablespoons apricot,
    strawberry, or plum jam
    Vegetable oil, for deep frying
    Confectioners' sugar, for dusting

In a large bowl with an electric mixer, or in the food processor with the dough blade (see Box) in place, combine the flour, yeast, sugar, and salt.

Heat the milk in a small saucepan over medium-high heat to scalding, then pour into a bowl and add the butter or oil, whisking until the butter is melted. Whisk in the eggs. Add the liquids to the dry ingredients all at once and mix or process until the dough is soft, smooth, and satiny. Cover and let rise in a warm place until doubled, about 1 hour.

Cover a large cutting board with a clean, woven tea towel and dust with flour. Turn the dough out onto a lightly floured surface and roll out to ⅓-inch thickness. Use a plain, round cookie or biscuit cutter about 2½ inches in diameter and press the dough lightly just to mark off circles on half the rolled-out dough. From the other half of the dough, cut out the same number of rounds as you've marked. Place 1 teaspoon jam or marmalade on the center of each of the marked rounds. Place the cut-out round over the jam. With the cutter, cut through the top and bottom rounds, following the top round as a guide, thus sealing the edges and separating the doughnuts. Place the cut-out doughnuts on the floured, cloth-covered board. Cover and let rise until doubled, about 30 minutes.

In a large heavy pot or deep fryer, heat the oil to 380°F. Lower the doughnuts into the oil with a slotted spoon and cook about 2 minutes until the bottoms are golden brown. Turn the doughnuts over and cook about 2 minutes longer until the second side is browned. Remove with a slotted spoon and cool on a wire rack placed over paper towels. Dust with confectioners' sugar.

Makes about 18 dozen doughnuts

NOTE: Although it isn't traditional, I prefer to bake the krapfen. Preheat the oven to 400°F. Place the filled doughnuts on a parchment-covered or lightly greased baking sheet instead of on the floured, cloth-covered board. Let stand, covered, until doubled, about 30 minutes. Bake for 10 to 15 minutes, until golden. Cool on a wire rack. Glaze with Lemon Icing.

Lemon Icing

1 cup confectioners' sugar
2 tablespoons fresh lemon juice
1 tablespoon unsalted butter,
  at room temperature
  Water, if necessary

Stir the confectioners' sugar, lemon juice, and butter together in a small bowl to make a smooth icing. If necessary, add water 1 teaspoon at a time, and mix until smooth.

 KNEADING BY MACHINE

The food processor dough blade has short, stubby, sturdy, strong blades that are designed to handle yeast doughs. The regular plastic blade, designed for light mixtures, is too weak to mix and knead yeast dough. Heavy-duty mixers, such as KitchenAids, come with a dough hook that is specifically designed for yeast doughs.

Soft Pretzels

In the days of the early Christian church it was a practice to form bread dough into thin ropes and then shape these ropes to resemble arms crossed across the breast in prayer. This bread was called bracalle, *meaning "little arms." In German, this bread was called* brezel, *from which came the English word* pretzel. *Making soft pretzels is fun and easy to do. The dough is a simple one to make, especially if you use a food processor. It is the hot water and baking soda bath that gives pretzels the evenly browned glaze once baked.*

3 cups all-purpose flour
1 package (2¾ teaspoons) active dry yeast
1 tablespoon sugar
1 teaspoon salt
1 cup very warm water (130°F)

Baking Soda "Bath"

6 cups water
4 tablespoons baking soda
Coarse salt, for sprinkling

In the work bowl of the food processor or in a large bowl with an electric mixer, combine the flour, yeast, sugar, and salt. If using a food processor, turn the motor on and slowly add the water, mixing until a dough forms and cleans the sides of the bowl. Process until the ball turns around the bowl about 25 times.

If mixing with an electric mixer, mix until dough is smooth and satiny, 3 to 5 minutes. If mixing by hand, stir with a wooden spoon until stiff, turn out onto a lightly floured surface, and knead for 5 to 10 minutes, until smooth.

Turn the dough onto a lightly oiled surface. Shape into a ball. Cover with an inverted bowl and let stand about 10 minutes.

Cover a large work area with waxed paper and coat with nonstick spray. Divide the dough into 12 equal parts. Shape each part into a strand about 20 inches long. Lay one strand horizontally in front of you. Grasp both ends with your hands. Pull the ends of the strand toward you and then cross them (like arms folded across your chest) above the center of the strand to shape a pretzel. Place on the waxed paper. Repeat with the other strands. Let the pretzels rise until almost doubled, about 30 minutes.

Preheat the oven to 400°F. Cover a baking sheet with parchment paper and coat with nonstick spray (the baked pretzels really stick!) or bake on a nonstick cookie sheet.

For the bath, combine 6 cups water and baking soda in a large stainless steel or enamel saucepan or Dutch oven (aluminum will discolor). Bring the water to boil. Carefully lift one pretzel, using a large pancake turner, and lower into the boiling water. Cook the pretzel for 15 seconds. Remove from the water using a slotted spoon and place it on the prepared baking sheet. Repeat for remaining pretzels, boiling them one at a time and placing them ½ inch apart on the baking sheet. Sprinkle with coarse salt.

Bake about 20 minutes, until golden. Remove from the baking sheet and cool on a wire rack.

Makes 12 soft pretzels

Coffeebread Pretzel

This bread is from the city of Viborg in the province of Karelia, which is now within the borders of Russia. This is another Lenten "prayer bread" symbolized by the shape of the pretzel. In the old days, it was proofed in boiling water (just as soft pretzels are) to give the surface a golden brown sheen; they were then baked on a bed of clean oat straw to impart a special flavor.

3 to 3½   cups unbleached all-purpose flour
1   package (2¾ teaspoons) active dry yeast
⅓   cup sugar
½   teaspoon salt
1   teaspoon freshly ground cardamom
¼   teaspoon freshly ground nutmeg
1   cup milk
2   tablespoons unsalted butter
1   large egg, lightly beaten

Glaze

1   large egg, lightly beaten with 2 tablespoons milk
Pearl sugar or coarsely crushed sugar cubes, for sprinkling

In a food processor or in a large bowl with an electric mixer, combine 2½ cups of the flour, yeast, sugar, salt, cardamom, and nutmeg. Heat the milk to scalding in a small saucepan over medium-high heat. Remove from the heat and add the butter. Stir until the butter melts and the mixture cools to very warm (130°F). Pour over the flour mixture along with the beaten egg. Process or mix until dough is smooth and satiny, adding more flour as necessary. Cover and let rise until doubled, about 1 hour.

Grease and flour a baking sheet or cover with parchment paper. Turn the dough out onto a lightly oiled work surface and roll out to make a 40-inch-long strand. Lay the strand horizontally in front of you on the prepared pan. Grasp both ends of the strand. Pull the ends toward you and cross them over the center of the strand (to resemble arms folded across the chest) to shape a pretzel. Cover with a towel and let rise until almost doubled, about 45 minutes.

Preheat the oven to 400°F. Brush the egg glaze over the bread. Sprinkle with the sugar.

Bake for 20 to 25 minutes, until golden; do not overbake. Remove from the oven and cool on a wire rack.

Makes 1 large pretzel, about 12 servings

Greek Easter Bread

 Eggs are the symbol of new life. I've always loved making Easter breads with eggs baked right into the braid. I wash the raw eggs in soapy water, rinse them, dry, and put them into a bowl of warm water with food color and about 1 teaspoon white vinegar added. When the eggs have tinted to the depth of color I like, I take them out of the liquid, place them on paper towels, and let them air dry. When the bread is baked, the eggs become hard cooked. I've suggested three pretty wreath shapes here, one that is braided, one that is curled, and one that is twisted.

Dough

5 to 6 cups unbleached all-purpose flour
2 packages (5½ teaspoons) active dry yeast
1 cup sugar
1 teaspoon grated lemon zest
1 teaspoon freshly ground cardamom
1 teaspoon salt
1 cup milk
¾ cup (1½ sticks) unsalted butter, cut into pieces
3 large eggs, beaten

Glaze, Finish, and Garnish

1 large egg, beaten with 1 tablespoon milk
1 to 6 colored uncooked eggs (see Easter Bread Rings, below)
Sliced, blanched almonds, for sprinkling (optional)
Sesame seeds, for sprinkling (optional)

In a large bowl, or in the food processor with the dough blade in place, combine 3 cups of the flour with the yeast, sugar, lemon zest, cardamom, and salt. Mix until blended. Heat the milk to boiling in a small saucepan over medium-high heat. Remove from heat and add the butter and stir until the butter is melted and milk is cooled to 130°F. Pour the milk mixture and the 3 eggs over the flour mixture. Stir with a wooden spoon, beat with the paddle or dough hook of a mixer, or process until dough is smooth and satiny but still rather soft and sticky. Add remaining flour to make a soft dough. Cover with plastic wrap and refrigerate at least 2 hours or overnight.

Punch down the dough. Shape, glaze, and decorate as directed for one of the three Easter Bread Rings, below. Preheat the oven to 400°F.

Bake for 20 to 25 minutes, until golden. Cool on a wire rack.

Makes 1 large loaf, 20 to 24 servings

Easter Bread Rings (Lambrokouloures)

Twisted Ring

Divide the dough in half. Roll each piece out to make a rope 24 inches long. Twist the ropes together and place on a greased baking sheet, curving them into a ring. Join the ends carefully. Wiggle 6 eggs in the spaces between the twisted ropes. Cover and let rise until almost doubled, about 1 hour. Brush with the egg-milk glaze.

Braided Ring

Divide the dough into 3 equal parts. Form each part into a rope about 30 inches long. Braid the three strands. Place the braid on a greased or parchment-covered baking sheet in the form of a ring. Place one colored egg on the join of the braid. Cover and let rise until doubled, about 1 hour, brush with the egg-milk glaze, and sprinkle with sliced almonds.

Curled Wheel Wreath

Divide the dough into 4 equal portions and roll each into a 12-inch strand. Place strands on a greased baking sheet, crossing the strands at the center of each to form the spokes of a wheel. Curl the outer ends of each strand. Make an indentation in the center of the hub (where all the strands cross). Place a colored egg in the center. Cover and let rise until doubled, about 1 hour. Brush with the egg-milk glaze and sprinkle with sesame seeds.

Hot Cross Buns

These small yeast buns, freckled with currants or raisins, and sometimes fruit and nuts, are traditionally served on Good Friday. They are slashed with a cross just before baking and the cross is filled with icing after they've cooled. I usually make them and freeze them unfrosted, ahead of time. Then on Easter morning I warm them in the oven and frost them for breakfast or brunch.

    3 cups unbleached all-purpose flour
    2 packages (5½ teaspoons) active
      dry yeast
    ¼ cup sugar
    ½ teaspoon salt
    ½ teaspoon grated fresh lemon zest
    ¾ cup milk
    ¼ cup (½ stick) unsalted butter,
      cut into pieces
    2 large eggs, beaten
    ½ cup raisins or currants
    ¼ cup chopped blanched almonds
    2 tablespoons chopped mixed
      candied fruits

Glaze

    1 large egg, beaten with 1
      tablespoon milk

Icing

       1 cup confectioners' sugar
    2 to 3 tablespoons cream or milk
       ½ teaspoon almond extract

LENT

The Lenten season is the forty days preceding Easter, which is a time for introspection about and study of the final days of Christ on earth. Depending on one's perspective, this can be a very solemn time or one of great hope. The practice of "giving up something important for Lent" has shifted in focus from one of self-sacrifice to one of self-discipline.

Measure the flour, yeast, sugar, salt, and lemon zest into a large mixing bowl or into the work bowl of a food processor.

Heat milk to boiling in a small saucepan over medium-high heat. Remove from heat and add the butter. Stir until the butter is melted. Stir in the eggs. Add the liquid ingredients to the dry ingredients, and process or mix with an electric mixer until the dough is smooth but soft, about 2 minutes. Mix in the raisins, almonds, and candied fruits.

Cover with plastic wrap and let rise for 1 hour. Cover a baking sheet with parchment paper.

Turn the dough out onto an oiled surface. Dust the dough with flour and knead to express air bubbles. Divide the dough into 16 equal parts. Shape each into a round ball. Place the balls of dough, smooth side up, about 3 inches apart on the prepared baking sheet. Let rise in a warm place, lightly covered, until almost doubled, for 45 minutes to 1 hour.

Preheat the oven to 400°F. Brush the tops of the buns with the egg glaze. Slash a cross in the center of each bun with a sharp knife.

Bake for 10 to 12 minutes, until golden. While the buns bake, mix the icing ingredients in a small bowl. Place the icing into a pastry bag with a small tip. Slide the parchment onto the countertop to cool or transfer the rolls onto a wire rack to cool. Pipe the icing into the shape of a cross on top of each bun. Serve warm.

Makes 16 buns

Osterpinzen "Austrian Easter Buns"

Even though these buns are always served on Easter, Osterpinzen also appear in Austrian bakeries during Lent. The texture of Osterpinzen is fine and almost cakelike. The faint flavor of anise comes from steeping aniseed in white wine. Egg yolks add to the browning quality of these light yeast buns, requiring baking in a slow oven for a rather long time so that they will cook through before they become too dark.

- 1 cup white wine
- 1 tablespoon whole aniseed
- 2 packages (5½ teaspoons) active dry yeast
- 5 to 5½ cups unbleached all-purpose flour
- ½ cup sugar
- 1 teaspoon salt
- 1 cup milk
- ½ cup (1 stick) unsalted butter, cut into pieces
- 4 large egg yolks
- Pinch of salt
- 1 teaspoon grated lemon zest

Glaze

- 1 large egg, beaten

Combine the wine and aniseed in a small bowl and allow to steep for 3 hours. Strain and reserve the wine. Measure the yeast, 3 cups of the flour, the sugar, and 1 teaspoon of salt into a large mixing bowl. Stir until well blended. Make a well in the center.

Combine the milk and butter in a saucepan. Heat and stir over medium heat until the butter is melted and the milk is hot. Pour the hot milk mixture into the well in the flour mixture. Stir until mixed, then beat until the batter becomes satiny and smooth. Beat in the egg yolks, the pinch of salt, the lemon zest, strained wine, and remaining flour. Mix until the dough is smooth and all the flour is incorporated. The dough will be soft.

Cover the dough and let rise for 45 minutes or until doubled. Lightly grease a baking sheet or cover with parchment paper. Turn

---

 ASH WEDNESDAY

Ash Wednesday marks the first day of Lent, which is the forty-day period before Easter. On this day, the faithful receive smudges of ash on their foreheads, as an emblem of their mortality, symbolizing the words "Dust thou art, and unto dust shalt thou return."

the dough out onto a floured surface. Divide into 12 equal parts. Shape each into a smooth, round ball. Place 3 inches apart, smooth side up, on the prepared baking sheet. Cover and let rise in a warm place until doubled, about 45 minutes.

Preheat the oven to 325°F. Brush the buns with the egg glaze. With a sharp knife slash a cross on the top of each bun, making the slashes about 1½ inches long.

Bake for 20 to 25 minutes, until golden. Cool on a wire rack.

Makes 12 buns

Danish Pastry

Perfect Danish pastry is so flaky and buttery that it melts in your mouth. And, it's the very best when it is hot out of the oven. Even though this is a short-cut method for making the pastry, the results are as close to perfection as one can find, except in Denmark, where Danish pastry is called "Viennabread." Don't be intimidated with the idea of making your own pastry; the simple mixing method is similar to that of making a pie crust, the difference being the addition of yeast. I like to do as much as I can with the help of a food processor. Once mixed, the dough is chilled and becomes quite easy to handle. You can make the dough a day or two before you plan to bake.

2 packages (5½ teaspoons) active dry yeast
½ cup warm water (about 105 to 115°F)
¼ cup sugar
3 large egg yolks
1 cup whipping cream
3½ cups all-purpose flour
1 teaspoon salt
1 cup (2 sticks) unsalted butter, chilled and cut into pieces
1 recipe Apple Almond Filling, Raisin Almond Filling, or Marzipan Filling (below)
1 large egg white
Pearl sugar, coarsely crushed sugar cubes, or sugar, for topping
Sliced or chopped almonds, for topping

In a large bowl, dissolve the yeast in the warm water. Add a pinch of the sugar and let stand 5 minutes, until the yeast foams. Stir in the remaining sugar, the egg yolks, and whipping cream, then set aside.

In a large bowl or in the work bowl of a food processor, combine the flour and salt. Cut in the butter until pieces are the size of kidney beans.

Turn the flour-butter mixture into the bowl with the liquid ingredients. Fold together just until dry ingredients are moistened throughout. Cover and refrigerate overnight or up to 3 days.

Prepare the filling of your choice (below).

Turn the dough out onto a lightly floured surface and dust with flour. Using a rolling pin, pound the dough until it is smooth and about ¾ inch thick. Roll out to a 24-inch square. Fold the dough into thirds to make a long, narrow strip. Cut lengthwise into two parts. Working with one part at a time, roll the dough into a rectangle, about 24 by 6 by ¼ inch. Spread half the filling in a 2-inch strip down the length of each dough strip. Brush the uncovered edges with egg white and fold over to seal in the filling, making a filled roll 24 inches long and about 3 inches wide. Brush the outside of the roll with egg white and press the sugar and sliced almonds on all sides. Repeat with the second half of the dough. Cut filled rolls into 12-inch lengths.

Lightly grease a baking sheet or cover with parchment paper. Place the rolls on the baking sheet. Cover and let rise in a warm place for 45 minutes; they will not double. Preheat the oven to 375°F.

Bake for 25 to 30 minutes or until golden. Remove from the baking sheet onto a wire rack to cool. Serve warm.

Makes four 12-inch-long pastries

Apple-Almond Filling

    6 cups sliced, cored tart apples,
        such as Granny Smith or Pippin
    1½ cups sugar
    1 cup ground almonds
    4 teaspoons ground cinnamon

In a large bowl, mix the apples, sugar, almonds, and cinnamon.

Raisin-Almond Filling

    1½ cups water
    1½ cups golden raisins
    ¼ cup (½ stick) unsalted butter,
        at room temperature
    ½ teaspoon freshly ground
        cardamom
    2 cups confectioners' sugar
    1 to 2 tablespoons whipping cream
    ½ cup chopped almonds

In a small saucepan bring the water to a boil over medium high heat and add the raisins. Remove from the heat and let stand 5 minutes; drain.

In a large bowl, cream the butter until soft, then add cardamom, confectioners' sugar, and enough cream to make a smooth, spreadable mixture. Mix in the raisins and almonds.

Marzipan Filling

    8 ounces almond paste
    ½ cup finely chopped
        blanched almonds
    ½ cup confectioners' sugar
    1 large egg white
    1 teaspoon almond extract

Crumble the almond paste into a mixing bowl and blend in the almonds, confectioners' sugar, egg white, and almond extract until well mixed. You can do this quickly in the food processor.

Spicy Easter Rabbit Cookies

I like to fill an Easter basket with these thin spicy cookies cut into rabbit shapes. If I tint the icing at all, I use pale yellow, pink, and green; I use silver dragées or silver candy cake decorations to make the bunnies' eyes. Sometimes I just melt white and dark chocolate in separate saucepans and dip the bunnies' ears, feet, and tails.

¼	cup packed brown sugar
¼	cup vegetable shortening, at room temperature
½	cup dark molasses
½	teaspoon baking soda
½	teaspoon ground ginger
½	teaspoon ground cloves
½	teaspoon ground cinnamon
¼	teaspoon salt
¼	teaspoon freshly ground nutmeg
¼	teaspoon ground allspice
2	cups all-purpose flour
2 to 3	tablespoons cold water

Royal Icing

1	large egg white, beaten
2	cups confectioners' sugar
¼	teaspoon lemon extract
	Food color if desired

Preheat the oven to 375°F.

In the food processor or a mixing bowl with an electric mixer, cream the brown sugar, shortening, and molasses together. Blend in the baking soda, ginger, cloves, cinnamon, salt, nutmeg, and allspice. Add the flour and mix until well blended, then add enough water to work the mixture into a thick but smooth dough.

Lightly grease 2 or 3 baking sheets or cover with parchment paper.

Roll out the dough as thin as possible, 1/16 inch or less. With a rabbit-shaped cookie cutter, cut out cookies and place them ½ inch apart on the cookie sheet.

Bake the cookies for 7 to 8 minutes. Remove the cookies to a wire rack to cool.

Make the frosting. In a small bowl, beat the egg white, confectioners' sugar, and lemon extract until smooth. Tint with food color, if desired. Keep covered until ready to use. Frost the tops of the cooled cookies with the icing. Let stand until set, about 15 minutes.

Makes 48 to 60 cookies

Lemon-Ginger Pound Cake

Originally pound cake was made with a pound each of flour, butter, eggs, and sugar. Over the years, the proportions have changed and a variety of other ingredients have given this category of cakes a wide range of flavors. The fresh flavors of lemon and ginger give this cake springtime flavors. The key resemblances to the original cake are the type of pan in which it is baked, a loaf pan, and the fine, close texture of the crumb.

1½ cups all-purpose flour
1½ teaspoons baking powder
½ teaspoon salt
½ cup (1 stick) unsalted butter, at room temperature
1 cup sugar
2 large eggs
½ cup milk
   Grated zest of 1 lemon
1 teaspoon freshly grated ginger

Lemon Glaze
¼ cup confectioners' sugar
1 tablespoon fresh lemon juice

Preheat the oven to 350°F. Butter and flour an 8 × 4 × 3-inch loaf pan.

In a medium bowl, stir the flour, baking powder, and salt together. In a large bowl with an electric mixer, cream the butter and sugar until smooth. Add the eggs one at a time and beat at high speed until light and fluffy, scraping the bowl often.

Add the flour mixture alternately with the milk, beating at low speed until well blended. Mix in the lemon zest and ginger. Pour into the prepared pan.

Bake for 60 to 65 minutes, or until a wooden skewer inserted into the loaf comes out clean. Let cool in the pan for 5 minutes, then turn out onto a wire rack.

To glaze, mix the confectioners' sugar and lemon juice until blended and brush over the top of the warm cake.

Makes 1 loaf cake, about 12 slices

Luscious Lemon Truffle Cake

This elegant silvery white cake is layered with a fresh lemon filling made with white chocolate and cream cheese. It is a lovely dessert for an Easter luncheon.

Cake
2¼ cups all-purpose flour
1⅔ cups sugar
3½ teaspoons baking powder
1 teaspoon salt
1¼ cups milk
¾ cup (1½ sticks) unsalted butter or white vegetable shortening, at room temperature

1 teaspoon vanilla
5 large egg whites

Lemon Truffle Filling

¾ cup sugar
3 tablespoons cornstarch
¼ teaspoon salt
1 cup water
2 large egg yolks
1 tablespoon unsalted butter
⅓ cup fresh lemon juice
1 teaspoon grated lemon zest
1 cup (6 ounces) chopped white
   chocolate or vanilla baking chips
1 (8-ounce) package cream cheese

Whipped Cream Frosting

1 cup whipping cream
3 tablespoons confectioners' sugar
Shaved white chocolate, for garnish

Preheat the oven to 350°F. Grease and flour two 9-inch round cake pans.

Make the cake. In a large bowl with an electric mixer, combine the flour, sugar, baking powder, salt, milk, and butter or shortening. Blend until the butter is evenly mixed. Add the vanilla. Beat at low speed for 1 minute, then increase the speed to high and beat for 2 minutes, scraping the bowl constantly, beating until the mixture is light and fluffy.

In a separate bowl, beat the egg whites until stiff. Gently but thoroughly fold the whites into the cake batter. Pour evenly into the prepared pans.

Bake for 35 to 40 minutes, until the cakes feel firm when touched in the center. Remove from the oven and cool on a wire rack. Split the cooled layers horizontally to make 4 layers in all.

To make the filling, combine the sugar, cornstarch, and salt in a medium saucepan. Whisk in the water until smooth. Cook over medium-high heat until the mixture comes to a boil, stirring constantly. Reduce the heat to low and cook 2 minutes longer, stirring constantly. Remove from the heat. In a small bowl, beat the egg yolks with a fork. Stir about ¼ cup of the hot mixture into the egg yolks; blend well. Add the egg yolk mixture to the mixture in the saucepan. Cook over low heat until the mixture boils, whisking constantly, then continue to cook for 2 minutes, stirring.

Remove from the heat and stir in the butter and lemon juice and zest. Transfer half of the hot filling to a small bowl and cool for 15 minutes. Add the white chocolate to the hot filling in the saucepan and stir until the chocolate is melted; set aside. In a small bowl, beat the cream cheese until fluffy. Beat in the white chocolate mixture until light and smooth.

Spread one-third of the white chocolate filling over one layer of the cake. Top with a second cake layer, then spread with one-third more of the filling; top with a third cake layer and spread the remaining filling over. Top with the last cake layer and spread with the reserved lemon mixture. Refrigerate, uncovered, 2 to 3 hours, until the filling is set.

Make the frosting. In another bowl, whip the cream and sweeten it with the confectioners' sugar. Frost the sides of the cake with half of the whipped cream frosting. Put the remaining frosting into a pastry bag and pipe decoratively around the top and bottom edge of the cake. Garnish with shaved white chocolate. Refrigerate up to 8 hours before serving.

Makes 16 servings

Ukrainian Easter Cheesecake (Syrniki Pyrih)

In the Ukraine, this is a traditional family dessert at Easter. It is made with what the Ukrainians call "farmer cheese," which is similar to ricotta, but silkier in texture. It's flavored simply with eggs, sugar, raisins, and lemon and enclosed in a rich, sweet pastry.

Pastry
- 2 cups all-purpose flour
- ½ cup sugar
- 1 teaspoon baking powder
- ½ teaspoon salt
- ¾ cup (1½ sticks) unsalted butter, chilled and cut into pieces
- 2 large egg yolks
- 4 tablespoons sour cream
- 1 teaspoon grated lemon zest

Cheese Filling
- 1 cup golden raisins
- 1 cup farmer cheese or ricotta
- 4 large egg yolks
- ½ cup sugar, divided
- 1 teaspoon vanilla
- 1 teaspoon grated lemon zest
- 2 tablespoons fresh lemon juice
- 4 large egg whites

Topping
- 1 large egg white, beaten with a little water
- 2 tablespoons pearl sugar or coarsely crushed sugar cubes

Make the pastry. In a food processor or a large bowl, combine the flour, sugar, baking powder, and salt. Add the butter and process, or cut in, until the mixture is the consistency of coarse crumbs. In another bowl, mix the egg yolks, sour cream, and lemon zest. Add to the flour mixture and process or mix just until the dough holds together. Press the dough into a ball, then remove one-quarter of the dough. Wrap the two pieces separately in plastic wrap and chill for 10 minutes.

Butter the bottom and sides of a 9- or 10-inch springform pan. Remove the larger portion of dough from the refrigerator and on a lightly floured surface, roll out to about ¼ inch thick (see Note). Using the pan as a guide, cut a circle of dough and fit it into the bottom of the pan. Cut the remaining rolled-out dough into 2-inch strips and "patch" them around the sides of the pan to cover, pressing them against the pan so they stay in place. Seal the edges around the bottom of the pastry. Refrigerate while preparing the filling.

Preheat oven to 350°F.

For the filling, place the raisins in a small bowl and cover with hot water. Let stand for a few minutes until plumped, then drain. Beat the farmer cheese, egg yolks, and $\frac{1}{4}$ cup of the sugar in a large bowl until fluffy. Add the vanilla, lemon zest and juice, and the raisins. In a small bowl, beat the egg whites with the remaining sugar until stiff and fold into the filling batter. Pour into the prepared pastry shell and spread evenly.

Roll out the reserved dough on a lightly floured surface to $\frac{1}{4}$-inch thickness and cut into $\frac{1}{2}$-inch strips that are 9 or 10 inches long, depending on the diameter of the pan. Arrange the pastry strips on top of the filling, weaving them into a latticework pattern. Crimp the edges of the pastry together to seal.

For the topping, brush with the egg white mixture and sprinkle with the sugar.

Bake for 1 hour to 1 hour 10 minutes, until the filling is set and the crust is pale golden brown. Remove from the oven and cool on a wire rack.

Makes 12 to 16 servings

NOTE: An easy way to roll out a sticky dough such as this is to place it between two sheets of plastic wrap. If the dough seems too sticky or soft to lift from the plastic, put it into the freezer for one or two minutes, until it stiffens, then peel off one part of the plastic wrap and lift the dough up from the second sheet of plastic.

April Fool's Day

Mock Apple Pie

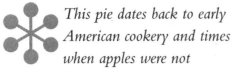

This pie dates back to early American cookery and times when apples were not available all year long.

Pastry for 1 single pie crust (see page 176) or use 1 purchased refrigerated pastry

Filling

30 whole wheat soda crackers or saltines
¼ cup (½ stick) unsalted butter, at room temperature

1½ cups cold water
1½ cups sugar
3 tablespoons fresh lemon juice
1 teaspoon ground cinnamon
½ teaspoon freshly ground nutmeg
1½ teaspoons cream of tartar
½ cup raisins

Topping

½ cup all-purpose flour
¼ cup packed brown sugar
¼ cup (½ stick) unsalted butter, cut into pieces
½ teaspoon ground cinnamon

FOOD SPOOFS FOR APRIL FOOL'S DAY

April Fool's Day, or "The Feast of the Fools," dates back to Medieval times according to some sources. The timing of the holiday seems to be related not only to old and new calendars but with the vernal equinox when nature fools us with sudden changes in weather.

Another account tells of the way in which the old calendar was deemed inaccurate, as it didn't match the earth's movement around the sun, so scientists created a new calendar, the one that we use today. Old habits die hard, and until 1564 the French continued to celebrate their New Year on the first day of spring, which for them was April 1. Finally, when Charles IX of France ordered that the new calendar be used, people rebelled by exchanging fake gifts such as candy boxes filled with straw and bouquets made of onions instead of flowers.

Whatever the actual history, it is still a day to serve a "fruitless" Mock Apple Pie or one of the other popular "mock" recipes of the past.

Preheat the oven to 450°F. Prepare the pastry and chill.

For the filling, spread the crackers with the butter, break them into 1-inch pieces, and place in a mixing bowl. In a saucepan, combine the water, sugar, lemon juice, cinnamon, nutmeg, and cream of tartar and heat to boiling over medium-high heat. Boil for 2 minutes, until the sugar is dissolved. Add the raisins to the crackers and pour the boiling syrup over them; let stand until the crackers have absorbed the liquid.

Roll out the chilled pastry on a lightly floured surface to fit a 9-inch pie pan. Line the pan with the pastry. Turn the cracker mixture into the pastry. In a bowl, stir the topping ingredients together until the mixture is crumbly. Sprinkle over the filling.

Bake for 20 to 25 minutes, until the pie is brown. Cool on a wire rack. Serve with whipped cream or ice cream, if desired.

Makes 6 to 8 servings

Mock Baby Ruth Bars

These rich bars taste like the popular candy bar, and are an especially big hit with kids.

Bars

    4 cups uncooked rolled oats
    1 cup packed brown sugar
    ¼ cup light corn syrup
    ¼ cup peanut butter
    1 teaspoon vanilla
    ¾ cup (1½ sticks) unsalted butter,
       at room temperature

Topping

    1½ cups semisweet chocolate chips
    ½ cup butterscotch chips
    ⅔ cup smooth or crunchy
       peanut butter

Preheat the oven to 400°F. Butter a 13 × 9-inch baking pan.

KIDS IN THE KITCHEN

Cooking with children is fun and educational; however, it is best to give kids jobs that they can easily accomplish. For Mock Apple Pie, kids can help by buttering the crackers and breaking them into quarters.

Get the kids to help by patting the mixture into the pan; then they can distribute the chocolate and butterscotch chips on top of the baked bars (be careful with the hot pan, however). Once the chips have melted and the pan has cooled, they can help by swirling the mixture over the surface of the bars.

Make the bars. In a large mixing bowl, blend together the rolled oats, brown sugar, corn syrup, peanut butter, vanilla, and butter. Spread into the prepared baking pan and pat into an even layer.

Bake for 12 minutes, until light brown. Remove from the oven and immediately sprinkle with the chocolate and butterscotch chips. When the morsels have softened, spread the top of the bars with the peanut butter, swirling the mixture over the surface. Cool in the pan, then cut into squares.

Makes 24 bars

Mock Cheese Soufflé

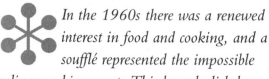 *In the 1960s there was a renewed interest in food and cooking, and a soufflé represented the impossible culinary achievement. This brunch dish became popular as a "cheater's" version of the intimidating soufflé.*

6 slices good white bread, crusts removed
2 tablespoons unsalted butter, at room temperature
2 cups shredded Cheddar cheese
4 large eggs
2½ cups milk
1 teaspoon dry mustard
1 teaspoon Worcestershire sauce

Spread each slice of bread with 1 teaspoon butter. Place the bread, buttered sides down and touching, into a 13 × 9-inch casserole. Sprinkle with the cheese. In a bowl, beat the eggs, milk, dry mustard, and Worcestershire sauce together and pour over the cheese layer. At this point, you can cover and refrigerate the soufflé for 8 hours or overnight.

Preheat the oven to 350°F. Uncover, if refrigerated. Place the casserole into a larger pan and fill the bottom pan with hot water. Bake for 1 hour to 1 hour and 15 minutes, until a knife inserted into the center comes out clean. Serve hot.

Makes 6 to 8 servings

Mock Cherry Pie

Made with cranberries, this is a delicious pie that fools you into thinking it is made with fresh, tart cherries.

Pastry for 1 double-crust 9-inch pie (see page 172) or use 1 purchased refrigerated pastry

Filling

1½ cups sugar

⅓ cup all-purpose flour

⅓ teaspoon salt

3 cups halved fresh or frozen cranberries

1 cup golden raisins

1 cup water

½ teaspoon almond extract

Prepare the pastry. On a floured surface, roll out half of the pastry to fit the bottom and sides of a 9-inch pie pan. Preheat the oven to 425°F.

In a large saucepan, combine the sugar, flour, salt, cranberries, raisins, and water. Bring to a boil over medium heat and boil gently for 5 minutes, stirring constantly. Remove from the heat and stir in the almond extract. Cool to room temperature. Pour filling into the pastry-lined pan.

On a floured surface, roll out the second half of the pastry. Place over the filling. Seal

 KIDS IN THE KITCHEN

Kids old enough to handle a knife (it need not be sharper than a butter knife) can help by cutting the cranberries into halves. They can also help by crimping the edges of the pie (it might have a unique look!).

and crimp the edges of the pie. Bake for 30 to 40 minutes or until the pie is light brown. Serve warm with ice cream or whipped cream, if desired.

Makes one 9-inch pie

Mock Mincemeat Pie

 Spicy and delicious, the combination of apples, zucchini, and carrots resembles that of mincemeat. Old-fashioned English mincemeat pie includes ground suet and meat. This one does not.

Pastry for 1 double-crust 10-inch pie (see page 172)

Filling

2 large Granny Smith apples, peeled, cored, quartered, and shredded

2 (8-inch) zucchini, scrubbed, unpeeled, and shredded

2 large carrots, peeled and shredded

½ cup chopped walnuts or pecans

½ cup raisins

¼ cup all-purpose flour

1½ cups packed brown sugar

¼ cup (½ stick) unsalted butter, melted

1 tablespoon ground cinnamon

1 teaspoon freshly ground nutmeg

1 teaspoon ground cloves

¼ teaspoon salt

1 tablespoon fresh lemon juice

Glaze

1 large egg, beaten

1 tablespoon water

Prepare the pie crust. On a floured surface, roll out half of the pastry to fit a 10-inch pie pan. Line the pan with the pastry. Preheat the oven to 425°F.

In a large bowl, combine the apples, zucchini, carrots, nuts, raisins, and flour; toss to mix.

In another bowl, mix the brown sugar and butter until blended and stir in the cinnamon, nutmeg, cloves, salt, and lemon juice. Mix into the apple mixture.

Turn the filling into the pastry-lined pan. On a floured surface, roll out the second half of the pastry and cut into ½-inch strips. Arrange on top of the filling in a lattice fashion. Trim and seal the strips to the bottom crust. In a small bowl, make the glaze by beating the egg and water together. Brush the mixture over the top and edges of the pie.

Bake for 40 to 50 minutes, or until the pie is set and the pastry is golden brown. Serve warm with whipped cream, if desired.

Makes one 10-inch pie

 KIDS IN THE KITCHEN

Kids can help by placing the buttered bread into the pan and sprinkling the cheese over it.

May Day

and Other Spring Holidays

Finnish May Day Pastries (Tippaleipä)

 The most eagerly awaited holiday in Finland is May Day because it marks the beginning of summer. On May Day, everybody enjoys this crispy, curled nest of pastry that is sold in bakeries throughout the country. Tippaleipä is similar to the Pennsylvania Dutch funnel cakes, as the batter is drizzled into hot oil to cook.

- 7 large egg whites, divided
- 1 large egg yolk
- ¾ cup sugar
- 1 cup all-purpose flour
  Vegetable shortening or oil
  Confectioners' sugar

In a large bowl, beat 4 of the egg whites, the egg yolk, and sugar. Stir in the flour. In another bowl, beat the remaining egg whites until stiff peaks form, and fold into the batter. Heat the oil in a deep fryer or a heavy, deep saucepan, to 370°F.

Pour 2 cups of the batter into a heavy-duty, zipper-lock plastic bag. Clip ¼ inch off the corner. Press the batter through the hole in the bag into the hot fat, swirling it to make a bird's nest–type shape. Cook until golden brown, about 30 seconds on each side. With a slotted spoon, remove pastry from the oil and drain on paper towels. Repeat until all the batter is used. Dust with confectioners' sugar.

Makes about 36 pastries

ON FRYING PASTRIES

Heat three to four inches of oil or fat for frying in a heavy kettle or deep-fat fryer. Place a candy thermometer into the fat and heat to the required temperature over medium to low heat. If using an electric deep-fat fryer, set the dial to the temperature required. The most common temperatures for deep frying are 370 to 380°F.

Be careful that water never touches the hot oil, which can cause splattering. Frying is not a good kitchen activity to let kids help with; rather, let them stir together the eggs and sugar, or frost or dust sugar on the fried pastries.

Use tongs, a metal spatula, or a slotted spoon to turn or lift foods from the hot fat. Place three to four paper towels on a wire rack for draining the hot, cooked pastries.

Orange-Date-Nut Scones

Springtime and scones seem to go together, especially these orange-perfumed scones that are speckled with dates and nuts.

2 cups all-purpose flour
1 cup uncooked rolled oats
½ cup sugar

4 teaspoons baking powder
¼ teaspoon salt
2 teaspoons grated orange zest
½ cup chopped dates
½ cup chopped walnuts
  or pecans
2 large eggs, beaten
¼ to ⅓ cup milk
½ cup (1 stick) unsalted butter, melted

MAY DAY

May 1 in Scandinavia marks the first day of summer, a holiday that is important in northern countries where winters are long, dark, and cold. University students in Sweden and Finland greet spring with a celebration that goes on all night, beginning on the afternoon of April 30, just before Walpurgis Night, which is the eve of May Day.

On the afternoon of April 30, students from Uppsala University in Sweden stand before the student library. A white velvet student cap, which hasn't been worn all winter, is tucked in each student's pocket. The rector of the university stands in front of them and at the exact moment when the clock strikes three, he takes out his cap and holds it above his head, signaling the students to pull out their caps and wave them wildly. At the same moment, they all put on their caps and greet spring with three loud cheers.

Then, the students join hands in long lines and run in rows down the wide street that leads to the town square. When a line reaches the square, it turns around and runs back up the hill, colliding with the lines that are still coming down. A chaotic, good-natured battle ensues, which is said to symbolize the war between winter and spring.

A similar ritual occurs in Helsinki, Finland, where students place their white caps on Havis Amanda, the statue of the goddess of the Baltic Sea. She stands at the foot of the Esplanade, near the waterfront in downtown Helsinki.

For tender scones, many of the same rules apply as for other quick breads:

1. Mix the dry ingredients with the liquids just until the dry ingredients are moistened. Overmixing results in a less tender texture.

2. Scones should not be overbaked, or they will be dry. Check them about five minutes before the suggested baking time is up (ovens vary, and the scones may be done sooner than the recipe states).

3. Baked scones can be frozen for serving later. Wrap them airtight and freeze as soon as possible after cooling. They will freeze well for up to two months. To thaw, remove from freezer and allow them to thaw, still wrapped; then reheat in a low oven (300°F) for about five minutes until heated through. Or unwrap the scones, place on a baking sheet, and simultaneously thaw and reheat at 300°F for ten to fifteen minutes.

Preheat the oven to 400°F. Cover a large baking sheet with parchment paper or coat with nonstick spray.

In a large mixing bowl, combine the flour, oats, sugar, baking powder, salt, orange zest, dates, and nuts. In another bowl, stir together the eggs, ¼ cup of the milk, and butter. With a fork, stir the liquids into the dry ingredients just until blended. Add the remaining milk, if necessary to make a dough that holds together. Divide the dough into 2 parts. Shape each part into a round ball. Place well apart on the baking sheet and flatten each to make 8-inch rounds. With a sharp knife, cut each round into 6 wedges, leaving the wedges in place.

Bake for 10 to 13 minutes or until golden brown. Serve warm with butter and orange marmalade, if desired.

Makes 12 scones

Currant Scones with Orange-Marmalade Butter

Quick to make, these scones have the texture of baking powder biscuits and the slight sweetness of a coffee cake.

    2 cups all-purpose flour
    1 tablespoon baking powder
    ¼ cup sugar
    ½ teaspoon salt
    ½ cup (1 stick) unsalted butter,
      chilled and cut into pieces
    ⅓ cup currants
    1 large egg, beaten
    ⅓ cup milk

For the Top
    Milk for brushing
    1 teaspoon sugar

Orange-Marmalade Butter
    4 tablespoons (½ stick) unsalted
      butter, at room temperature
    4 tablespoons orange marmalade

Preheat the oven to 400°F. Cover a baking sheet with parchment paper or coat lightly with nonstick spray.

In a large mixing bowl, combine the flour, baking powder, sugar, and salt. Cut in the butter until the mixture resembles coarse crumbs. Stir in the currants. In a small bowl, combine the egg and milk; stir into the flour mixture with a fork just until the dough gathers easily into a ball. Turn the dough out onto the baking sheet and pat into an 8-inch circle.

With a sharp knife, cut the dough into 8 wedges, leaving the wedges in place. Brush the top with milk and sprinkle with sugar.

Bake for 12 to 15 minutes, until light brown.

While the scones bake, make the orange-marmalade butter. In a small bowl, beat the butter until light and fluffy, then gradually beat in the orange marmalade.

Serve the scones warm with orange-marmalade butter.

Makes 8 scones

Sesame Cream Scones

These are the most delicate and tender when made with heavy cream, but if you are concerned about fat content, you can substitute half-and-half or milk.

    2 cups all-purpose flour
    1 tablespoon baking powder
    ¼ cup sugar
    ½ teaspoon salt
    ¼ cup (½ stick) unsalted butter,
      chilled and cut into pieces
    2 large eggs, beaten
    ¼ to ½ cup whipping cream,
      half-and-half, or milk

For the Top
    1 teaspoon water
    1 teaspoon sesame seeds
    1 teaspoon sugar

Preheat the oven to 400°F. Cover a baking sheet with parchment paper or coat lightly with nonstick spray.

In a large mixing bowl, combine the flour, baking powder, sugar, and salt. Cut in the butter until the mixture resembles coarse crumbs.

In a small bowl, combine the eggs with ¼ cup of the whipping cream and add to the flour mixture. Stir just until a dough is formed, adding more cream if necessary to make a soft dough.

Shape into a ball and place on the baking sheet. Pat into an 8-inch circle. With a sharp knife, cut into 8 wedges, leaving the pieces in place.

Brush the top of the scones with the water. Sprinkle with the sesame seeds and sugar.

Bake for 10 to 12 minutes, until golden. Serve hot with butter or cream cheese and strawberry jam, if desired.

Makes 8 scones

Coffee-Glazed Chocolate Chip Scones

 Rather indulgent, but these are a sure hit for a midmorning coffee party. They are quickly made, too.

1½ cups all-purpose flour
¼ cup sugar
2 teaspoons baking powder
¼ teaspoon salt
½ cup (1 stick) unsalted butter, chilled and cut into pieces
½ cup semisweet chocolate chips
½ cup chopped walnuts
1 large egg
½ cup milk

Coffee Glaze
1 cup confectioners' sugar
2 tablespoons hot, strong, brewed coffee

 ABOUT SCONES

This Scottish quick bread resembles our baking powder biscuit in texture and method of preparation. They take their name from the Stone of Destiny (or Scone), which is where Scottish kings were once crowned. The original scone was made of oat flour and baked on a griddle. Today, they are baked in the oven and most often made with wheat flour. Scones can be savory or sweet and are served with coffee or tea or as an accompaniment to a light meal such as soup or salad.

Preheat the oven to 400°F. Lightly grease a baking sheet or cover with parchment paper.

In a large bowl, combine the flour, sugar, baking powder, and salt. Cut in the butter until the mixture resembles coarse crumbs. Stir in the chocolate chips and walnuts. In a small bowl, beat the egg and milk and stir into the dry ingredients until they are just moistened.

Using a #12 ice cream scoop, or a ⅓ cup measure, scoop mounds of the dough onto the baking sheet, spacing them 1 inch apart.

Bake for 12 to 15 minutes, until golden.

To make the glaze, mix the confectioners' sugar with the coffee in a small bowl. Drizzle over the scones when they come out of the oven. Let stand until set; serve warm.

Makes 10 to 12 scones

Carrot-Spice Muffins

Glorious on a sunny morning in May, these fast and easy-to-make muffins are chock-full of flavor. I always think muffins are more interesting when they're made into either the giant size or the miniatures rather than the standard size. This recipe can go either way. Tiny muffins bake quickly and have lots of browned edges that appeal to the "crunchers" in the crowd, but you have to be careful not to overbake them or they can be dry. Giant muffins take a bit longer to bake but are satisfyingly moist and crumbly.

2 cups all-purpose flour
¾ cup sugar
2 teaspoons baking powder
½ teaspoon baking soda
½ teaspoon salt
1 teaspoon ground cinnamon
1 teaspoon freshly ground nutmeg
2 cups shredded fresh carrot
1 tart apple (such as Granny Smith), peeled, cored, and shredded
½ cup golden raisins
½ cup chopped pecans
3 large eggs, beaten
½ cup corn oil
2 teaspoons vanilla

Preheat the oven to 350°F. Grease 12 regular muffin cups, 36 miniature muffin cups, or 6 giant muffin cups, or line them with paper baking cups.

In a large mixing bowl, combine the flour, sugar, baking powder, baking soda, salt, cinnamon, nutmeg, carrot, apple, raisins, and pecans until all ingredients are well mixed. In another bowl, combine the eggs, oil, and vanilla. Stir into the flour mixture only until blended. Fill the prepared muffin cups three-quarters full with the batter.

Bake until a wooden skewer inserted in

the center of the muffins comes out clean. For regular muffins, bake 20 to 25 minutes; for miniature muffins, bake 15 to 20 minutes; for giant muffins, bake 25 to 30 minutes. Remove from pans and serve warm or cool on a wire rack.

Makes 12 regular muffins, 6 giant muffins, or 36 miniature muffins

Swedish Cream Puffs

 Swedes gather for a late supper after they have watched the bonfires and taken part in the merriment of Walpurgis Night, the evening before May 1. The menu is a simple one: soup, salad, bread, butter, and often cream puffs filled with whipped cream and the first strawberries of the season.

ABOUT MUFFINS

A perfect muffin has a rounded top, is tender, and is evenly textured with a golden brown crust, which may be pebbly or slightly rough. Imperfect muffins have peaked tops with tunnels or holes inside and are tough.

The secret to making good muffins is simple—be sure not to overmix. The simplest way to handle the mixing is to combine all of the dry ingredients first, then add special ingredients, such as nuts or fruits, if used. Mix the liquid ingredients separately and then add them to the dry ingredients; mix **only** until the dry ingredients are moistened—fifteen to twenty strokes, using a spoon or rubber spatula to gently fold or stir the ingredients together. The batter will look lumpy and rough, but the lumps will disappear when the muffins bake. The consistency of the batter will vary, depending on the individual flours and liquids used in the recipe. Scoop or spoon the batter gently into the muffin pans for baking. Be careful not to mix the batter during this process.

Always preheat the oven before baking. Muffins are usually baked at 350 to 400°F. Average muffins bake in twenty to twenty-five minutes. Miniature muffins take five to eight minutes less; giant-size muffins, five minutes more.

There are many textures that are acceptable for muffins, and that depends on the ingredients that are used. Muffins can be dense or light, moist or cake-like. Some are sweet and others are savory.

1 cup water
½ cup (1 stick) unsalted butter,
　cut into pieces
1 cup all-purpose flour
4 large eggs
　Confectioners' sugar, for dusting

Filling
2 cups whipping cream
　Sugar to taste
1 quart fresh strawberries

Preheat the oven to 425°F. Lightly grease a baking sheet or cover with parchment paper.

In a saucepan, combine the water and butter and bring to a boil. Cook over low heat until the butter has melted.

Add the flour, all at once, beating vigorously with a wooden spoon for a few seconds or until the mixture leaves the bottom of the pan. Remove the pan from the heat and let cool for a few minutes. Beat in the eggs, one at a time, until incorporated. Beat for 3 minutes more to make sure the ingredients are well blended and smooth. Scoop paste into twelve 2-inch balls and place them 3 inches apart on the prepared baking sheet.

Bake for 20 minutes. Reduce the heat to 375°F and bake for 15 minutes more or until light brown. Cut off the tops of each puff and pull out the moist inside. Let the shells cool on a wire rack, uncovered.

Just before serving, make the filling. Beat the whipping cream in a mixing bowl until thickened and sweeten with the sugar to taste. Slice the strawberries, saving a few whole for decoration. Fold the sliced berries into the cream and fill the puffs. Replace the tops and dust with the confectioners' sugar. Garnish with the reserved berries.

Makes 12 cream puffs

ANZAC DAY (APRIL 25)

ANZAC is the acronym for the Australian and New Zealand Army Corps. On April 25, 1915, during World War I, the combined forces landed on the Gallipoli Peninsula in Turkey in an attempt to capture the peninsula. The attack failed, and many soldiers died. This is a special day set for the remembrance of all those who lost their lives for Australia and New Zealand in service to their country.

Special cookies to commemorate this day, called ANZAC Cookies, are sold in most bakeries in Australia and New Zealand.

ANZAC Cookies

Australians still participate in the tradition of four o'clock afternoon tea, which can be a simple or formal occasion, and features a selection of sandwiches, scones, cookies, and cakes that are fancy and plain. This is the time to rest and "restoke the furnace." These thin, crisp oat and coconut drop cookies are a welcome part of the simplest or most elaborate tea.

- 1 cup uncooked rolled oats
- ¾ cup flaked sweetened coconut
- ¾ cup all-purpose flour
- ¾ cup sugar
- ½ cup (1 stick) unsalted butter, at room temperature
- 1 tablespoon honey or light corn syrup
- 3 tablespoons boiling water
- ½ teaspoon baking soda

Preheat the oven to 300°F. Lightly grease 2 baking sheets or cover with parchment paper.

Combine the oats, coconut, flour, and sugar into a medium-size mixing bowl and mix well. Add the butter and honey. Mix the boiling water and baking soda in a small bowl and add to the mixture.

Drop rounded teaspoonfuls of dough 3 inches apart onto the prepared baking sheets.

Bake for 10 to 12 minutes, until crisp and golden brown. Cool on the baking sheet for 30 seconds. Loosen with a thin spatula and cool on wire racks. If the cookies stick to the sheet, return to the oven for 1 minute, then loosen with a spatula. When cool, store in an airtight container.

Makes about 48 cookies

Dutch Almond Buttertart

In the Netherlands, citizens celebrate the springtime Festival of the First Fish. Everybody in the village crowds to the wharf to watch the herring fleets take off and race to the fishing grounds. The fishers quickly lower their nets into the water and haul them up as soon as they are full of herring. Then the fastest boat in each fleet takes the heavy net aboard and races back to the wharf, where other team members are waiting with an orange keg, orange being the official color of the Netherlands. They dump the herring into the keg and place it into a car that is decorated with streamers. The car races off to the royal palace, where the queen awaits their arrival and accepts the first team's offering of fish, officially beginning the village celebration.

Herring is generally served on small toasted rounds as canapés, or as an appetizer, with boiled new potatoes and a green salad. A favorite dessert for the Festival of the First Fish is this rich almond-filled tart.

1 cup (2 sticks) unsalted butter,
   at room temperature
1 cup sugar
1 large egg
2 cups all-purpose flour

For the Filling

2 cups toasted, finely ground
   blanched almonds
¼ cup sugar
1 large egg, beaten
1 teaspoon freshly grated lemon zest

Preheat the oven to 350°F.
In a large mixing bowl, cream the butter and sugar until blended, then add the egg and beat until light. Blend in the flour until the dough is firm. Divide the dough into 2 equal pieces and press one half into a buttered 8-inch tart pan with a removable bottom and sides that are about 1 inch high.

Make the filling. In the food processor, or in a large bowl with an electric mixer, mix the almonds with the sugar, egg, and lemon zest and process, or blend, until very smooth and fluffy. Spread this mixture over the dough in the pan.

Put the second half of the pastry between two sheets of plastic wrap. Roll out into a circle to fit the top of the pan. Peel off one layer of plastic. Place the dough on top of the filling and remove the second sheet of plastic. Trim and seal the edges. Roll any trimmings out between two sheets of plastic wrap and make cutouts with a cookie cutter to decorate the top of the tart. Brush the top with the egg glaze and place the cutouts on top. Cut 5 slits with the tip of a sharp knife to make vents. Brush again with glaze.

Bake for 1 hour or until golden. Cool the pan on a wire rack, then remove the tart from the pan and cut into wedges to serve.

Makes 12 servings

 TOASTING NUTS

Preheat the oven to 350°F. Spread the nuts on an ungreased baking sheet in a single layer. Toast in the oven for eight to fifteen minutes, or until the nuts are light brown (time will vary depending on type and size of nut). Watch that they don't burn; stirring or tossing them occasionally helps prevent this. Remove from the oven and cool.

Strawberry Savarin

Savarin, the rich, rum-soaked yeast cake, is named after Brillat-Savarin, the famous eighteenth-century food writer. The difference between Savarin and Rum Baba is that Savarin is classically made without raisins and typically baked in a rather shallow ring mold. The rum syrup makes the cake juicy and delicious.

    2 cups all-purpose flour
    2 tablespoons sugar
    ¾ teaspoon salt
    1 package (2¾ teaspoons) active
       dry yeast
    ½ cup milk
    ¾ cup (1½ sticks) unsalted butter,
       cut into pieces
    4 large eggs, beaten

Rum Syrup

    2 cups sugar
    1 tablespoon grated orange zest
    1 cup water
    ½ cup dark rum or orange-
       flavored liqueur

Garnish

    2 cups whipping cream
3 to 4 tablespoons sugar
    2 cups strawberries, washed, sliced,
       and sweetened to taste, if desired

In a large mixing bowl, stir the flour, sugar, salt, and yeast together. Heat the milk to boiling in a small saucepan over medium heat. Remove from the heat, add the butter and stir until the butter is dissolved. Cool to very warm (130°F). Pour the milk mixture over the flour mixture and add the eggs. With an electric mixer, beat at high speed until the batter is smooth. Cover and let rise until doubled, 45 minutes to 1 hour.

Butter an 8-cup Savarin or ring mold, or 8 individual ring molds or muffin tins. Beat the batter down and spoon evenly into the prepared pan or pans. Let rise in a warm place until almost doubled, about 1 hour.

Preheat the oven to 375°F. Bake for 35 to 40 minutes for the large mold or 12 to 15 minutes for small molds or until a wooden skewer inserted in the center comes out clean.

To make the syrup, combine the sugar, orange zest, and water in a saucepan. Heat to boiling over medium heat. Lower the heat and simmer for 6 minutes; remove from the heat and add the rum or orange liqueur.

Pierce the surface of the Savarin in many places while it is still warm in the pan. Spoon the syrup over. Let it soak in for a few minutes, then invert the Savarin onto a serving plate.

Pour the cream into a bowl and beat until soft peaks form. Beat in the sugar to sweeten.

Serve the Savarin with the sweetened whipped cream and berries.

Makes 8 servings

Mother's Day

Orange-Cappuccino Shortbread

 My editor, Katie Workman, says her mother just loves shortbread, and that is reason enough to include this recipe for Mother's Day. These tender, buttery, cookie wedges are perfumed with orange and finished with a coffee-flavored glaze.

Shortbread

2½ cups all-purpose flour
½ cup sugar
2 teaspoons grated orange zest
¼ teaspoon salt
1 cup (2 sticks) unsalted butter, chilled and cut into pieces

1 tablespoon water
1 teaspoon instant espresso coffee powder

Glaze

1 cup confectioners' sugar
2 to 3 teaspoons strong coffee

Preheat the oven to 300°F. Cover a baking sheet with parchment paper; draw two 7½ inch diameter circles on the paper, about 2 inches apart.

Make the shortbread. Mix the flour, sugar, orange zest, and salt in the work bowl of a food processor or in a large bowl. Process or cut the butter into the flour mixture until the mixture resembles coarse crumbs. Transfer into a large bowl if using a food processor. In a small bowl, with a fork, mix together

---

MOTHER'S DAY

Mother's Day is a rather modern invention, though there have been attempts made to link it to ancient cults of the mother goddess. Mother's Day was introduced in Scandinavia in 1919. But it wasn't an entirely new idea, since it had existed in England since the seventeenth century, forgotten, and then revived in 1913. In the United States, Mother's Day became a national holiday after much petitioning by Anna Jarvis, a West Virginia schoolteacher who was upset by the ill treatment of many elders by their children. She campaigned for three years before her efforts paid off. In 1910, West Virginia became the first state to observe Mother's Day. Then, in 1914, President Woodrow Wilson established the second Sunday in May as the official national day to honor our mothers.

the water and coffee powder. Stir the coffee mixture into the dry ingredients until the dough holds together in a ball.

Shape the dough into a smooth ball and cut the dough in half. Shape each half into a thick round disk, about 4 inches in diameter. Place the dough onto the center of each circle on the parchment paper. With fingers or a rolling pin, flatten the dough to meet the inside edge of the round. With a fork, make pricks on the top and edges of each round. With a sharp knife, cut the round into 8 wedges; leave the wedges in place.

Bake for 1 hour or until the shortbread is a very light golden color. With a sharp knife separate the wedges while still warm, leaving the wedges in place. Slide the shortbread, still on the parchment paper, onto the countertop to cool. In a small bowl, mix the confectioners' sugar and enough coffee to make a glaze, then drizzle it over the cooled shortbread.

Makes 16 wedges

Strawberry Layer Cake

This is the most popular Scandinavian celebration cake. Norwegians serve it on Sytende Mai (May 15). Finns consider it to be the only birthday cake. Swedes serve it always in the springtime, usually for Mother's Day. It's basically a sponge cake made with equal measures of eggs, sugar, and flour. I love it, too,

because it is such an easy recipe to remember and to multiply up or down. When other berries or fruits are in season I use them to fill the cake. In the wintertime, I'll substitute my own homemade strawberry jam and/or sliced bananas.

Cake

1	cup eggs (about 5 large)
1	cup sugar
1	cup all-purpose flour
1	teaspoon baking powder
½	teaspoon salt

Filling

1	pint strawberries, stemmed and sliced
3 to 4	tablespoons sugar
2	cups whipping cream
2 to 3	tablespoons confectioners' sugar
1	teaspoon vanilla
	Berries for garnish, if desired

Preheat the oven to 350°F. Butter and flour two 9-inch round cake pans.

For the cake, beat the eggs in a large bowl, with an electric mixer, until frothy. Slowly beat in the sugar and continue beating until light and lemon colored. Stir the flour, baking powder, and salt together in another bowl and sift into the beaten eggs. Beat on low for about 1 minute. Clean the beaters, and with a rubber spatula, scrape down the bowl and fold the mixture so that all of the dry ingredients are incorporated. Divide the batter evenly between the two cake pans.

Bake for 20 to 25 minutes, until the cake springs back when touched in the center. Loosen the edges and turn out onto a wire rack to cool. When cool, split the layers horizontally to make 4 cake layers in all.

For the filling, gently toss the strawberries with the sugar. In another bowl, whip the cream and blend in the confectioners' sugar and vanilla.

Place one cake layer on a serving plate with the cut side up. Top with one-third of the berries and spread with about ½ cup of the whipped cream. Top with a second cake layer, placing the cut side down. Top with one-third of the sliced berries and spread with about ½ cup of the whipped cream. Top with a third cake layer, cut side up. Top with the remaining strawberries and about ½ cup of the whipped cream. Place the remaining cake layer on top, cut side down. Pile the remaining whipped cream on top (the cake looks attractive when the sides are not covered with the cream). Garnish with additional whole berries, if desired.

Cover and refrigerate until ready to serve or up to 4 hours.

Makes 8 to 10 servings

Strawberry Pie in a Shortbread Crust

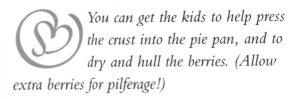 *You can get the kids to help press the crust into the pie pan, and to dry and hull the berries. (Allow extra berries for pilferage!)*

Shortbread Crust

1½ cups all-purpose flour
2 tablespoons sugar
½ teaspoon salt
½ cup corn oil
2 tablespoons milk

Strawberry Filling

3 pints fresh strawberries, rinsed, dried, and hulled
1 cup sugar
½ cup water
3 tablespoons cornstarch
⅛ teaspoon salt

Preheat the oven to 425°F. In a large bowl, mix the flour, sugar, and salt until blended. Add the oil and milk and stir with a fork until crumbly. Press evenly over the bottom and up the sides of an ungreased 9-inch pie pan. Press the edge up into a standing rim and flute or crimp. Pierce the crust all over with a fork.

Bake for 10 to 12 minutes, until the crust is golden. Cool on a wire rack.

Cover the bottom of the pie shell with the prettiest berries, arranging them with the pointed side up.

Fresh strawberries should always be washed just at the last minute before you plan to use them, or they will bleed and get mushy. For the prettiest berries, brush them clean with a very soft brush (such as one that is used for babies' hair). Or place the berries onto the center of a clean terry towel. Loosely fold the towel over the berries. Grasp the towel on each end with your hands and lift one end up at a time so that the berries roll down inside the towel. Then lift the other end up so that the berries roll down in the opposite direction. Repeat about five times. Open the towel. The berries will be shiny and clean. Using the tip of a sharp knife, or a strawberry-hulling tool, remove the stem from the berries.

For the filling, mash the remaining berries (about 2 cups) in a medium saucepan with a potato masher or fork. Add the sugar, water, cornstarch, and salt. Place over medium heat and stir until the mixture comes to a boil. Reduce the heat to medium-low and simmer until thickened and clear. Remove from the heat and cool to room temperature, covered.

Pour the cooled, cooked berries over the berries in the pie shell. Cover and refrigerate at least 3 hours, until set. The pie can be made a day ahead.

Makes one 9-inch pie

Frozen Strawberry Cream Torte

This is a gorgeous creation, made of layers of meringue filled with a strawberry cream. The whole thing can be made ahead in parts, or completed, and frozen for a time when you wish to whip out something beautiful—such as on Mother's Day. Mother's Day is just about the time that the first of the spring strawberries appear. The wild strawberries in our meadow don't ripen until about a month later, and when they do, I'll serve them along with slices of this torte. When one of our children asks if we can have wild strawberries for dessert, my answer is, "Certainly, if you pick them." This is one way to make a few berries go a long way. They need only to be very slightly sweetened, if at all, to make a perfect topping for this torte.

Meringue

- 5 large egg whites, at room temperature
- ¼ teaspoon cream of tartar
- ¼ teaspoon salt
- 1 teaspoon vanilla
- 1¼ cups sugar
- ¼ cup sliced almonds

Filling

- 1 teaspoon unflavored gelatin
- 1 tablespoon cold water
- 2½ cups whipping cream
- 3 tablespoons rum or orange-flavored liqueur

- 1 cup fresh strawberries, sliced, and sweetened with 2 to 3 tablespoon sugar

Preheat the oven to 200°F. Cover 2 baking sheets with parchment paper or grease and flour them. Trace two 6-inch-diameter circles on each of the baking sheets.

Combine the egg whites, cream of tartar, salt, and vanilla in a large bowl. With an electric mixer, beat at medium speed until the egg whites hold soft peaks. Gradually beat in ¾ cup of the sugar a tablespoon at a time, beating continuously. Continue beating until the meringue is stiff. Beat until the sugar is totally dissolved (see Box). Gently fold in the remaining sugar.

Spread a thin layer of the meringue within

MERINGUE

Meringue is beaten enough when a tiny bit, rubbed between thumb and finger, is no longer grainy. It should be stiff enough to hold its shape when formed with a pastry tube.

Meringues are "dried" rather than baked in the oven; this makes them tender. When baked until they begin to brown—or even show the slightest bit of tan—they are overbaked and are too chewy.

The best time to make meringues is in the evening. Then you can put them into the oven, turn the oven off, and let them dry overnight in the cooling oven.

The gelatin gives the whipped cream extra firmness so it can be put into a pastry bag to decorate the top of the torte. It can also be omitted.

each circle. Sprinkle one of the layers with the sliced almonds.

Bake for 15 minutes, turn off the oven, and without opening the oven door, let the meringues dry in the cooling oven for 4 to 5 hours or overnight. They should not brown at all.

When you are ready to assemble the torte, make the filling. In a heatproof cup or small bowl, soften the gelatin in the cold water. Set the cup in a pan of boiling water over medium heat until the gelatin mixture looks clear. In a well-chilled bowl, beat the whipping cream until it begins to thicken. Beat in the dissolved gelatin and continue beating until stiff (see Box). Beat in the rum or liqueur.

Combine the strawberries with two-thirds of the whipped cream mixture (refrigerate the remaining one-third of the whipped cream). Place one plain meringue on a serving plate and spread with one-third of the strawberries and cream. Top with a second layer of plain meringue and spread with another third of the strawberries and cream. Top with the third layer of plain meringue and spread with the remaining strawberries and cream. Place the almond-topped meringue on top. Freeze for 2 hours.

Spread the sides with the whipped cream mixture. Put the remaining whipped cream mixture into a pastry bag fitted with a ½-inch star tip. Make a border of rosettes around the top of the torte.

Freeze unwrapped. When completely frozen, the torte can be wrapped for storage and can be kept frozen up to 6 weeks. The meringue and cream cut the best while frozen rather than thawed. To serve, cut the frozen torte into wedges and serve immediately.

Makes 8 servings

Fresh Berry Tart with Mascarpone

Mascarpone is a buttery-rich double cream cheese made from cow's-milk cream. Ivory colored, soft, and delicate, it makes a wonderful base for fresh fruit in a tart shell. Besides being imported, mascarpone is also made in special Italian-style cheese plants in Texas, California, and Wisconsin. You can buy it in specialty food stores and Italian delicatessens. It is also available by mail order. Mascarpone is perishable and doesn't freeze well. With some experimentation, I've developed a method of making mascarpone in my kitchen, but you do need to plan in advance because it takes several days of draining in the refrigerator (see Box). I'll plan ahead any day to make this special tart when fresh berries are in season. In the spring, I like to make this with strawberries; when blueberries and raspberries come into season, I'll use them. This makes an all-summer holiday tart!

To make your own mascarpone, you'll need one cup of whipping cream, one teaspoon cream of tartar, cheesecloth, and a strainer. In a small, heavy saucepan over medium-low heat, heat the cream to scalding (200°F) or until small bubbles begin to form around the edge of the saucepan. Stir in the cream of tartar. Cover and cool to room temperature. The cream will set. Turn into a strainer that is lined with at least four layers of cheesecloth. Place over a bowl, cover, and refrigerate for one to two days or until the cheese feels firm to the touch. It is now ready to use. This makes about one cup of cheese. It will keep five to seven days, tightly covered.

Shortbread Crust

- 1½ cups all-purpose flour
- 2 tablespoons sugar
- ½ teaspoon salt
- ½ cup corn oil
- 2 tablespoons milk

Mascarpone Filling

- 4 large egg yolks
- 1 cup sugar
- 2 teaspoons vanilla
- 1 cup (8 ounces) mascarpone (see Box)

Topping

- 1 cup whipping cream
- 1 tablespoon confectioners' sugar
- 1 pint cleaned, fresh berries, such as halved strawberries, blueberries, or raspberries

Preheat the oven to 425°F. In a large bowl, mix the flour, sugar, and salt until blended. Add the oil and milk and stir with a fork until crumbly. Press evenly over the bottom and up the sides of an 11-inch tart pan with a removable bottom. Press the edge up into a standing rim and flute or crimp.

Pierce the crust all over with a fork. Bake for 10 to 12 minutes, until the crust is golden. Cool on a wire rack.

Make the filling. Fill an 8- to 10-inch skillet or double boiler halfway with water and bring to a boil over high heat. Put the egg yolks into a small, deep metal bowl. Beat with an electric mixer until the yolks are frothy, then gradually beat in the sugar. Place over the boiling water and beat until creamy and light. Beat at high speed for 5 to 10 minutes, or until the mixture reaches 160°F or until the custard coats the back of a wooden spoon. Remove from the heat and beat in the vanilla. Allow to cool for 5 minutes, then gradually beat in the mascarpone until the mixture is light, thick, and frothy. Cover and refrigerate until ready to use, at least 2 hours or overnight.

To finish the tart, make the topping. Whip the cream until stiff and blend in the confectioners' sugar to sweeten. Fill the tart shell with the mascarpone filling and top with the whipped cream and then the berries. Refrigerate until ready to serve, at least 2 hours or overnight.

Makes 6 to 8 servings

Almond-Cardamom-Fruit Shortcakes

For all of summer's celebrations— starting with Mother's Day and strawberries—shortcakes are a favorite dessert. This is one of my favorite basic shortcakes. I especially like the cardamom, which blends and brings out the flavors of fresh fruits, combined with the texture that the almonds give.

1½ cups all-purpose flour
1½ teaspoons baking powder
 1 teaspoon freshly ground cardamom
¼ cup sugar
½ cup chopped almonds
½ cup (1 stick) unsalted butter, chilled and cut into pieces
 1 large egg
½ cup plain yogurt or buttermilk

For the Top
 1 tablespoon sugar
¼ cup sliced almonds

For Serving
 1 pint fresh strawberries, cleaned, stemmed, and sliced or 2 cups fresh raspberries or sliced fresh peaches (when they come into season)
 3 tablespoons sugar
 1 cup whipping cream

Preheat the oven to 400°F. Lightly grease a baking sheet or cover with parchment paper.

Combine the flour, baking powder, cardamom, sugar, and almonds in a food processor or a large bowl. Add the butter and process or cut in until the mixture is in pea-size pieces.

In a small bowl, mix together the egg and yogurt. Add to the dry ingredients and blend quickly until dough forms (add a bit more yogurt, if needed). Scoop ½-cup mounds onto the prepared baking sheet about 3 inches apart. Sprinkle the tops with sugar and sliced almonds.

Bake for 10 to 15 minutes, until light brown. Remove from the pan and cool on a wire rack or slide the parchment onto a countertop to cool.

In a large bowl, combine the fruit and 2 tablespoons of the sugar. Whip the cream in another bowl until it forms soft peaks and blend in the remaining sugar.

Split the shortcakes horizontally and fill

with fruit and cream. Place the second half of the shortcake on top and top with more fruit and cream. Serve immediately.

Makes 6 servings

Cherry-Coconut Scones

Invite Mom over for afternoon tea and serve these scones (made with dried tart cherries) hot from the oven with whipped butter or cream cheese on the side. The crystallized ginger provides a burst of flavor, but it doesn't dominate the other flavors of the scones.

    1 cup dried tart cherries
       Boiling water
    2 cups all-purpose flour
    ⅓ cup sugar
    ½ teaspoon salt
    1 tablespoon baking powder
    ½ teaspoon baking soda
    ½ cup (1 stick) unsalted butter,
       chilled and cut into pieces
    ½ cup flaked sweetened coconut
    1 tablespoon finely chopped
       crystallized ginger
    1 egg
    ½ cup plain yogurt, low fat or nonfat

For the Top
    1 tablespoon milk
    1 tablespoon sugar

Preheat the oven to 400°F. Lightly grease a baking sheet or cover with parchment paper.

Cover cherries with boiling water for 1 minute; drain and dry thoroughly.

In a large mixing bowl, combine the flour, sugar, salt, baking powder, and baking soda. Cut in the butter until the mixture resembles coarse crumbs. Mix in the cherries, coconut, and ginger. In a small bowl, beat the egg and yogurt together. Add the egg mixture to the dry ingredients; stir with a fork until just mixed and the dough holds together in a ball.

Turn out onto a lightly floured surface. Divide the dough into 2 parts and pat each part into a round about 6 inches in diameter. Place the rounds well apart, on the baking sheet. With a straight knife, score each round into 6 wedges. Brush the top with milk and sprinkle with the sugar.

Bake for 10 to 12 minutes or until light golden brown. Remove the rounds from the baking sheet and cool on a rack or slide the parchment onto a countertop to cool. Divide into wedges where scored. Serve warm.

Makes 12 scones

Honey-Pecan Coffee Cake

A generous sprinkling of pecans and a drizzling of honey add a delicious finishing touch to this beautiful coffee cake. In Sweden, it is the custom for Mother to be greeted for breakfast with songs by her children and a freshly baked coffee cake on the table, along with flowers and a small gift. You can mix this coffee cake using the food processor, let it rise once, shape it, then wrap and refrigerate it so that all you need to do in the morning is bake it.

3 cups all-purpose flour
¼ cup (½ stick) unsalted butter, chilled and cut into pieces
¼ cup sugar
¾ teaspoon salt
1 package (2¾ teaspoons) active dry yeast
¾ to 1 cup very warm water (130°F)
1 large egg, at room temperature, beaten (see Box)
½ cup chopped pecans
¼ cup honey

Coffee Glaze (Optional)

1 cup confectioners' sugar
About 2 tablespoons hot, strong coffee
1 teaspoon unsalted butter

Measure the flour, butter, sugar, salt, and yeast into the work bowl of the food processor with the steel blade in place. Process until the butter is blended into the flour. With the motor going, add ¾ cup of the water through the feed tube, then add the egg. Process until the dough is smooth and satiny and pulls away from the side of the bowl, about 15 seconds. If the dough is too stiff, add the remaining ¼ cup water, a small amount at a time with the motor going.

Or measure the flour into a mixing bowl. Melt the butter in a small saucepan over medium-low heat and mix into the flour. Add the sugar, salt, and yeast. Make a well in the center of the flour mixture. Pour in ¾ cup of the water and the egg. Stir until the dough is stiff, adding more water if necessary. Cover and let stand for 15 minutes. Turn out onto a floured surface and knead for 5 minutes or until smooth and satiny.

 TO REMOVE THE CHILL FROM EGGS

If your eggs are cold, place them into a small bowl of very warm tap water for three to five minutes.

Place the dough in a greased bowl, cover, and let rise in a warm place for 1 hour or until doubled. Uncover the dough and roll out on a lightly floured surface to make a 6 × 10-inch rectangle. Cut lengthwise into 5 equally wide 10-inch strips.

Grease a 9-inch round cake pan. Arrange the dough strips in the cake pan by winding them, cut edges down, into a loose spiral. Pinch together ends of dough to form a continuous strip of dough. Sprinkle the pecans over the dough. Cover loosely with plastic wrap and let stand in a warm place until doubled, about 1 hour 15 minutes. (Or, after wrapping with plastic, before rising, place into the refrigerator overnight. Take out ½ hour before baking so cake can come to room temperature.)

Preheat the oven to 375°F. Drizzle the cake with the honey.

Bake for 25 to 30 minutes, until the coffee cake is golden brown. Remove from the pan immediately and cool on a wire rack.

Make the glaze, if desired. Stir together the confectioners' sugar, coffee, and butter in a small bowl to make a smooth glaze. Drizzle over the warm coffee cake and serve warm.

Makes one 9-inch coffee cake

Memorial Day
and
Early Summer

Most of the fresh soft fruits and berries that we enjoy are in season during the summer and into the fall. A variety of delicious and easy desserts are classic to American cuisine, but the names can be confusing. Here are a few descriptions:

Cobbler

A deep-dish dessert of stewed fruit topped with a biscuitlike crust. *Buckle* is another name for a cobbler.

Crumble

A British dessert in which fresh fruit is topped with a crumbly pastry mixture of flour, shortening, and spices and then baked.

Crisp

The American counterpart to the British crumble, which consists of fresh fruit topped with a crumbly mixture, usually made with brown sugar and often containing nuts.

Brown Betty

This is a fruit dessert that is made with layers of fruit and a crumb mixture that is finally used as a topping. The actual origin of the term *betty* is unknown, but recipes for fruit betties were printed as far back as 1864. Apple brown betty is well known.

Berry-Rhubarb Cobbler

I like to bake rather than stew the rhubarb and fruits when I make a cobbler. This preserves the shape and texture of the fruits. Although the rhubarb tastes wonderful all alone, I sometimes like to combine it with strawberries or blueberries or both.

5½ cups ½-inch pieces of fresh rhubarb, or any combination of cut-up rhubarb and stemmed, halved, and washed strawberries and washed blueberries

1 cup sugar

1 tablespoon cornstarch

¼ teaspoon ground ginger

¼ teaspoon ground cinnamon

Topping

1 cup all-purpose flour

¼ sugar

1 teaspoon baking powder

¼ teaspoon baking soda

¼ cup (½ stick) unsalted butter, chilled and cut into pieces

⅔ cup buttermilk or plain yogurt

Vanilla ice cream or whipped cream, for serving

Preheat the oven to 400°F. Butter a ceramic or glass 1½- to 2-quart shallow baking dish.

In a large bowl, combine the rhubarb and berries, sugar, cornstarch, ginger, and cinnamon. Spread the mixture into the baking dish. Bake for 10 to 15 minutes, until bubbly.

In a large bowl, mix the flour, sugar, baking powder, and baking soda; cut in the butter until the mixture resembles moist crumbs. With a fork, stir in the buttermilk or yogurt just until the dry ingredients are moistened and dough forms.

With an ice cream scoop or with a spoon, drop the dough into 8 mounds on top of the hot rhubarb mixture. Bake for 25 to 30 minutes, until the topping is light brown and the fruit is bubbly. Serve hot with ice cream or whipped cream.

Makes 8 servings

Deep-Dish Rhubarb Cake

Rhubarb is in season from April through June, and seems to be more of a "backyard" crop than a commercial one. Botanically, rhubarb is a vegetable, but we treat it as a fruit because it is so tart that it is usually combined with a considerable amount of sugar. As kids we used to chew on the celerylike stems that had been sprinkled with salt, which seemed to cut the sourness.

 RHUBARB

Rhubarb is probably the first spring crop in gardens across the country. The peak of the season extends from April through June. The thick, celerylike stalks, which range in color from pale green to bright red, are intensely tart and require a considerable amount of sugar. Rhubarb is delicious when used in combination with strawberries in cobblers, crisps, and pies. The British often stew rhubarb with ginger. Rhubarb is rather perishable but can be kept up to three days, well wrapped, in the refrigerator.

For the Pan

¼ cup (½ stick) unsalted butter

1 cup packed brown sugar

4 cups ½-inch pieces fresh rhubarb

Cake Batter

¼ cup (½ stick) unsalted butter,
   at room temperature

¾ cup sugar

1 large egg

1 teaspoon vanilla

1¼ cups all-purpose flour

1 teaspoon baking powder

1 teaspoon salt

½ cup milk
   Whipped cream or vanilla
   ice cream, for serving

Preheat the oven to 350°F. Put the butter into an 8- or 9-inch square glass or ceramic baking pan and place in the oven until melted. Remove from the oven and sprinkle the brown sugar evenly over the butter. Add the rhubarb in an even layer.

To make the batter, in a mixing bowl, cream together the butter and sugar. Add the egg and beat until light and fluffy, then blend in the vanilla. Stir the flour, baking powder, and salt together and add to the creamed mixture alternately with the milk. Mix until the batter is smooth. Pour evenly over the rhubarb.

Bake for 55 minutes or until light brown. Cut into squares and serve warm with whipped cream or ice cream.

Makes 9 servings

Ginger-Rhubarb Bars

The miraculous first signs of life in our northern garden are the round, pink shoots in the rhubarb bed that begin to peek through the last of the snow. My father says, "It's no use to plant the garden before Memorial Day." However, we can harvest the rhubarb, as by then the stalks are thick, short, juicy, and full of flavor. I use rhubarb for its tartness in this butter-crusted bar cookie. The combination of ginger and rhubarb is a British tradition.

1 cup all-purpose flour

⅓ cup confectioners' sugar

½ cup (1 stick) unsalted butter,
   at room temperature

Filling

2 large eggs

1½ cups sugar

¼ cup all-purpose flour

¼ teaspoon baking powder

½ teaspoon salt

2 cups thinly sliced and
   chopped rhubarb

1 tablespoon finely chopped
   crystallized ginger
   Confectioners' sugar,
   for dusting

Preheat the oven to 375°F. In a large bowl, blend together the flour and sugar. Cut in the butter, using a hand mixer or fork, until the texture resembles large-curd cottage cheese. Press evenly into a 13 × 9-inch baking pan.

Bake for 20 minutes, until light brown.

In another large bowl beat the eggs and sugar until frothy. Add the flour, baking powder, and salt. Stir in the rhubarb and ginger. Pour over the baked crust.

Bake for 35 minutes, until set. Remove from the oven and cool in the pan on a wire rack. Cut into bars when cool. Dust with confectioners' sugar.

Makes 32 bars

Fancy Brunch Torte

 Perfect for the morning when guests sleep late and breakfast runs into lunch (that's how brunch got its name). Make this torte up to two days ahead and keep it in the refrigerator. It tastes great chilled or warmed; we end up heating a slice at a time in the microwave as the breakfasters arrive on the scene. With a bowlful of strawberries to spoon onto the plate and a steaming cup of coffee in hand, a memorable Memorial Day has begun.

  5 large eggs
  1 tablespoon chopped fresh chives
  1 tablespoon minced fresh parsley
  1 teaspoon dried tarragon leaves
  ½ teaspoon salt
  2 tablespoons extra-virgin olive oil
  2 large red peppers, seeded and cut into 1-inch pieces

  2 cloves garlic, minced or pressed
  2 bunches (10 ounces each) fresh spinach, washed and stemmed
  ¼ teaspoon freshly grated nutmeg
  ¼ teaspoon salt
  ¼ teaspoon freshly ground pepper
  1 (15-ounce) package frozen puff pastry, thawed
  ½ pound Swiss cheese, thinly sliced
  ½ pound cooked ham, thinly sliced
  1 large egg, beaten, for glaze

Preheat the oven to 350°F. In a large bowl, whisk together the eggs, chives, parsley, tarragon, and salt. Brush a nonstick 8-inch skillet with some of the olive oil. Place over medium-high heat. Pour half of the egg mixture into the skillet. With a spatula, lift the omelet from the skillet so that the uncooked egg can run under the cooked egg. After about 30 seconds there should be no more uncooked egg on top of the omelet. Flip it over and brown the other side. Slide out onto a plate. Repeat with the remaining mixture and make another omelet. Place the second omelet onto a plate and reserve.

Add the remaining oil to the skillet and add the red peppers; stir-fry over moderately high heat until the peppers are crisp-tender. Remove and reserve. Add the garlic and spinach and sauté for 2 to 3 minutes. Season with the nutmeg, salt, and pepper, then remove from the skillet and reserve.

Coat an 8-inch springform pan with non-stick spray. Roll out one of the pieces of puff pastry on a lightly floured surface to fit the bottom and sides of the pan; trim corners and patch together to fill in holes as needed.

Layer the ingredients into the pastry: Place one omelet on the bottom. Top with half the spinach, half the cheese, half the ham, and all the red bell pepper. Top that with half the ham, half the cheese, half the spinach, and the second omelet. Roll the remaining pastry out to fit over the top. Trim to make an 8-inch circle and seal the edges to the bottom crust. Make fancy cutouts with the scraps. Brush the top of the torte with beaten egg and place the cutouts on top. Make slits on the top with the tip of a knife. Place the pan on a baking sheet.

Bake for 1 hour and 15 minutes or until the top is golden brown. Cool to room temperature on a wire rack.

Makes 8 servings

 # BREAKFASTS

This chapter includes many ideas for make-ahead breakfasts—from simple to complex—for weekend guests. Here are three menu ideas:

Menu #1

FRESH STRAWBERRIES AND CREAM (clean the berries the night before, cover, and refrigerate)

FANCY BRUNCH TORTE (page 78; make up to two days ahead, rewarm in individual pieces)

Menu #2

CHILLED STRAWBERRY/ORANGE JUICE IN COMBINATION (mix the night before: whirl fresh strawberries in a blender and add orange juice; serve over ice)

HONEY-PECAN-APPLE COFFEE CAKE (page 81; make the day before, wrap tightly, and rewarm for breakfast)

Menu #3

SLICED FRESH ORANGES AND GRAPEFRUIT (slice and arrange on a platter the day before; wrap tightly and chill)

COUNTRY EGG AND HAM BRUNCH (page 82; make refrigerated version and bake in morning)

ORANGE-DATE-NUT CAKE (page 80; freeze and rewarm)

Orange-Date-Nut Cake

 Memorial Day is a day when we are apt to have drop-in guests, and it is our custom to serve coffee and something to go with it. This is the perfect cake for the occasion. It's great to take along on a picnic, too.

- 1½ cups sugar, divided
- ¾ cup (1½ sticks) unsalted butter, at room temperature
- 2 large eggs, beaten
- 2 teaspoons grated orange zest
- 2½ cups all-purpose flour
- 1 teaspoon baking powder
- 1 teaspoon baking soda
- 1 cup chopped pitted dates
- 1 cup chopped walnuts
- 1 cup buttermilk
- 1 cup fresh orange juice

Preheat the oven to 350°F. Butter a 13 × 9-inch baking pan or a 10-inch fluted tube pan.

In a large mixing bowl, cream ¾ cup of the sugar and the butter together until smooth. Add the eggs and beat until light. Stir in the orange zest. In another bowl, mix the flour, baking powder, and baking soda together. Put the dates and walnuts into another small bowl and mix with 1 tablespoon of the flour mixture. Add the flour mixture and buttermilk alternately to the creamed mixture and beat until batter is light. Fold in the dates and nuts. Turn the batter into the prepared pan.

Bake for 35 to 40 minutes for the 13 × 9-inch cake, or 55 to 60 minutes for the tube pan, or until a wooden skewer inserted into the center of the cake comes out clean.

Meanwhile, combine the orange juice and the remaining sugar in a small saucepan. Heat to simmering over medium heat. Pour the simmering syrup over the hot cake when you take it out of the oven.

Cool the cake in the pan on a wire rack. Invert the tube cake onto a serving plate or cut squares from the 13 × 9-inch cake.

Makes about 16 servings

Cinnamon-Nut Coffee Cake

 Our friend Vladimir Hizhniak, from Kiev, has spent several weeks as a guest in our home; he calls me the "queen of cinnamon." I didn't realize that I use cinnamon so much, but if Vladimir said it, it must be true. I do love this cinnamony coffee cake, crunchy with nuts and perfumed with this spice that was once used in love potions.

1 cup (2 sticks) unsalted butter,
  at room temperature
1 cup sugar
2 large eggs
1 cup sour cream
2 cups all-purpose flour
1½ teaspoons baking powder
½ teaspoon baking soda
1 teaspoon vanilla
¾ cup chopped walnuts
1 teaspoon ground cinnamon
2 tablespoons packed
  brown sugar

Preheat the oven to 350°F. Butter and flour a 13 × 9-inch baking pan or a 10-inch fluted tube pan.

In a large bowl, beat the butter and sugar together until smooth and light. Add the eggs and beat until light and fluffy. Blend in the sour cream. Sift the flour, baking powder, and baking soda into a medium bowl. Stir into the egg mixture along with the vanilla. In a small bowl, mix the walnuts, cinnamon, and brown sugar. Spoon half the batter into the prepared pan. Sprinkle half the nut mixture over the batter in the pan. Top with the second half of the batter, then sprinkle with the remaining nut mixture.

Bake for 45 to 55 minutes for the 13 × 9-inch pan or 60 to 65 minutes for the fluted pan or until a wooden skewer inserted in the center comes out clean. Cool on a wire rack for 5 minutes, then turn out of the pan. Serve warm.

Makes 10 to 12 servings

Honey-Pecan-Apple Coffee Cake

Spoonfuls of light, yeast-raised batter bake atop a honey, pecan, and sliced-apple base. After baking, you invert it so that the topping will drizzle down onto the warm cake. The rising time is cut in half when you use rapid-rise yeast.

⅓ cup unsalted butter
1 cup chopped pecans
½ cup packed brown sugar
1 teaspoon ground cinnamon
2 tablespoons honey
1 tart apple (such as Granny Smith),
  peeled, cored, and thinly sliced
2 cups all-purpose flour
¼ cup whole wheat flour
1 package (2¾ teaspoons) active dry or
  rapid-rise yeast
¼ cup sugar
1 teaspoon salt
1 large egg
¼ cup (½ stick) unsalted butter, melted
¾ cup very warm water (about 130°F)

To freeze a baked coffee cake, first cool it completely. Then wrap airtight in aluminum foil and place the package into a plastic bag; date and label the bag and freeze for up to three months.

To serve, unwrap, leaving the coffee cake lightly covered, and allow to thaw completely at room temperature before reheating.

To reheat, place the thawed coffee cake on a baking sheet in a preheated 350°F oven. Heat for fifteen minutes. If the coffee cake has an icing or frosting, add it after reheating.

Lightly grease a 9-inch square pan. Melt the ⅓ cup butter in a nonstick skillet over medium heat. Add the pecans and heat until the butter is light brown and the pecans are toasted. Remove from the heat. Spread the mixture into the prepared pan. Mix the brown sugar and cinnamon in a small bowl and sprinkle over. Drizzle the honey over evenly. Arrange the apple slices over the mixture and set aside.

In a large bowl blend the flours, yeast, sugar, and salt together with an electric mixer. With the mixer on medium, add the egg, ¼ cup butter, and the water; beat until smooth. Drop the batter by spoonfuls onto the mixture in the baking pan. (The yeast dough needs to be spooned because it is so elastic it is difficult to spread.) Cover and let rise in a warm place until doubled, about 20 minutes if you used rapid-rise yeast or 45 minutes if you used active dry yeast.

Preheat the oven to 375°F. Bake the coffee cake for 30 to 35 minutes, until golden brown. Remove from the oven and immediately invert onto a serving plate and serve warm.

Makes 6 to 8 servings

Country Egg and Ham Brunch

You assemble this breakfast casserole the night before and while it bakes in the morning, there's time to set out plates, make coffee, stir up juice, and cut fruit. It is possible to de-fat this old classic with modern-day products: Use egg substitute in place of the whole eggs, skim milk instead of whole, and omit the butter. Turkey ham is low in fat, and you can substitute low-fat cheese for the whole-milk Cheddar.

12 large eggs, beaten

9 slices whole wheat bread, crusts removed, cut into ½-inch squares

4 tablespoons (½ stick) unsalted butter, cut into pieces

3 cups milk

6 green onions or scallions, chopped, including green tops

¼ cup chopped green bell pepper

¼ cup chopped red bell pepper

1 pound diced, cooked ham or turkey ham

2 cups (½ pound) shredded sharp Cheddar cheese

¼ teaspoon freshly ground pepper
Chopped fresh herbs (such as basil, chervil, or parsley), for garnish

Butter a 13 × 9-inch baking dish. In a large bowl, combine until well blended the eggs, bread, butter, milk, green onions, green bell pepper, red bell pepper, ham, and cheese. Season with the pepper.

Pour the mixture into the prepared dish, checking to see that all the ingredients are evenly distributed. Cover and refrigerate overnight or bake immediately.

Preheat the oven to 300°F. Uncover the casserole and bake for 1 hour or until set.

Garnish with the fresh chopped herbs and serve immediately.

Makes 8 to 12 servings

Father's Day

Hazelnut Bonbons

 These are little, round, chocolate-dipped butter cookies with a whole hazelnut (filbert) hidden in the center.

1 cup whole hazelnuts (filberts)
1 cup (2 sticks) unsalted butter, at room temperature
½ cup confectioners' sugar
1 teaspoon vanilla
2½ cups all-purpose flour
½ teaspoon salt

For Dipping

6 ounces white chocolate
2 teaspoons white vegetable shortening
6 ounces bittersweet or semisweet chocolate

Preheat the oven to 350°F. Lightly grease 2 baking sheets or cover with parchment paper.

Spread the nuts on an ungreased baking sheet and place in the oven. Toast for 8 to 10 minutes, shaking occasionally, or until aromatic. Remove from the oven and turn

---

 FATHER'S DAY

Father's Day has never met with quite the enthusiasm that Mother's Day has enjoyed. It started as a reaction to a Mother's Day sermon in 1909 by a woman from Spokane, Washington, whose father had raised six children after the death of his wife. But sixty-three years went by, and it wasn't until 1972 that Congress established the official holiday, which, like Mother's Day, has become commercialized.

In an effort to decommercialize Father's Day, I'm suggesting that you get the family together and cook for Dad. In Sweden, for instance, Father's Day is the day when Dad gets to choose his favorite foods, and his every whim is indulged.

Here are some ideas: Offer Dad breakfast in bed and make him a nice big Pannukakku—an oven pancake—served with bacon, sausages, fruit, and whatever else he loves. Or how about Raisin-Walnut Scones or a rich and gooey chocolate dessert after dinner? Check out the recipes in this section: My dad's favorite is the Finnish Rye Bread.

onto a terry towel. Rub off the papery skins and set the nuts aside.

In a large bowl with an electric mixer, cream the butter with the sugar and vanilla. Stir in the flour and salt; mix until the dough is smooth and pliable. Wrap about 2 teaspoons of dough around each nut, shaping the cookie into a perfect round. Place on the prepared baking sheets, 2 inches apart. Bake for 10 to 12 minutes, until light brown. Cool. Slide the parchment onto a countertop to cool or remove the cookies and cool on a rack.

For dipping the cookies, chop the white chocolate and place in a small heatproof bowl with 1 teaspoon of the shortening. Chop the bittersweet chocolate and place in another small heatproof bowl with the remaining 1 teaspoon shortening. Place the bowls, one at a time, over a saucepan of simmering water until the chocolate is melted. Stir occasionally.

Dip the cookies halfway in one of the chocolates. Place on waxed paper to harden. Dip the second half in the other chocolate. When the chocolates have hardened, place the cookies into paper bonbon cups. Store in an airtight tin in a cool place until ready to serve.

Makes about 48 bonbons

Cherry-Almond Tartlets

The simple-to-mix pastry is shaped into a roll and refrigerated to firm up. I just unwrap the roll and cut it into slices. I press the pieces into fluted tartlet pans or miniature muffin cups and fill them before baking.

Pastry

- ½ cup (1 stick) unsalted butter, at room temperature
- 4 ounces cream cheese
- 1½ cups all-purpose flour

Cherry-Almond Filling

- 4 tablespoons (½ stick) unsalted butter, melted
- ¾ cup sugar
- 1 large egg
- ¼ cup amaretto, or another almond-flavored liqueur
- ½ cup slivered almonds, toasted
- ½ cup dried tart cherries

To make the pastry, in a large bowl, cream the butter and cream cheese together until well blended. Add the flour and mix until the dough is smooth. Shape the pastry into a log, 2½ inches in diameter. Wrap in plastic wrap and chill 4 hours or overnight.

Preheat the oven to 350°F. Place 3 dozen tiny fluted tartlet tins, sandbakkel tins, or miniature muffin tins (1½ inches in diameter, and ¾ inch deep) on a baking sheet or sheets.

Unwrap the pastry. With a sharp, straight-edged knife, cut the pastry into 36 slices, ¼ inch thick. Press one slice at a time into the bottom and evenly up the sides of each tin or muffin cup.

To make the filling, beat the melted butter, sugar, egg, and amaretto together until smooth. Add the almonds and cherries. Spoon about 2 teaspoons of the mixture into each pastry-lined tin.

Bake for 15 to 20 minutes or until the filling is set and the pastry is light brown. Remove from pans and cool on a wire rack.

Makes 36 tartlets

Chewy Fudgy Brownies

Dad will have lots of help polishing off this pan of brownies if there are chocolate lovers in the house. These are perfect without an icing, but for extra gooiness go ahead and frost them!

Brownies
- 2 squares (2 ounces) unsweetened chocolate
- 6 tablespoons unsalted butter
- 1 cup sugar
- 2 large eggs
- ¾ cup all-purpose flour
- ½ teaspoon baking powder
- ¼ teaspoon salt
- ½ cup broken walnuts

Chocolate Icing
- 1 tablespoon unsalted butter
- 1 square (1 ounce) unsweetened chocolate
- 1½ tablespoons warm water
- 1 cup sifted confectioners' sugar

Preheat the oven to 350°F. Lightly grease an 8-inch square pan.

For the brownies, in a heavy saucepan, combine the chocolate and butter. Place over low heat and stir until the chocolate and butter are melted together. Remove from the heat and beat in the sugar and eggs until the mixture is light. In a small bowl stir the flour, baking powder, and salt together, then stir into the chocolate mixture until well blended. Mix in the walnuts. Spread into the prepared pan.

Bake for 25 to 30 minutes, or until the top has a dull crust and a slight imprint will remain when touched in the center. Cool on a wire rack.

Make the icing. Combine the butter and chocolate in a small glass bowl. Microwave on high power for 1 to 2 minutes, until the chocolate and butter are melted together. Stir in the water and sugar until the frosting is of spreading consistency. Spread over the cooled brownies. Cut into squares.

Makes sixteen 2-inch brownies

Unsweetened Chocolate

This is pure chocolate with no sugar or flavoring added. It is usually packaged in individually wrapped one-ounce squares. For an emergency substitution, use three tablespoons unsweetened cocoa plus one tablespoon melted butter or shortening.

Bittersweet Chocolate

This is pure chocolate with some sugar added. It is usually available in large bars. If unavailable, substitute half unsweetened chocolate and half semisweet chocolate.

Semisweet Chocolate

This is pure chocolate combined with sugar and extra cocoa butter. It's available in one-ounce squares, bars, chips, and chunks.

Milk Chocolate

This is pure chocolate with sugar, cocoa butter, and milk solids added. It's available in bars, chips, and stars.

Sweet Chocolate

This is pure chocolate combined with extra cocoa butter and sugar. It's available in bars.

White Chocolate

This is not considered to be real chocolate, because most or all of the cocoa butter has been removed and replaced by another vegetable fat. It's available in chips and bars.

Unsweetened Cocoa

This is made by extracting most of the cocoa butter from pure chocolate and grinding the remaining chocolate solids into a powder. It is low in fat.

Marble Brownies

White and chocolate batters, swirled together until marbled and baked, make these chewy brownies pretty and delicious.

    4   ounces (4 squares) semisweet
        chocolate
    5   tablespoons unsalted butter, divided
    1   small (3-ounce) package
        cream cheese
    1   cup sugar, divided
    3   large eggs
    1   tablespoon plus ½ cup all-purpose
        flour, divided
    ½   teaspoon vanilla
    ¼   teaspoon salt
    ½   teaspoon baking powder

Preheat the oven to 350°F. Butter a 9-inch square pan.

In a small, heavy saucepan, melt the chocolate and 3 tablespoons of the butter over very low heat. Or combine the chocolate and butter in a small glass bowl. Microwave on high power for 1 minute. Stir. Microwave 30 seconds to 1 minute longer, if necessary, until the chocolate is melted.

In a large bowl, cream the remaining 2 tablespoons butter and the cream cheese. Add ¼ cup of the sugar, beating until smooth. Beat in one of the eggs, 1 tablespoon of the flour, and the vanilla and beat until light. Set aside.

In another bowl, beat the remaining 2 eggs until light and lemon colored. Slowly add the salt and the remaining ¾ cup sugar. Beat until thickened and light. Add the baking powder and the remaining ½ cup flour. Stir in the melted chocolate mixture.

Turn half the chocolate batter into the baking pan. Top with the cream cheese mixture. Spoon the remaining chocolate batter evenly over the top. Swirl a knife back and forth through all three layers to create a marbled effect.

Bake for 25 to 30 minutes or until brownies feel firm to the touch in the center of the pan. Cool in the pan on a wire rack.

Makes 16 brownies

Raisin-Walnut Scones

These scones are especially good served with whipped cream cheese blended with shredded smoked Cheddar cheese.

    3   cups all-purpose flour
    1   tablespoon baking powder
    ½   teaspoon ground cinnamon
    ½   cup sugar
    1   cup (2 sticks) unsalted butter,
            chilled and cut into pieces
    1   cup raisins
    ½   cup chopped walnuts
    3   large eggs
    ½ to ⅔ cup plain yogurt or buttermilk
    1   tablespoon sugar, for sprinkling

Chocolate should be wrapped airtight and stored in a cool, dry place. Do not freeze or refrigerate pure chocolate. If unexposed to light and well wrapped, chocolate will keep at least a year.

Preheat the oven to 400°F. Lightly grease a large cookie sheet or cover with parchment paper.

Combine the flour, baking powder, cinnamon, and sugar in a food processor or a large bowl. Add the butter and process or cut in until the butter is in pea-size pieces. Turn mixture into a bowl, if using the food processor, and mix in the raisins and walnuts.

In a small bowl, mix the eggs and ½ cup of yogurt or buttermilk. Add to the dry ingredients and blend with a fork just until a dough forms (add a bit more yogurt or buttermilk if needed). Shape the dough into a smooth ball. Dust lightly with flour if sticky. Place on the baking sheet and flatten to a 7- to 8-inch circle. With a sharp knife, score into 12 wedges; leave the wedges in place. Sprinkle the top with sugar.

Bake for 15 to 20 minutes, until light brown. Cool on the baking sheet on a wire rack. To serve, break into wedges. Serve warm with butter or cream cheese.

Makes 12 scones

Chocolate-Glazed Fudge Brownie Cake

 Just because a lot of dads I know love chocolate, I think this is an appropriate Father's Day cake. This fudgy brownie is topped with an equally fudgy frosting.

Cake

- ½ cup dark corn syrup
- ½ cup (1 stick) unsalted butter
- 1 cup semisweet chocolate chips
- ½ cup sugar
- 3 large eggs
- 1 teaspoon vanilla
- 1 cup all-purpose flour
- 1 cup chopped walnuts

Chocolate Glaze

- ½ cup semisweet chocolate chips
- 3 tablespoons unsalted butter
- 2 tablespoons light corn syrup

Preheat the oven to 350°F. Butter and flour a 9-inch round cake pan.

In a large saucepan, combine the corn

syrup and butter. Bring to a boil over medium-high heat, stirring. Remove from the heat. Add the chocolate and stir until melted. Add the sugar, then stir in the eggs, vanilla, flour, and walnuts. Pour into the prepared pan.

Bake for 30 minutes or until a wooden skewer inserted in the middle of the cake comes out clean. Cool in the pan for 10 minutes. Remove. Cool completely on a wire rack.

To make the glaze, combine the chocolate, butter, and corn syrup in a heatproof bowl. Place over simmering water. Stir until the chocolate is melted and continue stirring occasionally until the glaze has cooled. Remove from the heat. Spread the glaze over the cooled cake, coating the top and sides evenly. Cool until the glaze is set, about 1 hour.

Makes 8 to 12 servings

Finnish Rye Bread

Unless there is rye bread in the bread box, my father doesn't think there's anything to eat. I learned to make this bread as a young girl. When I was fifteen, I demonstrated how to make Finnish Rye Bread and won the National Grand Championship in a 4-H bread baking competition. It was my father who suggested that I select rye bread as the topic for my demonstration. "Real food," he called it. I love this bread because of its simple rye flavor. It is a perfect base for open-faced sandwiches, and it is delicious with just butter.

>   2   cups bread flour or unbleached
>   all-purpose flour
> 1½   cups rye meal or dark rye flour
>   1   package (2¾ teaspoons) dry yeast
>   or rapid-rise yeast
>   1   tablespoon packed brown sugar
>   1   tablespoon melted butter or
>   vegetable oil
> 1½   teaspoons salt
> 1¼ to 1½   cups warm tap water
>   (about 130°F)

Measure the bread and rye flours into the work bowl of the food processor with the dough blade in place, or into a large bowl. Add the yeast, brown sugar, butter, and salt. Process or combine with an electric mixer until well blended.

Turn the motor on and slowly add 1¼ cups water; mixing or processing until the dough comes together in a smooth ball. If the dough is stiff and dry, add more water, a tablespoon at a time. If the dough is too sticky, add bread flour, a tablespoon at a time, until the dough has a smooth, satiny, springy consistency. Knead in the food processor for 25 turns, or in the bowl with a mixer for 5 minutes.

Cover and let rise in a warm place for 30 to 45 minutes, until doubled. Lightly grease a baking sheet or 9-inch round cake pan.

Turn the dough out onto a lightly oiled surface. Knead to punch out air bubbles. Shape into a round loaf. Place in the prepared pan. Cover and let rise until puffy, about 30 minutes.

Preheat the oven to 375°F. Bake for 45 to 55 minutes or until a skewer inserted in the center of the loaf comes out clean. Remove from the oven and brush with butter. Cool on a wire rack.

Makes one 9-inch round loaf

Walnut-Banana Cake

This is so quick and easy to stir up that kids can do it. Let them offer Dad a piece of this cake with his afternoon coffee. He'll probably snitch another piece at midnight to go with a glass of milk.

1½ cups all-purpose flour
¾ cup sugar
1 teaspoon baking powder
¼ teaspoon baking soda
⅛ teaspoon salt
⅔ cup walnuts, chopped
2 small, ripe bananas, mashed
⅓ cup vegetable oil
⅓ cup buttermilk
2 large eggs, beaten
1 cup whipping cream
1 tablespoon confectioners' sugar

Preheat the oven to 350°F. Lightly grease a 9-inch square cake pan.

Combine the flour, sugar, baking powder, baking soda, salt, and walnuts in a large bowl.

In another bowl, mix the bananas, oil, buttermilk, and eggs until smooth. Add the banana mixture to the dry ingredients and stir with a wooden spoon just until well blended.

Pour the batter into the pan and smooth out. Bake for 30 to 35 minutes, until a wooden skewer inserted in the center of the cake comes out clean. Cool in the pan on a wire rack. To serve, invert onto a serving plate. In a small bowl, whip the cream with the confectioners' sugar until stiff. Mound the whipped cream on top of the cake.

Makes 8 to 10 servings

Pannukakku

This is a super "quick Sunday brunch" dish. It's a recipe that appeals to the dads in our family because it is so logical. Basically, equal measures of eggs, milk, and flour with a little sugar and a little salt and a very hot oven is all you need to remember (see Note). Put out grilled sausages, a platter of fruit, a bowl of confectioners' sugar, and a bunch of lemon wedges, and the table will be ready when the pancake comes out of the oven, looking like a golden crater.

6 large eggs, beaten

1½ cups milk

1½ cups all-purpose flour

1 tablespoon sugar

1 teaspoon salt

½ cup (1 stick) unsalted butter

Toppings and Accompaniments

Lemon wedges

Confectioners' sugar

Cut fresh fruit

Whipped cream

Grilled breakfast sausages

Beat the eggs, milk, flour, sugar, and salt together until smooth. Let stand for 30 minutes at room temperature.

Preheat the oven to 450°F. Coat a 3-quart paella pan about 16 inches in diameter and 3 inches deep or a 3-quart baking dish with nonstick spray. Put the butter into the pan and place it in the oven until the butter is melted.

Immediately pour the batter into the pan. Place in the oven and bake for 20 to 25 minutes or until the pannukakku rises into a basket shape with golden, crisp edges.

Serve immediately cut into slices with lemon wedges and confectioners' sugar. Add fruit and whipped cream, if desired. Serve with grilled sausages.

Makes 4 servings

NOTE: If fat and/or cholesterol is a concern, you can make these adjustments: use 1½ cups egg substitute, skim milk, and coat the baking pan well with nonstick spray, omitting the butter.

Strawberry-Rhubarb Pie

 Fruits that are in season together, go together. Even though rhubarb is technically a vegetable we use it as a fruit. So it is with rhubarb and strawberries, making early summer the perfect time of year to enjoy the combination of strawberries at their tastiest and rhubarb at its juiciest. I do prefer to serve the pie cool or slightly chilled, to bring out the flavors of the fruits. Lard, as most farm women will say, makes the flakiest, tenderest pie crust. But, if you prefer, use vegetable shortening or butter, or a combination of the two.

Farmhouse Pastry (see Note)

1½ cups all-purpose or pastry flour

½ teaspoon salt

½ cup lard, butter, or vegetable shortening, chilled and cut into pieces

1 large egg white, slightly beaten

1 teaspoon vinegar

1 to 3 tablespoons ice water

Filling

1 cup sugar

¼ cup cornstarch

1 teaspoon grated lemon zest

¼ teaspoon salt

4 cups rhubarb, cut into 1-inch pieces

1 pint fresh strawberries, washed, hulled, and halved

Glaze

    Water

1 teaspoon sugar

Make the pastry. In a large bowl, stir the flour and salt together. Cut in the shortening until the mixture resembles coarse meal and is in pea-size pieces. In a small bowl, beat the egg white, vinegar, and 1 tablespoon ice water together. Pour over the flour mixture and stir with a fork until the mixture comes together in a coarse ball (add ice water a table-spoon at a time, if too dry). Turn out onto a lightly floured surface. Divide the dough in half and shape each piece into a 1-inch-thick disk. Wrap in plastic and chill at least 30 minutes or until you are ready for baking.

Preheat the oven to 425°F. On a floured surface, roll one part of the pastry out to fit a 9- or 10-inch pie pan with about 1 inch of pastry hanging over the sides and fit the pastry into the pan.

Make the filling. In a large mixing bowl, combine the sugar, cornstarch, lemon zest, and salt. Add the rhubarb and strawberries and toss until the pieces are coated. Turn into the pastry-lined pan.

Roll the second portion of pastry out on a lightly floured surface to fit over the top of the pie. Moisten the edges of the overhanging pastry and place the pastry on top. Trim the edges, seal, and flute. Cut several slashes in the top of the pastry for vents. Glaze the crust by brushing the top of the pie with water and then sprinkling with sugar.

Bake for 45 minutes or until the pie is golden and the filling is bubbly. Put on a wire rack to cool.

Makes 8 servings

NOTE: To save time, you can use purchased, refrigerated pie pastry instead of making your own. Follow the manufacturer's directions.

Applesauce Cake

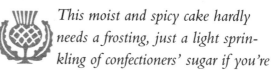 *This moist and spicy cake hardly needs a frosting, just a light sprin-kling of confectioners' sugar if you're baking it in a fancy tube pan. But the Brown Sugar Frosting on the layer or sheet cake turns the cake into confection.*

½ cup (1 stick) unsalted butter,
     at room temperature

1½ cups sugar

1 large egg, at room temperature

1½ cups applesauce

2 teaspoons baking soda

2 cups all-purpose flour

1 teaspoon ground cinnamon

¼ teaspoon ground cloves

¼ teaspoon salt

1 cup chopped pitted dates or
     raisins (optional)

1 cup chopped walnuts

Brown Sugar Frosting
(for layer cake)

¼ cup (½ stick) unsalted butter, at room temperature

⅓ cup light cream or undiluted evaporated milk

1 cup brown sugar, firmly packed

1½ to 2 cups confectioners' sugar

1 teaspoon vanilla

Preheat the oven to 350°F. Grease and flour two 9-inch round pans, a 10-inch bundt or fancy tube pan, or a 13 × 9-inch pan.

In a large bowl cream the butter and sugar with an electric mixer until smooth. Add the egg and beat until light.

In a small bowl, mix the applesauce with the baking soda.

In another bowl, stir together the flour, cinnamon, cloves, and salt.

Add the dry ingredients to the creamed mixture alternately with the applesauce mixture, and beat until smooth. Stir in the dates and walnuts with a wooden spoon. Pour the batter into the prepared pan. Bake for 30 to 35 minutes for the layers, 1 hour for the fancy tube pan, or 40 to 45 minutes for the 13 × 9-inch pan or until a toothpick inserted into the center of the cake comes out clean. Cool for 5 minutes in the pan, then turn out onto a wire rack to finish cooling.

TO MAKE THE BROWN SUGAR FROSTING

In a saucepan, combine the butter, cream, and brown sugar. Heat to boiling; boil for 2 minutes, stirring. Remove from heat and beat in the confectioners' sugar until the mixture is of spreading consistency. Stir in the vanilla.

To fill and frost the layers, place one layer on a cake plate. Spread about ½ cup of the frosting over the layer, then top with the second layer. Spread the remaining frosting over the top and sides of the cake. For the cake baked in the tube pan, drizzle the frosting over the top and sides of the cake or omit the frosting and sprinkle with confectioners' sugar. For the 13 × 9-inch pan, spread with the Brown Sugar Frosting.

Makes 16 servings

Midsummer's Day

Midsummer's Day is a holiday mostly observed by Scandinavians. Some scholars think that this festival is a continuation of the old pagan fire-festival in honor of Balder, the mild and beautiful sungod. Christians named the day for St. John the Baptist (Johannes Day). Whatever the name, June 24 is the longest day of the year, one on which the sun never sets in Scandinavia, so the celebrating goes on for twenty-four hours with no need for artificial light, with the sunlight energizing the people. There is dancing around the maypole, a tall mast, decorated with fresh flowers, birch branches, and colorful banners. It may seem strange to have a maypole for a June festival. The explanation is that *may* (maj in Swedish) does not refer to the month of May, but refers to an old Swedish word for "green leaf."

The traditional feast on Midsummer's Day includes salmon, chicken, strawberries, and of course, plenty of cakes, cookies, and breads. Strawberries are in season, chicken has traditionally been a delicacy reserved for festivals and parties, and salmon is at its best at this time of year.

Fruit Flan

Showcase various fruits atop this flan or tart as they come into season throughout the summer. If you were to visit Sweden during the Midsummer's celebration on June 24, you'd enjoy this lovely dessert with fresh strawberries.

Butter Pastry

 5 tablespoons unsalted butter,
    at room temperature

 ¼ cup sugar
 1 large egg yolk
 1 cup all-purpose flour

Vanilla Custard Filling

 1 cup light cream or
    half-and-half
 2 large egg yolks
 1 tablespoon sugar
 2 teaspoons cornstarch
 1 tablespoon vanilla or vanilla sugar
    (see Note)

Topping

   3 cups cleaned and sliced fresh fruit,
     such as strawberries; blueberries;
     raspberries; peeled, pitted, and
     sliced peaches; pitted and halved
     apricots; sliced bananas, or seedless
     green, red, or black grapes
   1 cup red currant jelly

Preheat the oven to 350°F. Butter a fluted 9-inch tart pan with a removable bottom. Cream the butter and sugar together until smooth, then add the egg yolk and beat until light. Blend in the flour until the dough is smooth. Press evenly onto the bottom and sides of the tart pan and trim the edges.

Bake for 10 to 15 minutes, until light golden brown. (There is no need to prick the tart or use weights when the pastry is pressed into the pan.) Let cool in the pan. Remove tart shell from the pan (see Box). Place the shell on a serving plate.

To make the filling, combine the cream, egg yolks, sugar, and cornstarch in a nonreactive saucepan. (If you use an aluminum pan, the custard will turn a light green.) Heat to a simmer, over medium-low heat, stirring continuously, and cook until thickened, about 3 minutes. Let cool, covered. When cooled, stir in the vanilla.

Fill the shell with the cooled vanilla custard. Arrange the fruit on top. Place the jelly into a small saucepan over low heat and stir until melted. Spoon evenly over the fruit. Chill ½ hour before serving.

Makes 8 servings

NOTE: To make your own vanilla sugar, split a vanilla bean and sink it into a pint jar filled with confectioners' sugar. Cover and let it stand for a week for the flavor to permeate. The vanilla bean may be reused.

Mazarins

This is the beloved almond-paste–filled butter pastry of Europe. I like to make them in miniature muffin cups for two-bite treats. They're perfect pastries to keep on hand in the freezer for a quick dessert or to go with tea or coffee.

Pastry

   ½ cup (1 stick) unsalted butter,
     at room temperature
   ⅓ cup sugar
   1 large egg yolk
  1⅓ cups all-purpose flour

Filling

   ½ cup (1 stick) unsalted butter,
     at room temperature
   ¼ cup sugar
   ½ pound almond paste
   3 large eggs
   ¼ cup all-purpose flour

Frosting

   1 cup confectioners' sugar
   2 tablespoons water

Preheat the oven to 350°F. Lightly butter 24 miniature muffin cups.

To prepare the pastry, in a mixing bowl, with an electric mixer or a wooden spoon, cream the butter and sugar until smooth. Add the egg yolk, mixing well. Stir in the flour until the dough is stiff and smooth.

Shape the dough into a long log and cut into 24 pieces. Place each piece into a muffin cup and press to cover the bottom and sides of each cup.

Make the filling. In a mixing bowl, cream the butter and sugar together until smooth. Crumble the almond paste into the bowl and mix until smooth. Beat in the eggs one at a time; then stir in the flour just until combined. Spoon the filling into the pastry-lined muffin tins.

Bake for 20 to 25 minutes or until golden. Cool in the tin for 5 minutes, then gently unmold and finish cooling on a wire rack.

To frost, stir the confectioners' sugar and water together in a small bowl to make a thin glaze. Spread on top of the pastries while still slightly warm. Or you can simply sift the confectioners' sugar over the pastries. Serve warm or at room temperature.

Makes 24 mazarins

BAKING AHEAD

Although most baked goods taste their very best fresh out of the oven, most can be baked ahead and kept frozen for several weeks without significant loss of quality. Except for cream-filled pies, the majority of cakes, cookies, yeast breads, pies, and tarts can be frozen successfully. Cream fillings lose quality and break down after thawing, but fruit-filled freeze better. Popovers, oven pancakes, fritters, doughnuts, and other deep-fried pastries do not freeze well.

Always wrap baked goods airtight so that the surface moisture will not evaporate or collect ice in the freezer, which causes sogginess when the products are thawed. Careful wrapping will keep flavors fresh.

While freezing is an excellent way to preserve freshness, refrigerating baked goods causes them to get stale faster than if they were at room temperature, even though refrigeration does retard the growth of mold on bread.

Norwegian Bløtkake

This cake is part of all important celebrations in Norway. Norwegians serve it not only on Midsummer's Day but also on birthdays, anniversaries, and Sytende Mai—May 17—which is Norwegian independence day, celebrated by both Norwegians and Americans of Norwegian descent. It is perfect because fresh strawberries are in season, and that's what makes this cake so good.

Sponge Cake

- ¾ cup all-purpose flour
- 1 teaspoon baking powder
- 6 large eggs, separated
- 1 cup sugar

Filling

- 3 large egg yolks
- 2 tablespoons unsalted butter
- 2 tablespoons cornstarch
- 1½ cups half-and-half
- ¼ cup sugar
- 2 teaspoons vanilla
- ½ cup strawberry jam
- 2 pints fresh strawberries, washed and hulled

Topping

- 1½ cups whipping cream
- 2 tablespoons confectioners' sugar
- 1 teaspoon vanilla

Preheat the oven to 350°F. Butter and flour two 9-inch round cake pans.

Make the cake. Sift the flour with the baking powder and set aside. In a large bowl, beat the egg whites with an electric mixer until frothy; gradually add the sugar and beat until stiff and meringuelike. In a small bowl, beat the yolks until frothy; fold the yolks and flour into the egg whites just until incorporated. Divide the batter evenly between the pans.

Bake for 30 minutes or until the centers spring back when touched. Cool in the pans on a wire rack (centers of the cakes may sink slightly).

To prepare the custard filling, in a small nonreactive saucepan, mix the egg yolks, butter, cornstarch, half-and-half, and sugar. Cook, stirring, over medium heat until the mixture is smooth and thick. Remove from the heat, cover, and cool. Stir in the vanilla.

To assemble the cake, cut the layers horizontally, making 4 layers in all. Place the bottom layer on a cake plate and spread with half the custard. Top with the next layer. Spread with the jam. Reserve a few of the nicest strawberries for garnish on top of the cake, then slice the remainder and arrange on top of the jam layer. Top with a third layer of cake. Spread with the remaining custard. Top with the remaining layer of cake.

No more than 1 hour before serving, make the topping. Whip the cream and flavor with the confectioners' sugar and vanilla. Pile whipped cream on top of the cake and garnish with the reserved berries.

Makes about 16 servings

Spiced Butter Sponge Cake

For a Midsummer's coffee treat, offer pieces of this sponge cake with a scoop of freshly made coffee ice cream and top it with a rich chocolate sauce.

Dried bread crumbs, for coating pan
3 large eggs
1 cup sugar
1⅓ cups all-purpose flour
2 teaspoons baking powder
1 teaspoon freshly ground cardamom
1 teaspoon ground cinnamon
½ teaspoon ground ginger
¼ teaspoon ground cloves
½ cup (1 stick) unsalted butter, melted
⅓ cup warm water

Preheat the oven to 350°F. Butter a 6-cup ring mold and sprinkle it with dry bread crumbs to coat.

In a large bowl with an electric mixer, beat the eggs and sugar until thick and light. Sift the flour, baking powder, cardamom, cinnamon, ginger, and cloves over the batter and stir into the batter along with the melted butter. Add the water and blend well. Pour the batter into the prepared pan.

Bake for 40 to 45 minutes or until a wooden skewer inserted in the center comes out clean. Remove from the oven and cool in the pan for 5 minutes, then invert the cake onto a wire rack to finish cooling.

Makes about 8 servings

Swedish Breakfast Crackers

This recipe is from a Swedish country inn in Tallberg, where every summer there is a huge Midsummer's celebration. Crispy twice-baked breads are a regular offering at the inn's breakfast buffet.

¾ cup (1½ sticks) unsalted butter, at room temperature
⅓ cup sugar
1 large egg
4 cups whole wheat flour
2 cups all-purpose flour
6 teaspoons baking powder
1 teaspoon salt
1½ cups milk

Preheat the oven to 400°F. Lightly grease two 17 × 14-inch baking sheets without sides.

In a large mixing bowl, cream the butter with the sugar; add the egg and beat until light.

In another bowl, stir the flours together with the baking powder and salt. Add to the creamed mixture along with the milk and mix until the dough is well blended. Divide the dough into 2 equal parts.

Flatten each half of the dough and place one on each baking sheet. Sprinkle lightly with flour. With a rolling pin, roll the dough out directly on the baking sheet, adding flour as necessary to keep from sticking, until the dough is 12 × 15 inches and about ¼ inch thick. Pierce all over with a fork. With a straight knife, cut into 2 × 3-inch rectangles, leaving them in place.

Bake for 12 to 15 minutes or until light brown. Remove from the oven and, with a sharp knife, cut the crackers where they were scored to separate, leaving them on the baking sheet. Turn off the oven and return the crackers to the oven to crisp, about 10 minutes.

Makes about 48 crackers

Swedish Punch Cake

The Swedes enjoy a liqueur called "punch" which has a rumlike flavor. They serve it warm in demitasse cups, add it to sweets as a flavoring, and soak sponge cake layers with it.

    1 cup (4 to 5 large) eggs,
        at room temperature
    1 cup sugar
    1 cup all-purpose flour
    1 teaspoon baking powder
    1 teaspoon vanilla

Swedish Punch Syrup
  ½ cup water
  ¼ cup sugar
  ½ cup golden rum

Filling
    2 cups whipping cream
    2 tablespoons confectioners' sugar

    1 teaspoon vanilla
2 to 4 cups cubed fresh fruit or berries,
        or 2 cups fruit-flavored jam

Preheat the oven to 350°F. Line the bottoms of two 9-inch round cake pans with parchment paper and coat with nonstick cooking spray.

In a large bowl with an electric mixer, beat the eggs until frothy. Increase the speed to high and add the sugar gradually, beating until thick and lemon colored, scraping the sides of the bowl often. Stir together the flour and baking powder in another bowl. Reduce the speed of the electric mixer to low and slowly add the flour mixture to the whipped eggs. Mix just until blended. Stir in the vanilla. Pour the batter evenly into the prepared pans and smooth the tops.

Bake for 25 to 30 minutes or until the center of the cake bounces back when touched. Remove the cake layers from the oven and cool in the pans on a wire rack.

Make the syrup. In a small saucepan, combine the water and sugar and place over medium heat until the mixture boils. Stir until the sugar is completely dissolved, about 2 to 3 minutes. Cool the sugar syrup. Then combine the rum and sugar syrup in a small bowl.

Make the filling by whipping the cream in another bowl, until stiff peaks form. Blend in the sugar and vanilla.

Remove the cakes from the pans. Invert one layer on a serving plate so that the flat side is up. Split the cake horizontally into 2 parts. Remove the top half of the layer.

Drizzle the cut side with one-quarter of the syrup. Spread with one-quarter of the whipped cream and one-third of the fruit or jam. Top with the upper half of the layer. Drizzle with another one-quarter of the syrup and one-third of the fruit; top with one-quarter of the whipped cream.

Split the second cake layer. Place the bottom half of the layer on top of the assembled cake. Drizzle with one-quarter of the syrup. Spread with the remaining fruit and another quarter of the whipped cream. Top with the last upper part of the layer, with the smooth top up, and drizzle with the remaining syrup. Spread the remaining whipped cream on top.

Refrigerate for up to 2 hours or serve immediately. Cover with a large bowl or a cake bell so the topping doesn't get disturbed.

Makes 8 to 12 servings

Bread-Machine-Caraway-Rye Bread

Freshly baked breads are important to midsummer's celebrations because they are used not only as a base for sandwiches but also sliced and buttered to accompany a meal. I added caraway seed to my favorite Finnish rye bread and then converted the recipe for use in a bread machine with excellent results. In fact, I tested the recipe in five different machines that make a 1½-pound loaf with excellent results. What we really enjoy is setting the machine so that the bread is ready in the morning, allowing us to rise to that wonderful yeasty aroma. What a great way to have homemade bread without heating up the kitchen!

1	cup water
2	tablespoons light molasses
1	tablespoon unsalted butter, cut into pieces
1	teaspoon salt
2	teaspoons caraway seed
1	cup dark rye flour
2	cups bread flour
1½	teaspoons active dry yeast

Measure all of the ingredients in the order in which they are listed into the mixing container of the bread machine. If your machine requires that the liquid ingredients be added last, simply reverse the order. Program the machine according to the manufacturer's directions for a standard loaf of bread, medium darkness. This bread can be programmed for delayed mixing and baking, or you can start it immediately.

Makes one loaf, 1½ pounds

Fresh Fruit Muffins

You can bake blueberries, blackberries, chopped apple, diced peaches or, my favorite, raspberries into these muffins depending on what's in season at the moment. Just be sure that you handle the soft berries gently so they will not get smashed in the dough.

2 cups all-purpose flour
½ cup sugar
3 teaspoons baking powder
½ teaspoon salt
1 teaspoon grated orange zest
1 cup fresh berries or fresh fruit, in ½-inch dice
¾ cup milk
½ cup (1 stick) unsalted butter, melted
1 egg, slightly beaten

For the Top
1 to 2 tablespoons sugar

Preheat the oven to 400°F. Lightly grease 12 muffin cups or line them with paper baking cups.

In a large mixing bowl, stir together the flour, sugar, baking powder, salt, and orange zest. Sprinkle 1 tablespoon of the mixture over the fresh fruit and mix gently to coat.

In a small bowl, combine the milk, butter, and egg. Pour the liquid ingredients over the dry ingredients and stir just to moisten, about 15 strokes. Fold in the fruit.

Fill the muffin cups ⅔ to ¾ full. Sprinkle the tops of the muffins with sugar. Bake for 20 to 25 minutes or until light golden brown. Cool 1 minute, then remove from the muffin cups. Serve warm.

Makes 12 muffins

Bread-Machine Oatmeal Bread

This recipe, adapted from a recipe from my friend Mary Boman, I tested in five different brands of bread machines. They all make a 1½ pound loaf. The original recipe requires that you soak the rolled oats in boiling water until the mixture is cooled down to room temperature.

1¼ cups boiling water
½ cup quick-rolled oats
2 tablespoons light molasses
1 tablespoon unsalted butter, cut into pieces
1 teaspoon salt
2½ cups bread flour
2 tablespoons wheat germ
1½ teaspoons active dry yeast

Pour the boiling water into the container of your bread machine. Add the un-cooked rolled oats, stir, and let stand for 30 minutes or until the mixture is cooled to room temperature.

Add the remaining ingredients in the order in which they are listed to mixing container of the bread machine. If your machine instructions have you add the liquid ingredients last of all, combine the boiling water and oats in a small bowl and let stand for 30 minutes or until the mixture has cooled to room temperature. Place the remaining ingredients into the container of the bread machine in the reverse order, starting with the yeast and ending with the cooled-oat mixture.

Program the machine according to the manufacturer's directions for a standard loaf of bread, medium darkness. This bread can be programmed for delayed mixing and baking, or you can start it immediately.

Makes one loaf, 1½ pounds

Fourth of July

Chicken and Vegetable Pasties

 These chicken and vegetable pies are great picnic fare. If you make them half size (see Variation), they can be eaten out of hand.

Boiling-Water Pastry

1 cup lard (see Note) or vegetable shortening
1¼ cups boiling water
1 teaspoon salt
4 to 4½ cups all-purpose flour

Chicken and Vegetable Filling

4 medium potatoes, peeled and cut into ½-inch dice
½ cup finely chopped onion
1 cup shredded carrots
1 cup broccoli florets, broken into ½-inch pieces
1 red pepper, seeded and diced into ½-inch pieces
2 teaspoons salt
½ teaspoon freshly ground pepper
1 pound skinless, boneless chicken breasts, diced
2 tablespoons unsalted butter, at room temperature, plus additional for serving, if desired

To make the pastry, in a large bowl, mix the lard or shortening with boiling water and salt and stir until the fat is melted. Add enough flour to make a stiff dough. Cover and refrigerate 1 hour or more. Divide into 8 parts. On a lightly floured surface, roll out each part to make a 9-inch round.

Preheat the oven to 350°F. Line 2 baking sheets with parchment paper or brown paper.

Combine all of the filling ingredients. Scoop 1 cup of the filling mixture in the center of each pastry round. Gently lift the edges

---

 AMERICAN INDEPENDENCE DAY, JULY 4

The thirteen rebel American colonies voted in favor of independence on July 2, 1776. John Adams insisted that the day should be observed with pomp and parade, games and sport, guns, bells, and bonfires from one end of the country to another. The Declaration of Independence was then officially adopted on July 4. People celebrate the day by playing in a band, marching in a parade, having a barbecue or a picnic, or visiting our nation's capital. We usually plan a party with friends and later we watch fireworks.

of each pastry up around the filling. Pinch the seam firmly lengthwise across the top of the pastry to make a seam about ½ inch wide that stands upright. Pinch with 2 fingers and thumb to make a pretty ropelike design. Place the pasties on the prepared baking sheets 1 inch apart.

Bake for 1 hour or until golden. Remove from the oven and brush lightly with the soft butter. Serve hot or at room temperature on a wire rack.

The cooked pasties can also be frozen. To thaw and reheat, place on a baking pan in a preheated 300°F oven for about 10 minutes.

Serve with a pat of butter on top, if desired.

Makes 8 pasties

OTHER DAYS OF INDEPENDENCE

MAY 5 is Cinco de Mayo, a holiday celebrated in Mexico to commemorate the anniversary of the Battle of Puebla. Mexican Independence Day is September 16, when Mexico won independence from Spain in 1821.

MAY 17, 1814, is the date when Norway adopted a constitution and was declared a free and democratic country. Norway was forced to unite with Sweden, but was promised equality and was permitted to keep its new constitution. In 1905 the two countries separated peacefully, and with parades, flags, and feasting Norway continues to celebrate May 17 as its independence day.

JUNE 2 is Italian National Day, which celebrates the day in 1946 when Italy voted to become a republic.

JUNE 6 is Swedish Flag Day, which commemorates the day in 1523 when Gustavus I ascended the throne of Sweden. Gustavus I has been called the founder of modern Sweden.

JULY 1 is Canadian Dominion Day, also called Canada Day. On this day in 1867, four eastern provinces of Canada joined to form the Dominion of Canada.

DECEMBER 6 is Finnish Independence Day, commemorating the day in 1917 when Finland declared its independence from Russia.

NOTE: Lard is the classic shortening used in this pastry, giving it a flakiness unmatched by any other fat. If you choose vegetable shortening, the pastry will be tender, but not quite so flaky.

Small Pasties

For pasties that you can eat out of hand, cut the dough into 16 pieces and roll each piece out to a 6-inch round. Scoop ½ cup filling onto each round. Crimp and seal as directed. Reduce the baking time to 45 minutes.

French Cheese Puff, Gougère

 Choux paste (cream puff dough) with shredded Swiss or Emmentaler cheese added makes a quick, crusty, puffy bread that's perfect for any time of day. For a savory summertime breakfast, serve it with fresh fruit and hot coffee, with a salad for lunch, or for dinner with soup or grilled meat. Because it is at its very best hot out of the oven, you can get it ready for baking, cover lightly, and hold at room temperature up to two hours before you pop it into the oven.

   1 cup water
  ¼ cup (½ stick) unsalted butter
  ½ teaspoon salt
  1 teaspoon Dijon mustard

  1 cup all-purpose flour
  4 large eggs
  1 cup (4 ounces) shredded
     Swiss cheese

Preheat the oven to 375°F. Lightly grease a baking sheet or cover with parchment paper.

Combine the water, butter, salt, and mustard in a medium saucepan and heat over medium-high heat until the butter is melted and the mixture comes to a rolling boil. Add the flour all at once and beat with a wooden spoon until the mixture comes away from the sides of the pan, about 1 minute. Remove from the heat. Beat in the eggs one at a time, beating until the mixture is a smooth paste. Mix in ½ cup of the cheese.

With an ice cream scoop, or 2 large spoons, scoop out 7 mounds of dough, using three-quarters of the dough, and place the mounds close together to make a 9- or 10-inch circle on the prepared baking sheet. They will touch each other as they rise during baking; you can serve this as a wreath and have your guests pull the puffs apart. Spoon or scoop the remaining dough into 7 smaller mounds and place them on top of each of the larger mounds. Sprinkle with the remaining cheese.

Bake for 50 minutes, or until the puffs are brown and crisp. Serve immediately.

Makes 7 servings

Caraway-Beer Burger Buns

 For your Fourth of July barbecue menu, these are perfect with burgers, or they can be shaped into oblongs for grilled sausages. They're not an all-day project either. With an extra measure of yeast and a machine—either a heavy-duty mixer with a dough hook or a large food processor—you can have them, fresh baked, in about an hour. For a pronounced malt flavor, use a dark stout.

4	cups all-purpose flour
1	tablespoon sugar
1	tablespoon caraway seeds
1½	teaspoons salt
2	packages (5½ teaspoons) active dry or rapid-rise yeast
1½	cups (12 ounces) beer
¼	cup vegetable oil

Measure the flour, sugar, caraway seeds, salt, and yeast into the work bowl of a food processor with a dough blade or into a large bowl. Process or mix with an electric mixer just until blended.

Heat the beer in a saucepan over medium heat to 130°F. Turn on the machine or mixer. Pour the warm beer and the vegetable oil into the dry ingredients. Mix until the dough is soft, pliable, and just slightly sticky. If the dough feels too dry and stiff, add warm water a tablespoon at a time while mixing. If the dough is too soft and sticky, add additional flour a tablespoon at a time.

Cover the dough in the bowl or the processor and let stand for 5 minutes.

Cover a baking sheet with parchment paper or coat lightly with nonstick spray. Turn out onto a lightly oiled surface. Shape into a long roll and cut into 12 equal pieces and shape into balls or oblongs. Place each ball or oblong of dough onto the baking sheet 3 inches apart and flatten to a ½-inch thickness. Cover and let rise in a warm place for 25 minutes.

Preheat the oven to 425°F. Bake for 10 to 15 minutes, until golden brown. Slide the parchment with the buns onto the countertop to cool or remove the buns to cool on a wire rack.

Makes 12 buns

Fresh Raspberry Tart

 This tart consists of a simple but tender press-in crumb crust baked with a filling of fresh raspberries. Because raspberries tend to have a sharp flavor when they are warm, I prefer to chill the tart and serve wedges with a topping of fresh raspberries and whipped cream.

Crust

        2 cups all-purpose flour
        2 tablespoons sugar
    ½ teaspoon salt
    ¼ teaspoon baking powder
    ½ cup (1 stick) unsalted butter,
        chilled and cut into pieces
4 to 5 tablespoons milk

Filling

    2 pints fresh raspberries
    1 tablespoon fresh lemon juice
    1 cup sugar
    3 tablespoons cornstarch

Topping

    1 pint fresh raspberries, washed
    4 tablespoons confectioners' sugar
    1 cup whipping cream
    1 teaspoon vanilla

Preheat the oven to 400°F. In a large bowl, mix together the flour, sugar, salt, and baking powder. Cut in the butter until the mixture resembles fine crumbs. Add the milk a tablespoon at a time and toss with a fork until the mixture resembles large-curd cottage cheese. Press the mixture into the bottom and sides of an 11-inch round tart pan with removable bottom.

In a bowl, toss the raspberries with the lemon juice, sugar, and cornstarch until the raspberries are evenly coated. Turn into the pastry-lined pan.

Bake for 30 to 40 minutes, until the crust is light brown and the filling is set. Remove from the oven, cool on a wire rack, then chill.

Before serving, remove the sides of the tart pan and place the tart on a serving plate. Top with the fresh raspberries and dust with 2 tablespoons of the confectioners' sugar. In a bowl, whip the cream until stiff and mix in the remaining 2 tablespoons confectioners' sugar and the vanilla. Fill a pastry bag with the whipped cream and pipe onto the top of the tart, or serve dollops of the cream with wedges of the tart.

Makes 8 to 10 servings

 MIXING UP THE FRUITS OF SUMMER

Summer fruits are the "soft" fruits: berries, peaches, nectarines, plums, apricots, and cherries. Most of these fruits can be substituted for one another in such preparations as pies, tarts, upside-down cakes, shortcakes, cobblers, crisps, and crumbles. They can be used alone or in combination.

Peach Cream Pie

I just can't wait for peaches to be in full season so that I can make this luscious pie.

Press-in Pastry Shell

- 1 cup all-purpose flour
- 1 tablespoon sugar
- ¼ teaspoon salt
- ¼ cup (½ stick) melted butter
- 1 tablespoon corn oil
- 2 tablespoons milk

Peach Filling

- 4 cups peeled, pitted, and sliced peaches, 3 large
- ¾ cup sugar
- ¼ cup all-purpose flour
- ¼ teaspoon salt
- ¼ teaspoon freshly ground nutmeg
- ⅔ cup whipping cream

Preheat the oven to 400°F.

In a mixing bowl, stir the flour, sugar, and salt together. In a small bowl, whisk the butter, oil, and milk together until well blended. Stir into the flour mixture until the mixture resembles moist crumbs. Press into a 9-inch pie pan.

In the same mixing bowl, combine the peaches with the sugar, flour, salt, and nutmeg; fold gently until the peaches are evenly coated. Turn into the pastry shell, distributing the fruit evenly. Pour the cream over.

Bake for 35 to 45 minutes, or until the fruit is bubbly and the pastry is light brown. Cool on a wire rack, then chill before serving.

Makes 6 to 8 servings

 BUYING AND STORING SUMMER FRUITS

Although most fruits are available all year round, thanks to modern transportation and storage, fruits that are in season always taste the best.

When buying fruits, choose them for ripeness, color, and firmness; of course, make sure they're free from decay. Smelling the fruit is an excellent way to evaluate ripeness. Whenever possible, buy fruit that has been grown locally. It will be fresher and tastier.

Store fresh fruits in the refrigerator. Do not wash soft fruits until you are ready to serve them. Place fruit, preferably in a single layer, in a moistureproof container lined with paper towels. This is an especially good way to keep berries. You can store larger fruit in a plastic bag in the refrigerator.

Peach Upside-Down Cake

This irresistible cake is also a very special treat for breakfast or brunch.

Fruit Layer

½ cup (1 stick) unsalted butter, melted
½ cup packed brown sugar
⅛ teaspoon freshly ground nutmeg
2 to 3 large peaches, peeled, pitted, and sliced ¾ inch thick

Cake

1 cup all-purpose flour
½ cup whole wheat flour
2 teaspoons baking powder
¼ teaspoon salt
¼ cup (½ stick) unsalted butter, at room temperature
1 cup sugar
2 large eggs, at room temperature
½ cup milk
1 teaspoon vanilla
Vanilla ice cream or whipped cream, for serving

Preheat the oven to 350°F.
Make the fruit layer. Pour butter into a 9-inch square baking pan. Mix the brown sugar and nutmeg together in a small bowl. Sprinkle evenly over the butter. Arrange the peach slices over the brown sugar.

Make the cake. In a small bowl, mix the flours, baking powder, and salt. In a large bowl, cream the butter and sugar together until smooth. Add the eggs and beat until light and fluffy. Add the dry ingredients alternately with the milk and vanilla to the creamed mixture and mix until smooth. Spread the batter evenly over the peach layer.

Bake for 50 to 55 minutes or until a wooden skewer inserted into the center of the cake comes out clean. Loosen the edges with a knife and invert the cake onto a serving plate or platter. Serve warm with the ice cream or whipped cream.

Makes 8 servings

Plum and Nectarine Streusel

There are many varieties of plums, and all of them are good in combination with nectarines in this down-home dessert.

Plum-Nectarine Filling

½ cup packed brown sugar
3 tablespoons cornstarch
⅛ teaspoon salt
2 pounds ripe plums, pitted and sliced ½ inch thick
4 medium nectarines, peeled, pitted, and sliced ½ inch thick

Streusel

  1 cup all-purpose flour

  ½ cup packed brown sugar

  ½ cup (1 stick) unsalted butter, chilled and cut into pieces

  1 teaspoon ground cinnamon

  ¼ teaspoon salt

  ½ cup finely chopped almonds (optional)

     Ice cream or whipped cream, for serving

Preheat the oven to 350°F. Butter a 2-quart shallow baking dish.

Make the filling. In a large bowl, mix the brown sugar, cornstarch, and salt. Add the plums and nectarines and fold together until the fruit is evenly coated. Turn into the prepared pan.

To make the streusel, in a food processor or mixing bowl, combine the flour, brown sugar, butter, cinnamon, salt, and almonds. Process or blend until the mixture is moist and crumbly. Sprinkle over the fruit in the pan.

Bake for 45 to 50 minutes, until the fruit is bubbly and the topping is crisp. Serve warm with ice cream or whipped cream.

Makes 6 servings

Summer Berry Pie

 Three seasonal berries are combined to make this delicious, old-fashioned pie with a lattice top.

Butter Pastry

  2 cups all-purpose flour

  2 tablespoons sugar

  ¾ teaspoon salt

  ¾ cup (1½ sticks) unsalted butter, chilled and cut into pieces

  1 tablespoon fresh lemon juice

6 to 8 tablespoons ice water

Filling

  2 cups fresh strawberries, stemmed and halved

  2 cups fresh blueberries

  2 cups fresh raspberries

  ¾ cup plus 1 tablespoon sugar

  ⅓ cup minute tapioca (see Note)

  1 tablespoon unsalted butter, chilled and cut into tiny pieces

In a medium bowl or in the food processor, combine the flour, sugar, and salt. Process or cut the butter into the flour mixture until the mixture is in pea-size pieces. If using the food processor, transfer the mixture into a large bowl. In a small bowl, mix the lemon juice with 6 tablespoons of the ice water. Sprinkle over the flour mixture, tossing with a fork until the dough holds together in a ball. Add more ice water, a tablespoon at a time, if too dry. Wrap in plastic wrap and refrigerate for 30 minutes.

FREEZING UNBAKED PIE FILLING

To Freeze Unbaked Fruit Pie Fillings

1. Line a nine-inch pie pan with heavy foil, pressing it smoothly across the bottom and sides of the pan. Allow the foil to extend about six inches beyond the rim.
2. Fill the lined pan with uncooked pie filling mixture.
3. Place into the freezer until the filling is frozen.
4. When the filling is frozen solid, remove the foil and filling from the pan, fold the extending foil over the top of the filling, and seal. Label and date. Freeze.

To Bake Pies with Frozen Filling

1. Line a nine-inch pie pan with unbaked pastry shell.
2. Unwrap the filling and place into the pastry. Dot with one to two tablespoons butter, if desired.
3. Cover with a top crust; seal the edges of the pie. Brush the top of the pie with milk. To prevent excess browning of the rim, wrap the pie's edge with a two- to three-inch-wide strip of foil. Set the pie on a rimmed baking sheet.
4. Preheat the oven to 425°F. Bake for thirty to thirty-five minutes. Remove the foil and bake for twenty to thirty minutes longer or until the fruit is tender and bubbly. Remove from the oven and cool in the pan on a wire rack.

Basic Fruit Pie Mixture for Freezing (for one pie)

6 cups whole berries such as blueberries, blackberries, pitted cherries, strawberries, cut-up rhubarb, sliced apple, and sliced peaches

1 tablespoon fresh lemon juice

1 to 1½ cups sugar, depending on sweetness of fruit

4 tablespoons cornstarch or minute tapioca

1½ teaspoons ground cinnamon (if desired)

¼ teaspoon ground ginger (if desired)

In a large bowl combine the fruit of your choice, lemon juice, sugar, cornstarch or tapioca, cinnamon, and ginger. Turn into a foil-lined pie pan. Freeze as directed (above). Bake pie as directed (above).

Fourth of July • 115

Preheat the oven to 425°F. Divide the pastry into 2 halves and roll 1 part out on a lightly floured surface to fit a 9-inch pie pan. Line the pan with the pastry.

Measure the berries into a bowl—you can use any proportion of the three berries; depending on availability, you should have 6 cups of loosely packed berries in total. Stir in ¾ cup of the sugar and the tapioca and let stand for 20 minutes, stirring occasionally. Turn into the pastry-lined pan. Dot with the butter. Roll out the second half of the dough on a lightly floured surface to ¼-inch thickness. Cut into ½-inch strips. Place the strips in a latticework fashion over the top of the pie. Moisten the edges and trim, seal, and crimp. Sprinkle the top with the 1 tablespoon sugar.

Bake for 40 minutes or until pastry is golden and the filling is bubbly. Remove from the oven and cool on a wire rack.

Makes one 9-inch pie

NOTE: Tapioca is the thickener in this pie. You can substitute cornstarch, but due to the sweet and the tart chemistry of the pie, cornstarch will sometimes break down and the pie may be runny.

Three-Berry Shortcake

 Just right for the Fourth of July, this red, white, and blue topping is very festive on a light and airy sponge cake base.

Sponge Cake Base

  1½ cups all-purpose flour
  1½ teaspoons baking powder
   ½ teaspoon salt
   3 large eggs, at room temperature
   1 cup sugar
   1 teaspoon vanilla
   ¾ cup milk
   3 tablespoons unsalted butter

Topping

   1 pint whipping cream
   3 tablespoons confectioners' sugar
   1 teaspoon vanilla
   2 cups fresh strawberries, hulled and quartered
   2 cups fresh blueberries
   1 cup fresh raspberries
    Confectioners' sugar, for dusting

Preheat the oven to 350°F. Lightly grease a 13 × 9-inch pan.

In a medium bowl, stir the flour, baking powder, and salt together; set aside.

In a large bowl with an electric mixer, beat the eggs until frothy. At high speed, beat in the sugar, 1 tablespoon at a time, until very light and creamy. Beat in the vanilla.

In a small saucepan, combine the milk and butter and place over medium heat until the butter is melted and the mixture comes to a boil.

Meanwhile, fold the flour mixture into the egg mixture until well blended. When the milk and butter come to a boil, remove from the heat immediately and stir into the batter until blended. Pour into the prepared pan.

Bake for 25 to 30 minutes or until the cake feels firm in the center when touched. Remove from the oven and cool on a wire rack. Turn the cake out of the pan and place onto an oblong serving plate or a cutting board. (I like to cover a cutting board with foil, then top it with a paper doily.)

In a mixing bowl, whip the cream until stiff and fold in the confectioners' sugar and vanilla. Spread over the cake. Top with the berries; you can either mix the berries and pour them over the cake or arrange them in rows. Dust with additional confectioners' sugar. Serve immediately or refrigerate up to 4 hours until ready to serve.

Makes 12 to 16 servings

Fresh Wisconsin Bing Cherry Pie

 When bing cherries are in season, I love to treat myself to a fresh cherry pie at least once. It may seem like a nuisance to pit fresh cherries, but with a special little tool designed for the purpose, you can get the job done while you're talking on the phone because it is a rather "mindless" chore. At other times of the year, you can use frozen, unsugared cherries. Pastry for a double crust pie (see page 172).

¾ cup plus 1 tablespoon sugar
3 tablespoons cornstarch
½ teaspoon ground cinnamon
½ teaspoon salt
4 cups pitted fresh or frozen bing cherries
1 tablespoon fresh lemon juice
¼ teaspoon almond extract
1 tablespoon unsalted butter, cut into little bits

Prepare and chill the pastry. Preheat the oven to 425°F. Divide the pastry into 2 halves and roll 1 part out on a lightly floured surface to fit a 9-inch pie pan. Line the pan with the pastry.

In a large bowl, combine the ¾ cup sugar, cornstarch, cinnamon, and salt. Add the cherries, lemon juice, and almond extract and mix with a rubber spatula until the cherries are evenly coated. Turn the cherries into the pastry-lined pan. Dot with the butter. Roll out the second half of the dough on a lightly floured surface to ¼-inch thickness. Fold the dough into quarters and position the point of the fold on the center of the pie. Unfold to cover the filling. Moisten the edges and trim, seal, and crimp. Sprinkle the top with the 1 tablespoon sugar.

Bake for 15 minutes at 425°F, then reduce the head to 350°F. Continue baking for 40 minutes longer, until the crust is golden and the filling is bubbly. Remove from the oven and cool on a wire rack.

Makes one 9-inch pie

Blueberry Bars

 In July, when blueberries are in season, it's the perfect time to bake these bars. For a mixed cookie tray, cut these into small bars or cut larger squares for a wonderful afternoon dessert. I picture myself at our friend's cabin on an island on Lake Namakon on the Minnesota-Canadian border, enjoying these bars, freshly baked and made with the wild blueberries that we gathered ourselves. This can happen only if we don't absolutely load our pancakes with wild blueberries in the morning!

Butter Pastry

2½ cups all-purpose flour
½ teaspoon baking powder
½ cup sugar

1 cup (2 sticks) unsalted butter,
　　room temperature
1 egg, slightly beaten

Blueberry Filling

2 cups fresh blueberries
¼ cup sugar
1 tablespoon fresh lemon juice
1 teaspoon grated lemon zest
2 tablespoons cornstarch
　　Dash salt
1 tablespoon sugar

In a large bowl with an electric mixer, combine the flour, baking powder, and sugar. With the electric mixer, blend in the butter until the mixture resembles coarse crumbs. Add the egg and mix until a smooth dough forms. Wrap in plastic wrap and chill for 30 minutes.

In a medium saucepan, combine the berries, sugar, lemon juice and zest, cornstarch, and salt. Cook over low heat, stirring, until the mixture is blended. Increase the heat to medium and cook, stirring until thickened. Cool to room temperature.

Preheat the oven to 375°F. Butter a 13 × 9-inch jelly roll pan. Remove ¼ of the chilled dough. On a lightly floured surface, roll out the large portion of dough to fit the bottom and sides of the baking pan. To transfer the dough, roll it around the rolling pin and then unroll onto the baking pan. Spoon the cooled filling evenly onto the pastry-lined pan. On a floured surface, roll out the reserved dough to ⅛-inch thickness and about 12 inches square. With a pastry wheel or a sharp knife, cut the dough into ½-inch strips. Lay the strips in a latticework pattern over the blueberry filling. Trim and crimp the edges of the pastry to seal. Sprinkle the top with 1 tablespoon sugar.

Bake for 25 to 30 minutes or until the lattice is golden brown. Cool in the pan on a wire rack. To serve, cut into 1½ × 3-inch bars or 3-inch squares for dessert.

Makes 12 dessert servings or 24 bars

Blueberry-Cream Cheese Coffee Cake

 Remember this coffee cake when you want to serve something extra special for brunch on a summer morning. The buttery crust encases a cream cheese layer with fresh blueberries and an almond streusel topping baked into it.

2¼ cups all-purpose flour
1 cup sugar
¾ cup (1½ sticks) unsalted butter, at room temperature
1½ teaspoons baking powder
¼ teaspoon salt
¾ cup sour cream
2 large eggs
1 teaspoon almond extract
1 (8-ounce) package cream cheese, at room temperature
2 cups fresh blueberries, cleaned
½ cup slivered almonds

Preheat the oven to 350°F. Lightly grease the bottom and sides of a 10-inch springform pan and dust with flour.

In a large mixing bowl, mix the flour and ¾ cup of the sugar. With a pastry blender or fork, cut in the butter until the mixture resembles coarse crumbs. Reserve 1 cup of the mixture.

Add the baking powder, salt, sour cream, 1 of the eggs, and the almond extract to the remaining flour mixture. Mix until a stiff dough forms. Press the dough over the bottom and 2 inches up the sides of the pan; it will be about ¼ inch thick on the sides.

In a small bowl, with an electric mixer, beat the cream cheese, remaining ¼ cup sugar, and remaining egg until well blended. Pour the mixture over the dough in the pan and spread evenly. Arrange the blueberries over the top. Mix the almonds with the reserved crumb mixture and sprinkle over the blueberries.

Bake for 50 to 55 minutes or until the filling is set and the crust is golden brown. Cool 15 minutes, then remove sides of the pan and finish cooling. Serve warm.

Makes 12 to 16 servings

Labor Day
and
Early Fall

Autumn Fruit Kuchen

 When plums, nectarines, peaches, pears, and apples are in season, this is one of my favorite coffee cakes to bake. Serve it hot out of the oven for breakfast, brunch, coffee break, or dessert. The kuchen batter is a cross between a pastry and a cake. Tender and delicious, it is made without leavening.

½ cup (1 stick) unsalted butter, at room temperature

½ cup sugar

3 large eggs

½ teaspoon vanilla

1 cup all-purpose flour

⅛ teaspoon salt

Fruit Topping

14 to 16 purple plums, halved and pitted; or 3 large apples, peeled, cored, and cut into 1-inch-thick slices; or 3 large pears, peeled, cored, and thickly sliced; or 3 large ripe nectarines or peaches, peeled, pitted, and thickly sliced

¼ cup sugar

1 tablespoon unsalted butter, cut into tiny pieces

Preheat the oven to 375°F. Butter and flour an 11-inch round tart pan with a removable bottom or a 9-inch square cake pan.

In a large bowl, cream the butter with the sugar until smooth; beat in the eggs until

BAKER'S TIP

Kuchen is the German word for "cake," but we have come to know it as a yeast-risen fruit- or cheese-filled cake that is often served for breakfast.

light and fluffy. Stir in the vanilla, flour, and salt. Spread the batter evenly in the prepared pan.

Press the fruit evenly into the batter, sprinkle with the sugar and dot with the butter.

Bake for 40 minutes or until a wooden skewer inserted in the center of the cake comes out clean. Serve warm or cool on a wire rack. Serve with a topping of slightly sweetened whipped cream, if desired. The kuchen can also be frozen, well wrapped. Thaw and reheat in a 300°F oven for 10 to 15 minutes.

Makes 12 servings

Upside-Down Caramel Apple Pie

 This has always been my favorite version of apple pie. When we were kids, my mother called this "Down-Side-Up Apple Pie," much to our delight.

Pastry

1 cup all-purpose flour
2 teaspoons sugar
½ teaspoon salt
½ cup (1 stick) unsalted butter, chilled and cut into pieces
2 to 4 teaspoons ice water

Filling

6 large Granny Smith apples (about 3 pounds)
5 tablespoons unsalted butter
¾ cup sugar
2 teaspoons ground cinnamon

In a bowl or in a food processor, combine the flour, sugar, and salt. Process or cut in the butter until the butter is in pea-size pieces. Turn the mixture into a large bowl if using a food processor. Add 2 tablespoons of the ice water and stir with a fork until the dough gathers into a ball. Add more water if needed. Turn onto a floured surface and lightly knead once or twice. Wrap in plastic wrap and chill at least 1 hour.

Preheat the oven to 375°F.

To make the filling, peel, core, and slice the apples into quarters. Butter a 10-inch pie pan and dust with sugar. Combine the butter and sugar in a saucepan over medium heat and stir until the sugar dissolves. Pour the syrup into the pie pan, covering the bottom evenly. Arrange the apples in concentric circles, leaving no open spaces. Sprinkle with the cinnamon.

Roll out the pastry on a lightly floured surface to fit the top of the pie. Transfer it to

LABOR DAY

The first Labor Day celebration was held in New York City in 1882 to applaud the industrial spirit of the nation. It was organized by Irish-American labor leader Peter J. McGuire, who was a carpenter by trade and the president of the United Brotherhood of Carpenters and Joiners. The event was such a success that it was adopted in thirty states by 1893. In 1894, Congress decreed that Labor Day be an official national holiday.

cover the apples, tucking in the edges of the pastry down between the apples and the sides of the pan. Slash the top of the pastry to make air vents.

Bake for 50 to 55 minutes or until the pastry is golden and juices bubble through the slits. Cool about 5 minutes on a wire rack. Invert onto a serving platter. Do not cool in the pan too long or the caramel will harden and stick to the pan.

Makes 8 servings

Rustic Apple Pie

Before there were pie pans (which are an American invention), sliced apples were piled on a sheet of pastry, the edge of the pastry was flopped over to hold in the filling, and the top of the "pie" was left open, something like this.

Pastry

1½ cups all-purpose flour
2 tablespoons sugar
½ cup (1 stick) unsalted butter
3 tablespoons water

Filling

¾ cup chopped almonds
¼ cup finely crushed zwieback or fine, unseasoned dry bread crumbs

½ cup sugar
3 medium Granny Smith apples
2 tablespoons unsalted butter or margarine, cut into tiny pieces

Make the pastry. In a food processor or large bowl, combine the flour and sugar. Process or cut in the butter until the mixture resembles coarse crumbs. Add the water and mix until the dough just forms a ball that will hold together. Wrap the dough in plastic wrap and chill while you prepare the filling.

Preheat the oven to 425°F. Lightly grease a baking sheet and dust with flour.

In a small bowl, blend the almonds with the zwieback crumbs and sugar. Roll the pastry out to make a 14-inch circle directly on the baking sheet. Sprinkle with half the almond mixture to within 1 inch of the edge.

Peel, core, and thinly slice the apples. Distribute the apples over the almond mixture. Sprinkle with the remaining almond mixture. Fold the edges up over the filling and pinch to crimp. Dot the exposed apples with the chilled butter.

Bake for 45 minutes or until the apples are bubbly and the pastry is brown. Remove from the oven and cool in the pan on a wire rack. Serve warm with whipped cream, crème fraîche, or soft ice cream, if desired.

Makes 6 to 8 servings

Dessert Apple Pizza

When we made this tart in a cooking class in the south of France, I thought, My gosh, this could be called an apple pizza! But, actually, in France it's called tarte au pommes.

Sweetened Butter Pastry

1½ cups all-purpose flour
 2 tablespoons sugar
 ⅛ teaspoon salt
 ½ cup (1 stick) plus 1 tablespoon unsalted butter, chilled and cut into pieces
 1 large egg yolk beaten with 3 tablespoons cold water

Filling

 1 cup strained apricot preserves
 5 large Granny Smith or Golden Delicious apples, peeled and cored
 ¼ cup sugar

Glaze

 ½ cup confectioners' sugar
 1 tablespoon apricot preserves
 ¼ cup slivered almonds, toasted
   Whipped cream, for serving

In a large bowl or a food processor, mix the flour, sugar, and salt. Cut or process the butter into the flour mixture until the butter has the texture of rolled oats. If using a food processor, transfer the mixture to a large bowl. Add the egg yolk–water mixture to the flour mixture and toss with a fork until the flour is moistened. Press the dough into a ball. Wrap in plastic wrap and chill for 30 minutes.

Preheat the oven to 400°F. Lightly grease a 12-inch round pizza pan.

Roll out the pastry to fit the pizza pan. Place in the pan and press the edges upward and crimp. Brush the whole surface with 1 cup of apricot preserves.

Slice the apples crosswise very thinly. Arrange the slices on top of the crust in a circular pattern, covering the whole pan. Sprinkle with the granulated sugar. Bake for 40 to 45 minutes, until the apples are tender and the crust is brown.

In a small saucepan, mix the confectioners' sugar with 1 tablespoon apricot preserves and heat over low heat until runny. Drizzle the glaze over the hot tart and sprinkle with toasted almonds. Cut into wedges and serve with whipped cream.

Makes 8 to 10 servings

Swedish Apple Torte

This is my all-time favorite apple torte. A multilayered creation, it includes a butter pastry; a thick layer of apples, raisins, and hazelnuts, another layer of pastry; and finally a brown sugar and hazelnut topping. It's baked in a springform pan, which I place on a rimmed pizza pan in order to prevent the juices from dripping onto the bottom of the oven.

Pastry

- 2½ cups all-purpose flour
- 1 cup (2 sticks) unsalted butter, chilled and cut into pieces
- ¼ cup sugar
- 1 large egg
- 2 tablespoons cold water

Apple Filling

- 4 large tart cooking apples, such as Granny Smith (about 2 pounds)
- ½ cup fine, dry unseasoned bread crumbs
- ½ cup sugar
- ½ cup golden raisins
- ½ cup chopped, toasted hazelnuts (filberts)

Buttered Hazelnut (Filbert) Topping

- ⅓ cup unsalted butter, at room temperature
- ⅓ cup packed brown sugar
- ¼ cup chopped toasted hazelnuts (filberts)
- Confectioners' sugar, for dusting
- Whipped cream, for serving

To make the pastry, measure the flour into a mixing bowl. Cut the butter into the flour until the mixture is the texture of coarse crumbs. Add the sugar, egg, and water and mix just until a dough forms. Wrap the dough in plastic wrap and chill about 1 hour.

Lightly grease a 10-inch springform pan. Divide the dough into halves and roll one part out on a lightly floured surface to make a 12-inch circle. Fit one circle into the bottom of the prepared pan, bringing the edge up about 1 inch on the sides.

Peel, core, and thinly slice the apples. Sprinkle the pastry-lined pan with 2 tablespoons of the bread crumbs. In a small bowl, combine the remaining bread crumbs, sugar, raisins, and nuts. Arrange half the apple slices in an even circle on top of the crumbs, overlapping the slices. Sprinkle with half of the bread crumb mixture. Layer the rest of the apples over the crumbs in an overlapping circle and sprinkle with the remaining bread crumb mixture.

Roll out the second half of the pastry on a lightly floured surface to a 12-inch circle. Top the torte with the second round of pastry. Press the pastry around the edges to seal to the bottom layer of pastry.

Preheat the oven to 400°F.

To make the topping, cream the butter and sugar in a small bowl, then stir in the chopped nuts. Spread over the top of the pastry and pierce all over with a fork. Place the pan on another rimmed pan or baking sheet to catch any butter that may ooze out of the torte.

Bake for 45 to 50 minutes, until golden brown. Cool in the pan on a wire rack to room temperature. Dust with confectioners' sugar. To serve, remove the sides of the pan, cut into wedges, and top with whipped cream.

Makes 10 to 12 servings

APPLES

APPLE VARIETY	FLAVOR	FRESH	BAKING	SEASON
Beacon	Mild, mellow	Good	Fair	August to September
Cortland	Mild	Excellent	Very good	October to January
Delicious, golden	Sweet, semifirm	Excellent	Very good	September to May
Delicious, red	Sweet, crisp	Excellent	Fair	September to June
Granny Smith	Tart, crisp	Very good	Very good	April to July
Gravenstein	Tart, crisp	Good	Good	July to September
Greening	Slightly tart	Poor	Very good	October to March
Jonathan	Tart, tender	Very good	Poor	September to January
McIntosh	Slightly tart, tender	Excellent	Very good	September to June
Paula Red	Tart, crisp	Very good	Poor	September to October
Pippin	Slightly tart, firm	Very good	Excellent	September to June
Red Rome	Slightly tart, firm	Good	Excellent	October to June
Spartan	Fairly tart	Excellent	Fair	September to May
Wealthy	Tart, soft	Good	Fair	August to December
Winesap	Slightly tart,	Excellent	Good	October to June

Puffy Apple Pancake

This basic pancake has been a family favorite of ours for years. I grew up thinking it was Finnish, only to find out that almost every nationality claims a puffy oven pancake as its own. Sometimes we bake it without the apples and then add fresh fruit to the center of the big, puffy shell that it forms. This is a great Sunday-morning brunch dish.

¾ cup (3 to 4 large) beaten eggs
¾ cup milk
¾ cup all-purpose flour
1 tablespoon sugar
¼ teaspoon salt
2 tablespoons unsalted butter
2 medium-size tart cooking apples, peeled, cored, and thinly sliced

For Serving

Confectioners' sugar
Slightly sweetened whipped cream

In a bowl or blender, measure the eggs, milk, flour, sugar, and salt. Mix until all the flour is incorporated and the batter is smooth. Let stand for 30 minutes.

Preheat the oven to 450°F.

Put the butter into an 11-inch ovenproof skillet or shallow baking pan (preferably with sloping sides). Place in the oven as the oven heats. When the butter is melted, pour the batter into the hot pan. Cover the batter with the apple slices.

Bake for 15 minutes or until the pancake is puffy and brown around the edges. Dust with the confectioners' sugar and cut into quarters to serve. Pass the whipped cream at the table.

Makes 4 servings

Apple-Date-Nut-Cake

This moist and delicious cake has stood the test of time in our family, coming to me from my mother-in-law, Grace. Sometimes I double the amount of apples and the result is a moist apple pudding.

1 cup sugar
½ cup (1 stick) unsalted butter, at room temperature
2 large eggs
2 teaspoons unsweetened dark cocoa
1 teaspoon ground cinnamon
⅛ teaspoon ground cloves
1 teaspoon baking soda
2 cups all-purpose flour
½ cup cold, strong coffee
4 tart apples (such as Granny Smith), peeled, cored, and chopped (about 4 cups)
½ cup chopped dates
½ cup chopped walnuts or pecans
Caramel Frosting (recipe follows)

Preheat the oven to 350°F. Butter an 8-inch fancy tube pan or a 13 × 9-inch baking pan.

In a large mixing bowl, cream the sugar and butter until smooth. Add the eggs and beat until light and frothy. Add the cocoa, cinnamon, cloves, and baking soda and mix until well blended. Add the flour and coffee and mix until the batter is smooth. Fold in the apples, dates, and nuts. Turn the batter into the prepared pan.

Bake for 1 hour for the tube pan or for 35 to 40 minutes for the 13 × 9-inch pan or until a wooden skewer inserted into the center of the cake comes out clean. Cool the tube cake for 5 minutes in the pan, then turn out onto a wire rack to finish cooling. Cool the rectangular cake completely in its pan on a wire rack. Ice with the Caramel Frosting.

Makes 1 cake, 8 to 10 servings

Caramel Frosting

½ cup whipping cream
½ cup sugar
1 tablespoon dark corn syrup
⅛ teaspoon salt
1 teaspoon unsalted butter
1 teaspoon vanilla
    Confectioners' sugar (if needed)

Combine the cream and sugar in a saucepan. Bring to a boil over medium heat and cook for 2 minutes, stirring. Add the corn syrup, salt, butter, and vanilla and stir to combine. If the mixture seems too thin, stir in some confectioners' sugar. Spread on the cake while the cake is still warm.

Peanut Butter-Toffee Bar Cake

There's just a hint of peanut butter flavor in this light-textured cake that we cut into squares and serve right out of the pan. This is a cake that's perfect for a picnic or to take to the cabin for the last weekend of summer.

Bars

¾ cup (1½ sticks) unsalted butter, at room temperature
¼ cup smooth or crunchy peanut butter
1½ cups sugar
4 large eggs, at room temperature
½ cup buttermilk
1 teaspoon vanilla
3 cups all-purpose flour
3 teaspoons baking powder
½ cup water

Frosting

½ cup peanut butter
2 cups confectioners' sugar, sifted after measuring
4 to 5 tablespoons milk
2 (1.4-ounce) English toffee bars (such as Heath Bars), coarsely crushed

Preheat the oven to 350°F. Butter a 13 × 9-inch cake pan. To make the bars, in a large bowl cream the butter, peanut butter, and sugar until smooth; add the eggs and beat until light.

Mix in the buttermilk and vanilla.

Stir the flour and baking powder together in another bowl and add to the creamed mixture along with the water, mixing until smooth. Pour into the prepared pan.

Bake for 45 to 55 minutes or until a wooden skewer inserted in the center comes out clean. Remove from the oven and cool in the pan on a wire rack.

To make the frosting, cream the peanut butter with the confectioners' sugar in a mixing bowl, then add 4 tablespoons of the milk and mix until smooth. Add more milk if necessary. Spread over the cake. Sprinkle with the crushed toffee bars.

Makes one 13 × 9-inch cake

Apricot-Apple Bars

An easy press-in butter base is topped with a delicious combination of apricot jam, almonds, and shredded apple. You can serve this in squares for dessert, topped with a puff of whipped cream or a small scoop of vanilla ice cream and call it "apricot apple tart."

Cookie Base

2 cups all-purpose flour
½ cup confectioners' sugar
1 cup (2 sticks) unsalted butter, at room temperature

Filling

2 large eggs
¾ cup sugar
¼ teaspoon salt
¾ cup ground almonds
⅓ cup raisins
3 large tart cooking apples (such as Granny Smith), peeled, cored, and shredded
½ teaspoon ground cinnamon
6 tablespoons apricot jam
¼ cup (½ stick) unsalted butter, melted
½ cup sliced almonds

Preheat the oven to 350°F. Combine the flour and sugar in a large bowl or in the food processor. Process or cut in the butter until the mixture resembles moist crumbs that hold together when you pinch it. Press into the bottom of a 13 × 9-inch baking pan.

To make the filling, beat the eggs in a large bowl and add the sugar and salt. Beat until the mixture is thick and lemon colored. Stir in the ground almonds and raisins and then stir in the apples and cinnamon.

Brush the bottom of the unbaked pastry with the apricot jam. Spread the apple mixture evenly over the jam. Bake for 25 minutes.

Remove from the oven and drizzle with the melted butter; then sprinkle with the sliced almonds. Bake for 15 minutes longer or until the filling is set and the almonds are toasted. Cool in the pan on a wire rack. Cut into 36 squares or bars or, for dessert, cut into 12 to 16 squares and serve with whipped cream or ice cream, if desired.

Makes 36 bars or 12 to 16 dessert servings

Greek Olive Bread

Nuggets of feta cheese and olives stud this delicious loaf, perfect with grilled or barbecued lamb or chicken on those last cookouts of the season.

3 to 3½ cups bread or unbleached all-purpose flour
1 package (2¾ teaspoons) active dry yeast or rapid-rise yeast
1 tablespoon sugar
1 teaspoon salt
2 tablespoons extra-virgin olive oil
1 cup very warm water
1 cup coarsely chopped pitted oil-cured or black olives
½ cup crumbled feta cheese
2 teaspoons extra-virgin olive oil, for brushing

In a large mixing bowl stir 3 cups of the flour, the yeast, sugar, and salt together.

Make a hole in the center of the dry ingredients and pour in the 2 tablespoons olive oil and the water. Stir until all the dry ingredients are moistened. Cover and let stand for 15 minutes.

Sprinkle a work surface with flour. Scrape dough out onto the floured surface. Dust the top of the dough with flour. Knead until the dough is smooth and develops small bubbles just under the surface, about 5 minutes, adding more flour if the dough gets sticky. Place in a clean, greased bowl, turning to grease all over. Cover and let rise in a warm place until doubled, 1 to 1½ hours.

Punch down the dough and pat it into a ½-inch-thick circle. Sprinkle with the olives and cheese. Knead the dough lightly to incorporate the ingredients, then shape into a ball. Pat out to make a circle 8 inches in diameter.

Place on a greased baking sheet. With a 3-inch round cutter, cut a circle in the center but leave the round of dough in place. (You can bake the removed center alongside the bread; it will probably cook faster than the circular loaf.) Brush the dough with the 2 teaspoons of oil. Cover and let rise until puffy, 30 to 45 minutes.

Preheat the oven to 375°F. Bake for 25 minutes or until the crust is a rich golden brown and the loaf sounds hollow when tapped. Cool the bread on a wire rack before slicing.

Makes 1 round loaf

Danish Apple Cake

When you press apples into this kuchenlike butter batter, the cake bakes up around the apples to make a cake that's not only beautiful to look at but moist and delicious as well. A Danish friend gave me this recipe several years ago, and I have enjoyed it ever since.

    4 tart cooking apples, such as
       Red Romes, peeled
       Fresh lemon juice
  ¾ cup (1½ sticks) unsalted butter,
       at room temperature
  ¾ cup sugar
    3 large eggs, at room temperature
  ¼ teaspoon salt
    1 teaspoon vanilla
1½ cups all-purpose flour
  ½ teaspoon baking powder
    2 tablespoons milk
    2 tablespoons unsalted butter, melted
    2 tablespoons sugar, for sprinkling

Preheat the oven to 425°F. Butter an 11-inch tart pan with a removable bottom or a 9-inch square cake pan.

Cut the apples into halves down the length of the core. With a melon baller, teaspoon, or paring knife, remove the cores from the apple halves, leaving the apple halves intact. Brush the surfaces with lemon juice to prevent browning. Place the apples cut side down on a cutting board. With a sharp knife, cut crosswise every ⅛ inch almost all the way through each apple; do not cut all the way through, keeping the halves intact.

In a mixing bowl, cream the butter and ¾ cup sugar together. Add the eggs, salt, and vanilla and beat until light and fluffy. Stir the flour and baking powder together in a small bowl and add to the creamed mixture along with the milk, beating until the batter is smooth.

Spread the batter in the prepared pan. Press the apple halves with the cut side down into the batter, spacing them evenly. Brush with the melted butter. Sprinkle with the 2 tablespoons sugar. Bake for 30 minutes or until the apples are tender and the cake is golden brown.

Remove from the oven and cool in the pan on a wire rack.

Makes 8 servings

Rosh Hashanah

Rosh Hashanah is the Jewish new year and is celebrated by Jews the world over. It marks the beginning of a ten-day penitence before God, involving self-examination, and a time when Jews show sorrow for the wrongs they have done during the previous year. This purely religious holiday honors God's role as ruler of the universe and celebrates new beginnings.

As the new year begins, at sundown, Jewish people eat sweet foods, like apples dipped in honey, honey cake, honey cookies, and sweet potato pudding. This symbolizes their wish for a "sweet" year. Special foods for Rosh Hashana include new fruits of the season such as grapes, pomegranates, and apples and the braided bread called challah, which is shaped into a circle at this holiday to symbolize the cyclical and eternal nature of life. Challah, apple cake, and honey cake have come to be some of the most traditional foods for the new year celebrations.

Yom Kippur, the Day of Atonement, comes at the end of the ten days of penitence. To make amends for all their sins, Jewish adults fast from the beginning of the holiday at sundown to the end of the holiday at sunset the next day. Yom Kippur is the holiest day of the year, and many Jews spend most of the day praying in the synagogue.

Cinnamon-Walnut Kamish Bread

This is a delicious, twice-baked (biscotti-like) cookie from the East European Jewish tradition. Some families enjoy this exclusively as a Rosh Hashanah treat; others eat it all year long. There are different versions of Kamish Bread, some of which are rolled up with a filling.

- 3 large eggs
- 1¼ cups sugar
- ¾ cup vegetable oil
- 2 teaspoons vanilla extract
- 1 teaspoon grated orange zest
- 3 cups all-purpose flour
- 2 teaspoons baking powder
- ½ teaspoon salt
- ½ cup finely chopped walnuts or pecans
- 1 teaspoon ground cinnamon

In a large bowl, beat the eggs and 1 cup of the sugar until fluffy. Slowly beat in the oil, vanilla, and orange zest. In a small bowl, mix together the flour, baking powder, and salt. Mix the dry ingredients into the liquid ingredients, stirring until a smooth dough forms. Mix in the nuts. Cover and chill the dough for 30 minutes until the dough is firm but not hard.

Preheat the oven to 350°F. Cover 2 cookie sheets with parchment paper or lightly grease them.

Cut the chilled dough into 4 equal parts. Shape each part into a roll about 1½ inches thick and 16 inches long. Place 2 rolls on each of the prepared cookie sheets, spacing them about 4 inches apart.

Stir together the remaining ¼ cup sugar and the cinnamon. Sprinkle each roll with a tablespoonful of the sugar-cinnamon mixture.

Bake for 25 minutes or until the rolls feel firm to the touch.

Remove from the oven and immediately, with a sharp knife, cut into ½-inch diagonal slices. Place the slices with the cut sides up, close together on one cookie sheet. Return to the oven and reduce the temperature to 250°F. Bake for 30 minutes or until the cookies are crisp and dry. Store in an airtight container.

Makes about 80 cookies

Challah

A round challah is one of the most symbolic foods at Rosh Hashanah.

This bread represents the image of a prayer rising heavenward. At this holiday, the bread is formed in a circle, not left as a straight bread as it is all year, signifying the hope for a long life span and the hope that the coming year will be complete, unbroken by tragedy. Sometimes the dough is shaped into a long, thick rope and coiled up like a snail. In the Ukraine, however, challah is made in the shape of a bird. The idea comes from Isaiah 31:5: "As birds flying, so will the Lord of hosts defend Jerusalem."

The dough for challah is wonderful to handle and to shape into a pretty braided loaf, glazed with egg and garnished with poppy seeds. The eggs provide a lightness and richness to the crumb and are the reason why the braid rises so high and browns so beautifully. Vegetable oil for shortening also provides a nice handling quality to the bread. This is a perfect bread for mixing in the food processor, using the dough blade (see Note).

3½ to 4 cups unbleached all-purpose or bread flour
    ¼ cup sugar
     1 teaspoon salt
     1 package (2¾ teaspoons) instant active dry yeast

1 cup very warm water
   (about 130°F)
3 tablespoons vegetable oil
2 large eggs, at room temperature
1 large egg yolk mixed with
   1 teaspoon water, for glaze
2 teaspoons poppy seeds, for
   sprinkling

Mix 3 cups of the flour, the sugar, salt, and yeast in a large mixing bowl. Make a well in the center of the flour mixture and pour in the water, oil, and 2 eggs. Beat until the dough is smooth and elastic, about 5 minutes. Cover the dough and let rest for 15 minutes. Beat in the remaining flour until the dough is stiff. Turn out onto a floured board and knead until smooth and satiny, about 10 minutes. Or if using an electric mixer with a dough hook, knead 5 to 10 minutes, until smooth, adding flour until the dough feels just "tacky," not dry and not overly sticky. Shape into a ball and place into a large oiled bowl, turn over to grease the top, and cover. Let rise for about ½ hour or until doubled.

Cover a large baking sheet with parchment paper.

Divide the dough into 3 parts. Shape each portion into a rope about 1 inch in diameter. Braid the 3 parts together and place on the prepared baking sheet in a ring shape. Or coil up like a snail, starting from the center and working outward. Tuck the ends under. Let rise, covered, in a warm place for 20 to 30 minutes, until puffy. Preheat the oven to 350°F. Brush the top of the loaf with the egg mixture and sprinkle with the poppy seeds.

Bake for 25 to 30 minutes or until golden. Remove from the oven and cool on a rack.

Makes 1 large loaf

NOTE: To mix the dough in the food processor, combine 3 cups of the flour, sugar, salt, and yeast in the work bowl. Turn the processor on to mix the ingredients. With the motor going, add the water, oil, and 2 eggs through the feed tube and process 30 seconds. Remove the cover and add ½ cup flour; process 30 seconds. Add more flour a little at a time and process until the dough comes together in a smooth, soft ball. Let the dough stand for 2 minutes. Feel the dough. It should feel "tacky" but not sticky. If the dough is sticky, or too soft, add more flour a tablespoon at a time. If the dough seems too stiff, add more water, a tablespoon at a time, processing between the additions until the dough is satiny and smooth. Cover and let rise for 30 minutes until doubled. Proceed as directed above.

Apple Cake

 This recipe is from my friend Marge Portella, who is a caterer and an excellent cook. She says, "This is the best apple cake recipe I know . . . a truly traditional flavor and texture." I agree; this is a rich, moist, and delicious cake. Marge bakes it in a tube pan with half the apples on the bottom and the rest on top. I make it in a rectangular baking pan.

3 cups all-purpose flour
3 teaspoons baking powder
1 teaspoon salt
2¾ cups sugar
1 cup vegetable oil
4 large eggs
1 cup fresh orange juice
1 tablespoon vanilla

6 medium apples (such as Jonathan or Red Romes) peeled, cored, and thinly sliced (about 4 cups)
1 tablespoon ground cinnamon
Whipped cream, for serving

Preheat the oven to 350°F. Grease a 13 × 9-inch cake pan or a 9- or 10-inch tube pan, such as an angel food or sponge cake pan.

In a large mixing bowl, combine the flour, baking powder, salt, and 2 cups of the sugar. Mix the oil, eggs, orange juice, and vanilla. Stir into the flour mixture. Beat with an electric mixer until light.

Mix the apples in a large bowl with the remaining sugar and the cinnamon until the apples are well coated. Arrange half the apples in the bottom of the pan. Pour the batter evenly over the top. Arrange the remaining apples on top.

TO FREEZE SLICED FRESH APPLES

Peel, core, and thinly slice the apples. Place in a single layer on a baking sheet. Place into freezer until frozen solid. Remove the apples from the baking sheet and pack into freezer bags or plastic freezer containers. When you wish to use the apples for baking, simply remove as much as you need from the freezer. Return remaining apple slices to freezer, sealed, before they thaw. Frozen apples can be used just like fresh for baking. No need to thaw them for most recipes such as pies, crisps, cobblers, and cakes.

Bake for 1 hour and 15 minutes or until a wooden skewer inserted into the center of the cake comes out dry, the cake is brown, and the apples are tender. Remove from the oven and cool the rectangular cake in the pan on a rack. If using a tube pan, allow to cool in the pan for 10 minutes, and then loosen the edges. Place a plate onto the top of the pan; invert to remove the cake. Replace any apples that might have adhered to the baking pan, then place a serving dish onto the cake and invert again so that the topside is up. Serve warm with whipped cream.

Makes 10 to 12 servings

Honey-Nut Brownies

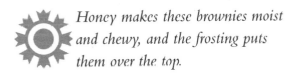

Honey makes these brownies moist and chewy, and the frosting puts them over the top.

6 tablespoons vegetable oil or unsalted
   butter, at room temperature
½ cup sugar
½ cup honey
2 teaspoons vanilla
2 large eggs
½ cup all-purpose flour
⅓ cup dark, unsweetened cocoa
½ teaspoon salt
1 cup chopped walnuts or pecans

Cocoa Frosting

1 cup confectioners' sugar
2 tablespoons dark, unsweetened cocoa
2 tablespoons fresh orange juice
   or water
1 teaspoon vanilla

Preheat the oven to 350°F. Grease a 9-inch square pan.

In a bowl with an electric mixer or spoon, cream together the oil or butter, sugar, honey, and vanilla until smooth. Beat in the eggs, one at a time until well mixed.

In a small bowl, stir the flour, cocoa, and salt together and then add to the creamed mixture. Mix or beat until smooth. Stir in the nuts. Pour into the prepared pan.

Bake for 25 to 30 minutes, until brownies are set but still soft in the center. Do not over-bake or brownies will be dry. Remove from the oven and cool in the pan on a rack.

In a small bowl, stir together the confectioners' sugar, cocoa, orange juice or water, and vanilla to make a smooth frosting. Spread over the top of the cooled brownies. Cut into squares.

Makes 12 brownies

Plum Strudel

Plums of all varieties are in season in the late summer and autumn and are absolutely irresistible baked within thin and crispy sheets of phyllo dough. If you make the strudel ahead and freeze it, be sure to wrap it well so that it isn't damaged in the freezer. To thaw the strudel before serving, unwrap it completely and place it on a cookie sheet, and reheat in a 300°F oven until the filling is hot, at least 140°F (you can check the temperature by inserting an instant-reading thermometer into the strudel's center), 15 to 20 minutes.

2 pounds Italian prune plums or other purple plums, pitted and cut into ½-inch dice

⅓ cup dark brown sugar, packed

1 tablespoon all-purpose flour

⅛ teaspoon ground cloves

⅛ teaspoon ground nutmeg

1 package (16 ounces) phyllo dough, thawed as directed on package

¾ cup (1½ sticks) unsalted butter, melted

Preheat the oven to 450°F.

In a large bowl, mix the plums, brown sugar, flour, cloves, and nutmeg until thoroughly combined; set aside.

Line an 11 × 17-inch baking sheet with parchment paper.

For easier rolling of the filled strudel, lay a sheet of plastic wrap on the countertop in front of you. Have the long edge nearest you.

Place a sheet of phyllo on the plastic wrap. Using a pastry brush, lightly brush the dough with some of the butter. Place the second sheet of dough perpendicular to the first, so that the 2 sheets overlap in the middle. Lightly brush this sheet with butter. Continue overlapping and buttering the dough in this manner until all the sheets are used. Reserve ½ tablespoon of the butter to brush the filled roll.

Spread the plum filling in an even mound along the long bottom edge of the phyllo dough, leaving a ¾-inch border on each end. Using the plastic wrap to lift the dough, roll it into a neat log, tucking in the ends as you roll. Remove the plastic wrap and place the log on the parchment-covered baking sheet with the seam side down. Brush the roll with the reserved butter. Using a sharp knife, score the strudel crosswise on the diagonal to divide it into 10 equal-sized portions, making the cuts about an inch apart.

Bake for 20 to 25 minutes, until the phyllo is golden brown. Let cool on the tray for about 15 minutes before cutting.

Makes 10 servings

Lemon–Poppy Seed Cake

Poppy seeds fleck this tender, white, lemon-scented cake. You can bake it in layers and use lemon curd, either purchased or your own homemade variety, for a filling. Soaking the poppy seeds in milk overnight enhances their flavor, so plan accordingly.

¾ cup poppy seeds
¾ cup milk
¾ cup (1½ sticks) unsalted butter, at room temperature
1 teaspoon grated lemon zest
1½ cups sugar
4 large egg whites, at room temperature
2 cups cake flour
2 teaspoons baking powder
¼ teaspoon salt

Lemon Glaze

1 cup confectioners' sugar
2 tablespoons unsalted butter, softened
2 to 3 teaspoons fresh lemon juice

Preheat the oven to 350°F. Grease a 10-inch tube-type pan and dust the pan with flour.

In a small bowl, combine the poppy seeds and milk. Cover and refrigerate overnight.

In a large bowl, cream the butter, lemon zest, and sugar until creamy. Add the egg whites and beat at high speed with an electric mixer until the mixture is light and fluffy. Place the cake flour, baking powder, and salt into a sieve and set it over the bowl. With a spoon, stir the mixture until it is sifted into the creamed mixture. Add the poppy seed–milk mixture and with an electric mixer at medium speed beat until the batter is light and fluffy, scraping the sides of the bowl often.

Pour the batter into the prepared pan and bake for 45 to 55 minutes or until a wooden skewer inserted in the center comes out clean.

Let the cake cool in the pan for 5 minutes, then invert it out onto a wire rack to finish cooling.

TO MAKE THE LEMON GLAZE

In a small bowl, stir together the confectioners' sugar, butter, and lemon juice. Drizzle the icing over the cake.

Makes about 12 servings

Halloween

Raisin-Chip-Peanut Butter Cookies

 These cookies have been a family favorite for more years than I care to relate! Our kids took them to school and sold them at fund-raisers, we made them for Halloween parties, we gave them away as gifts stacked and wrapped in cellophane, and we sold them at the church bazaar. They were always the first to go. My original recipe makes fifty jumbo cookies and the amount of dough was so large that we had to mix the dough in a dishpan. I've scaled this down to a reasonable amount. Yes, there is no flour in this recipe!

½ cup (1 stick) unsalted butter, at room temperature

½ cup peanut butter, creamy or chunky

1 cup packed brown sugar

¼ cup granulated sugar

1 teaspoon vanilla

1 large egg

2 cups old-fashioned rolled oats

½ teaspoon baking soda

1 cup semisweet chocolate chips

1 cup raisins

1 cup chocolate-covered raisins

½ cup chopped walnuts

Preheat the oven to 350°F. Coat two baking sheets with parchment paper or nonstick spray.

THE ORIGIN OF HALLOWEEN

Originally the Druids, an ancient religious cult in Britain, celebrated the Celtic new year near the end of October. They built bonfires on hilltops to frighten away witches and evil spirits, and they also made human and animal sacrifices to the Lord of the Dead (called Saman) and to the sun.

The holiday was fueled by Pope Gregory III in the eighth century when he designated November 1 to be All Hallows' Day, meaning "the day of all holy people," to honor all saints. The evening before became known as "All-hallow e'en," or the eve of All Hallows' Day, which we now observe on October 31.

Today All Hallows' Day is celebrated as All Saints' Day by the Christian church to memorialize loved ones who have died. The Mexicans call it "The Day of the Dead" and make a special bread called Pan de Muertos for their celebration. The bread is traditionally decorated with bones and tears that are made out of bread dough.

In a large bowl, with an electric mixer, cream the butter, peanut butter, brown sugar, and granulated sugar together until smooth. Add the vanilla and egg and beat until light.

Stir in the rolled oats and baking soda. Add the chocolate chips, raisins, chocolate-covered raisins, and walnuts and mix well.

Using a #12 ice cream scoop or a ⅓ cup measure, scoop dough from the bowl and place the mounds 3 inches apart on the baking sheet. Flatten slightly using a fork.

Bake for 10 to 15 minutes or until light golden brown. Cool for 2 or 3 minutes on the baking sheet, then remove and cool completely on a wire rack.

Makes fifteen 4½- to 5-inch cookies

Chocolate-Chunk Platter Cookies

These pizza-size cookies can be cut into wedges for serving. For a birthday party drizzle them with melted chocolate and decorate with candles.

- 1 cup (2 sticks) unsalted butter, at room temperature
- 1 package (8 ounces) cream cheese
- 1 cup packed brown sugar
- ½ cup granulated sugar
- 2 large eggs, at room temperature
- 2⅓ cups all-purpose flour
- 1 teaspoon baking soda
- ¼ teaspoon salt
- 1 package (12 ounces) semisweet chocolate chunks
- 1 cup coarsely chopped walnuts or pecans

Preheat the oven to 375°F. Lightly grease two 12-inch pizza pans.

In a large bowl with an electric mixer, cream the butter, cream cheese, brown sugar, and granulated sugar. Add the eggs and beat at high speed until fluffy.

In another bowl, stir together the flour, baking soda, and salt. Add to the creamed mixture, mixing until the dough is stiff. Stir in the chocolate chunks and walnuts.

Divide the dough in half and press each half evenly into a prepared pan, press the top down with a fork dipped in water.

Bake for 20 to 25 minutes or until light brown around the edges and firm in the center. Cool in the pan on a wire rack. Cut into wedges to serve.

Makes two 12-inch platter cookies

Crinkle-Faced Ginger Monsters

These are chewy, yet crisp; spicy, yet mellow. Sugar and water create the crinkled top on the cookies as they bake.

¾ cup (1½ sticks) unsalted butter
1 cup packed brown sugar
1 large egg
¼ cup dark molasses
2 teaspoons baking soda

1 teaspoon ground cinnamon
1 teaspoon ground ginger
¼ teaspoon salt
2¼ cups all-purpose flour
  Sugar, for dipping
  Water, for sprinkling

Preheat the oven to 375°F. Lightly grease 2 baking sheets or cover with parchment paper.

In a large bowl with an electric mixer, cream the butter with the brown sugar. Add the egg and molasses and beat until light and

---

 MONSTER COOKIE PARTY

This is a fun party idea for kids as young as four or five years old. Have the kids select ahead of time which "monster-size" cookies they would like to make. Plan to have one adult supervisor for every two children, who will make one batch of cookies. Children can take home a sampling of their baking. Provide sandwich bags, plastic wrap, or aluminum foil for transporting the cookies.

Some tips for a safe and fun party:

- Read the recipe carefully
- Have children wash and dry their hands before beginning
- Tie back the kids' hair if it is long
- Roll up long sleeves and have kids wear washable clothing
- Teach safety: Use thick, dry mitts or pot holders when putting pans into and taking pans out of the oven
- Stress that knives and electrical appliances should be used only with adult supervision

fluffy. Beat in the baking soda, cinnamon, ginger, and salt. Add the flour and mix until the dough is stiff.

Using a #12 ice cream scoop or a ⅓ cup measure, scoop the dough from the bowl. Dip the tops of the balls of dough into sugar and place them 3 inches apart, sugar side up, in the prepared pan. Sprinkle each cookie with 5 to 6 drops of water.

Bake for 12 minutes, until just set.

Makes twelve 4- to 5-inch cookies

Hermits

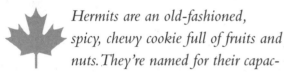

Hermits are an old-fashioned, spicy, chewy cookie full of fruits and nuts. They're named for their capacity to keep well, actually tasting better when hidden away like a hermit for several days. In the aging, the spices, which can seem too pronounced when the cookies are first baked, mellow and blend together. Keep them in a covered container in a cool place or freeze them.

½ cup (1 stick) unsalted butter, at room temperature
1 cup packed brown sugar
1 large egg
½ cup sour cream
1½ cups all-purpose flour
½ teaspoon baking soda
¼ teaspoon salt
½ teaspoon ground cinnamon
½ teaspoon freshly ground nutmeg
¼ teaspoon ground cloves
¼ teaspoon ground allspice
1¼ cups raisins
1 cup chopped walnuts

Glaze
½ cup confectioners' sugar
1 to 2 tablespoons strong, hot coffee

Preheat the oven to 400°F. Lightly grease 2 baking sheets or cover with parchment paper.

In a mixing bowl, cream the butter and brown sugar until smooth, then add the egg and beat until light. Mix in the sour cream. Stir the flour, baking soda, salt, cinnamon,

---

 FREEZING COOKIES

Package the cooled cookies in heavy-duty freezer bags or airtight containers. Freeze fragile cookies in single layers on baking sheets; when frozen solid, transfer to airtight containers in single layers separated by waxed paper. Bar cookies can be frozen, uncut, in the pan. Be sure to cover tightly.

nutmeg, cloves, and allspice together in another bowl and add to the creamed mixture, mixing until the dough is smooth. Stir in the raisins and walnuts.

Using a #12 ice cream scoop or a ⅓ cup measure, scoop dough from the bowl and place the mounds 3 inches apart in the prepared pan. Bake for 10 to 12 minutes or until cookies feel firm when touched in the center; do not overbake.

To make the glaze, mix the confectioners' sugar and coffee in a small bowl to make a thin glaze. Brush the glaze over the hot cookies. Return to the oven for 1 more minute until the glaze appears crackly. Slide the cookies on the parchment onto the countertop to cool, or lift with a spatula onto a wire rack.

Makes 12 large cookies

Jumbo Sugar Jumbles

 This simple drop sugar cookie dates back to the 1800s. Even the youngest kids like these.

½ cup unsalted butter,
   at room temperature
½ cup sugar
 1 large egg
1½ cups all-purpose flour
¼ teaspoon baking soda
¼ teaspoon salt

Water, for dipping
Sugar, for dipping

Preheat the oven to 375°F. Lightly grease a baking sheet or cover with parchment paper.

In a large bowl with an electric mixer, cream the butter and sugar together well. Add the egg and beat until light.

Stir the flour, baking soda, and salt together in another bowl. Add to the creamed mixture and mix until the dough is stiff.

Using a #12 ice cream scoop or a ⅓ cup measure, scoop dough from the bowl and place 6 equal-size mounds 3 inches apart in the prepared pan. Flatten with a fork or a flat-bottomed tumbler, dipped in the water and then in sugar.

Bake for 12 to 15 minutes, until light brown. Remove from the oven and cool on a wire rack.

Makes 6 jumbo cookies

Lemon-Almond Cookies

 These big six-inch cookies are flavored with lemon zest and topped with sliced almonds, which toast as the cookies bake.

½ cup (1 stick) unsalted butter,
    at room temperature
1 cup sugar
1 large egg
1 teaspoon grated lemon zest
1¾ cups all-purpose flour
⅛ teaspoon salt
1 teaspoon baking powder
3 tablespoons fresh lemon juice
¼ cup sliced almonds

In a large bowl, cream the butter and sugar until smooth. Beat in the egg and lemon zest until the mixture is light and fluffy. Mix the flour, salt, and baking powder in another bowl and add to the creamed mixture along with the lemon juice. Mix until the dough is smooth. Wrap in plastic wrap and chill for 1 hour.

Preheat the oven to 375°F. Lightly grease a baking sheet or cover with parchment paper. On a lightly floured surface roll the dough out to ¼ inch thick. Cut out circles with a 6-inch cookie cutter. Place the cut-out cookie on the baking sheet about 2 inches apart. Press the almonds lightly into the tops of the cookies.

Bake for 8 minutes or until golden. Remove from the pan and cool on a wire rack.

Makes 8 large cookies

Peanut Butter Monsters

 Peanut butter was first developed in 1890 as a health food and was exhibited at the 1904 St. Louis World's Fair; its popularity has steadily increased since then. Cookies made with peanut butter are an all-time favorite in most households, and these monsters should satisfy any craving! The perfect peanut butter cookie needs to be tender, peanutty, and not dry or crumbly. Although the recipe is very good with commercial peanut butter, which often contains sugar and additives to improve creaminess, I think it is the very best made with natural peanut butter, which is made from only peanuts and peanut oil.

½ cup unsalted butter (1 stick) or
    vegetable shortening, or a
    combination
½ cup peanut butter, creamy or chunky
½ cup coarsely chopped dry
    roasted peanuts
⅓ cup granulated sugar
⅓ cup packed brown sugar
1 large egg
2 teaspoons vanilla
1¼ cups all-purpose flour
½ teaspoon baking powder
½ teaspoon baking soda
¼ teaspoon salt

Preheat the oven to 375°F. Lightly grease 2 baking sheets or cover with parchment paper.

In a large bowl with an electric mixer, cream the butter or shortening with the peanut butter, peanuts, sugars, egg, and vanilla. Stir the flour, baking powder, baking soda, and salt together in another bowl. Mix the dry ingredients into the creamed ingredients until well blended.

Using a #12 ice cream scoop or a ⅓ cup measure, scoop dough from the bowl, and place the mounds 3 inches apart in the prepared pans. Flatten with a fork dipped in flour. Bake for 10 to 15 minutes or until light brown. Remove from the pan and cool on a wire rack, or slide the parchment off onto the countertop.

Makes 10 large cookies

Pumpkin-Glazed Pumpkin Cookies

These are soft, chewy cookies. I like to wrap them individually in plastic wrap and freeze them so that they are all ready to tuck into lunch boxes, or to offer one at a time to cookie-hungry monsters.

½ cup (1 stick) unsalted butter,
    at room temperature
1½ cups packed brown sugar
2 large eggs
1 cup fresh cooked or canned
    puréed pumpkin
1 teaspoon vanilla

2½ cups all-purpose flour
3 teaspoons baking powder
1 teaspoon ground cinnamon
½ teaspoon allspice
¼ teaspoon ground ginger
¼ teaspoon salt
1 cup chopped walnuts

Pumpkin Glaze

1½ cups confectioners' sugar
2 tablespoons unsalted butter,
    at room temperature
1 teaspoon ground cinnamon
¼ teaspoon allspice
3 tablespoons fresh cooked or
    canned puréed pumpkin

Preheat the oven to 375°F. Lightly grease 2 baking sheets or cover with parchment paper.

In a large bowl with an electric mixer, cream together the butter and brown sugar until smooth. Add the eggs and beat until light. Add the pumpkin and vanilla. Stir together the flour, baking powder, cinnamon, allspice, ginger, and salt in another bowl. Add to the creamed mixture and mix until well blended. Stir in the walnuts.

Using a #12 ice cream scoop or a ⅓ cup measure, scoop dough from the bowl and place the mounds 3 inches apart in the prepared pans.

Bake for 12 to 15 minutes, until the cookies feel firm when touched in the center. Remove from the cookie sheet and cool on a wire rack.

Wash the pumpkin and cut it in half, crosswise. Remove the seeds and strings. Place it in a baking pan, with the skin side up, and bake in a 325°F oven for one hour or until the flesh can be easily pierced with a fork. Remove from the oven and allow to cool. Scrape the pulp from the shell and press through a food mill or whirl in the food processor until very smooth.

To make the glaze, stir together in a small bowl the confectioners' sugar, butter, cinnamon, allspice, and pumpkin. Spread over the cookies while they are still slightly warm.

Makes 16 to 18 cookies

Spiced Raisin Apple Jumbos

 These are healthy jumbos made with whole wheat flour and rolled oats, fresh apple chunks, and raisins.

¼ cup (½ stick) unsalted butter, at room temperature
¼ cup vegetable oil
¾ cup packed brown sugar
1 large egg, at room temperature
1 teaspoon vanilla
¾ cup whole wheat flour
½ teaspoon baking soda
1 teaspoon ground cinnamon
¾ cup uncooked rolled oats
1 cup chopped fresh tart apple, such as Granny Smith
½ cup raisins

Preheat the oven to 350°F. Lightly grease 2 baking sheets or cover with parchment paper or coat with nonstick spray.

In a large bowl with an electric mixer, cream together the butter, oil, and brown sugar until smooth. Add the egg and vanilla and beat until light.

Stir the flour, baking soda, and cinnamon together in another bowl. Add to the creamed mixture and mix until well blended. Stir in the oats, apple, and raisins until well combined.

Using a #12 ice cream scoop or a ⅓ cup measure, scoop dough from the bowl and place the mounds 3 inches apart on the baking sheet; flatten slightly using a spatula or a fork.

Bake for 10 to 15 minutes, until the cookies feel firm to the touch. The cookies may sink in the center slightly as they cool. Remove from the baking sheet and cool on a wire rack.

Makes eight 4- to 5-inch cookies

Pumpkin-Spiced Monkey Bread

Monkey bread is a pull-apart bread baked in a tube pan. This spicy, nutty Halloween version is golden with pumpkin.

5 cups all-purpose flour, divided

½ cup nonfat dry milk powder

2 packages (5½ teaspoons) active
 dry yeast or rapid-rise yeast

1½ cups sugar, divided

1 cup (2 sticks) unsalted butter,
 melted, divided

1 teaspoon salt

1 cup very warm water (130°F)

2 cups (one 16-ounce can)
 puréed pumpkin

3½ teaspoons pumpkin pie spice, divided

½ cup finely chopped walnuts
 or pecans

In a large mixing bowl, combine 3 cups of the flour, the dry milk, yeast, ½ cup of the sugar, ¼ cup butter, and salt; mix well. Make a well in the center of the dry ingredients and pour in the water. Add the pumpkin and 2 teaspoons of the pumpkin pie spice. Beat at low speed with an electric mixer for 3 minutes, scraping down the bowl often. Gradually beat in enough remaining flour to make a stiff dough. Turn the dough onto a lightly floured surface and knead until smooth, adding flour as necessary. Wash the bowl, grease it, and place the dough into the bowl; turn the dough over to grease the top. Cover and let rise in a warm place until doubled, about 40 to 50 minutes (rising time will be less with rapid-rise yeast).

Lightly grease a 10-inch tube pan. In a small, shallow bowl, combine the remaining sugar with the remaining pumpkin pie spice. Punch down the dough and divide into thirds. Turn out onto a lightly oiled surface

MONKEY BREAD

This is a sweet yeast bread constructed of balls of dough that are laid next to one another in a baking pan. A savory version calls for the dough to be shaped into balls and dipped into garlic butter. It has been suggested that the name comes from its resemblance to the monkey puzzle tree, a tree that has funny, bulbous shapes on its limbs. Others have thought that the baked bread resembles a bunch of monkeys packed together. Another possibility is that the name comes from the fact that you just pull the bread apart to eat it—the way a monkey might eat it.

and shape each third into a smooth 18-inch rope; then cut each rope into 18 equal pieces. Shape each piece into a smooth ball. Dip each ball in the remaining melted butter and roll in the sugar mixture. Arrange 18 balls in the bottom of the pan and sprinkle with one-third of the nuts. Top with another layer of 18 balls, staggering the balls, and sprinkle with one-third of the nuts. Repeat with the remaining balls and nuts. Cover the pan lightly and let rise in a warm place, about 45 minutes until doubled.

Preheat the oven to 350°F. Bake for 55 to 65 minutes or until a wooden skewer inserted into the center comes out clean. Cool in the pan on a wire rack for 20 minutes and invert onto a serving plate. Serve warm, breaking apart the bread with two forks.

Makes 12 to 16 servings

Pumpkin Pecan Waffles

A cheerful Halloween breakfast to get everyone in the mood, or ideal anytime during the autumn season. These are great topped with cinnamon-spiced whipped cream and/or pure maple syrup.

 2 cups all-purpose flour
 3 teaspoons baking powder
 2 teaspoons pumpkin pie spice
 ½ teaspoon salt
 3 large eggs, separated
 1½ cups milk
 ½ cup fresh cooked or canned puréed pumpkin
 ½ cup (1 stick) unsalted butter, melted
 1 cup chopped pecans

Preheat a waffle iron. In a large bowl, stir together the flour, baking powder, pumpkin pie spice, and salt. In a medium bowl, beat the egg yolks with the milk, pumpkin, and butter. Add the liquids to the dry ingredients, mixing until well blended. Stir in the nuts. In another bowl, beat the egg whites until stiff and fold into the batter. Grease the hot waffle iron and pour on 1 cup of the batter. Close and cook for 3 to 5 minutes, until golden brown. Repeat with the remaining batter. Keep the cooked waffles warm in a 300°F oven.

Makes about twenty 4-inch waffles

Mexican All Saints' Day Bread, or Pan de Muertos

Literally translated, pan de muertos *means "the bread of the dead," which is made for All Saints' Day in Mexico. All Saints' Day is November 1 and is usually celebrated in the Christian church on the last weekend of October. Mexicans traditionally decorate this bread with shapes of bones and tears made out of dough. These breads are often works of art, as beautiful to look at as they are delicious to eat. Being a bread baker, I love to "sculpt" bread dough, and I find that my version of this bread, which is based on a refrigerator dough, is easy to handle and fun to work with. The bread is delicious with orange and anise flavors. I serve it with a simple, country-style stew.*

2 packages (5½ teaspoons) active
   dry yeast
1 cup warm water (105 to 115°F)
½ cup (1 stick) unsalted butter, melted
½ cup sugar
3 large eggs, at room temperature
½ teaspoon grated orange zest
¼ teaspoon ground aniseed
1 teaspoon salt
4½ to 5 cups all-purpose flour
1 large egg, beaten with 1 tablespoon
   water, for glaze
1 tablespoon sugar, for sprinkling

In a large mixing bowl, dissolve the yeast in the warm water. Let stand for 5 minutes, until the yeast begins to bubble. Add the butter, sugar, eggs, orange zest, aniseed, salt, and 2 cups of the flour. Beat with an electric mixer until very smooth.

With a wooden spoon, stir in 2 cups more flour, 1 cup at a time, stirring until all the flour is moistened. Slowly stir in ½ cup more flour if the mixture is moist enough to absorb it.

Cover the bowl with plastic wrap and refrigerate at least 2 hours or up to 2 days.

Sprinkle a work surface with some of the remaining flour. Remove the dough from the refrigerator and turn out onto the floured surface. Sprinkle the dough with a small amount of the flour. Knead lightly until dough makes a smooth ball, about 1 minute.

Lightly grease a baking sheet or cover with parchment paper.

Pinch off about ⅓ cup of the dough. Shape the remaining dough into a smooth, round ball. Place on the baking sheet with the smooth side up. Flatten to about a 2-inch thickness. The loaf will be about 10 inches in diameter.

Divide the reserved dough into 3 equal-size pieces. Roll 2 of the pieces of dough into two 8-inch-long ropes. Flatten the ends to resemble bones. Brush the loaf with the egg glaze. Place the ropes over the loaf, crossing them in the center. Shape the third piece of dough into a ball. Divide the ball into 2 parts. Shape 1 part into a ball, moisten its bottom with the egg glaze, and press it into the center of the crossed ropes. Cut the remainder of the dough into 4 pieces and roll into teardrop shapes. Place them on the loaf, pressing them into the dough. Brush with the egg glaze. Let rise, covered, in a warm place for 30 to 45 minutes or until puffy.

Preheat the oven to 375°F. Brush the loaf again with the egg glaze and sprinkle with 1 tablespoon sugar.

Bake for 30 to 35 minutes or until the loaf is brown and a skewer inserted in the center comes out clean. Cool on a wire rack.

Makes 1 large loaf

Moist and Chewy Pineapple Cookies

Crushed pineapple keeps these cookies quite moist. I like them shaped into 2-inch cookies, but made into "mini monsters" they're great for trick-or-treaters. Browned butter and pineapple juice give the glaze an especially nice flavor.

- ¾ cup (1½ sticks) unsalted butter, at room temperature
- 1¼ cups packed brown sugar
- 2 large eggs, slightly beaten
- 1 (20-ounce) can crushed pineapple, very well drained (reserve juice)
- 2½ cups all-purpose flour

- 1 teaspoon baking soda
- 1 teaspoon baking powder
- ½ teaspoon salt
- ½ cup chopped walnuts

Pineapple Glaze

- ¼ cup (½ stick) unsalted butter
- 2 cups confectioners' sugar
- 3 to 5 tablespoons reserved pineapple juice

Preheat the oven to 375°F. Lightly grease or cover 2 baking sheets with parchment paper.

In a large mixing bowl, using an electric mixer, cream the butter with the brown sugar. Add the eggs and beat until light. Stir in the pineapple.

In a small bowl, combine the flour, baking soda, baking powder, and salt. Stir the flour mixture into the creamed mixture until well blended. Mix the nuts.

Using a #12 ice cream scoop, or a ⅓ cup measure, scoop dough from the bowl and place 6 equal-sized scoopfuls 3 inches apart on the baking sheet.

Bake for 12 to 15 minutes or until golden around the edges. Remove from the pan and cool on a wire rack.

TO MAKE THE PINEAPPLE GLAZE
Meanwhile, in a heavy saucepan over medium heat, melt the butter until it turns a nut brown. Stir in the confectioners' sugar and enough of the reserved pineapple juice to make a smooth glaze.

Frost the cookies with the glaze while they are still slightly warm.

Makes 16 to 18 large cookies or 48 two-inch cookies

Giant Whole Wheat–Pumpkin Muffins

 These hearty whole-grain muffins are quick to make and great served with a hearty stew on a chilly autumn day.

2 cups whole wheat flour
⅔ cup all-purpose flour
⅔ cup packed brown sugar
2 teaspoons baking powder
1 teaspoon baking soda
1 teaspoon pumpkin pie spice
1½ cups buttermilk
1 cup puréed or canned pumpkin
¾ cup raisins

Preheat the oven to 350°F. Lightly grease 6 large, 4-inch muffin cups. In a large mixing bowl, stir together the whole wheat flour, all-purpose flour, sugar, baking powder, baking soda, and pumpkin pie spice.

In a medium-sized bowl, stir together the buttermilk and pumpkin. Add to the dry ingredients, mixing just until the flour mixture is moistened. Fold in the raisins. Spoon the mixture into the prepared muffin cups. Bake for 35 to 40 minutes or until a toothpick inserted in the center comes out clean. Remove from pans and cool on a wire rack.

Makes 6 giant muffins

Thanksgiving

Breads • Pies • Desserts

B R E A D S

Bolillos

In Mexico, these buns are sold in open-air stands for snacks. They are called "bolillos" because they look like the bobbins used for making lace. Baked in tiny round rolls, they make great appetizers. Mexican cooks split the rolls in half, spread the cut sides with refried beans, sprinkle with a grated sharp cheese, and top with chopped cooked chicken that has been seasoned with lemon juice, minced onion, and salsa. This is a great way to serve any extra turkey from Thanksgiving dinner. Offer shredded lettuce, guacamole, and chopped olives on the side to be added just before eating. Mexicans use lard as the shortening in this bread; however, you can use butter instead, which results in a different but acceptable texture.

1¼ cups boiling water
3 tablespoons lard or unsalted butter
2 teaspoons sugar
1½ teaspoons salt
4 cups bread flour or unbleached all-purpose flour
1 package (2¾ teaspoons) active dry yeast

THANKSGIVING

The first Thanksgiving was observed by the Pilgrims after a particularly bad growing season. A combination of bad seed (brought from England) and the late arrival of warm weather had contributed to a disappointing harvest. But they did have corn and for that they decided to have a day of thanksgiving. Some of the men were sent out to hunt, and with the help of ninety Native American men, they brought in deer, duck, goose, and turkey. Other items enjoyed that day were clams, shellfish, smoked eel, corn bread, leeks, watercress and other greens, wild plums, and dried berries. There was also wine made from wild grapes. The first Thanksgiving was a great success, and the Pilgrims repeated it, creating a holiday tradition in New England. In 1863, President Abraham Lincoln proclaimed the last Thursday in November as Thanksgiving Day nationwide. Today Americans observe the holiday on the fourth Thursday in November.

Glaze

    1 teaspoon cornstarch dissolved in
      4 teaspoons water

In a medium bowl, pour the water over the lard or butter and stir in the sugar and salt. Let stand, stirring occasionally until the shortening melts and the mixture has cooled to very warm (about 130°F).

In a large mixing bowl or in the food processor, combine the flour and yeast. Pour in the liquids and stir or process until a dough forms. If mixing by hand, turn out onto a lightly floured surface and knead until smooth and elastic. If using a food processor, process until the dough is smooth (it may not clean the sides of the work bowl). Place the dough into a clean, greased bowl. Turn the dough over to grease the top, cover, and let rise in a warm place for 45 minutes or until doubled.

Turn the dough out onto a lightly floured surface and knead to express all air bubbles. Divide into 8 equal pieces. Shape each piece of dough into an oval, pinching and pulling the ends into points. Place on a lightly greased or parchment-covered baking sheet. Cover with a towel and let rise until puffy, 30 to 45 minutes.

Preheat the oven to 375°F. Stir the cornstarch mixture to recombine and brush it onto the rolls. With a sharp razor or knife make a 2-inch slash on top of each roll about ¾ inch deep.

Bake for 20 to 25 minutes or until brown and crusty. Remove from the baking sheet and cool on a wire rack.

Makes 8 rolls

Crunchy Breadsticks

Sometimes I snip one end of each of the sticks to simulate stalks of wheat, as they curve slightly when they bake. I'll stand them up in crocks at the table for a neat edible centerpiece. Or you can run the dough through the fettucini blade of your pasta maker to make pencil-thin sticks. Kids love to help with this!

3 to 3½ cups all-purpose flour
    1 tablespoon sugar
    1 teaspoon salt
    2 packages (5½ teaspoons) active
       dry yeast
 1¼ cups very warm water
       (about 130°F)
   ¼ cup extra-virgin olive oil or
       vegetable oil
       Extra-virgin olive oil or
       vegetable oil, for coating the
       sticks
    1 large egg white, beaten with
       1 tablespoon water
       Kosher salt, sesame seeds, or
       poppy seeds

In the work bowl of a food processor with the dough blade in place, or in a large mixing bowl, combine the flour, sugar, salt, and yeast. Pour the water over the mixture, then pour the oil over. Process or mix until the dough is smooth and satiny. This dough does not need to be kneaded, just be sure to stir until all the flour is mixed in.

Shape the dough into a log and with a knife cut it into 20 equal-size pieces. Roll each piece of dough into a rope that is 16 to 20 inches long or as long as your baking sheet. Coat each stick generously with the additional oil and place the sticks side by side, about 1 inch apart on 2 baking sheets.

Let rise for 15 minutes, until puffy. With a soft brush paint each stick with the egg white wash. Sprinkle the sticks with salt or seeds. If desired, now's the time to snip one tip of each breadstick on both sides to simulate stalks of grain; use scissors that have small pointed tips.

Preheat the oven to 300°F. Place both baking pans of sticks into the oven and bake for 40 to 50 minutes or until light brown all over. Switch the pans halfway through baking to ensure even browning. Serve the breadsticks warm, or cool on a wire rack.

Makes 20 sticks

Dinner Rolls in One Hour

You really can do these rolls from beginning to end in an hour! I use the food processor to mix the dough and hasten the rising by using rapid-rise yeast. This yeast is so finely milled that it dissolves right in the flour mixture, and it can stand a higher temperature, giving the dough a boost for the single necessary rising.

2½ cups all-purpose flour
1 package (2¾ teaspoons) rapid-rise yeast
5 tablespoons instant nonfat dry milk
2 tablespoons sugar
½ teaspoon salt
¾ cup very warm water (about 130°F)
2 tablespoons extra-virgin olive oil
3 tablespoons unsalted butter, melted

In a food processor or in a mixing bowl, mix the flour, yeast, milk, sugar, and salt. Add the water and oil and stir or process until a thick, sticky dough forms. Let stand for 5 minutes.

Butter an 8-inch round cake pan. Turn the dough out onto a floured board. (Gently round up the dough.) With a floured knife or dough scraper cut the dough into quarters. Cut each quarter into quarters, and shape the dough into balls, adding flour to prevent stickiness. Place the dough pieces close together in the prepared pan. Cover and let rise in a warm place for 20 to 25 minutes or until the rolls are puffy.

Preheat the oven to 400°F. Drizzle the melted butter over the rolls. Bake for 20 minutes or until golden.

Makes 16 pull-apart rolls

Giant Cinnamon-Pecan Rolls

S*Big, fat yeast rolls never taste so good to me as in the fall, when mornings have a nip to them and the day is sunny, dry, and warm. With a food processor, the mixing is a snap, but you can do the mixing and kneading by hand, too. Rapid-rise yeast cuts the rising time in half.*

Dough
- 2½ cups all-purpose flour
- 3 tablespoons sugar
- ½ teaspoon salt
- 1 package (2¾ teaspoons) rapid-rise yeast
- 1 cup milk, scalded and cooled to very warm (about 130°F)
- 2 tablespoons unsalted butter, at room temperature

Filling
- 2 tablespoons unsalted butter, melted
- ¼ cup packed brown sugar
- ½ teaspoon ground cinnamon
- ½ cup chopped pecans

Glaze
- 1 cup confectioners' sugar
- 2 tablespoons hot, strong coffee

Make the dough. In a food processor with the dough blade in place or in a large mixing bowl, combine the flour, sugar, salt, and yeast. Combine the milk and butter. Pour the milk mixture over the dry ingredients and mix or process until a dough forms.

Let the dough rest for 10 minutes. Grease 6 large muffin cups or one 9-inch round cake pan. Turn out onto a floured surface and roll out to make a 13 × 8-inch rectangle. Fill the dough by spreading it with the melted butter. Sprinkle with the brown sugar, then the cinnamon and pecans. Roll up from the short side.

Cut the roll into 6 equal-size slices. Place the cut side down into the muffin cups. Or place the rolls, evenly spaced, into the prepared round pan. Cover and let rise in a warm place until doubled, about 25 to 35 minutes.

Preheat the oven to 375°F. Bake for 20 to 30 minutes or until light brown and a skewer inserted into the center of a roll comes out clean. Remove from the cups or baking pan and cool on a wire rack.

To make the glaze, mix the confectioners' sugar and coffee together in a small bowl and drizzle over the warm rolls. Serve warm.

Makes 6 large rolls

Mincemeat Minimuffins with Sherry Butter

These little muffins are a nice addition to the bread basket on Thanksgiving Day and also a high point of any holiday breakfast or brunch.

1 cup all-purpose flour
¾ cup whole wheat flour
¼ teaspoon freshly ground nutmeg
3 teaspoons baking powder
¼ teaspoon salt
¼ cup sugar
½ cup chopped walnuts or pecans
1 cup plain yogurt, stirred
2 large eggs
1 cup prepared mincemeat (from a jar)

2 tablespoons unsalted butter, melted and cooled
Sherry Butter (below)

Preheat the oven to 400°F. Butter 36 miniature muffin cups.

In a mixing bowl, combine the flours, nutmeg, baking powder, salt, sugar, and nuts.

In a small bowl, combine the yogurt, eggs, mincemeat, and butter. Add the mincemeat mixture to the dry ingredients and blend just until combined; don't overmix.

Scoop the batter into the muffin cups and bake for 10 to 15 minutes or until a wooden skewer inserted in the center of a muffin comes out clean. Remove from cups and cool on a wire rack. Serve warm with Sherry Butter.

Makes 36 miniature muffins

 MINCEMEAT

The recorded history of mincemeat can be traced to King Henry V of England when it was served at his coronation in 1413. This rich, spicy fruit preserve usually includes chopped cherries, dried apricot, apples, pears, raisins, candied citrus peel, nuts, beef suet, spices, and cooked chopped meat, which gives this condiment its name. However, many modern mincemeats do not include the suet and the meat. Homemade mincemeats should be aged for a month to allow the flavors to blend.

King Henry VIII liked his Christmas pie to be a main-dish pie filled with mincemeat. In America, mincemeat pie became a dessert, and today commercially prepared all-fruit mincemeat is available in jars, especially around Thanksgiving and Christmas.

Sherry Butter

¼ cup (½ stick) unsalted butter,
  at room temperature

¼ cup confectioners' sugar

1 tablespoon cream sherry

In a small bowl, cream together all of the ingredients. With an electric mixer beat at high speed until light and fluffy. Turn into a serving bowl and serve without chilling.

Old-Fashioned Dinner Rolls

 With this kneading-free yeast dough you can make a variety of dinner rolls.

4 to 4½ cups all-purpose flour

2 packages (5½ teaspoons) active
  dry yeast

½ cup sugar

1 teaspoon salt

1 cup milk

½ cup (1 stick) unsalted butter,
  cut into pieces

3 large eggs, beaten

In a large bowl, mix 4 cups of the flour, the yeast, sugar, and salt until well blended. Heat the milk to boiling in a small saucepan over medium heat. Remove from the heat and add the butter. Stir until the butter is melted and the mixture has cooled to 130°F.

Pour the mixture over the dry ingredients in the bowl and pour the eggs over. Stir until well mixed using a wooden spoon or the paddle of an electric mixer.

Scrape down the dough. Cover with plastic wrap and refrigerate at least 2 hours or up to 3 days.

When you are ready for baking, remove the dough from the refrigerator and shape the dough into one or two of the following variations.

Cloverleaf Rolls

Divide the dough into 2 parts. Return 1 part to the refrigerator. Turn the other half of the dough onto a lightly floured surface and knead lightly, dusting with flour as needed. Divide the dough into 12 parts. Grease 12 muffin cups. Divide each of the 12 parts of dough into 3 pieces, and shape each piece into a small ball. Fit 3 balls into each muffin cup to make cloverleaf-shaped rolls. Repeat with the rest of the dough, if desired. Let rise, covered, until almost doubled, about 45 minutes.

Preheat the oven to 375°F and bake for 15 to 20 minutes or until golden. Remove from the baking sheet into a serving basket. Serve hot.

Makes 24 rolls, if all dough is used

Parker House Rolls

Roll out half the dough to a ½-inch thickness, keeping the other half covered in the refrigerator. Using a 3-inch round cutter, cut 12 rounds. Brush each round with melted butter. Make a crease just off center of each round. Firmly fold each roll at the crease, pressing the larger half of each round over the smaller half to seal (they tend to open up in rising and baking). Place on a parchment-covered or greased baking sheet. Repeat with the rest of the dough, if desired. Let rise, covered, until almost doubled, about 45 minutes.

Preheat the oven to 375°F and bake for 15 to 20 minutes or until golden. Remove from the baking sheet into a serving basket. Serve hot.

Makes 24 rolls, if all dough is used

Crescent Rolls

Roll out half the dough to make a 12-inch circle. Cut into 8 wedges. Brush the tops with melted butter. Roll up each piece starting from the wide side and rolling toward the tip. Place on a parchment-covered or lightly greased baking sheet with the tip under the roll and pull in the ends to turn each roll into a crescent shape. Repeat with the rest of the dough, if desired. Let rise, covered, until almost doubled, about 45 minutes.

Preheat the oven to 375°F and bake for 15 to 20 minutes or until golden. Remove from the baking sheet into a serving basket. Serve hot.

Makes 16 crescents, if all dough is used

Pecan-Pineapple Scones

The most notable difference between scones and baking powder biscuits is that scones use eggs. Basic scones are such a quick-and-easy bread, perfect for company breakfast or brunch. Vary the flavor by using dates, chopped dried apple, pears, or prunes for the raisins and pineapple. Or eliminate all the fruits and nuts and serve the scones with your favorite fruit jam or jelly and Devonshire cream (available in gourmet stores or high-quality supermarkets).

3 cups all-purpose flour
3 tablespoons sugar
2 tablespoons grated orange zest
4 teaspoons baking powder
½ teaspoon salt
½ cup unsalted butter or margarine, chilled and cut into pieces
3 large eggs, beaten
⅓ cup milk
½ cup raisins
½ cup chopped pecans
½ cup chopped dried or candied pineapple (see Note)

For the Top
2 teaspoons water
1 tablespoon sugar

Preheat the oven to 450°F. Lightly grease a large baking sheet or cover with parchment paper. Dust with flour.

In a large bowl or a food processor, mix the flour, sugar, orange zest, baking powder, and salt. Process or cut in the butter until the mixture resembles coarse crumbs. In a small bowl, mix together the eggs and milk. Add to the flour mixture and mix just until blended; don't overmix.

Fold in the raisins, pecans, and pineapple.

Turn the dough out onto the prepared baking sheet. Dust your hands with flour and pat the dough into an 8-inch-diameter round. With a straight-edged knife, cut the dough into 8 wedges, leaving the wedges in place. Brush the top with water and sprinkle with the sugar.

Bake for 15 to 18 minutes, until golden. Slide the parchment paper with the scones on top onto a rack to cool. Serve warm, in wedges.

Makes 8 servings

NOTE: I buy my dried pineapple at the local whole foods cooperative store. It has no extra sugar added, and the flavor is sweet and intense. Commercially packaged candied pineapple works fine, too.

Raisin–Sweet Potato Bread

In Eric Copage's book Kwanzaa, *he recommends serving this delicious golden, raisin-nut–studded bread with a hearty vegetable stew for a Kwanzaa supper. This is my adaptation of the bread, which would complement any fall or winter dinner nicely.*

1 small (8-ounce) sweet potato or yam, peeled and cubed
3 cups bread or unbleached all-purpose flour
1 package (2¾ teaspoons) rapid-rise yeast
2 tablespoons packed brown sugar
1 teaspoon salt
½ cup raisins
½ cup chopped walnuts

Place the potato cubes into a 2-quart saucepan; add water to cover. Heat to boiling over medium-high heat and cook until the potato is tender when pierced with a wooden skewer or a fork, about 20 minutes. Drain, reserving ⅔ cup of the cooking liquid and cool to very warm (about 130°F). Mash the potato; you should have about ½ cup.

In a large bowl or in a food processor, mix the flour, yeast, brown sugar, and salt together. Add the cooled mashed sweet potato. Add the reserved cooking liquid and mix or process until the dough is smooth and satiny (see Box).

Place into a lightly greased bowl, turning

ABOUT MOISTURE IN FLOUR

If bread dough seems dry or too stiff, add more water, a tablespoon at a time, to the mixture until it is soft, tender, and resilient but not sticky. Wait a few minutes after adding more water or if you think the dough has become a little too wet; this allows the gluten in the flour to absorb the liquid. Usually, after 5 minutes the dough will become satiny on the surface. If it is still too wet, add flour a tablespoon at a time until it doesn't feel sticky. There will be a difference in the dryness of flour during different seasons. In humid conditions, the flour will be moister, to start out, so you may need to add more so the dough isn't sticky. When the air is very dry, usually in the colder weather, you'll use less flour, because it will absorb more moisture.

to grease the top, cover, and let rise about ¾ hour or until doubled.

Grease an 8½ × 3¾-inch loaf pan. Turn the dough out onto a lightly floured surface and flatten out into an 8 × 12-inch rectangle. Press the raisins and walnuts evenly into the surface of the dough. Roll up tightly starting from the 8-inch end. Pinch the seams to seal and fit into the loaf pan. Cover and let rise in a warm place until the dough fills the pan, about 30 to 45 minutes.

Preheat the oven to 375°F, and bake until the loaf is golden and a wooden skewer inserted in the center comes out clean, 35 to 45 minutes. Remove the loaf from the pan and cool on a wire rack.

Makes 1 loaf

Plum Biscuits

Reminiscent of the flavors of Czech plum dumplings, these sugary topped plum-filled biscuits are great for breakfast or brunch. They are also lovely for a late-afternoon snack with a cup of hot tea.

    2 cups all-purpose flour
    1 tablespoon baking powder
    ¼ cup sugar
    ⅛ teaspoon salt
    ½ teaspoon grated lemon zest
    ¼ cup (½ stick) unsalted butter,
       chilled and cut into pieces
    1 large egg, beaten
    ½ cup whipping cream

Topping

12 fresh Italian prune plums,
halved and pitted

4 tablespoons (½ stick) unsalted butter,
at room temperature

6 tablespoons sugar

Preheat the oven to 400°F. Lightly grease a baking sheet or cover with parchment paper.

In a large bowl or in a food processor, combine the flour, baking powder, sugar, salt, and lemon zest. Process or cut in the butter until the mixture resembles coarse meal. Turn into a mixing bowl if using a food processor. Beat the egg and cream together in a small bowl. Add to the flour mixture and stir with a fork until the dough holds together in a ball. Turn out onto a lightly floured surface and knead once or twice to compact the ball.

Roll out to 1-inch thickness. Using a 2¾-inch biscuit cutter, cut out rounds. Place in the prepared pan. Press a plum half into the center of each round. Dot each with ½ teaspoon butter and sprinkle each with 1 teaspoon sugar.

Bake for 20 to 25 minutes, until golden. Slide the parchment onto the countertop to cool or place the biscuits onto a wire rack to cool. Serve warm.

Makes 24 biscuits

Rosemary-Raisin Focaccia

This Italian yeast bread is shaped into a large, flat round, much like a pizza crust, but thicker. The wonderful-tasting combination of rosemary and raisins makes this a bread I like to serve with simple foods, like grilled chicken for dinner or a chicken or fruit salad for lunch. I first tasted focaccia in a train station in Florence, Italy, where there were at least a half dozen varieties to choose from. This is quick and easy to mix up in the food processor.

3 to 3½ cups bread flour or
unbleached all-purpose flour

1 package (2¾ teaspoons) instant
active dry or rapid-rise yeast

1 teaspoon salt

1 tablespoon chopped fresh
rosemary leaves

1 cup very warm water (about 130°F)

4 tablespoons extra-virgin olive oil

⅓ cup golden raisins
Fresh rosemary sprigs

1 teaspoon coarse salt

In the food processor with the dough blade in place or in a large bowl, combine 3 cups of the flour, the yeast, salt, and chopped rosemary. With the motor running, add the water and 3 tablespoons of the olive oil through the feed tube. Process until the dough is smooth

FREEZING BREADS

aked bread freezes well. Cool completely after baking, then wrap in plastic wrap or seal in a plastic bag. Place into the freezer. To thaw, remove from the freezer, unwrap, and place in a 300°F oven for about ten to fifteen minutes or until the bread has heated through. Or remove from the freezer and allow the bread to stand at room temperature, still wrapped, for about one hour, until thawed. Unwrap and serve.

and satiny and comes away from the sides of the bowl. Add more flour if the dough is too soft. Process until the dough is smooth, then add the raisins and process just until they are blended in. Leave the cover on the food processor and let the dough rise to fill the bowl, 30 to 35 minutes. Or if mixing by hand, make a well in the center of the flour mixture, add the water and 1 tablespoon oil, and stir until the dough is stiff and the flour is absorbed. Turn the dough out onto a floured surface and knead until the dough is smooth and springy, 5 to 10 minutes. Place into a clean, greased bowl, cover, and let rise until doubled, 30 to 35 minutes.

Line a baking sheet with parchment paper. Turn the dough out onto a lightly floured surface and knead until smooth, 2 to 3 minutes. Shape into a smooth ball. Place the dough on the baking sheet and roll out to about a 1-inch thickness. Cover and let rise until puffy, about 20 minutes.

Preheat the oven to 400°F. With your fingers poke holes all over the top of the focaccia. Drizzle with the remaining tablespoon of olive oil. Poke fresh sprigs of rosemary into the top of the focaccia. Sprinkle with the coarse salt.

Bake for 15 to 20 minutes until the loaf is golden brown and sounds hollow when tapped on the bottom. Remove from the pan and cool on a wire rack.

Makes 1 loaf

Wild Rice and Pecan Bread

Wild rice and pecans combine to give a delicious, nutty flavor to this loaf.

To get a crispy crust on these loaves, I bake them in a very hot oven directly on pre-heated baking tiles. I line the upper rack in my oven with unglazed tile (from a floor tile shop). I preheat the oven for about thirty minutes, and when the loaves are ready for baking, I place them directly onto the hot tiles; I throw a glass of water into a preheated pan on the rack below, close the oven door, and let them bake until golden. That "burst" of steam allows the crust to develop a wonderful crunch and keeps the interior of the bread moist and spongy. The bread can also be baked in the bread pans.

- 2 packages (5½ teaspoons) active dry yeast
- 4½ cups bread flour or unbleached all-purpose flour
- ½ cup chopped pecans
- ½ cup cooked, cooled wild rice
- 2 teaspoons sugar
- 2 teaspoons salt
- 2 cups very warm water (about 130°F)

In a large mixing bowl combine the yeast, 4 cups of the flour, the pecans, wild rice, sugar, and salt. Pour in the water all at once and stir with a wooden spoon until well mixed. Cover and let rise for 15 minutes.

Sprinkle the dough with another ¼ cup flour. Sprinkle a work surface with the remaining flour. Turn the dough out onto the surface and knead gently until the flour is worked into the dough, about 5 minutes. Put the dough into a clean, greased bowl, turn over to oil the top, cover, and let rise until doubled, 45 minutes.

Turn the dough out onto a lightly oiled surface (see Note). Divide the dough into 2 equal parts. Shape each part into an oblong or round loaf.

Pan-Baked Loaves

Place each half into two 5 × 9-inch loaf pans or two 9-inch cake pans. Cover and let rise for about 45 minutes, until doubled.

Preheat the oven to 375°F. Bake for 30 to 35 minutes, until a wooden skewer inserted into the loaf comes out clean. Turn the loaves out onto a wire rack to cool.

Crusty Loaves

Leave the loaves right on the oiled surface, covered with a towel to rise, about 45 minutes.

Place one oven rack in the center of the oven and cover it with unglazed tiles. Place a shallow pan on the bottom rack. Preheat the oven to 450°F. Fill a tumbler with water and have it near the oven.

With a sharp knife, make 3 or 4 parallel diagonal slashes about ⅛-inch deep, on each loaf. Pick up the loaves with both hands (one at a time) and place onto the preheated tiles in the oven.

All at once, pour the water from the tumbler onto the preheated pan in the oven. This should result in a burst of steam in the oven. Close the oven door quickly to enclose the steam in the oven.

Bake for 15 to 20 minutes, until loaves are crusty and golden and sound hollow when tapped. Remove the breads from the oven and cool on a rack.

To be sure the loaves have baked sufficiently, check them with an instant-reading thermometer. Insert the thermometer into the center of the loaf (on the bottom side so you don't destroy the looks of the top). Properly baked, the loaf should register 200°F. If the bread isn't finished baking, it can be returned to the oven without sacrificing the crispiness of the crust.

Makes 2 loaves

NOTE: When shaping bread dough, a very lightly oiled surface will prevent the dough and your hands from sticking. If you get too much oil on the surface, the dough will be difficult to handle because it will slide around between your hands and the surface. Too much oil may also add oily streaks to the dough. Pour a small amount of oil onto a paper towel, then rub it gently on your work surface.

PIES

Pumpkin-Pecan Pie

Two favorite holiday pies are combined in one here. While the pie bakes, the pecans come to the top as the creamy pumpkin filling bakes beneath them.

- 3 large eggs, slightly beaten
- ¾ cup sugar
- ½ cup dark corn syrup
- 1 cup fresh cooked or canned puréed pumpkin
- 1 cup whipping cream or undiluted evaporated milk
- 1 tablespoon dark rum, bourbon, or 1 teaspoon vanilla
- 1 cup pecan halves
- 1 9-inch unbaked pie crust (see page 176)

Preheat the oven to 375°F. In a large bowl, blend the eggs, sugar, corn syrup, pumpkin, cream, and rum. Fold in the pecan halves. Turn the mixture into the pie shell and bake for 55 to 60 minutes or until a knife inserted near the center of the pie comes out clean. Cool on a wire rack.

Makes one 9-inch pie

Gingered Apple and Apricot Pie

 Freshly grated ginger adds a bit of heat, while apricots add a delicious hint of tartness to this spicy apple pie.

1 cup chopped, dried apricots
½ cup water
¾ cup sugar
¼ cup all-purpose flour
2 teaspoons grated fresh ginger
1 teaspoon ground cinnamon
½ teaspoon freshly ground nutmeg
6 cups thinly sliced peeled and cored Granny Smith or Golden Delicious apples

Pastry for a double crust pie (see page 172)
2 tablespoons unsalted butter, at room temperature
1 teaspoon milk, for brushing
2 teaspoons sugar, for sprinkling

Preheat the oven to 425°F. In a saucepan, combine the apricots and water. Heat to boiling over medium heat. Lower heat to simmer and cook for 10 minutes, stirring often. Remove from the heat and cool.

In a large bowl, combine the sugar, flour, ginger, cinnamon, and nutmeg. Add the apples and mix until the apples are coated with the flour mixture.

 FREEZING PIES

To Freeze a Baked Fruit Pie
Cool the pie completely on a wire rack after baking. Wrap in plastic wrap or put in a zipper-closure plastic bag or into a sturdy plastic container. Place into the freezer until frozen, four to six hours. To thaw and serve, remove from the freezer and allow to thaw to room temperature. To refresh, bake in a 350°F oven for fifteen minutes or until heated through.

To Freeze an Unbaked Fruit Pie
Brush the prepared pie with one egg yolk mixed with one tablespoon milk. Freeze unwrapped, then when firm, wrap and return to the freezer. To bake, place the frozen pie on the lower shelf of a preheated 450°F oven. Bake for forty-five minutes to one hour, until the crust is brown and the filling is bubbly.

Divide the pastry into 2 halves. Roll out one part on a lightly floured surface to fit a 9-inch pie pan and fit the pastry into the pan. Turn the apple mixture into the pastry-lined pan. Dot with 1 tablespoon of the butter. Top evenly with the apricot mixture. Dot with the remaining butter. Roll out the second part of the dough on a lightly floured surface and fit it over the top of the pie. Moisten the edges, trim, seal, and flute. Cut slits into the top of the crust. Brush the top with milk and sprinkle with sugar

Bake for 40 to 50 minutes or until the crust is brown and the juices begin to bubble through the slits. Remove from the oven and cool on a wire rack.

Makes one 9-inch pie

Banbury Tarts

 Because these fruity, oval-shaped pies with a sugary top encase an irresistible nut, spice, and raisin filling, they make a perfect individual tart to serve as a dessert for Thanksgiving or other holiday meals. Sometimes called Banbury cakes, these pies originated in Banbury, England. Using frozen puff pastry shells, they are quick and easy to make.

  1 (10-ounce) package frozen puff
      pastry shells or 1 recipe
      Quick Flaky Pastry

BAKER'S TIP

To remove the sides from a tart pan, place the tart on top of a jar and let the sides drop down. Slide the shell on the pan's bottom onto a serving platter.

Filling

  ½ cup chopped walnuts
  ½ cup currants
  ½ cup golden raisins
  ⅛ teaspoon freshly ground nutmeg
  ⅛ teaspoon ground cinnamon
  ⅛ teaspoon allspice
  ¼ cup sugar
  2 tablespoons unsalted butter, melted
  1 egg white, beaten, for brushing
      Sugar, for sprinkling

Preheat the oven to 425°F. Cover a baking sheet with parchment paper.

For the puff pastry, thaw the pastry according to package directions, or prepare the pastry recipe below. If using thawed puff pastry shells, roll the rounds out to 6 inches in diameter.

For the filling, blend the walnuts, currants, raisins, nutmeg, cinnamon, allspice, sugar, and butter together in a large bowl, and divide the filling evenly between the 6 rounds. Lift 2 opposite sides of the pastry rounds up to meet in the middle and pinch

For perfect tender, flaky pastry, be sure to measure, mix, and handle the dough carefully. Too much flour or too much handling toughens the pastry. If the pastry has too little liquid it will be crumbly and unmanageable. If it has too much liquid it will be sticky.

The standard proportion of shortening to flour is one to three, or one cup shortening to three cups flour. Shortening, lard, or butter is *cut* into the flour until the particles are about the size of small peas. This is done with a pastry blender, two table knives, a pastry fork, or in the food processor using on/off bursts with the steel blade.

Solid Vegetable Shortening
This produces a tender pastry, and is usually used at room temperature.

Lard
Many old-fashioned pie bakers insist that the only really flaky pastry is made with lard. Lard has a very low melting point and needs to be chilled before being cut into the flour.

Butter
Butter pastry is ideal for quiches or tarts or any time you want a richer crust. It can take a little more handling without becoming tough. It can be either rolled out or pressed into the pan.

Oil
Oil will never produce a flaky pastry (because for flaky pastry you need to have tiny, pea-size pockets of fat rolled into the flour mixture). An oil pastry can, however, be very tender. Oil pastries can often be pressed into the pan.

To Add Moisture to the Pastry
Sprinkle the flour and fat mixture with ice cold water (or another liquid if the recipe indicates it). With a fork or a spatula, lightly toss the liquid with the flour until the mixture has the appearance of cottage cheese. Gather the pastry into a

ball. If the dough makes a double crust, divide into two parts. Shape each part into a flattened disk about one inch thick. Wrap in plastic and chill at least thirty minutes.

To Roll Out Dough

Place the chilled dough on a lightly floured surface. Place the rolling pin on the center of the dough and start rolling from the center outward toward the edges with even, light strokes. Lift the rolling pin slightly as it comes to the edge of the dough so that the edge will not be thinner than the middle. Lift and turn the dough a quarter turn after each roll, but do not overhandle the dough. Keep it very lightly dusted with flour.

To Fit Pastry into the Pan

Fold the pastry into quarters. Place the tip of the folded pastry onto the center of the pie pan. Unfold, then press the pastry into the pan without stretching. The dough shrinks when it bakes if it has been stretched. Trim and crimp the edges decoratively, or fill and place the second rolled-out pastry on top of the pie. Seal the edges and trim and crimp decoratively.

---

together to make a seam all the way across the top of the filling so that the resulting shape is an oval with 2 pointed ends. Brush the edges with water and seal. Place the ovals with the seam side down on the baking sheet. Brush with beaten egg white and sprinkle with sugar. With a sharp knife or razor blade, cut a small cross on top of each tart, making the cuts about 1 inch long. Bake for about 15 minutes or until golden.

Makes 6 tarts

Quick Flaky Pastry

2	cups all-purpose flour
½	teaspoon salt
¾	cup (1½ sticks) unsalted butter, chilled and cut into pieces
5 to 7	tablespoons ice water
4	tablespoons (½ stick) unsalted butter, at room temperature

Combine the flour and salt in a large bowl or food processor. Cut in or process the ¾ cup of butter into the flour until the mixture resembles coarse crumbs. If using a food processor, turn the mixture into a bowl. Sprinkle the ice water over a tablespoon at a time and stir with a fork until the dough will hold together in a ball. Chill, wrapped in plastic wrap, for 30 minutes. On a floured surface, roll the dough out to 20 inches in diameter. Spread with the 4 tablespoons of soft butter. Roll the dough up loosely, as you would a jelly roll. With a rolling pin, flatten out the roll to make a long rectangle about 6 by 36 inches. With a 5- or 6-inch round cutter, or using a plate as a guide, cut out 6 rounds, rerolling the dough scraps as necessary. Fill the rounds as directed in the basic recipe.

Cran-Apple Pie

Not only is the rosy filling in this pie pretty, but the cranberries provide a burst of tartness and flavor. Instead of making your own pastry for this pie, you can use store-bought refrigerated pie crusts.

Double Crust Pastry (recipe follows)

Cranberry-Apple Filling

  1 cup fresh cranberries

 ¾ cup sugar

  1 tablespoon cornstarch

  2 tablespoons port wine or water

 ⅔ cup sugar

  2 tablespoons cornstarch

  5 cups peeled, cored, and sliced tart apples (such as Granny Smith) (about 4 large)

  1 teaspoon milk, for brushing

  2 teaspoons sugar, for sprinkling

Prepare the pastry and chill it wrapped in plastic wrap.

In a saucepan, combine the cranberries, ¾ cup sugar, 1 tablespoon cornstarch, and the wine or water. Heat to boiling over medium heat, stirring, and boil for 5 minutes. Cool for 15 to 20 minutes.

Preheat the oven to 425°F. In a large bowl, combine ⅔ cup sugar and 2 tablespoons cornstarch; add the apples and toss to coat; add the cooled cranberry mixture and stir.

On a lightly floured surface, roll out half the pastry to fit a 9-inch pie pan. Fit the pastry into the pan and add the filling. Roll out the second half of the crust on a lightly floured surface and place over the filling. Moisten the edges with water. Trim both the top and bottom crusts to within ½ inch of the edge of the pan. Fold the top and bottom crusts under and crimp the edges with your fingers or with a fork.

Cut slits into the top crust. Brush with the milk and sprinkle with sugar. Bake for 45 to 55 minutes or until golden brown.

Makes 8 servings

Double Crust Pastry

1½ cups all-purpose flour

 ½ teaspoon salt

 ½ cup (1 stick) plus 1 tablespoon unsalted butter, chilled and cut into pieces, or ½ cup lard, chilled

  1 large egg, lightly beaten

  2 teaspoons fresh lemon juice

3 to 4 tablespoons ice water

Combine the flour and salt in a large mixing bowl or in the work bowl of a food processor. Process or cut in the butter or lard until the fat is in pea-size pieces. If using a food processor, turn the mixture into a large bowl. In a small bowl, whisk the egg, lemon juice, and 3 tablespoons ice water together. Drizzle the liquids over the crumbly mixture. With a fork, mix until the pastry holds together in a ball, adding more ice water if necessary. Turn out onto a lightly floured surface and knead once or twice, lightly, to shape the dough into a ball. Wrap in plastic wrap and refrigerate at least 30 minutes before rolling out.

Harvest Festival Pie

 The last of the garden's zucchini finds its way onto the dessert buffet at Thanksgiving in this spicy pie filling. This is one way to use a zucchini that got away and blew up into a monster. Just remember to remove the seeds before shredding if you're using an overblown squash.

Pastry for one double-crust pie
(see page 172)

Filling

2 cups shredded, unpeeled, cored tart apples, such as Pippins, Greenings, or Golden Delicious

BAKER'S TIP

For a more interesting top to this pie, and others as well, instead of covering the pie with the top crust, roll the second half of the crust to about ⅛-inch thickness on a lightly floured surface. With a leaf- or fruit-shaped cookie cutter, cut the dough into shapes. Place them on top of the pie, allowing some of the filling to show through, using your best "decorating" eye when you place them.

1 cup shredded unpeeled zucchini
1 cup shredded carrots
½ cup chopped walnuts or pecans
3 tablespoons all-purpose flour
1 cup packed brown sugar
¼ cup (½ stick) unsalted butter, melted
1 tablespoon pumpkin pie spice
¼ teaspoon salt
1 tablespoon fresh lemon juice
1 teaspoon grated orange zest
2 large eggs, beaten

Glaze

1 large egg, beaten with
1 tablespoon water

Prepare the pie crust and chill, wrapped in plastic wrap, for at least 30 minutes. Roll out half to fit a 9-inch pie pan. Line the pan with the pastry. Roll out the remaining half of the pastry, and with leaf-, apple-, or turkey-shaped cookie cutters, cut out as many shapes as you can; reserve to decorate the top of the pie.

Preheat the oven to 425°F. In a large bowl, combine the apples, zucchini, carrots, nuts, and flour and toss to coat. In another bowl mix the brown sugar and butter until blended. Add the pumpkin pie spice, salt, lemon juice, orange zest, and eggs and blend well. Turn into the apple mixture and mix well.

Turn the filling into the pastry-lined pan. Arrange the pastry cutouts on top of the filling. Brush the edges and pastry cutouts with the egg glaze.

Bake for 40 to 50 minutes or until the pie is set and the pastry is golden brown. Remove from the oven and cool on a wire rack. Serve warm with whipped cream, if desired.

Makes one 9-inch pie

French Apple Tart (Tarte Tatin)

This is an upside-down apple tart made by covering the bottom of a shallow baking dish with butter and sugar, then apples, and finally, a pastry crust.

The sugar and butter create a caramel that becomes the topping when the tart is inverted onto a serving plate. The tart was supposedly created by two unmarried French sisters who lived in the Loire Valley and earned their living making it; thus the name tarte des demoiselles Tatin, *which is translated verbatim as "the tart of two unmarried women named Tatin." Several years ago, I spent a week cooking with Simone Beck in southern France. This is an adaptation of the recipe I received from her in her cooking school. Select apples that have a rich, tart flavor but are not too juicy, such as Pippins or Greenings.*

Pastry

1 cup all-purpose flour
1 tablespoon sugar
¼ cup (½ stick) unsalted butter, chilled and cut into pieces
1 tablespoon vegetable shortening
2½ to 3 tablespoons ice water

Filling

8 large (about 4 pounds) crisp cooking apples, peeled, cored, and quartered
⅔ cup granulated sugar, divided
1 teaspoon ground cinnamon
½ cup (1 stick) unsalted butter, at room temperature, divided
¼ cup packed brown sugar
⅓ cup confectioners' sugar, for sprinkling

1. If the pie has a cream filling, be sure that it stays cold (below 40°F) to prevent bacterial growth.

2. If the pie has a meringue, protect the meringue with an inverted pie pan or a bowl, preferably the same diameter as the pie pan, so that the rim of the bowl can sit on the rim of the pie pan. Tape the edges together. Wrap the pie with the bowl attached in plastic wrap or place into a large plastic bag. Place into a cooler or plastic-lined box with ice; close the top.

3. If the pie is a fruit pie, be sure that it has cooled completely. Wrap well with plastic wrap. Transport in a box or container with the edges buttered and a sturdy top so that it will not slide around and get damaged.

Preheat the oven to 375°F.
To make the pastry, mix the flour and sugar in a bowl. Cut in the butter and the shortening until the mixture resembles coarse crumbs. Sprinkle with the ice water and stir with a fork until the dough gathers together into a ball. Knead 2 or 3 times, then wrap in plastic wrap and chill.

Cut the apple quarters crosswise into $\frac{1}{8}$-inch slices. Toss them in a bowl with $\frac{1}{3}$ cup of the granulated sugar and the cinnamon.

Melt 4 tablespoons of the butter over medium-low heat in a heavy baking dish or ovenproof cast iron skillet. Add the brown sugar and stir until the sugar is melted. Arrange the apple slices over the syrup in layers, sprinkling with the remaining $\frac{1}{3}$ cup granulated sugar as you go. Melt the remaining butter and drizzle over the apples.

Roll out the pastry on a lightly floured surface to fit over the top of the tart with 1 inch to spare all around. Place on top of the apples and tuck the edges into the side of the dish. Slash in 4 or 5 places.

Bake in the lower third of the oven for 45 to 60 minutes, until the pastry is golden and filling bubbles through. Unmold immediately onto a heatproof serving dish and sprinkle with confectioners' sugar. Preheat the broiler and broil for a few minutes until caramelized. Serve warm.

Makes 6 to 8 servings

Sweet Potato Pie

S*I love this pie because it goes all out for spiciness and sweetness. It looks and tastes a lot like pumpkin pie, only the flavors are all much more intense and the color, brighter and deeper.*

Pastry for a single pie crust
(recipe follows)

Filling

2 large (1¾ to 2 pounds)
     sweet potatoes or yams
2 cups sugar
½ cup (1 stick) unsalted butter, melted
⅓ cup whipping cream
2 tablespoons ground cinnamon
1 tablespoon freshly ground nutmeg
3 tablespoons vanilla
½ teaspoon ground cloves
½ teaspoon ground mace
½ teaspoon ground ginger
3 large eggs, beaten

Prepare the crust and roll out on a floured surface to line a 9-inch pie pan. Fit the pastry in the pan.

Place the sweet potatoes in a saucepan and add water to cover. Heat to a boil over medium-high heat and boil until the potatoes are tender. Drain, cool, peel, and mash the potatoes. Measure 1½ cups mashed potato into a large bowl. Beat in all of the remaining ingredients, then pour the filling into the pastry-lined pan.

Preheat the oven to 350°F and bake for 50 to 60 minutes or until the filling is set and the center of the pie feels firm to the touch. Cool on a wire rack.

Makes one 9-inch pie, about 8 servings

Pastry for a Single Pie Crust

1 cup all-purpose flour
½ teaspoon salt
6 tablespoons unsalted butter,
     chilled and cut into pieces
2 teaspoons fresh lemon juice
3 to 4 tablespoons ice water

Measure the flour and salt into a large bowl or a food processor. Cut in the butter or process until the mixture resembles coarse crumbs.

In a small bowl, mix the lemon juice and 3 tablespoons of the ice water. Sprinkle over the flour mixture and toss with a fork until blended. Press the dough together into a ball, adding more water if necessary. Wrap in plastic wrap and chill for at least 30 minutes.

Sour Cream–Raisin–Cranberry Pie

 Dried cranberries add a pleasant tartness to contrast the sweetness of the raisins.

1 unbaked single crust 9-inch pie shell (see page 176), or store bought

Filling

1 cup raisins
1 cup fresh cranberries
½ cup light rum or water
¾ cup packed brown sugar
2 tablespoons all-purpose flour
½ teaspoon ground cinnamon
¼ teaspoon salt
2 large eggs, beaten
1 cup sour cream

For Top

½ cup sour cream

Preheat the oven to 450°F. Prepare the pie shell according to recipe or package directions if using a ready-to-bake pie shell. On a lightly floured surface, roll the pastry out to fit a 9-inch pie pan. Line the pastry with foil and fill the pie with pie weights, dried beans, or rice. Bake for 10 to 11 minutes or until partially baked. Remove the crust from the oven, and remove the pie weights and foil. Reduce the oven temperature to 375°F.

Make the filling. In a large saucepan, combine the raisins, cranberries, rum, brown sugar, flour, cinnamon, and salt. Heat to boiling over medium heat and cook, stirring, for 5 minutes. Remove from the heat and cool until just warm to the touch. Whisk in the eggs and sour cream. Pour into the partially baked pie shell.

Bake for 35 minutes or until the filling is set and the center of the pie feels slightly firm to the touch. Remove from the oven and cool on a wire rack. Before serving, spread the top with sour cream.

Makes one 9-inch pie

White Chocolate–Pecan Pie

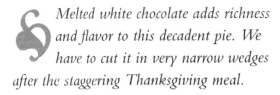 *Melted white chocolate adds richness and flavor to this decadent pie. We have to cut it in very narrow wedges after the staggering Thanksgiving meal.*

Pastry for a single-crust pie (see page 176)

Filling

4 ounces white chocolate, chopped, or 1 cup white chocolate morsels
3 large eggs
½ cup light corn syrup
2 tablespoons unsalted butter, melted
1 teaspoon vanilla
1½ cups pecans, chopped
½ cup pecan halves

Prepare and chill the pastry, wrapped in plastic wrap.

Preheat the oven to 425°F. Place the chocolate into a small bowl and set over a pan of hot (not boiling) water. Stir until the chocolate is melted and smooth. In a large bowl, beat the eggs, syrup, butter, and vanilla until smooth. Blend in the melted chocolate, then stir in the chopped pecans.

Roll the pastry out to fit a 9-inch pie pan and line the pan with the pastry. Trim the edges. Reroll the scraps and cut out leaves using a cookie cutter and reserve them to decorate the top. Pour the pecan mixture into the pastry-lined pan. Arrange the pecan halves and pastry cutouts on top of the filling.

Bake for 15 minutes. Reduce the temperature to 350°F and bake for 30 minutes longer or until the pie is set. The pie will feel firm when touched in the center. Cool on a wire rack.

Makes one 9-inch pie, 8 to 12 servings

Apple Strudel (Apfelstrudel)

When our daughter Cathy married Gerhard from Graz, Austria, I didn't dream that Gerhard's mother, Hati, would actually volunteer to bake enough strudel to feed one hundred and fifty people. But she did. She slapped and stretched batch after batch of strudel dough and encased a delicious apple filling in the eggshell-thin pastry. I was surprised that she divided the dough into small portions, stretching and rolling one loaf-size strudel at a time. I am including the directions for mixing and stretching homemade strudel dough, but as a simpler alternative, I suggest using a one-pound package of frozen strudel leaves, sometimes called filo, or phyllo dough (see Note). This recipe, however, does not serve one hundred and fifty! It makes two strudels, each serving about six.

Strudel Dough

  1½ cups all-purpose flour
  1 large egg
  ¼ teaspoon salt
  1½ tablespoons corn oil
  ⅓ cup warm water
  ¼ cup (½ stick) unsalted butter, melted, for brushing

Apple Filling

¼ cup fine, dry bread crumbs

½ cup sugar

1 teaspoon ground cinnamon

5 large, tart apples (such as
   Granny Smith) peeled, cored,
   and thinly sliced

1 tablespoon lemon juice

¼ cup raisins

1 cup finely chopped walnuts

1 tablespoon confectioners' sugar

To make the strudel dough, measure the flour into a large bowl and make a well in the center of it. In a small bowl, beat the egg, salt, oil, and water until blended. Pour the liquids into the well in the flour and mix until a soft dough forms. Pick up the dough with one hand (coat your hand lightly with oil to prevent sticking) and slap the dough into the bowl or onto a lightly oiled surface about 100 times. (Or place the dough into an electric mixer with dough hook and beat at high speed for 10 minutes.) The dough will be sticky at first, but then will become elastic and will leave the board and hands clean. Divide the dough into 2 lightly oiled bowls and let rest, covered, for 10 minutes.

Cover a table with a smooth, plastic tablecloth and rub very lightly with an oil-soaked cloth. Dust one of the parts of dough lightly with flour and invert the bowl onto the plastic tablecloth–covered surface. Dust the top with flour. Pat the dough down as flat as possible, then with a lightly floured rolling pin, roll out to make a circle about 10 inches across. Working from the underside of the dough with palms up, gently and slowly stretch the dough until it measures 30 inches each way and is paper thin. Brush the dough with 2 tablespoons of the melted butter.

Make the filling. In a small bowl, mix the crumbs, ¼ cup of the sugar, and ½ teaspoon of the cinnamon. Sprinkle the dough evenly with 2 tablespoons of this mixture. In a large bowl, mix the apples with the lemon juice,

 PHYLLO DOUGH

You can find filo or phyllo dough in the pastry section of the frozen foods department of a supermarket. Purchased filo sheets are paper thin, and, therefore, will dry very quickly. Once thawed and unrolled, you need to keep the leaves covered with a damp dish towel to prevent the pastry from drying and cracking. Handle with care and be prepared to lose a few sheets until you get the hang of this delicate pastry.

the remaining sugar, and cinnamon. Sprinkle the dough with half the apple mixture and half the raisins and the chopped walnuts, leaving about one-quarter of one end of the dough uncovered, and 6 inches from 2 opposite ends uncovered. Lift the 2 opposite sides of unfilled edges up over the filling. Brush the fold edges with 1 tablespoon more of the melted butter. Starting from the filled edge of the dough, lift the plastic cloth so that the strudel will roll up, rolling toward the unfilled edge of the dough, forming a roll.

Place the roll on a buttered baking sheet with the seam side down. Brush the roll with 1 tablespoon more melted butter. Repeat the stretching, filling, and rolling procedure with the second half of the dough and the remaining filling ingredients.

Preheat the oven to 400°F. Bake for 35 to 45 minutes or until golden brown. Dust with confectioners' sugar. Cut in slices to serve.

Makes 2 strudels, about 6 servings each

NOTE: To make Apple Strudel using frozen strudel leaves, thaw the frozen phyllo dough according to the package directions. To keep strudel leaves from drying out as you work with them, place on a dampened towel on the work surface. Lay a dry towel on top of the dampened towel. Unroll the thawed dough and place on the dry towel. Top with a dampened towel.

Remove a single sheet of dough from the pile, replacing the dampened towel after each sheet of dough is removed. Brush with

melted butter, top with 6 to 8 more sheets of dough (or about half of the total), brushing between each sheet with melted butter.

Make the filling as directed above. Pile half of the apple filling along one long edge of dough, leaving about 2 inches at the top and bottom of the filling. Fold the ends in to enclose the filling, then roll up toward the empty edge of dough. Lightly grease a baking sheet or cover with parchment paper. Place the roll on the baking sheet with the seam side down. Brush the top with melted butter. Repeat for the second half of dough and filling. Place the 2 rolls on the same baking sheet about 3 inches apart.

Preheat the oven to 400°F. Bake for 35 to 45 minutes or until golden brown. Dust with confectioners' sugar. Cut in slices to serve.

Carrot Pudding

This started out as a steamed pudding, a Thanksgiving dessert that has been a favorite of mine. But since steaming puddings can be awkward and involved, I bake the pudding, with consistently good results. Serve it with Danish Butter Sauce and/or Lemon Sauce.

½ cup (1 stick) unsalted butter,
     at room temperature
½ cup packed brown sugar
 1 large egg, beaten

1 cup shredded raw carrots
2 teaspoons grated lemon zest
1 cup currants
½ cup raisins
1¼ cups all-purpose flour
1 teaspoon baking powder
½ teaspoon baking soda
½ teaspoon salt
½ teaspoon freshly ground nutmeg
½ teaspoon ground cinnamon
Danish Butter Sauce (recipe follows)
or Lemon Sauce (recipe follows)

Preheat the oven to 350°F. Butter an 8-cup tube mold or 8 individual fancy molds.

In a large mixing bowl, cream the butter and brown sugar. Add the egg and beat until light. Add the carrots, lemon zest, currants, raisins, flour, baking powder, baking soda, salt, nutmeg, and cinnamon and stir until well mixed. Pour into the buttered mold or molds. Place the molds into a larger pan filled with boiling water. Bake for 1 to 1½ hours for the large mold, or about 45 minutes for the small molds, or until a wooden skewer inserted in the center of the pudding comes out clean. (The cooking time varies greatly, depending on what material the mold is made out of as well as its depth; very deep molds will take longer to cook.) Invert while warm onto a serving platter or individual plates and serve with one of the following sauces.

Makes 8 servings

Danish Butter Sauce

½ cup (1 stick) unsalted butter, at room temperature
1 cup packed brown sugar
1 large egg
1 tablespoon white wine vinegar
Dash freshly ground nutmeg
1 teaspoon vanilla
1 cup whipping cream, whipped

In the top of a double boiler or in a large heatproof bowl placed over a pan of simmering water, cream the butter with the brown sugar. Add the egg and vinegar and beat until very light and fluffy. Blend in the nutmeg. Raise the heat to medium-high until the water boils and cook the mixture over the water, stirring constantly with a whisk, for 10 minutes or until thickened. Add the vanilla. Cover and chill. Just before serving, fold in the whipped cream.

Makes 3 cups

Lemon Sauce

½ cup fresh lemon juice
1¾ cups water
1 cup packed brown sugar
¼ cup granulated sugar
¼ cup (½ stick) unsalted butter
⅛ teaspoon salt
2 tablespoons cornstarch

In a saucepan, combine the lemon juice, 1½ cups of the water, the sugars, butter, and salt. Bring to a boil over medium-high heat and cook for 2 minutes, stirring constantly. In a small bowl, mix the cornstarch and ¼ cup water until smooth. Stir into the boiling mixture and cook, stirring, until smooth and thickened. Serve hot.

Makes 3 cups

Cinnamon– Wild Rice Pudding

In the areas where wild rice is harvested, it is an important part of all meals. Served simply cooked with a topping of maple syrup, wild blueberries, and cream, it makes a wonderfully tasty breakfast. Baked into this pudding, it is a delicious dessert.

¾ cup golden or dark raisins
½ cup maple syrup
2 large eggs
½ teaspoon ground cinnamon
¼ teaspoon freshly ground nutmeg
1 teaspoon vanilla
2 cups cooked wild rice (see Note)
2 cups light cream or half-and-half
2 tablespoons sugar
1 teaspoon ground cinnamon

Preheat the oven to 350°F. Grease a 1½-quart casserole or soufflé dish.

Combine the raisins, maple syrup, eggs, ½ teaspoon cinnamon, the nutmeg, vanilla, wild rice, and cream in a large bowl. Mix and pour into the prepared dish. In a small bowl, stir the sugar and 1 teaspoon cinnamon together and sprinkle evenly over the top of the rice

---

 WILD RICE

Wild rice, the all-American "grain," was introduced to Europeans by Native Americans. Indigenous to the northern part of our country, along the Canadian border, wild rice is harvested in the late summer. This delicious grain is really a grass, botanically related to barley, that grows in lakes and marshy areas.

In recent years, wild rice growers in California and Minnesota have cultivated the rice in paddies, providing a greater supply to the public. Basically, it's still a wild, natural product and varies in aroma and flavor depending on where it is grown. Native Americans who live in northern Minnesota can simply whiff a sample of uncooked wild rice and determine where it came from!

mixture. Place the casserole into a larger pan and fill it halfway with boiling water.

Bake for 1 hour or until the pudding is set or a knife inserted into the center of the pudding comes out clean. Remove from the oven and cool on a wire rack. Serve warm or chilled.

Makes 8 to 10 servings

NOTE: To cook wild rice, measure ⅔ cup uncooked rice. Rinse in hot tap water three times to remove any dust. Put the rice into a saucepan, add 2 cups water, and bring to a boil over medium-high heat. Stir, lower the heat to medium-low, cover, and simmer for 35 to 45 minutes or until the rice is tender and has absorbed all of the water.

Brandied Cranberry Pudding

 So simple, this dessert is a bright and tangy end appropriate for almost any holiday meal.

　4　cups fresh whole cranberries, washed and dried
1½　cups sugar
　½　cup chopped walnuts
　¼　cup cognac, brandy, or water
　2　large eggs
　1　cup all-purpose flour
　½　cup (1 stick) unsalted butter, melted

Preheat the oven to 325°F. Butter a shallow 1½-quart baking dish. Spread the cranberries evenly over the bottom of the dish. Sprinkle ¾ cup of the sugar and the walnuts on top. Pour the cognac around the cranberries in the dish.

In a bowl, beat the eggs until foamy. Add the remaining sugar and beat until light and fluffy. Fold in the flour and melted butter. Spoon the batter over the top of the cranberries. Bake for 45 to 55 minutes or until the pudding is golden. To serve, spoon into individual serving dishes and top with whipped cream or vanilla ice cream, if desired.

Makes 8 servings

Fruits that are in season from late summer through autumn include the following ones:

Apples

Although we generally know about only a few of them, there are thousands of varieties of apples grown in the temperate zones throughout the world. Apples range in color from yellow to bright yellow-green to bright red. The textures range from tender to crisp; their flavors, from sweet to tart. Available all year round, the peak season is from September through November, when they are newly harvested. Look for apples that are firm, with a smooth skin that's free of bruises and a fresh fragrance. Because there are so many choices, select the best apples for your specific baking needs (see the chart on page 126).

Pears

There are more than five thousand varieties of pears grown throughout the world. They can be spherical to bell shaped and have hues of green to golden yellow to red. Ripe pears are juicy and may be spicy or sweet. Select pears that are free of blemishes and firm. Pears that are slightly underripe will ripen quickly at room temperature; refrigerate when ripe. Pears do not need to be peeled before using, but if they are peeled, dip them in water mixed with a little lemon juice, lime juice, or vinegar to prevent browning.

Quinces

Although the quince has been around for some four thousand years, it is not popular in America. It is a fruit that looks like a cross between an apple and a pear and has a dry texture with an astringent, tart flavor. Quinces have a high pectin content, making them popular for jams, jellies, and preserves.

Persimmons

Available from October through February, persimmons are a slightly elongated fruit with a pointed base and a red-orange skin and flesh. The skin should be smooth, glossy, and brightly colored. Ripe fruit should be stored in the refrigerator up to three days. Persimmons are used in baked goods, and other desserts, and are delicious eaten out of hand.

Tangerines

These are a variety of the mandarin orange, which is a loose-skinned orange. It is named after the city of Tangier, Morocco.

Grapes

Most varieties of grapes—red, black, green, with and without seeds—are in season in the autumn. Tiny champagne grapes are expensive and in season for only a short time but make an attractive garnish for baked cakes, pies, and desserts.

Pomegranates

About the size of a large orange with a thick, leathery skin, pomegranates are in season from October through November. They can be kept, refrigerated, for up to two months. Cut the pomegranate in half and pry out the pulp-encased seeds. Remove and discard the light membrane. Pomegranates are used to garnish baked goods, salads, and fruit platters, and the juice can be extracted for cooking.

Cranberries

Grown in huge, sandy bogs on low, trailing vines, cranberries are in peak season from October through December. They're usually packaged in 12-ounce plastic bags. Discard any discolored or shriveled berries. They keep, refrigerated, for up to two months. They can be frozen up to a year. Cranberries are not only used in the traditional Thanksgiving sauce, but are delicious in a variety of baked goods, both alone or combined with apples or dried apricots. Sweetened dried cranberries can be used in baked goods or eaten as snacks, just like raisins. They are available all year round in many supermarkets.

Frosty Pumpkin Crunch Squares

This is a great make-ahead Thanksgiving dessert. A spicy, crunchy baked base is topped with a mixture of coffee ice cream and pumpkin, then frozen. Pull it out of the freezer ten minutes before you're ready to serve.

- 2 cups uncooked old-fashioned or quick rolled oats
- ½ cup (1 stick) unsalted butter, melted
- ½ cup packed brown sugar
- ¼ cup hot water
- 1 teaspoon ground cinnamon
- ½ teaspoon freshly ground cardamom

Filling
- 1 quart coffee-flavored ice cream, softened
- 1 cup canned or freshly cooked puréed pumpkin
- ¾ teaspoon freshly ground cardamom
- ½ teaspoon ground cinnamon

For Serving
- 1 cup whipping cream
- 2 tablespoons confectioners' sugar
- 1 teaspoon vanilla

Preheat the oven to 350°F. Lightly butter a 9-inch square baking dish.

In a mixing bowl, combine the oats, butter, brown sugar, water, cinnamon, and cardamom. Stir with a fork until the mixture is crumbly.

Spread into the bottom of the baking dish. Bake for 20 to 25 minutes, until light brown. Cool the pan on a wire rack.

Combine the ice cream, pumpkin, cardamom, and cinnamon in a large bowl. Pour over the cooled crust. Cover tightly and freeze about 6 hours, until firm.

Remove from the freezer 10 minutes before serving. Place the whipping cream into a small bowl. With an electric mixer or a whisk, beat the cream until stiff. Mix in the sugar and vanilla. Cut the dessert into squares and top with whipped cream.

Makes 9 to 12 servings

Pear Upside-Down Cake

Fresh autumn pears are spicy and juicy, and this is the best time to enjoy them baked into this upside-down cake. Pass the orange butter sauce at the table. Bosc pears are the best for baking. If you cannot get them, use Bartletts or Seckels.

- 3 fresh Bosc pears (about 1½ pounds)
- ¾ cup (1½ sticks) unsalted butter, at room temperature, divided
- ¼ cup packed brown sugar
- 1 cup granulated sugar
- 1 large egg
- 1 teaspoon vanilla
- 2 teaspoons baking powder
- ½ teaspoon salt

1⅔ cups all-purpose flour

½ cup milk

Orange Butter Sauce

1 cup fresh orange juice

1 tablespoon cornstarch

½ cup sugar

1 tablespoon unsalted butter

½ teaspoon ground ginger

Peel, halve, and core the pears; set aside. Preheat the oven to 350°F. Put ¼ cup of the butter into a 10 × 6-inch baking pan and place into the oven as it preheats. Remove from the oven when the butter is melted.

Sprinkle the brown sugar evenly over the melted butter. Arrange the pears in a single layer over the brown sugar with the cut side down.

In a large bowl, cream the remaining ½ cup butter with the granulated sugar, egg, and vanilla. Mix in the baking powder and salt. Add the flour alternately with the milk, mixing until the batter is smooth.

Pour the mixture evenly over the pears. Bake for 45 minutes or until a wooden skewer inserted into the center of the cake comes out clean. Invert while warm onto a serving plate and serve warm with the orange butter sauce.

While the cake bakes, make the sauce. Combine the orange juice, cornstarch, sugar, butter, and ginger in a small saucepan. Heat to boiling over medium-high heat, stirring. Cook, stirring, until thickened. Remove from the heat.

Makes 6 servings

Apricot Baba

This is a variation from the classic baba au rhum, the rich, light yeast cake soaked in a rum syrup, invented in the 1600s by a Polish king who soaked a stale kugelhopf in rum and named the dessert after Ali Baba, the storybook hero. The classic baba is baked in a tall, straight-sided mold. If you bake it in a ring mold, it then is a "savarin" (see page 61).

1 package active dry yeast

2 cups all-purpose flour

½ cup sugar

½ teaspoon salt

½ cup milk

¾ cup (1½ sticks) unsalted butter, cut up

4 large eggs, at room temperature, lightly beaten

½ cup finely chopped dried apricots

Apricot Syrup

¾ cup (6 ounces) apricot nectar

¾ cup sugar

1 teaspoon lemon juice

¼ cup light or dark rum

1 cup whipping cream, for serving

1 tablespoon confectioners' sugar

In a large mixing bowl, stir together the yeast, flour, sugar, and salt.

In a small saucepan, heat the milk to boiling. Add the butter; remove from the heat and stir until the butter is melted. Cool at 130°F.

Stir the butter-milk mixture and the eggs into the flour mixture until the mixture is smooth. Stir in the chopped apricots. Beat until the batter is very smooth and satiny. Cover and let rise in a warm place for 45 minutes or until dough has doubled.

Butter a 7- to 8-cup baba mold or fancy ring mold. Stir the batter down and pour it into the prepared mold. Let rise until the mixture has almost doubled, about 30 minutes.

Preheat the oven to 450°F. Bake the baba for 10 minutes, reduce the temperature to 350°F, and bake 30 minutes longer or until a toothpick inserted in the cake comes out clean. Let cool 5 minutes, loosen the cake from the mold, then return it to the mold.

TO MAKE THE APRICOT SYRUP

In a small saucepan, heat the apricot nectar, sugar, and lemon juice to boiling. Add the rum to the syrup. Spoon it over the warm baba. Let the syrup soak in. When ready to serve, invert the baba onto a serving plate.

In a small bowl, whip the cream and confectioners' sugar until stiff. Cut the baba into slices and spoon whipped cream over each serving.

Makes 8 to 10 servings

NOTE: To make the Apricot Baba ahead and freeze it, wrap the cooled, soaked cake in its baking pan in a plastic freezer bag. Before serving, remove from the wrapping and place the cake in the pan at preheated 300°F oven for about 20 minutes, until heated through.

Gingerbread with Lemon Sauce

S I think of gingerbread as a comfort dessert. It reminds me of autumn Sundays home on the farm. That's why I probably associate it with Thanksgiving. We used to make a Crumb Cake that was much like this, in which you remove part of the dry cake mixture and save it for the topping.

½ cup sugar
¼ cup (½ stick) unsalted butter, softened
1 cup all-purpose flour
1 teaspoon ground ginger
1 teaspoon ground cinnamon
½ teaspoon ground allspice
¼ teaspoon salt
½ teaspoon baking soda
½ cup nonfat plain yogurt or buttermilk
¼ cup light molasses
1 large egg, slightly beaten

Lemon Sauce
½ cup sugar
¼ cup (½ stick) unsalted butter
2 tablespoons lemon juice
1 teaspoon grated lemon zest
¼ cup water

Preheat the oven to 375°F. Lightly grease an 8-inch square or round cake pan.

In a large bowl, cream together the sugar and butter.

In another bowl, combine the flour, ginger, cinnamon, allspice, and salt. Mix the dry ingredients into the creamed ingredients until the mixture resembles moist crumbs. Remove and reserve ⅓ cup of the mixture.

Add the baking soda to the remaining mixture and stir in the yogurt, molasses, and egg. Stir with a wooden spoon until the batter is evenly blended. Pour into the prepared pan. Sprinkle evenly with the remaining mixture. Bake for 20 to 25 minutes or until a toothpick inserted in the center comes out clean.

TO MAKE THE LEMON SAUCE

In a small saucepan combine the sugar, butter, lemon juice, lemon zest, and water. Place over medium-heat and bring to a boil, stirring constantly. Reduce heat to low and simmer for 4 minutes, stirring until the mixture is clear and slightly thickened. Serve warm over squares of the gingerbread.

Makes 8 to 9 servings

Advent Through Christmas

Christmas Breads • A Fancy Cookie Sampler • Favorite and Classic Cookies • A Gift of Bars and Brownies • Christmas Cakes and Fruitcakes • Festive Christmas Desserts • Quick Breads • Special Pastries

CHRISTMAS BREADS

Italian Pine Nut Panettone

In Milan, Italy, this tender, light fruited bread studded with pine nuts, candied fruit, and raisins is traditional at Christmas. It is delicious for breakfast or to accompany tea or coffee. Although it's customarily baked in tall, cylindrical pans that are especially made for Panettone, you can use any tall, straight-sided round pan or dish such as a two-quart soufflé dish, a metal charlotte mold, or a springform pan fitted with a paper collar.

4½ cups all-purpose flour
2 packages (5½ teaspoons) active dry yeast
½ teaspoon salt
¼ cup pine nuts
¼ cup dark raisins
¼ cup mixed candied fruits, finely diced
1 teaspoon aniseed
1 teaspoon grated lemon zest
¾ cup sugar
1 cup milk
½ cup (1 stick) unsalted butter
3 large eggs

Icing and Decoration
1 cup confectioners' sugar
3 to 4 tablespoons whipping cream
Additional pine nuts and candied fruits

In a large mixing bowl, stir together 3 cups of the flour, the yeast, salt, pine nuts, raisins, fruits, aniseed, lemon zest, and sugar. In a saucepan, scald the milk over medium-high heat. Remove from the heat and add the butter; let stand until the butter is melted and the mixture is cooled to very warm (130°F). Make a hole in the center of the flour mixture and add the milk mixture and the eggs. Beat with a spoon until smooth. Cover and let rise in a warm place until doubled. Or combine the dry ingredients in a food processor with the dough blade in place (see page 9). With the machine running, add the liquids through the feed tube. Process until the dough is smooth, soft, and satiny, then cover and let rise in a warm place until doubled, about 1 hour.

Butter 2 large (about 2-pound) coffee cans or 2 quart-size charlotte molds, or fit two 9-inch soufflé dishes or springform pans with a collar (see Note). With a spoon, beat the dough to remove air bubbles. Divide the dough between the two pans. Cover and let rise in a warm place for 45 minutes or until almost doubled.

Preheat the oven to 350°F. Bake for 40 to 45 minutes or until a skewer inserted through the center comes out clean.

Remove from the oven and turn out of the pans. Cool on a wire rack. Before serving, mix together the confectioners' sugar and cream in a small bowl. Brush this glaze onto the breads and decorate with pine nuts and candied fruits.

Makes 2 loaves

NOTE: To make a collar, cut a piece of parchment paper long enough to wrap around the inside of a 9-inch round pan plus 2 inches. Fold the strip lengthwise to make it 3 inches wide. Grease the bottom and sides of the pan. Fit the folded strip of paper inside the pan, so that it rises above the rim of the pan by 2 inches and overlaps at the ends by 2 inches. Fasten the ends together with a paper clip.

Another novel way to bake Panettone was done in *Sunset Magazine* in the sixties. Fold the tops down on two brown paper lunch bags. Grease the insides of the bags thoroughly. Bake the Panettone as directed, placing the filled bags upright on a cookie sheet while baking.

HOLIDAY BREADS FOR TODAY

The breads I bake for Christmas today seem to fill more varied purposes than they did in the past. A stuffed bread could be the main course for a light meal or something I take to a party at a friend's house. One with fruits and spices could be something I keep on hand for coffee, snacks, or breakfast. And festive ethnic bread makes a great gift.

Now when I bake, I often make an extra loaf to freeze. I like to keep an assortment on hand for the holidays for different occasions and times of the day. My favorite still is the cardamom bread "pulla," so great for coffee breaks, snacks, and breakfasts, even for gifts. But I've grown to love the dense, fruit-and-nut–stuffed loaves that come from other traditions. And instead of dealing with huge batches of dough, I'd rather bake a single loaf, or sometimes two, using the food processor or my heavy-duty mixer instead of kneading the dough by hand. With today's technology, baking bread in the home kitchen has never been easier.

Swedish St. Lucia (Saffron) Bread

December 13 is St. Lucia Day, marking the beginning of the Christmas festivities for Swedes. On this day, there are parades in Swedish villages and cities over which the lucky young woman appointed to be the fair-haired Lucia presides, looking like a shimmering dream figure. Even the most reserved Swedish hearts melt.

There are many legends about who Lucia was and why she became so important to the Swedes. An old folk tale from Varmland, a province in western Sweden, relates a time of suffering under a great famine; Lucia suddenly appeared on board a ship that brought food for the starving people.

Traditionally, young Swedish girls present their mothers with breakfast in bed, consisting of hot coffee and St. Lucia's buns shaped in fancy twists. Swedish teachers, too, receive a similar tray, carried in by the "Lucia" of the classroom. St. Lucia Breads may take the shape of a braided wreath or fancy individual buns. This dough shapes easily because it is refrigerated, and it's simple to make because it requires no kneading.

  2   packages (5½ teaspoons)
        active dry yeast
4 to 4½   cups all-purpose flour
  ¾   cup sugar
  1   teaspoon salt
  1   cup milk
  ⅛   teaspoon powdered saffron or
        ½ teaspoon saffron threads
  ½   cup (1 stick) butter, cut up
  2   large eggs, slightly beaten

Glaze and Decoration
  1   large egg beaten with
        2 tablespoons milk
  ½   cup sliced almonds (optional)
        Up to ¼ cup golden raisins
        (optional)
  ½   cup pearl sugar or coarsely
        crushed sugar cubes (optional)

In a large mixing bowl, combine the yeast, 2 cups of the flour, the sugar, and salt. In a small saucepan, heat the milk to simmering over medium heat, then remove from the heat. Add the saffron and butter; stir until the butter is melted and the mixture has cooled to very warm (130°F). Stir the liquids into the flour mixture and add the eggs. Beat with a wooden spoon until the batter is smooth and satiny. Beat in the remaining flour a cup at a time until the dough is stiff but not dry. Cover and refrigerate for at least 2 hours or up to 24 hours.

To Make a St. Lucia Wreath
Cut off one-third of the chilled dough and reserve. Cut the remaining dough into 3 parts. On a lightly floured board, roll each of the 3 parts out to make a rope 36 inches long.

Yeast is a living organism that, once given moisture and food, will actually grow. During growth, yeast produces tiny bubbles of carbon dioxide that leavens dough (as it is trapped in the gluten network of the dough) and gives the bread a wonderful flavor. Yeast is a microscopic plant, a biological rather than chemical leavening agent. In the past, most bread bakers used cake-style compressed fresh yeast, which has to be refrigerated and used before it spoils. Compressed yeast is available in health food stores as well as most supermarkets. An active, granular dry yeast has been developed that has a much longer shelf life because without moisture the yeast is dormant. When reconstituted in warm liquid (between 105 and 115°F), the yeast becomes active. If the liquid is cooler than 105°F, the yeast gets a slow start, and your bread will take a long time to rise. Yeast will not become active at temperatures below 50°F and begins to die between 115° and 120°F.

There are two basic methods for using dry yeast. In one method, the yeast is reconstituted in a small amount of warm water, then added to the dough. The other method, which is very easy for the baker, is to add the yeast to the dry ingredients (but usually not all of the flour) before adding the liquid ingredients to the mixture. When using this method, the liquid needs to be very warm (about 130°F) because the dry ingredients will cool the mixture down quickly. The advantage of the first method is that you can check out the activity of the yeast, as the yeast will begin to bubble within minutes after adding the liquid. The advantage of the second method is convenience.

Active dry yeast is available today in two forms: regular and rapid-rise. Although they are different strains of yeast, they can be used interchangeably. Rapid-rise yeast, however, is not recommended for refrigerated doughs (it is designed for a quick, warm rise rather than a slow, refrigerated rise). Rapid-rise yeast cuts rising time by about half. For proper use, refer to the package directions. Both types of dry yeast are available in quarter-ounce envelopes as well as in bulk. All dry yeast should be stored in a cool, dry place, and can be refrigerated or frozen. A package of active dry yeast is equal to one scant tablespoon dry yeast or one cake of compressed fresh yeast.

Braid the 3 ropes together. Cover a 17 × 14-inch rimless baking sheet with parchment paper or lightly grease the baking sheet. Place the braids in a wreath shape on the baking sheet, trim off about 1 inch from each end of the braids, and fit the cut ends together; pinch to seal. Reserve the trimmings.

For the small bread, divide the reserved two-thirds portion of dough into 3 parts. On a lightly floured board, roll each piece into a strand 36 inches long and braid these as well. Brush the large braid with the egg glaze. Sprinkle with almonds. Center the small braid on top of the large braid. Trim the ends of the braids and fit together; pinch to seal. Reserve the trimmings.

On a floured board, roll the dough trimmings to about a 1/4-inch thickness. Cut into leaf shapes using a knife or cookie cutter. With a knife, score the leaves to simulate veins. Brush both braids with the egg glaze. Roll the leftover scraps to make thin strands and twine the strands along the top of the braids like vines. Decorate with the leaf cutouts and brush again with the egg glaze. Let the wreath rise, covered, until doubled, about 1 to 1 1/2 hours.

Preheat the oven to 375°F and bake for 25 to 35 minutes or until golden. Cool on a wire rack.

Makes 1 wreath

To Make a Golden Christmas Cake

Lightly grease 2 baking sheets or cover with parchment paper. Divide the refrigerated dough into 2 parts, then divide each part into 9 equal parts. Shape each part into a strand about 10 inches long by rolling the dough between your palms and a lightly floured board. Curl one strand into a tight spiral shape and place in the center of one of the prepared pans. Tuck one end of each of the 8 remaining strands under the center curl; pinch to seal each strand to the center spiral and curl the ends of each strand so that they are all pointing in the same direction around the center. (This shape is called Christmas chariots in some parts of Sweden.) Repeat for the second half of the dough and place on another baking sheet. Cover with a towel and let rise in a warm place until the dough is almost doubled, about 1 to 1 1/2 hours. Brush with the egg glaze and press a raisin into the center of each curl.

Preheat the oven to 375°F and bake for 20 to 25 minutes, until just golden. Cool on wire racks.

Makes 2 cakes

To Make Lucia Cats

Cover 2 baking sheets with parchment paper or lightly grease them. Divide the dough into 6 equal portions, then divide each portion into 8 equal pieces. Roll each piece between the palms of your hands to make 6-inch ropes. Place 2 ropes side by side, pinching them together in the middle. Curl all 4 ends toward the center and place on a baking sheet. Repeat with the rest of the ropes. Cover with a towel and let rise until puffy, about 45 minutes.

Preheat the oven to 400°F. Press a raisin

into the center of each curl and brush with the egg glaze. Sprinkle with sugar, then bake for 8 to 10 minutes, until just golden. Cool on a wire rack.

Makes 24 Lucia cats

Christmas Boars

Cover 2 baking sheets with parchment paper or lightly grease them. Divide the dough into 24 equal portions. Roll each part out to make an 8-inch rope, then curl each rope into a tight S shape and place on the baking sheet. Cover with a towel and let rise until puffy, about 45 minutes.

Preheat the oven to 400°F. Press a raisin into the center of each curl on the S. Brush with the egg glaze and sprinkle with sugar. Bake for 8 to 10 minutes, until just golden. Cool on a wire rack.

Makes 24 Christmas Boars

Golden Nut-Stuffed Brioche

Brioche, the golden, egg-rich French bread in its traditional form has a top knot and is baked in a flared, fluted pan. I like to stuff the brioche with a delicious nut-based filling and serve it for a special holiday breakfast or brunch.

  3 cups all-purpose flour
  1 package (2¾ teaspoons) active
     dry yeast

  ¼ cup sugar
  ½ teaspoon salt
  ½ cup milk, scalded and cooled
     to about 130°F
  3 large eggs, slightly beaten
  ½ cup (1 stick) unsalted butter,
     at room temperature

Honey-Nut Filling

  3 cups (12 ounces) ground pecans
     or walnuts
  ¾ cup undiluted evaporated milk
  ¾ cup sugar
  ⅓ cup honey
  ½ teaspoon vanilla

Cinnamon-Almond Filling

  12 ounces almond paste
  2 large egg whites
  ¾ cup ground almonds
  2 teaspoons ground cinnamon
  ¼ teaspoon almond extract
  1 egg beaten with 1 tablespoon milk,
     for brushing
  ½ cup sliced almonds, for sprinkling

Combine 2 cups of the flour, the yeast, sugar, and salt in a food processor or in the bowl of an electric mixer with a dough hook. Add the milk and eggs and process until the mixture is smooth. Add the remaining flour and the butter and process until the dough is smooth and cleans the sides of the work bowl. Let the dough stand, covered, in the work bowl for 30 minutes.

Process again until the dough turns around the bowl about 25 times, or about 30 seconds.

Gluten

While gluten is not usually an ingredient called for in a recipe, it is such an important component of flour that to omit discussion of it risks misunderstanding its role in bread. Pure gluten is a tough, elastic, grayish substance that when moistened has the texture of chewing gum. High-gluten flour, available in health food stores, can be added to whole grain breads in order to add elasticity to the dough. The elasticity allows the dough to expand, yet traps the carbon dioxide gases produced by the yeast. The amount of gluten in a loaf determines the strength of the dough. Hard-wheat flours, or "strong" flours, contain the most gluten and are the best for yeast-bread baking. Soft-wheat flours have less gluten and are best for cakes, cookies, pastries, and quick breads.

Types of Flour

All-purpose flour, either unbleached or bleached, is milled from a mixture of hard (high-gluten) and soft (low-gluten) wheat. Depending on the manufacturer, the amount of gluten in flour labeled "all-purpose" varies from eleven grams of protein (gluten) per cup to thirteen grams per cup. Bread bakers prefer bread flour, which contains fourteen grams of protein per cup (usually only thirteen grams of protein in Southern brands, such as White Lily). The more protein, the stronger the flour, and the better it is for yeast-bread baking because the strong gluten structure retains more of the tiny bubbles of carbon dioxide formed by the growth of the yeast. While high-protein flour is preferable for baking with yeast, it makes a tougher texture in non-yeast-baked goods such as quick breads, cakes, cookies, and pastries. For non-yeast baking, select all-purpose flour with eleven or twelve grams of protein per cup. Whole wheat flour is ground from the entire wheat kernel and is low in gluten. Rye flour also contains little gluten, and both must be combined with wheat flour in most doughs. Bran, wheat germ, cornmeal, corn germ, cracked wheat, and wheat berries (the wheat kernels) are grain components and not actually flours. They add fiber, crunch, nutrition, and flavor to breads.

Let the dough stand, covered, in the work bowl for another 30 minutes. Meanwhile, prepare one of the fillings.

To make the honey-nut filling, combine the nuts, milk, and sugar in a 2-quart saucepan. Stir in the honey. Bring to a boil over medium-high heat, stirring constantly, and let boil for 1 minute. Remove from the heat and add the vanilla. Cover and let cool to room temperature.

To make the cinnamon-almond filling, in a bowl, mix together the almond paste, egg whites, almonds, cinnamon, and almond extract. Form into a roughly shaped square and place between 2 sheets of plastic wrap. Roll out to make a 12-inch square and set aside.

Turn the yeast dough onto a lightly greased surface. Pinch off about ½ cup of the dough, shape into a smooth ball, and reserve. Roll out the remaining dough to make a 12-inch square.

To fill with the honey-nut filling, spread the cooled filling evenly across the dough square.

To fill with the cinnamon-almond filling, peel the top sheet of plastic wrap from the almond paste mixture and flip the paste over onto the dough square. Peel off the plastic from the top.

For either filling, roll the square up as for a jelly roll; then bring the ends together to form a ring.

Place the ring of dough, seam side down, in a buttered 2-quart brioche pan (see Note).

Shape the reserved dough into a teardrop shape and poke it, pointed side down, into the center of the dough ring. Cover and let rise until the dough reaches the top of the pan, 1 to 1½ hours. Brush with the beaten egg and milk mixture and sprinkle with the sliced almonds.

Preheat the oven to 350°F. Bake for 40 to 45 minutes or until golden and a wooden skewer inserted in the center comes out clean. If the brioche begins to brown too quickly, cover lightly with foil until the loaf tests done. Cool in the pan for 10 minutes, then turn out of the pan and finish cooling on a wire rack. Serve warm.

Makes 1 large filled brioche

NOTE: If you do not have a brioche pan, you can use a regular cake pan or a springform pan. Shape the bread, let rise, and bake as described. The brioche can also be baked in a tube pan such as an angel food pan or kugelhopf pan, but then do not reserve the ½ cup dough for the topknot. Fill and shape the entire batch of dough, eliminating the topknot step. Baking time will remain the same.

Cherry-Nut Christmas Wreath

The colorful cherry-nut filling is exposed in a ropelike twisted wreath. To achieve this effect, you follow the same procedure as if you were making cinnamon rolls. However, instead of slicing the filled yeast roll crosswise into buns, you cut it lengthwise into two pieces, exposing the filling along the cut. Twist the strands into a rope as you place them on the baking sheet in the shape of a wreath.

- 2 packages (5½ teaspoons) active dry yeast
- 3 cups all-purpose flour
- 3 tablespoons sugar
- ¾ teaspoon salt
- ½ teaspoon freshly ground cardamom
- ⅓ cup hot water
- ¼ cup (½ stick) unsalted butter, melted and cooled
- 2 large eggs, lightly beaten

Cherry-Nut Filling

- ¾ cup chopped walnuts, pecans, filberts, or almonds
- ½ cup chopped candied cherries
- ¼ cup all-purpose flour
- ¼ cup (½ stick) unsalted butter, at room temperature
- 2 tablespoons packed brown sugar
- ½ teaspoon almond extract

Almond Icing

- 1 cup confectioners' sugar
- 2 tablespoons milk
- ½ teaspoon almond extract

Combine the yeast, flour, sugar, salt, and cardamom in the work bowl of a food processor; mix until blended. Or combine in a mixing bowl and make a well in the center. In a small bowl, mix together the water and butter. Pour the water-butter mixture and the eggs into the flour. Process or mix until the dough is smooth and satiny. If using the food processor, process until the dough turns around the bowl about 25 times. If necessary, add additional water a tablespoon at a time until the dough has a soft, satiny, springy texture. If the dough seems to be too soft, add flour 1 tablespoon at a time, processing between each addition until the dough is no longer sticky. If mixing by hand, turn the dough out onto a floured surface and knead until the dough is smooth and satiny, then return to the bowl, cover, and let rise until doubled, about 1 hour. If you have used the food processor, cover the bowl of the food processor and let the dough rise until doubled, about 1 hour.

In a mixing bowl, combine the filling ingredients.

Turn the dough out onto a lightly oiled surface. Roll the dough into a 24 × 9-inch rectangle with a lightly floured rolling pin. Spread with the filling. Roll up starting from a long side into a 24-inch roll and pinch the seam to seal. Carefully cut the roll in half lengthwise using a sharp knife. Turn each half cut side up. Pick up each half of the dough and carefully lift one side over the other, twisting them into a rope, keeping the smooth side down and the exposed filling side up. Place on a lightly greased or parchment-covered cookie sheet and shape into a wreath or circle, pinching the ends together. Let the wreath stand in a warm place, covered, until puffy, 20 to 30 minutes.

Preheat the oven to 375°F. Bake for 20 to 25 minutes, until brown. Mix the icing ingredients in a small bowl, then drizzle the baked wreath with the icing while still warm. Serve warm.

Makes one 14-inch wreath

Czech Christmas Vánocka

This delectable and beautiful lemon and almond loaf bread is a three-layer construction consisting of a large braid on the base topped by a smaller braid and finally by a twisted rope on top. It's a perfect bread to show off on a buffet table and can be sliced and reassembled ahead of time.

    2 packages (5½ teaspoons) active
      dry yeast
    4 cups all-purpose flour or more
      as needed

    ½ cup sugar
    1 teaspoon salt
    1½ cups milk
    ½ cup (1 stick) unsalted butter
    1 large egg
    ½ teaspoon grated lemon zest
    1 teaspoon vanilla
    ¼ cup raisins
    ⅓ cup blanched slivered almonds
    2 tablespoons chopped citron
      (see Note)
    1 large egg, beaten
    2 tablespoons sliced almonds
      Confectioners' sugar, for sprinkling

In the large bowl of an electric mixer with a dough hook or in the work bowl of a food processor, combine the yeast, flour, sugar, and salt. In a heavy saucepan, scald the milk over medium heat, then remove from heat and add the butter. Stir until the butter is melted, then add the egg, lemon zest, and vanilla. Stir until the mixture has cooled to very warm (130°F). Turn on the electric mixer or food processor and add the liquid mixture; process or mix until the dough is smooth and satiny. (The dough can also be kneaded by hand on a lightly floured surface until smooth and satiny.) Add up to ¼ cup additional flour if necessary.

Place the dough into a clean, oiled bowl and turn to coat. Cover with a cloth and let rise in a warm place until the dough is doubled, about 1 hour. Punch down the dough and, on a lightly floured surface, knead in the raisins, blanched almonds, and citron.

Cover a baking sheet with parchment paper or lightly grease it. Divide the dough into 4 equal parts. Roll 3 parts into ropes 24 inches long. Braid the ropes and place on the baking sheet to make a straight loaf. Divide the remaining dough into 4 equal parts. Roll 3 parts into ropes about 24 inches long. Braid, pinch the ends together, and center on top of the large braid. Cut the remaining dough into 2 parts. Roll into 2 ropes about 24 inches long and twist together. Place on top of the braids and tuck ends under the large braid. To keep the braids and twist from falling over while rising and baking, press 3 to 5 wooden skewers through the twist and braids to "nail" them together. Cover with a cloth and let rise until almost doubled, about 1 hour.

Preheat the oven to 375°F. Brush the loaf with the beaten egg and sprinkle with the sliced almonds.

Bake for 30 to 35 minutes, until a skewer inserted into the center of the loaf comes out clean and dry. Sprinkle the warm bread with confectioners' sugar.

Makes 1 large braid

NOTE: Citron is a semitropical citrus fruit that looks like a large, lumpy, yellow-green lemon. It grows six to nine inches long, is very sour, and has a thick peel that is candied and used in baking. It is available in the baking section in supermarkets and specialty foods stores during the Christmas season.

Danish Christmas Kringle

An almond filling is encased in a buttery, flaky yeast pastry that is crusted with sugar and almonds and traditionally shaped in a large pretzel. This legendary Danish specialty has always been a Christmas favorite of ours. This Christmas treat symbolizes Danish hygge, or the "comfortable and good life." Danes use a variety of fruit or nut fillings in a kringle, although the almond filling is the most popular. I have included two fruit fillings as alternatives to the nut filling.

I often make two horseshoe-shaped coffee breads instead of a pretzel. The pastry is actually quite simple to make, because it is based on a refrigerated dough that is easy to handle.

Dough

2 packages (5½ teaspoons) active dry yeast
½ cup warm water (105 to 115°F)
¼ cup undiluted evaporated milk, at room temperature
1 teaspoon freshly ground cardamom (optional)
¼ cup sugar
3 large egg yolks
1 cup whipping cream
3½ cups all-purpose flour
1 teaspoon salt
¾ cup (1½ sticks) unsalted butter, chilled and cut into pieces

Nut Filling

1 cup (about ½ pound) almond paste
1 cup finely chopped almonds, pecans, or walnuts
½ cup confectioner's sugar
1 large egg white
1 teaspoon almond extract

Cranberry Filling

1 package (12 ounces) fresh or frozen cranberries
⅓ cup fresh orange juice
1 tablespoon orange zest
1 small, tart apple (such as Granny Smith), peeled, cored, and chopped
½ cup golden raisins
1 cup sugar
1½ teaspoons ground cinnamon
Pinch of freshly ground nutmeg

Apricot-Apple Filling

1½ cups (about 8 ounces) dried apricots, cut into pieces
1 cup fresh orange juice
1 tablespoon grated orange zest
1 tart apple (such as Granny Smith), peeled, cored, and chopped
1 cup sugar

Glaze and Topping

1 large egg white, lightly beaten
Pearl sugar, coarsely crushed sugar cubes, or granulated sugar, for sprinkling

Sliced almonds or chopped walnuts or pecans, for sprinkling

Make the dough. In a medium bowl, dissolve the yeast in the warm water. Let stand for 5 minutes. Add the milk, cardamom, sugar, egg yolks, and whipping cream and blend well; set aside.

In a large bowl, or in the work bowl of a food processor with the steel blade in place, combine the flour and salt. Cut in the butter until the pieces are the size of kidney beans. If using a food processor, turn into a large bowl. Add the yeast mixture, mixing only until the dry ingredients are moistened. Cover with plastic wrap and refrigerate for 12 to 24 hours.

Meanwhile, prepare the filling of your choice.

To make the nut filling, in a bowl with an electric mixer or a food processor break the almond paste into pieces and blend with the chopped nuts, confectioners' sugar, egg white, and almond extract until well mixed.

To make the cranberry filling, combine the cranberries, orange juice and zest, apple, raisins, sugar, cinnamon, and nutmeg in a 2-quart saucepan. Cook over medium heat, stirring occasionally, until the mixture is thick, about 20 minutes. Remove from the heat and cool to room temperature.

To make the apricot-apple filling, combine the apricots, orange juice and zest, apple, and sugar in a 2-quart saucepan. Cook over medium heat, stirring often, until the fruits are soft and the mixture is thick, about 10 minutes. Remove from the heat and cool to room temperature.

Remove the dough from the refrigerator, turn out onto a lightly floured surface, and dust the dough lightly with flour. Using a rolling pin, pound the dough until smooth and about ½ inch thick. Roll out to make a 24-inch square. Fold the dough into thirds to make a long and narrow strip. With the rolling pin, roll again until about ¼ inch thick and about 36 inches long and 8 inches wide.

Spread the filling in a 3-inch strip down the length of the dough. Overlap the edges of the dough to enclose the filling; pinch the ends to seal. Brush with the egg white to seal the ends and the seam. Brush the entire roll with egg white and coat generously with sugar and nuts on all sides.

Lightly grease and flour a baking sheet or cover with parchment paper.

To make the kringle shape, place the roll on the baking sheet in the shape of a large pretzel. To do this, place the baking sheet horizontally in front of you. Lift the filled roll from both ends firmly and center the middle of the roll onto the baking sheet as if you were forming a circle. Pull the ends of the roll so that they make a cross above the roll, then pull the ends down and tuck the ends under the top part of the roll so that the ends stick out from under the roll.

For the horseshoe shapes, cut the filled strip crosswise at the center point to make two strips. Place on 2 prepared baking sheets and form each strip into a horseshoe. Seal the ends of each horseshoe. Brush with the egg white and sprinkle with the sugar and nuts.

Cover and let rise in a warm place for 45 minutes. It will not double. Preheat the oven to 375°F.

Brush the kringle again with the egg white and bake for 25 to 30 minutes or until golden. Cool on a wire rack.

Makes one 15-inch-diameter pretzel or two 12-inch horseshoes

Hungarian Christmas Mákos és Diós Kalács

 Hungarians look forward to this Christmas cake that is made jelly-roll fashion with a poppy seed and nut filling. It can be made at least a week in advance or more, if wrapped and frozen.

   2 packages (5½ teaspoons) active
     dry yeast
4 to 4½ cups all-purpose flour
   ½ cup sugar
 1½ teaspoons salt
   1 cup warm milk
   ¼ cup (½ stick) unsalted butter,
     at room temperature
   3 large eggs

Poppy Seed–Walnut Filling

- 1½ cups poppy seeds
- 1½ cups chopped walnuts
- 1 cup sugar
- 2 teaspoons freshly grated lemon zest
- ½ cup raisins
- 1 (12-ounce) can undiluted evaporated milk
- 1 large egg, slightly beaten, for glaze

In a large bowl of an electric mixer, combine the yeast, flour, sugar, and salt. In a heavy saucepan, scald the milk over medium heat, then remove from the heat and add the butter, stirring until it is dissolved. Mix in the eggs. Make a well in the center of the flour mixture and pour in the milk mixture. Beat until the dough is smooth and soft. Divide the dough evenly into 3 well-greased bowls. Cover and let rise in a warm place for 1 hour, until doubled.

For the filling, combine the poppy seeds and walnuts in a blender or food processor. Process until finely pulverized. Mix the sugar, lemon zest, raisins, and milk in a heavy saucepan. Cook over medium heat, stirring constantly, until the sugar is dissolved. Add the poppy seeds and walnuts and heat to boiling over medium-high heat. Boil for 1 minute, stirring. Remove from the heat and let cool.

Lightly oil a large work surface and grease three 9-inch round pans. Do not punch down the dough. Invert one of the bowls of dough onto the countertop. Dust the dough with flour; flatten and then roll out to a rectangle about ¼ inch thick, measuring about 24 by

OTHER IMPORTANT BREAD INGREDIENTS

Liquids

Water and milk are the most common liquids used in making yeast breads. Water gives the loaf a crunchy crust. Milk gives the loaf a velvety crumb and a soft crust. Breads made with milk stay moist longer than breads made with water.

Salt

Besides enhancing the flavor of bread, salt controls the growth of the yeast. Too much salt kills the yeast; none may produce a porous loaf.

Fats

Butter, margarine, oils, and lard add flavor and moistness to bread. Doughs that are high in fat require more yeast than low-fat doughs.

12 inches. Spread one-third of the filling over the dough, leaving a 2-inch margin on one long edge uncovered. Roll up like a jelly roll starting with the filling-covered long edge. Form the roll into a coil and, with the seam side down, place in a prepared pan, then brush with the beaten egg. Repeat with the remaining portions of dough and filling. Let rise, covered, in a warm place for 30 minutes, until the rolls appear slightly puffy. Brush again with the egg glaze. Using a long skewer, pierce the rolls to break any large air bubbles.

Preheat the oven to 325°F. Bake the loaves for 45 minutes or until light brown. Remove from the pans and cool on a wire rack.

Makes 3 round 9-inch loaves

Viennese Kugelhopf

This festive, rich, easy-to-make batter bread with almonds, raisins, and lemon peel is popular not only in Austria but in Germany and southern France as well. I love this bread for the ease of its preparation, because batter breads do not require any kneading. By allowing the batter to rise once in the bowl before pouring it into the baking pan, the bread bakes up with a cakelike texture.

    1 package (2¾ teaspoons) active
       dry yeast
    1 cup sugar
    4 cups all-purpose flour
    1 teaspoon salt
    1 cup raisins
    ¾ cup slivered or sliced almonds
    1 tablespoon grated lemon zest
    1 cup milk
    ¾ cup (1½ sticks) unsalted butter
    4 large eggs, at room temperature
    1 teaspoon vanilla

Decoration
    Sugar and sliced almonds, for pan
    Confectioners' sugar, for dusting

In a large mixing bowl, stir together the yeast, sugar, flour, salt, raisins, almonds, and lemon zest.

In a heavy saucepan, scald the milk over medium-high heat. Remove from the heat and add the butter; stir until the butter is melted and the mixture has cooled to very warm (130°F).

Make a hole in the center of the flour mixture and pour in the milk mixture, then add the eggs and vanilla. Stir or beat with an electric mixer on high speed until the dough is very smooth.

Cover and let rise for 45 minutes or until about doubled. Heavily butter a large, fancy, tube pan (at least 12-cup capacity); sprinkle the bottom with sugar and sliced almonds. Stir down the batter and pour it into the pan (see Note). Cover and let rise for 45 minutes or until puffy.

Preheat the oven to 350°F. Bake for 50 to 60 minutes or until a wooden skewer inserted in the center comes out clean. Remove from the oven and cool in the pan on a wire rack; remove from the pan after 10 minutes of cooling. Before serving, dust with confectioners' sugar.

Makes 1 large loaf

NOTE: To freeze the unbaked batter, let it rise once, then pour it into the buttered baking pan, wrap well, and freeze for up to 1 month. To thaw and bake, remove from the freezer and allow to thaw in the refrigerator overnight; then let rise at room temperature, covered, for about 1 hour until puffy. Bake as directed above. Or, if you wish, you can pour the mixed batter into a heavy-duty plastic bag; close tightly and freeze. Remove from the freezer, allow to thaw in the refrigerator overnight, then pour into the greased baking pan and allow to rise at room temperature, covered, until doubled.

Norwegian Julekage

 Studded with fruits and flavored and perfumed with cardamom, this Christmas cake is popular in Denmark and Sweden as well as in Norway. I've learned to make it quickly using the food processor as the mixing and kneading tool.

4 cups unbleached all-purpose flour
2 packages (5½ teaspoons) active dry yeast

½ cup sugar
2 teaspoons freshly ground cardamom
½ teaspoon salt
1 cup milk
½ cup (1 stick) unsalted butter, chilled and cut into pieces
1 large egg, beaten
½ cup raisins
1 cup candied cherries or mixed chopped candied fruit

Glaze
1 large egg, beaten

Icing and Decoration
½ cup confectioners' sugar
1 tablespoon cream or milk
½ teaspoon almond extract
Toasted sliced almonds

In a food processor with the dough blade (see page 9) in place, or in a large bowl, mix 2 cups of the flour, the yeast, sugar, cardamom, and salt. In a heavy saucepan, scald the milk over medium-high heat. Stir in the butter until it is melted and remove from the heat.

With the food processor running, or stirring with a wooden spoon, add the milk mixture and the egg to the flour; process or beat until the dough is soft, smooth, and satiny. Add the remaining flour and process or mix until the dough gathers into a ball and turns around the bowl 15 to 20 times. Turn the dough into a greased bowl, turning to coat the dough completely. Cover and let the dough rest for 15 minutes.

Turn the dough out onto a floured board and pat out to make a rough rectangle. Sprinkle with the raisins and other fruit. Fold the dough over the fruit, kneading the fruit into the dough. Place the dough back into the greased bowl and let rise, covered, for 1 hour or until doubled.

Punch the dough down and shape into a round ball. Place into a greased 9-inch round pan. Let rise, covered, until almost doubled, about 1 hour. Brush with the beaten egg. Preheat the oven to 375°F and bake for 20 to 25 minutes, until a wooden skewer inserted into the center of the bread comes out clean. Turn out of the pan onto a wire rack to cool.

In a small bowl, mix the confectioners' sugar, cream, and almond extract to make a smooth icing. Spread over the top of the warm loaf. Sprinkle with sliced almonds.

Makes 1 loaf

Finnish Pulla

 The aroma of this bread brings me back to my childhood when my mother baked "biscuit" on Saturdays. We didn't call it pulla until Aunt Ida demanded it. "Biscuit is not a Finnish word," she insisted. "It's English. This bread is pulla." Some American Finns still call it nisu, which stems back to the old Finnish word for wheat. Wheat was such a precious commodity in the Scandinavian countries that it was only used to make fancy breads and cakes for the holidays. Coffee breads are still called "wheat bread" throughout Scandinavia. Pulla is not just for celebrating, but no celebration or holiday is complete without it.

For Christmas and other holidays Finns often add golden raisins and candied orange peel to the dough. For variety, I like to shape pulla into individual buns and stuff them with butter, sugar, and almonds.

 CARDAMOM

For the best flavor, crush cardamom seeds fresh each time you use them. Cardamom is available in pod form (you need to open up the pods to remove the black seeds), or you can buy the loose seeds. Cardamom that is already ground has lost much of its flavor. To grind cardamom, use a mortar and pestle, a grinder/processor or a coffee grinder. (I like to use the coffee grinder so that my next pot of coffee will have just a hint of cardamom flavor.)

2 cups milk

2 packages (5½ teaspoons) active dry yeast

¾ cup sugar

5½ to 6 cups unbleached all-purpose flour

2 teaspoons salt

2 teaspoons freshly ground cardamom (see Box)

3 large eggs

½ cup (1 stick) unsalted butter, melted

Glaze

1 large egg, beaten with 2 tablespoons milk

Pearl sugar and sliced almonds, for sprinkling

Filling for Sugar-Almond Butter Buns (optional)

½ cup (1 stick) unsalted butter, chilled and cut into 36 cubes

6 tablespoons sugar

In a small heavy saucepan, scald the milk over medium-high heat, then remove from the heat and cool to very warm (130°F).

In a large mixing bowl or the bowl of an electric mixer, combine the yeast, sugar, 4 cups of the flour, the salt, and cardamom. Add the milk, eggs, and butter and beat until the dough is soft and satiny smooth. Add enough of the remaining flour to make a soft dough. Let stand, covered, for 30 minutes.

Turn the dough out onto a lightly floured surface and knead until smooth and satiny and small blisters appear on the surface of the dough, about 10 minutes. Place in a greased bowl and turn to coat the dough. Let rise, covered, in a warm place until doubled, about 1 hour. Turn the dough out onto a lightly oiled work surface.

One Large Braided Ring

Divide the dough into 3 parts. Roll each part out to make strands 36 inches long. Braid the strands together and place on a parchment-covered or lightly greased baking sheet in the form of a wreath. Pinch the ends together to seal.

Two Straight Braided Loaves

Divide the dough into halves and divide the halves into thirds. Roll each part into a strand 30 inches long. Braid 3 strands together and place the braid on one end of a large parchment-covered or lightly greased baking sheet. Form the second braid and place it on the baking sheet about 4 inches away from the other braid. Let rise until puffy, about 45 minutes. Brush the braids with the egg mixture and sprinkle with the sugar and sliced almonds.

Sugar-Almond Butter Buns

Divide the dough into 36 equal-size pieces and shape each into a round ball. Place on 2 parchment-covered or lightly greased baking sheets, evenly spaced. Cover and let rise in a warm place until puffy, 35 to 45 minutes. Press a small cube of butter into the center of each bun. Top each with ½ teaspoon sugar. Brush with the egg glaze and sprinkle with pearl sugar or sliced almonds or a combination.

Preheat the oven to 375°F for the braids or to 400°F for the buns. Bake braided loaves for 25 to 30 minutes or until golden. Bake the buns for 12 to 14 minutes until golden. Do not overbake. Cool on a wire rack.

Makes 1 large wreath, 2 braids, or 36 buns

Pulla People

My mother used to make these little dough people for us. She didn't have a cookie cutter, so she used her all-purpose kitchen knife to slash pieces of dough to shape the legs, arms, and head of the dough-boys and doughgirls. A large gingerbread person cookie cutter works well. Working with chilled dough is a lot of fun because it is very easy to handle.

    2 packages (5½ teaspoons) active
        dry yeast
    1 cup warm water (105 to 115°F)
    ½ cup (1 stick) unsalted
        butter, melted
    ½ cup sugar
    3 large eggs
    1 teaspoon salt
    1 teaspoon freshly ground cardamom
4 to 4½ cups all-purpose flour
    1 large egg beaten with 2 tablespoons
        milk, for glaze
        Raisins, for garnish

In a large bowl, combine the yeast and warm water. Let stand for 5 minutes or until the yeast foams. Stir in the butter, sugar, eggs, salt, and cardamom. Stir in 4 cups of the flour 1 cup at a time, until the dough is stiff, adding the remaining ½ cup flour if needed. Cover and refrigerate at least 2 hours or up to 4 days.

Lightly grease a baking sheet or cover with parchment paper. Dust the dough with flour and turn out onto a lightly floured surface. Roll or flatten the dough to 1 inch thickness. With a large gingerbread person cookie cutter, cut out people shapes. Place in the prepared pan.

Or cut the dough into 12 parts. Roll each part into a 6 × 3-inch rectangle. With the tip of a knife or with scissors, cut out snips of dough where the person's neck would be, to shape the head. Then, to shape the arms, make cuts about 1 inch lower than the neck, making the cuts on opposite sides of the body. With fingers, smooth out the body of the dough person. Starting from the center of the bottom of the dough, make a 3-inch slash to make the legs. Place in the prepared pan, separating the legs slightly so they will not bake together. Roll out one of the little snips of dough into a ball. Make a little hole where the dough person's nose would be and place the dough into the hole. Roll out the other snip of dough into a skinny strand and place it over the top of the head to make hair. Repeat with the other dough parts.

Let rise, covered, for 45 minutes or until puffy.

Preheat the oven to 375°F. Brush the dough people with the egg glaze, then press raisins into the dough to make eyes, mouths, and buttons. Bake for 12 to 15 minutes or until light brown. Remove from the pan and cool on a wire rack.

Makes 12 pulla people

Short-Cut Refrigerator Danish

Keep this easy pastry on hand in the refrigerator up to 4 days before you bake it. There are many ways you can shape this dough. Make traditional Danish Pastry Rolls (page 212), cinnamon rolls, or try the Raspberry-Almond Christmas Tree (page 211). For the best results, use active dry yeast or compressed yeast rather than rapid-rise yeast.

1½ cups milk
 1 teaspoon freshly ground cardamom (optional)
¼ cup sugar
 1 teaspoon salt
 2 packages (5½ teaspoons) active dry yeast
 2 large eggs, lightly beaten
 3 cups all-purpose flour
1½ cups (3 sticks) unsalted butter, chilled and cut into pieces

Combine the milk and cardamom in a small saucepan and scald over medium-high heat. Remove from the heat and stir in the sugar and salt. Pour into a medium bowl and cool to warm (between 105 and 115°F). Sprinkle the yeast over the top, stir in the eggs, and let stand for 5 minutes, until the yeast foams.

Measure the flour into a large mixing bowl. Using a fork or pastry cutter, cut the butter into the flour until the mixture resembles coarse crumbs. Pour the liquid ingredients over the flour mixture. Mix lightly with a fork until the flour is just moistened. Cover with plastic wrap and refrigerate at least 4 hours or up to 4 days. Shape and bake the dough as directed in one of the following recipes.

Makes 1 Raspberry-Almond Christmas Tree or 24 Danish Pastry Rolls

THE SYMBOLISM OF CHRISTMAS BREADS

Christmas breads are especially beautiful in their shapes, often studded with jewellike fruits and nuts, symbolizing the royalty of the newborn Jesus and that of the visitors from the East. The golden color and aroma of these special breads (from egg and/or saffron) are symbolic of gold, frankincense, and myrrh—the gifts of the three kings (or wisemen or prophets) who visited the manger in Bethlehem.

The wreath shape, in most cultures, symbolizes eternity. Animal shapes, not only for breads but for cookies as well, in the Scandinavian tradition go back to the ancient practice of sacrificing a goat, lamb, or a pig as a burnt offering. The old practice is gone, but the shapes are still part of the baker's art. In Finland, the pig-shaped cookies still hail the beginning of the Advent season.

Raspberry-Almond Christmas Tree

 Your family and guests will have a hard time leaving this delicious coffee cake alone until it is all gone.

 1 recipe Short-Cut Refrigerator
    Danish (see page 210)
½ pound almond paste
½ cup seedless raspberry jam
¼ cup (½ stick) unsalted butter,
    at room temperature
 1 cup confectioners' sugar
 1 tablespoon unsalted butter, melted
1 to 2 tablespoons raspberry-flavored
    liqueur or water

Prepare and refrigerate the pastry as directed. In a small bowl, cream together the almond paste, raspberry jam, and the ¼ cup butter. Set aside.

Turn the dough out onto a lightly floured surface and knead briefly to shape into a ball. With a rolling pin, pound the dough into an evenly thick mass. Roll out to about a 14-inch square. Fold into thirds. Roll out again to about a 24 × 8-inch rectangle that is ½ inch thick. Fold into thirds again, folding the short sides in toward the center, resulting in a square shape. Roll out again to make a 14-inch square. Fold into thirds to form a long and narrow rectangle.

Cut off one-third of the dough from one short end. Fold the remaining dough in half to make a square. Roll the small portion of dough out very thinly to make a rough diamond shape by rolling diagonally from one corner to the other. It should measure 26 inches the long way and about 12 inches the other way. Fold the bottom half up making a Christmas tree shape (the fold will be at the bottom of the tree). Place on a lightly greased cookie sheet.

Roll the remaining dough out to make a 16-inch square. Spread the almond and raspberry filling all the way to the edges. Roll up tightly. With a sharp knife, cut into thirty-two ½-inch slices. Arrange the slices, overlapping slightly, on the pastry base, using one of the slices to make the trunk of the tree. Let rise, covered, until almost doubled, about 1 hour.

Preheat the oven to 350°F. Bake for 25 to 30 minutes, until golden. Remove onto a wire rack to cool.

In a small bowl, mix together the confectioners' sugar, melted butter, and liqueur to make a thin glaze. Drizzle over the warm baked tree.

Makes 1 Christmas Tree Bread

Danish Pastry Rolls

 We simply call them "Danish," but in Denmark there is a separate name for each of the shapes, with no distinction between the many different types of fillings. The traditional fillings range from creamy vanilla and lemon custards to mixtures of candied fruits to almond and hazelnut fillings. Here I offer a variety of fillings—each recipe will fill two dozen Danish—and suggest different ways to shape the pastries. Feel free to mix and match the fillings, shapes, icings, and toppings as you desire. Although the fillings yield different amounts, each will fill one pastry recipe.

1 recipe Short-Cut Refrigerator Danish pastry (see page 210)
1 recipe filling (recipe follows)
1 recipe icing, if desired (recipe follows)
   Topping, if desired (recipe follows)

Prepare and refrigerate the pastry as directed. Prepare one of the following variations. Preheat the oven to 400°F. Cover the pastries and let rise for 30 to 45 minutes, until puffy.

Bake for 12 to 15 minutes, until golden. Remove from the baking sheet and cool on a rack. Drizzle with icing while pastries are warm, if desired.

Makes 24 Danish

Almond or Hazelnut Bear Claws

Divide the pastry into 4 portions. Roll each portion, one at a time, into a 12-inch square. Spread Almond Paste Filling or Hazelnut Filling down the center of the pastry. Fold the top third over the filling; then fold the bottom third over to make a strip about 4 inches wide. Press the pastry to seal it together. Roll lightly to widen the strip and even it out. Cut the dough crosswise into 2-inch pieces. Then make 4 parallel cuts along the long side of each piece, cutting to within ½ inch of the edge. Repeat with the other 3 pieces of dough.

When all pieces have been cut, prepare 2 bowls: Fill one with water and one with sugar. Dip the uppermost side of each bear claw into water, then into sugar. Press sliced almonds onto the top of each bear claw, if desired. Place on a parchment-covered or lightly greased baking sheet with the sugared side up. Let rise and bake as directed.

Vanilla or Lemon Custard Danish Packages

Roll the pastry out to make a 24 × 16-inch rectangle. Cut into twenty-four 4-inch squares. Put a teaspoonful of either Vanilla Custard or Lemon Custard into the center of each square. Fold the 4 corners so that they meet in the center of each square, covering the filling. Press down firmly to seal. Place on a lightly greased or parchment-covered baking sheet. Let rise and bake as directed.

Fruit and Almond Snails

Roll the pastry out to make a 24-inch square. Spread the Fruit and Almond Filling to the edges. Roll the dough up like a jelly roll. Cut into 1-inch slices. Place each piece in the center of a paper cupcake liner. Place the filled cupcake liners on a baking sheet. If you don't wish to use liners, simply place on a lightly greased baking sheet; the snails will not have quite as neat a shape using this method. Let rise and bake as directed.

FILLINGS

Almond Paste Filling

  ½ cup almond paste
  ¼ cup (½ stick) unsalted butter, at room temperature
  ½ cup confectioners' sugar

In a mixing bowl using a wooden spoon or an electric mixer, or in the food processor, cream the almond paste, butter, and sugar together until well blended and smooth. Store in the refrigerator, covered, until ready to use. Allow to return to room temperature before using.

Makes about 1 cup

Hazelnut Filling

  1 cup hazelnuts (filberts)
  1 cup sugar
  2 tablespoons unsalted butter, at room temperature
  1 egg

Preheat the oven to 350°F. Put the nuts on a baking sheet and toast for 8 to 10 minutes or until nuts are crisp and begin to brown. Turn the nuts into a clean terry towel and rub off the brown skins. Turn the nuts into a food processor with the steel blade in place. Process until the nuts are very fine. Add the sugar, butter, and egg and process until smooth. Refrigerate, covered, until ready to use. Allow to return to room temperature before using.

Makes about 2 cups

Vanilla Custard
    1 cup whipping cream
    2 tablespoons all-purpose flour
    3 tablespoons sugar
    2 large egg yolks
    1 teaspoon vanilla

In a small, heavy saucepan, mix the cream, flour, sugar, and egg yolks. Stir over medium heat until the mixture comes to a boil. Cook until thickened. Remove from the heat and stir in the vanilla. Cool, cover, and refrigerate until ready to use.

Makes about 1 cup

Lemon Custard
    ¼ cup (½ stick) unsalted butter
    1 teaspoon grated lemon zest
    ⅓ cup fresh lemon juice
    ¾ cup sugar
    1 tablespoon cornstarch
    2 large egg yolks

In a small, heavy nonaluminum (see Note) saucepan, over medium heat, melt the butter. Add the lemon zest and juice, sugar, cornstarch, and egg yolks. Stir to blend well. Lower the heat to medium-low and cook the custard, stirring constantly until thickened and smooth. Cool, cover, and refrigerate until ready to use. Allow to return to room temperature before using.

Makes about 1 cup

NOTE: Aluminum will discolor the filling.

Fruit and Almond Filling
    1 cup finely chopped candied mixed fruit such as cherries, pineapple, and orange peel
    ⅓ cup finely chopped blanched almonds

In a bowl, stir the fruit and almonds together.

Makes 1⅓ cups

ICINGS AND TOPPINGS

Almond Icing
    1 cup confectioners' sugar
    2 tablespoons water
    1 teaspoon corn oil
    ½ teaspoon almond extract

In a small bowl, stir the sugar with the water, oil, and almond extract until smooth.

Add more water if necessary to make an icing that can be drizzled.

Makes ¹/₂ cup

Coffee Glaze

 1 cup confectioners' sugar
 2 tablespoons hot strong coffee or
  1 teaspoon instant coffee dissolved
  in 2 tablespoons water
 2 tablespoons unsalted butter,
  at room temperature

In a small bowl, stir all of the ingredients together until smooth. Store in the refrigerator, covered, until ready to use. Allow to return to room temperature before using.

Makes ¹/₂ cup

Toasted Sliced Almonds

Preheat the oven to 350°F. Place sliced almonds on a baking sheet. Toast the nuts for 8 to 10 minutes. Remove from the oven and allow to cool on the baking sheet.

 PEARL SUGAR

Pearl sugar is available in food shops that carry Scandinavian ingredients. It is usually sold in one-pound cartons. If you cannot find pearl sugar, substitute coarsely crushed sugar cubes.

Mexican Three Kings Bread, or Rosca de Reyes

 Garnished with candied fruits, this rich, fruited bread is served on King's Day, January 6, the day that the Three Kings brought Jesus their gifts. Traditionally, there is a little baby doll or a wrapped coin hidden in the cake. Whoever gets the prize must host a party on February 2, which is El Dia de la Candelaria (the Day of the Candle Mass). Mexican bakers use lard for the shortening, which results in a characteristic texture, crust, and flavor. If you'd rather, you can use shortening, butter, or margarine; however, the bread's characteristics will be altered, but you'll still have a delicious bread. This is really more of a yeast-raised cake than a bread; no kneading is necessary.

 2 packages (5¹/₂ teaspoons) active
  dry yeast
 ¹/₄ cup warm water (105 to 115°F)
 ²/₃ cup milk
 ¹/₂ cup sugar
 1¹/₂ teaspoons salt
 ¹/₃ cup lard, shortening, butter,
  or margarine, at room temperature
 3 large eggs, beaten
 4 cups all-purpose flour
 2 cups candied fruits or raisins
  Melted butter or lard for
  brushing loaf

Icing and Decoration

1 cup confectioners' sugar
2 to 3 tablespoons milk, cream, or
  water
  Candied fruits or pecan or
  walnut halves

In a small bowl, dissolve the yeast in the warm water. In a small heavy saucepan, bring the milk to a boil over medium-high heat. In large bowl, combine the milk, sugar, salt, and shortening. Cool to lukewarm. Add the yeast mixture, eggs, and 2 cups of the flour; beat with a wooden spoon or an electric mixer until smooth and satiny. With a wooden spoon stir in 2 cups more flour and the candied fruits or raisins. Mix until stiff and smooth and all the flour has been incorporated into the dough. Scrape down the bowl with a rubber spatula to work all the flour into the dough. Cover with plastic wrap and let rise until doubled, about 1 hour.

Grease 2 tube pans. Divide the dough into 2 parts. On a lightly floured surface, shape each half into a 20-inch-long log. Place the prepared pans so the ends touch. Tuck a tiny ovenproof china doll or foilwrapped coin into each loaf, if desired; cover with dough so they will not show. Let rise, covered, until doubled in bulk, about 1 to 1¼ hours.

Preheat the oven to 375°F. Bake the rings for 25 to 30 minutes or until golden and a toothpick inserted in the center comes out clean. Brush the rings with the melted butter and turn them out of the pans onto a wire rack to cool.

For the icing, in a small bowl mix the confectioners' sugar with enough milk to make a mixture that can be drizzled. Drizzle the icing over the cooled rings, then decorate with bits of candied fruit or nuts.

Makes 2 rings

Stollen

Stollen (pronounced shtoh-luhn) is a traditional Christmas bread from Germany. The bread varies slightly from one area of Germany to another, so that one hears of Dresden, Bavarian, or other regional stollens. The bread is often stuffed with fruits and sometimes nuts. The traditional shape is that of a large, folded oval that resembles a large Parker House roll. This version has been our family's favorite. I often make it a month or six weeks ahead and then freeze it. On Christmas morning, I unwrap it, and reheat it in a warm (300°F) oven, and we enjoy it with coffee and hot chocolate. This recipe makes two loaves, and I usually give one as a gift with reheating instructions written on a Christmas card.

Dough

1 cup mixed chopped candied fruits
½ cup golden raisins
½ cup currants
½ cup halved candied cherries

ON FREEZING BREADS

To preserve freshness, breads should be frozen as soon as possible after they have cooled. I do not like to freeze breads that are hot from the oven because they can get soggy and lose their beautiful baked sheen when they are wrapped while they are still warm. To freeze, cool the breads on a rack. Wrap them airtight in plastic or in a large bag with a firm closure (such as the type with a zipper lock), squeezing out as much air as possible. For really fancy breads, I like to first wrap them tightly in plastic, then slip them into a comfortably large freezer bag, leaving a little air in the bag to act as a cushion to prevent damage in the freezer. If the breads have a frosting, it will be prettier if you frost them just before serving, after reheating.

There are two ways in which you can thaw bread. One is to remove the wrapped bread and let it stand, still wrapped, at room temperature for about one hour. Or, if time is short, unwrap the bread, place it in a 300°F oven for fifteen to twenty minutes or until it is heated through.

¼ cup diced citron (see Note on page 201)

¼ cup dark rum

2 packages (5½ teaspoons) active dry yeast

5 cups all-purpose flour

½ cup sugar

½ teaspoon salt

1 cup milk

¾ cup (1½ sticks) unsalted butter, chilled and cut into pieces

3 large eggs, beaten

Filling and Finishing

5 tablespoons unsalted butter, melted

4 tablespoons granulated sugar

2 to 3 tablespoons confectioners' sugar

2 to 3 tablespoons brandy or rum

To make the dough, combine the candied fruits, raisins, currants, candied cherries, citron, and rum in a bowl, and mix to coat all the fruits with rum. Marinate at least 1 hour. In a large bowl or the bowl of an electric mixer, mix the yeast with 3 cups of the flour, the sugar, and salt. In a heavy saucepan, heat the milk to boiling over medium-high heat. Remove from the heat. Add butter and stir until the butter is melted and the mixture has cooled to very warm (130°F).

Add the milk mixture and eggs to the flour mixture and beat until the mixture is smooth, satiny, and has an elastic quality to it. Cover the bowl and let the dough rest for 15 minutes.

Stir in the remaining flour a cup at a time and mix until the dough is stiff. If using a mixer with a dough hook, knead the dough for 5 minutes at low speed, scraping the sides of the bowl. Or turn out onto a floured board and knead, adding flour as necessary to make a light and springy dough. Knead or mix in the fruit-rum mixture. Place the dough in an oiled bowl, cover, and let rise for 1 to 1½ hours, until doubled.

Lightly grease a baking sheet or cover with parchment paper. To fill and finish the stollen, punch down the dough and divide into 2 parts. On a lightly oiled surface, pat each half into an oval about 12 inches long and 8 inches wide at its widest point. Brush each oval with ½ tablespoon melted butter and sprinkle with 1 tablespoon of the granulated sugar.

Make a crease down the length of each oval. Fold each loaf in half lengthwise along the crease to enclose the sugared surface. Place the loaves on a baking sheet spaced well apart. Cover and let rise until puffy, but not doubled, 30 to 45 minutes. Brush each loaf with ½ tablespoon melted butter and sprinkle with 1 tablespoon of the granulated sugar.

Preheat the oven to 375°F and bake for 20 to 25 minutes or until a wooden skewer inserted in the center of the loaf comes out clean and dry. If the stollen begins to brown excessively, cover lightly with foil to finish baking. While the loaves are still hot, brush each loaf with ½ tablespoon melted butter and sprinkle with 1 to 1½ tablespoons confectioners' sugar. Drizzle each loaf with 1 to 1½ tablespoons brandy or rum. Remove from the sheet and cool on a wire rack. Brush with the remaining butter. Wrap the loaves in plastic, then in foil and store in a cool place for 2 to 3 days until ready to serve or freeze up to 3 months.

Makes 2 loaves

Norwegian Potato Lefse

Our Norwegian friends make this potato lefse early in December so that it is ready for special holiday meals, snacking, and celebrations. They make this flat crepelike bread throughout the year for special celebrations, too, like weddings, anniversaries, baptisms, and special birthdays. When they serve it with cookies, cakes, and coffee, they butter the lefse, sprinkle it with either plain sugar or cinnamon sugar, roll it up tightly, and then cut the rolls into 1-inch pieces. For picnics in the summertime, our friends roll lefse around hot dogs, but for special holiday meals, it is simply buttered, folded, and enjoyed for its own flavor. Lefse rolling pins have narrow grooves carved into them which either go lengthwise on the roller or around the roller. *In the old days, people carved their own rolling pins out of a 16- to 18-inch log of birch, usually with the grooves going the length of the pin. Today, the rolling pins are commercially grooved on lathes and the grooves go around the pin.*

> 5 to 6 large (2 pounds) russet potatoes,peeled and diced
> 1 teaspoon salt
> 2 tablespoons unsalted butter, at room temperature
> 1½ to 2 cups all-purpose flour

In a medium saucepan over medium heat, cook the potatoes in water to cover until tender but not mushy, about 20 minutes. Drain well. Press the potatoes through a ricer or grate finely. (There should be 3⅓ cups riced potatoes.) In a large bowl, stir the potatoes, salt, and butter together. Cool to room temperature. Stir in 1½ cups flour, then add enough of the remaining flour to make a stiff dough.

Divide the dough into 4 parts. Divide each part into 4 equal pieces to make 16 portions of dough in all. Preheat a large electric griddle to 400°F or heat a large skillet over medium-high heat. On a lightly floured surface, roll 1 piece of dough at a time to make a paper-thin 10- or 11-inch circle, preferably using a grooved lefse rolling pin to get an authentic gridlike texture. Bake the dough circle on the dry, preheated griddle or skillet, 1 to 2 minutes on each side until brown in spots. The lefse will look dry, but will be flexible, not crisp. Fold in half, then in half again. Stack on a piece of waxed paper. Repeat with the remaining pieces of dough. To serve, unfold and spread with butter. To freeze, do not butter; wrap the folded breads airtight and freeze for up to 3 months. Thaw, wrapped. Serve warm, reheating in a low oven, or at room temperature.

Makes 16 lefses

Swedish Christmas Limpa

The Christmas season in Scandinavia begins *on Christmas Eve. This is when all the special cheeses, pressed meats, cold-sliced meats, and sausages that have been prepared for the season are laid out on the buffet tables. This rye bread is among the holiday specialties. Seasoned with orange, anise, and molasses and made with a strong Swedish malt beer (vört) it has a distinctive flavor that goes well with the foods of the Christmas smorgasbord. In old Sweden, it was traditional to make an elaborately shaped loaf of bread using this dough, sculpted with ropes, which became the centerpiece of the holiday table.*

4 cups dark or medium rye flour

2 packages (5½ teaspoons) active dry yeast

1 tablespoon sugar

1 teaspoon salt

½ cup chopped candied orange peel

2 tablespoons freshly grated orange zest

2 tablespoons ground aniseed or fennel seeds

3 tablespoons lard (see Note) or unsalted butter

1 (12-ounce) bottle dark stout beer

1 cup warm water

¾ cup dark molasses

2 cups bread flour or unbleached all-purpose flour

Glaze

2 tablespoons molasses

2 tablespoons water

In a large mixing bowl, mix the rye flour, yeast, sugar, salt, candied orange peel, orange zest, and aniseed or fennel seeds. Heat the lard or butter, beer, water, and molasses in a saucepan until very warm (130°F). Make a well in the center of the flour mixture, add the liquids, and mix until the dough is smooth and firm. Mix in the bread or all-purpose flour until completely incorporated and the dough is stiff. Cover and let rise in a warm place until almost doubled, about 1 hour.

Punch the dough down and pinch off 2 balls of dough, each about 3 inches in diameter; set aside. Grease a baking sheet. Shape the remaining dough into a smooth ball. Place in the prepared pan and flatten into a 10-inch round.

Gently roll each of the 3-inch balls between your hands to make a 15-inch-long rope. With a razor blade or a sharp floured knife, cut a 5-inch-long slash into each end of the 2 ropes. Place the ropes on the loaf, crossing them at the center; do not press down. Curl the slashed sections away from the center of each rope.

Let the bread rise in a warm place, covered, until almost doubled, about 1 hour.

Preheat the oven to 350°F. Bake the bread for 35 to 45 minutes or until a skewer inserted in the center of the loaf comes out clean and dry. To make the glaze, mix the molasses with water. Brush the loaf about halfway through baking with half of the glaze. Remove the bread from the oven and cool on a wire rack. Brush with the remaining glaze.

Makes 1 large loaf

NOTE: For the most authentic flavor and texture use lard. Bread made with butter will be good, but the texture of the crust will not be as tender.

Spiced Sweet Potato Muffins with Walnut Streusel

 This is adapted from Eric Copage's book Kwanzaa, *which offers a vivid and detailed description of this African-American holiday. Kwanzaa is a non-religious holiday designed to celebrate the African heritage of black Americans. It's celebrated from the day after Christmas to New Year's.*

There are no specified foods for this holiday, but most of the foods reflect a Southern (as in these muffins, which are made with sweet potatoes), Caribbean, Creole, or African theme. These are delicious, spicy, and soft-textured muffins with a crunchy topping.

1 sweet potato or yam
½ cup milk
2 large eggs, beaten
¼ cup (½ stick) unsalted butter, melted
2 cups all-purpose flour
½ cup sugar
1 tablespoon baking powder
1 teaspoon freshly ground nutmeg
1 teaspoon freshly ground cardamom
½ teaspoon salt

Walnut Streusel

2 tablespoons coarsely chopped walnuts
2 tablespoons packed brown sugar
2 tablespoons all-purpose flour
¼ teaspoon ground cinnamon
1 tablespoon unsalted butter, at room temperature

Preheat the oven to 400°F. Butter 12 muffin cups or line with paper liners.

Peel and cube the potato. Place into a saucepan, add water to cover, and cook over medium heat until just tender, about 20 minutes. Drain, cool, and mash in a mixing bowl. You should have about 1 cup mashed potato.

Stir together the sweet potato and milk. Beat in the eggs and butter. In another bowl, mix the flour, sugar, baking powder, nutmeg, cardamom, and salt. Stir the dry ingredients into the potato mixture just until blended.

Make the streusel in a small bowl. Stir the walnuts, brown sugar, flour, and cinnamon together. Add the butter; mix until crumbly. Spoon the batter into the muffin cups, filling them two-thirds full. Sprinkle with the streusel mixture and gently pat it .

Bake for 20 to 25 minutes. Remove from the cups and cool on a wire rack.

Makes 12 muffins

A FANCY COOKIE SAMPLER

BAKING COOKIES AND COOKIE-BAKING TIPS

Although I never learned her name, there was one woman who has always been my "Christmas cookie queen." She was the "ice cream lady," the one who handed out samples of ice cream at the supermarket. Each December she kept me up to date on the progress of her Christmas cookie baking. Her goal was always to make two dozen different kinds of cookies. She gave them as gifts, and presented them like boxes of chocolates. Tiny fancy cookies, nestled in bonbon cups in flat boxes. Each year she gave more and more of them away to friends and neighbors, shut-ins, and people in nursing homes. She collected pretty boxes during the year, covered them with gift wrap, and bought colorful fluted paper cups.

Baking fancy cookies is time-consuming but very satisfying when you step back to admire your work all displayed on a beautiful cookie platter. When you break

the work up into sections, it is a lot more manageable. It isn't a new idea, but all tedious work makes perfect party activity. Every year at holiday time, the women at our church get together to make their old-time Norwegian specialties in the church kitchen. They bake hundreds of rosettes, krumkake, butter cookies, breads, and lefse, all in one day! They have a wonderful time making all these delicious baked goods mass-production style.

I have my own method of individual "mass production." That is, I group the work, mixing butter cookie doughs one day, shaping and baking them on another day. I usually freeze cookies until I have time to do the final touches of decorating and finishing them. I do all "iron work" at once, such as pizzelle and krumkake. If I decide to make deep-fried pastries, I will do them all the same day, too, to save me from cleaning up and cleaning out the resulting odors for more than one day.

The advantages to grouping the work are obvious. Mixing the doughs usually requires similar equipment: measuring cups, measuring spoons, a bowl, a hand mixer, a food processor, and a wooden spoon. I scrape the dough into a heavy-duty plastic bag and refrigerate or freeze it for baking later. Butter cookie doughs scrape cleanly out of the bowl, so clean you don't even need to wash the bowl between batches. I keep measuring cups right in the flour and sugar containers when I'm on a baking spree.

Many cookie doughs need to be refrigerated before shaping and baking. There is good reason for this step. It gives the butter flavor a chance to develop in a butter cookie dough. Spicy cookie dough mellows and blends during refrigeration. Most cookies actually taste better when the dough has "aged" for a day or two before shaping and baking, and chilled dough is easier to handle.

It is a good idea to mix all the similar kinds of dough in a day: shaped cookie dough, rolled cookie dough, drop cookie dough, and so on. Wrap each of the doughs tightly in plastic and either refrigerate or freeze them. Start with light-colored dough and continue with darker doughs, such as those that contain spices and cocoa or chocolate. This way you can mix several kinds of dough without having to wash the equipment between each batch. But, if you make many doughs ahead, be sure to label and date them!

Shape and bake all the similar cookies at one time. Bake all the cut-out cookies one day, molded or shaped cookies another, drop cookies on another day, and so on.

Almond Sandbakkels

 Sandbakkels, cookies that are baked in a tiny fluted tin, are a Scandinavian classic. This recipe is from my friend Peg Fox, who makes them with a little brown sugar to give them a caramel flavor. These small shells are usually served with their pretty bottoms up. Some people might fill them with jam or whipped cream, but I like to serve them just plain because they taste so good.

   1 cup (2 sticks) unsalted butter
  ½ cup granulated sugar
  ½ cup packed light brown sugar
  1 large egg
  ½ teaspoon almond extract
  1 teaspoon vanilla
  ⅓ cup blanched almonds, finely ground
2 to 2½ cups all-purpose flour

In a large bowl, cream the butter and sugars until smooth. Beat in the egg, almond extract, and vanilla until light and fluffy. Stir

Baking cookies with kids of all ages is an enjoyable activity as long as you keep your expectations in focus. Very little children might not even understand what they are trying to do, but they'll enjoy the experience. I believe kids of all ages can have fun in the kitchen. Here is a list of things that you might try doing with kids of different ages, starting with the very young.

1. Very young children (three to four years old) can help by dumping measured ingredients into a mixing bowl. You can offer to let them stir it a little. Once the dough is mixed (which you will probably have to finish yourself), they can help by rolling dough into balls or strands (don't expect perfection). Kids this age might not be able to handle a rolling pin yet.

2. Preschoolers (four to five years old) can probably assist in measuring ingredients, mixing the dough, and by rolling small pieces of dough out with a rolling pin. They may even be able to use cookie cutters to make shapes, although you will have to transfer them to the baking sheet. (All kids are different and learn coordination at different ages, so again, don't expect perfection.) Kids this age love to spread frosting on cookies and to decorate them with raisins, gumdrops, sprinkles, chocolate chips, colored sugar, and other decorations.

3. Depending on their age, kids in grade school (ages six and up) can help decide what cookies to make. They may be able to read and interpret the recipe. Under supervision, they can handle getting out all of the tools, help set the oven temperature, measure out the ingredients, and mix the dough. Some kids are incredibly precise in shaping cookies to the exact size, while for others, it isn't as important. (Expect variations among kids and cookies.) Kids of these ages will enjoy making cookies designated for gifts. They can help decorate, package, and deliver the gifts to the recipient.

Mail deliverer

Teachers

Janitor at school

Bus driver

Grandma and Grandpa

Uncles and aunts

People in nursing homes

Children in special homes

Prisoners (they are often forgotten)

Families of prisoners

People living alone

UPS, Federal Express, and other courier service deliverers

Hairdresser and manicurist

Friends

Neighbors

Elevator operator (in your apartment or office)

Baby-sitter or day care provider

---

in the almonds and flour; mix well. Wrap the dough in plastic wrap and chill for 1 hour.

Preheat the oven to 350°F. Butter small, fancy fluted molds or sandbakkel tins. Divide the dough into 4 equal portions. Shape each portion into a log and cut each log into 12 equal pieces. Press each piece into a sandbakkel tin using your thumbs to make a thin, even shell of dough in each.

Place the shells on a baking sheet. Bake for 10 to 12 minutes or until light golden. Invert the tins onto a wire rack. Let cool for 3 to 4 minutes, then gently tap the bottom of each tin to remove the cookies.

Makes about 4 dozen sandbakkels

Amaretti

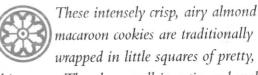

These intensely crisp, airy almond macaroon cookies are traditionally wrapped in little squares of pretty, thin paper. They keep well in a tin and make a wonderful gift packed in a glass jar.

1 large egg white

2 teaspoons amaretto or almond liqueur

1⅔ cups finely ground almonds

1½ cups confectioners' sugar
Confectioners' sugar, for dusting

Preheat the oven to 350°F. Line baking sheets with parchment paper. In a small bowl whisk together the egg white and amaretto until light and frothy but not stiff.

GETTING KIDS INVOLVED
IN COOKIE BAKING

Many cooks today began their kitchen careers by baking cookies. Getting kids involved depends on their age and ability to comprehend what they are doing. Very young children may simply have fun handling cookie dough. Cookie baking is a good time to talk about family traditions and fond holiday memories. Kids love to hear about their parents' childhood and life in the "olden" days (even though it doesn't seem very long ago to us).

What can you allow kids to do?

Ask children which of two recipes they'd rather make. Kids respond to having a choice.

Involve the kids in the preparation. Have them help make shopping lists, check equipment needed, and mark the baking day on the calendar. Kids love to have something to look forward to.

Structure the activity so that the tasks are clear: reading the recipe, lining up the tools and equipment, lining up the ingredients, measuring the ingredients, and following the steps of the recipe. Kids understand things much better when the directions are clear.

Talk about the ingredients and what they do. Taste the ingredients. Taste the dough once the ingredients are put together. See if kids can identify the various ingredients in the mixture by taste.

Have kids help package cookies, store them, and wrap them for gifts. Let them designate which cookies will be gifts for which people, and be sure to ask them why.

Have kids help deliver the gifts. Give them a chance to talk about the cookies they baked especially for that person.

Combine the almonds and sugar in a large bowl and add the egg white mixture. Mix until dough is pastelike.

Shape rounded tablespoons of dough into 36 balls; place on the baking sheet about 2 inches apart. Bake for 15 minutes or until light brown. Dust the hot cookies with confectioners' sugar. Slide the cookies off the baking sheet still on the parchment paper onto a wire rack to cool. Store airtight in a cool place for up to 6 weeks.

Makes 36 amaretti

Brown Sugar–Pecan-Praline Cookies

When time is short and I need to produce a lot of cookies, this is the recipe I choose. The cookie base gets its butterscotch flavor from brown sugar. The dough is rolled out directly on an ungreased baking sheet, scored, and topped with pecan praline before baking.

Dough

- 1 cup (2 sticks) unsalted butter, at room temperature
- ½ cup packed brown sugar
- ½ cup granulated sugar
- 1 teaspoon vanilla
- 1 large egg
- ½ teaspoon baking soda
- ¼ teaspoon salt
- 3 cups all-purpose flour

Pecan Praline

- ½ cup heavy cream or undiluted evaporated milk
- ½ cup packed brown sugar
- ½ cup chopped pecans

Chocolate Drizzle

- 2 ounces white chocolate, chopped
- 2 ounces semisweet or bittersweet chocolate, chopped

Make the dough. In a large bowl, cream the butter and sugars. Add the vanilla, egg, baking soda, and salt. Beat until light and fluffy. Stir in the flour until the dough is stiff and well blended. Shape into a ball, wrap in plastic, and chill for 1 hour or refrigerate up to 4 days.

To make the praline, bring the cream, brown sugar, and pecans to a boil in a heavy saucepan over medium-high heat. Boil for 2 to 3 minutes, stirring, until thick. Remove from the heat and cool.

Preheat the oven to 375°F. Divide the dough into 4 pieces. Shape each piece into a smooth log about 12 inches long. Place logs lengthwise on an ungreased, rimless cookie sheet, about 5 inches apart. Flatten with your palm. With a rolling pin, roll out the dough

A holiday cookie swap party can be a lot of fun for all who take part in it. Each of four to six friends selects and bakes a variety of cookies, and at the party, everybody trades cookies and goes home with a much greater variety. The more organized you can be, the better. It may be preferable for the cookie recipes to be preselected by the group or by one member of the group so that there will be no overlap. Of course, the most successful cookie swaps result when everybody agrees on the rules (such as no "ordinary" oatmeal or chocolate chip cookies).

to the length of the cookie sheet and 3 inches wide. The 2 strips should be about 2 inches apart. Trim the ends and sides to make straight-sided rectangles. With a straight-edged knife, score the dough into 1½-inch squares. Drop about ½ teaspoonful of the pecan praline filling onto the center of each square. Bake for 10 to 12 minutes or until golden on the edges. Remove from the oven, and while still warm separate the cookies along the score marks using a straight-edged knife. Place the white and semisweet or bittersweet chocolate into separate little bowls. Place over hot water until the chocolates have melted. Drizzle the chocolate over the cookies decoratively. Leave the cookies in place on the cookie sheet and cool until the chocolate is set.

Makes 4 to 5 dozen cookies

Candy Cane Cookies

These are fun to make. My friend Peg Fox makes these every year in a fancy cookie class that she teaches. She uses these daintily shaped treats to decorate her elaborate cookie plates.

¾ cup (1½ sticks) unsalted butter, softened
¾ cup sugar
1 large egg
2 cups all-purpose flour
½ teaspoon vanilla or coconut extract
⅓ cup finely pulverized coconut (see Note)
½ teaspoon peppermint extract
Red food color

Preheat the oven to 350°F. Cover 2 baking sheets with parchment paper.

In a large bowl or the bowl of an electric mixer, cream the butter and sugar until smooth. Add the egg and beat until light. Add the flour until a smooth dough forms. Divide the dough into 2 parts. Add the vanilla or coconut extract and the pulverized coconut to 1 part and mix well. Add the peppermint extract and a few drops of red food color to the other half.

Working with a small amount of each batch at a time, roll the dough into ¼-inch-wide strips, trimming to even the sides. Cut the strips into 3-inch lengths and twist a red strand with a white strand for each cookie. Place on the parchment-covered baking sheet and shape into candy canes; place about 2 inches apart.

Bake for 8 to 10 minutes or until just barely brown. Slide the parchment paper off the cookie sheet onto a wire rack to cool.

Makes 5 dozen cookies

NOTE: To pulverize the coconut, put it into a blender or food processor and run the motor until the coconut is very fine.

Caramel Acorns

 These carmel-dipped little cookies are quite pretty, especially when presented in little paper bonbon cups.

1 cup (2 sticks) unsalted butter, at room temperature
¾ cup packed brown sugar
3 large egg yolks
1 teaspoon vanilla
2¾ cups all-purpose flour
½ teaspoon baking powder

Caramel for Dipping the Cookies

1 cup sugar
1 cup whipping cream
2 tablespoons dark corn syrup
½ cup finely chopped walnuts or pecans

Preheat the oven to 350°F. Cover 2 baking sheets with parchment paper.

In a large mixing bowl, cream the butter with the brown sugar until smooth, then add the egg yolks and vanilla and beat until light. In a small bowl, stir the flour and baking powder together and add to the creamed mixture; mix until the dough is smooth. Roll the dough into small, 1-inch balls. Pinch with 2 fingers and a thumb to make a small point at the top of each. Place, pointed side up, 1 inch apart on the baking sheet. Bake for 10 to 12 minutes, until light brown and firm. Remove from the oven and slide the cookies

When selecting cookies to serve on a cookie platter, keep in mind the principles of variety and contrast: For instance, select cookies that have different shapes (rounds, squares, stars, logs, sandwiches, and curls), textures (soft, crispy, and chewy), and flavors (vanilla, chocolate, spicy, fruity, and nutty). Don't forget to include cookies that offer a splash of color to the tray. An uneven number of varieties is another classic rule. Scandinavians try to serve three, five, or seven varieties of cookies on their cookie trays.

on the parchment off onto a wire rack to cool.

Make the caramel. In a large saucepan, combine the sugar and whipping cream. Heat to boiling over medium-high heat and boil until the mixture is at the hard-ball stage (260°F). Stir in the corn syrup. Place the chopped nuts in a small bowl or on a plate.

Dip the cookies, holding them by the point, first into the warm caramel, and then into the chopped nuts. Place on waxed paper and let stand until firm.

Makes about 60 cookies

Christmas Bells

Simpler to shape than you'd think, the dough is chilled like an icebox cookie, sliced, then folded to make a bell shape. A cherry is the clapper.

- ¾ cup (1½ sticks) unsalted butter, at room temperature
- ½ cup sugar
- 1 large egg yolk
- 1¾ cups all-purpose flour
- ½ teaspoon vanilla
- 12 glacéed or maraschino cherries, drained and halved
- Confectioners' sugar, for dusting

In a large bowl, cream together the butter and sugar. Add the egg yolk and beat until fluffy. Stir in the flour and vanilla until the dough is smooth. Shape the dough into a roll 1½ inches thick. Wrap in plastic and chill for at least 2 hours or up to 24 hours.

Preheat the oven to 375°F. Cover 2 baking sheets with parchment paper.

Unwrap the cookie dough and cut the log into ¼-inch slices. Place the slices 1 inch apart on the baking sheet. Fold 2 edges of each cookie over the center so that they overlap and each cookie has a point on one end and a rounded bell shape on the other. Tuck a cherry half into each cookie. Bake for 10 to 12 minutes or just until the cookies are pale golden. Slide the parchment paper off the baking sheet onto the countertop with the cookies on top. When the cookies are cool, dust with the confectioners' sugar. Store in an airtight container.

Makes about 2 dozen cookies

Brown Sugar Christmas Trees

These are the cookies I bake every year when there's hardly any time for fussing. The basic procedure is that of mass production. The dough is rolled out right on the cookie sheet and scored into elongated triangles. I press an almond into the triangles, turning them into a miniature Christmas trees. After baking, I drizzle them with green and white icing and sprinkle them with colored nonpareils.

  1 cup (2 sticks) unsalted butter,
    at room temperature

  ½ cup packed brown sugar
  ½ cup granulated sugar
  1 teaspoon vanilla
  1 large egg
  ½ teaspoon baking soda
  ¼ teaspoon salt
  3 cups all-purpose flour
  ¾ cup slivered almonds

White Icing
  1 cup confectioners' sugar
  2 tablespoons cream or milk
  ½ teaspoon vanilla

Green Icing
  1 cup confectioners' sugar
  2 tablespoons green crème de menthe

Decoration
  Colored sugar or nonpareils

In a large mixing bowl, cream the butter with the sugars until smooth. Add the vanilla, egg, baking soda, and salt and beat until light and fluffy.

Mix in the flour thoroughly until the dough is stiff and shape into a ball. Divide the ball into 4 parts and wrap separately in plastic wrap. Chill for 30 minutes.

Preheat the oven to 375°F.

Remove the dough from the refrigerator 2 pieces at a time, and divide each part in half. Knead each piece slightly and shape each into a roll 2 inches in diameter.

Working with 2 rolls at a time, place the rolls lengthwise on a 16 × 11-inch rimless baking sheet and flatten with the palms of your hands. Roll the 2 strips of dough out right on the baking sheet to make each 3 inches wide and 16 inches long, spaced about 2 inches apart. With a straight-edged knife, score into elongated triangles. Leave the dough in place and press a piece of slivered almond onto the edge of the short side of each triangle, where the trunk of the tree should be.

Bake for 10 to 12 minutes or until light brown. Remove from the oven and separate the triangles with a straight-edged knife along the scored lines while still warm, but leave them in place. Trim the uneven edges to straighten while cookies are still warm.

Mix the ingredients for the white icing and the green icing in 2 separate small bowls. Drizzle the icings decoratively over the Christmas trees and while the icing is still wet, sprinkle with the colored sugar or nonpareils. Let the icing set.

Makes about 64 cookies

Coconut Melting Moments

 Cathy, our daughter, loves anything made with coconut. I think she was the original Mounds Bar kid. So, to please her, I added ground coconut to this old favorite recipe.

> ¾ cup (1½ sticks) unsalted butter, at room temperature
> ½ cup confectioners' sugar
> 1 cup all-purpose flour
> ¼ cup cornstarch
> ¼ teaspoon salt
> 1 cup finely ground flaked coconut Confectioners' sugar, for dusting

Preheat the oven to 325°F. Cover 2 baking sheets with parchment paper.

In a large mixing bowl, cream together the butter and sugar. Add the flour, cornstarch, salt, and coconut and mix until a smooth dough is formed. Wrap in plastic wrap and chill just until the dough firms up enough to handle, 15 to 20 minutes.

Divide the dough into 4 portions. Using your palms, shape each portion into a ½-inch-thick rope and cut each rope into 1-inch pieces. Roll each piece between your palms into a ball and place on the baking sheet, spaced about 1 inch apart. Bake for 12 to 15 minutes, until the cookies are firm to the touch and light brown around the edges. Slide the parchment paper with the cookies on it onto the countertop to cool. Dust the cookies heavily with confectioners' sugar.

Makes about 48 cookies

Fruit Drop Cookies

These are beautiful little bite-size fruitcakes. This is the first cookie I bake in December because when I hide them well, they keep well. I like to leave the fruits and nuts in rather big pieces, so that each cookie looks different. For a really festive appearance, bake them in little paper petit four cups and glaze them with the corn syrup.

½ cup (1 stick) unsalted butter, at room temperature

½ cup packed brown sugar

1 large egg, beaten

1 teaspoon vanilla

1¼ cups all-purpose flour

½ teaspoon baking soda

½ teaspoon salt

½ teaspoon ground cinnamon

2 cups (½ pound) pitted dates, quartered

1 cup diced candied pineapple

1 cup halved candied cherries

½ cup walnut pieces

½ cup pecan halves

½ cup hazelnuts (filberts)

Corn syrup, for glaze (optional)

Preheat the oven to 350°F. Lightly grease 2 baking sheets or cover with parchment paper.

In the bowl of electric mixer, or in a large bowl, cream together the butter and sugar until smooth. Add the egg and vanilla and beat until light. In a small bowl, stir the flour, baking soda, salt, and cinnamon together. In another bowl combine the dates, pineapple, and cherries. Stir the flour mixture, the fruits, and the nuts into the creamed mixture until well combined. Drop the dough by small spoonfuls onto the baking sheets (or into baking cups), spacing them about 2 inches apart.

Bake for 12 to 15 minutes or just until set. If you use parchment paper, slide the cookies on parchment paper off the baking sheet onto the countertop to cool. If not, remove the cookies and cool on a wire rack.

If you want to glaze the cookies, warm the corn syrup in a custard cup in the microwave oven or in a small saucepan over low heat. With a small brush, paint the top of each cookie. Allow to cool until set.

Makes about 48 cookies

Place the nuts on a baking sheet in a single layer and heat them in a pre-heated 350°F oven for ten minutes or until the skins begin to flake. Turn the nuts into a towel and rub off the papery skins.

Hazelnut Crescents

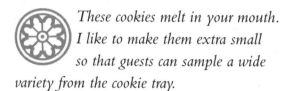

These cookies melt in your mouth. I like to make them extra small so that guests can sample a wide variety from the cookie tray.

½ cup (1 stick) unsalted butter, at room temperature

⅓ cup sugar

1 large egg yolk

1 teaspoon vanilla

½ cup hazelnuts (filberts), toasted, skinned, and ground (see Box)

1¼ cups all-purpose flour

Frosting

½ cup semisweet chocolate chips, melted

Preheat the oven to 350°F. Cover 2 baking sheets with parchment paper.

In the bowl of an electric mixer or in a large bowl, cream the butter and sugar. Beat in the egg yolk and vanilla until the mixture is light. Add the hazelnuts and flour and mix until the dough is smooth and well blended.

Divide the dough into 4 portions. Shape each into a long log and cut each log into 12 parts. Roll each piece between your palms to make a short log, about 1½ inches long and tapered on each end. Place each piece 2 inches apart on the prepared baking sheet and shape into a crescent.

Bake for 12 minutes, until the cookies feel firm and are very light brown. Slide the cookies on the parchment off onto the countertop to cool. Melt the chocolate in a small bowl over hot water. Dip both ends of each cookie into the melted chocolate and leave to harden on the parchment paper.

Makes 48 crescents

Hazelnut Spritz

The difference between hazelnuts and filberts is one of breeding. Hazelnuts generally refer to the wild nuts that grow on the hazel tree in temperate climates around the world. They are cultivated in Oregon and Washington, and it is these cultivated nuts that are known as filberts.

½ cup hazelnuts (filberts), toasted
  (see Box on page 234)
1 cup (2 sticks) unsalted butter,
  at room temperature
½ cup confectioners' sugar
1 teaspoon vanilla
2 cups all-purpose flour

Chocolate Frosting

½ cup semisweet chocolate chips
2 tablespoons heavy cream

Preheat the oven to 350°F. Cover 2 baking sheets with parchment paper or use 2 ungreased baking sheets.

Put the nuts into the food processor and grind them until very fine. In a large bowl, cream the butter, sugar, and vanilla with an electric mixer until light. Add the ground nuts and flour. Mix until smooth. Put the dough into a cookie press with a star or ridged tip and press into long, narrow strips. Cut the strips into 4-inch pieces and shape into rings and place on the baking sheet.

Bake for 10 minutes just until light brown. Slide the baked cookies on the parchment off the baking sheet onto the countertop to cool or lift the cookies from the baking sheet onto a wire rack to cool.

While the cookies bake, combine the chocolate chips and cream in a small glass bowl. Microwave on high power for 1 minute; stir. Repeat, stirring after each minute, until the frosting is smooth. Or combine in a bowl and place over a small saucepan of simmering water, stirring until the chocolate is melted. Dip the cooled cookies ½ inch into the chocolate so that one side is coated. Place on the parchment or on waxed paper to harden.

Makes about 60 cookies

 SPRITZ

Spritz are rich and buttery cookies shaped by pressing the dough through a cookie press. Spritz hold their shape and design in baking because they have a higher proportion of butter and flour with less sugar and little or no liquid added to the dough as compared with a drop cookie.

Macadamia Nut Cookies

 Macadamia nut oil enhances the flavor of chopped macadamia nuts in this delicate cookie that melts in your mouth. Because the oil has a wonderful nutty flavor, it is not necessary to add macadamia nuts in order to flavor these cookies, but the chopped nuts do add a crunchy texture.

½ cup macadamia nut oil
  (see Box) or corn oil
½ cup (1 stick) unsalted butter,
  at room temperature
½ cup confectioners' sugar
½ cup granulated sugar
1 large egg
2 cups all-purpose flour
½ teaspoon baking soda
½ teaspoon cream of tartar
¼ teaspoon salt

½ cup chopped macadamia nuts
  (optional if using macadamia nut oil)
Sugar, for dipping

Preheat the oven to 350°F. Lightly grease 2 baking sheets or cover with parchment paper.

In a large bowl, cream the oil, butter, and sugars together with an electric mixer until light. Add the egg and beat until light and fluffy.

In a separate bowl, stir the flour, baking soda, cream of tartar, and salt together. Stir into the creamed mixture along with the chopped macadamia nuts if used. Chill at least 30 minutes or overnight, covered.

Shape the dough into 1-inch balls. Place on the prepared baking sheet, about 2 inches apart. Dip the bottom of a glass in sugar, then use to flatten the cookies.

Bake for 8 to 10 minutes, until light brown.

Makes about 48 cookies

 ## MACADAMIA NUT OIL

Macadamia nut oil is pressed from macadamia nuts and has a pronounced macadamia nut flavor. It is produced and marketed by:

LORIVA SUPREME FOODS INC.
40-1 Oser Avenue
Hauppauge, NY 11788

HAWAIIAN MACADAMIA NUT OIL CO.
P.O. Box 685
Waialua, HI 96791

Meringue Stars

 When I have leftover egg whites, I make these easy meringues. I use them to decorate simple desserts, like rice pudding or a scoop of ice cream. For the daintiest stars, use a tiny star tip on the pastry bag. The stars keep well if stored in an airtight container.

2 large egg whites,
  at room temperature
½ teaspoon vanilla
¼ teaspoon cream of tartar
½ cup sugar

Preheat the oven to 300°F. Line a large baking sheet with parchment paper. In a small bowl, beat the egg whites, vanilla, and cream of tartar until frothy with an electric mixer. Turn the beater to high speed and add the sugar 1 tablespoon at a time until stiff, glossy peaks form.

Scrape the mixture into a pastry bag with a ½-inch star tip. Press out stars onto the cookie sheet, placing the stars about 1 inch apart.

Bake for 15 minutes. Turn the oven off and let the cookies dry in the oven with the door closed, about 30 minutes.

Makes about 40 cookies

Mocha Logs

A coffee-flavored, buttery spritz dough is shaped into a log, and after baking, the ends of the logs are dipped into chocolate. These are daintiest and best when you make them tiny. A little bit of shortening melted with the chocolate gives the glaze a sheen.

1 cup (2 sticks) unsalted butter,
  at room temperature
¾ cup sugar
1 large egg
1 teaspoon vanilla
2 tablespoons instant coffee granules
  dissolved in 1 tablespoon water
2¼ cups all-purpose flour
½ teaspoon baking powder

Chocolate Dip
1 cup semisweet chocolate chips
1 teaspoon solid vegetable shortening

Cream the butter and sugar together in a large bowl until smooth. Add the egg, vanilla, and coffee and beat until light and fluffy. Stir in the flour and baking powder until the dough is stiff. Chill for 30 minutes, covered.

Preheat the oven to 350°F. Press the dough through a cookie press or pastry bag fitted with a ½-inch star tip into logs the length of an ungreased baking sheet, placing the strips about 2 inches apart. Cut into 2-inch lengths, but leave the cookies in place.

Bake for 10 to 12 minutes or until light brown. Remove from the pan and cool on wire racks.

Meanwhile, place the chocolate morsels and shortening into a small bowl. Place over hot water and stir until the chocolate is melted. Stir well. Dip the ends of the cooled cookies into the chocolate. Place on waxed paper to harden.

Makes 60 to 72 cookies

Chocolate-Pistachio Cookie Sticks

These cookies are utterly irresistible, and you don't need any fancy tools to make them look pretty. The dough molds easily into smooth, fat sticks, and after they're baked they're dipped into chocolate and chopped pistachios.

- 1 cup (2 sticks) unsalted butter, at room temperature
- ½ cup confectioners' sugar
- 1 teaspoon vanilla
- 2¼ cups all-purpose flour

For Decoration

- 1 cup semisweet chocolate chips
- 1 teaspoon corn oil
- ½ cup finely chopped pistachios

Preheat the oven to 350°F. Cover 2 baking sheets with parchment paper.

In a large bowl, cream the butter and sugar together with an electric mixer until smooth. Add the vanilla and mix well. Add the flour a little at a time, beating at high speed until the dough is smooth.

Press the dough through a pastry tube with a #5 star tip or through a cookie press with a star tip directly onto the prepared cookie sheet to make 2½-inch sticks, spaced about 2 inches apart.

Bake for 10 minutes, until the cookies feel firm and are just beginning to brown. Slide the cookies on the paper onto a countertop to cool.

While the cookies bake, combine the chocolate chips and oil in a small glass bowl. Heat in the microwave, for about 2 minutes, stirring every 10 seconds until the chocolate is smooth and shiny. Or place the bowl over hot water and stir until melted. Place the chopped pistachios in a small bowl.

To decorate the cookies, dip one end of each stick into the melted chocolate, then into the pistachios. Place on the parchment paper and let sit until the chocolate is firm.

Makes about 48 cookies

Pizzelle

Italian pizzelles are crisp, anise-flavored cookies that are baked in a hinged, fancy iron heated on a stovetop burner. My favorite iron produces round ruffled cookies 5 inches in diameter. To keep both sides of the iron hot, it needs to be turned over every minute or so. Electric pizzelle irons are available today that maintain a steady heat; they're something like waffle irons. For a mail-order source, see the Note.

2 cups all-purpose flour
1 cup sugar
2 teaspoons ground aniseed
½ teaspoon baking powder
½ teaspoon baking soda
¼ teaspoon salt
¼ cup oil
3 large eggs, slightly beaten

In a large mixing bowl, blend the flour, sugar, aniseed, baking powder, baking soda, and salt. In another bowl mix the oil and eggs. Stir the egg mixture into the dry ingredients and mix until the dough is smooth. Cover and chill for 30 minutes. Shape into 1-inch balls and keep them chilled.

Place the pizzelle iron over medium heat. Heat on both sides until a drop of water bounces and sizzles on an inside surface of the iron. Turn over the iron occasionally during cooking to keep both surfaces hot.

Coat the heated iron on both sides of the interior surface with nonstick cooking spray.

Place a ball of dough onto the center of the heated iron and flatten it slightly by carefully pressing it against the iron with your finger (remember that it's hot!). Close the iron and cook over medium heat for 30 to 45 seconds, then turn over and cook on the other side for another 45 seconds or until the pizzelle is pale golden. Remove the pizzelle from the iron with a fork and cool on a wire rack (see Note).

Makes about 20 cookies

NOTE: To make pizzelle in the shape of cups, drape the warm, still-flexible cookie over the bottom of a small juice glass; cool. Fill with ice cream, sherbet, or berries and cream to serve.

Mail-order sources for pizzelle irons are Maid of Scandinavia, 3244 Raleigh Avenue, Minneapolis, MN 55416 (1-800-328-6722) and Vitantonio Mfg. Co., 34355 Vokis Drive, Eastlake, OH 44095 (1-800-732-4444).

Raspberry
Ribbons

 When I don't have much time for Christmas cookie baking but I'd like something special to serve with a soft dessert such as ice cream, rice pudding, or fruit, I make these cookies. They don't look as quick and simple as they are!

Dough

    1 cup (2 sticks) unsalted butter,
        at room temperature
    ½ cup confectioners' sugar
    1 large egg yolk
    1 teaspoon vanilla
    2½ cups all-purpose flour

Filling and Decoration

        About ½ cup raspberry jam
    ½ cup confectioners' sugar
    2 teaspoons fresh lemon juice
    1 teaspoon cream, milk, or water

Preheat the oven to 375°F. Make the dough. In a large bowl, cream the butter and confectioners' sugar together with an electric mixer. Add the egg yolk and vanilla and beat until light. Add the flour, a little at a time, and mix until the dough is smooth.

Divide the dough into 4 parts. On the countertop, use your palms to roll each part into a strand about ¾ inch in diameter and the length of your cookie sheet. Place the strands about 2 inches apart on an ungreased cookie sheet.

With the side of your little finger, press a groove down the center of the length of each strand. Bake for 10 minutes until the cookies feel firm to the touch.

Remove the cookies from the oven and spoon jam into the grooves. Return to the oven for 5 to 10 minutes or until the cookies are light golden brown.

To make the decoration, mix the confectioners' sugar, lemon juice, and cream in a

---

 HOW TO FREEZE DELICATE COOKIES

Plastic or metal containers are great for freezing cookies because they protect the cookies from being squashed in the freezer. When packing cookies for freezing, pack them a layer at a time separated by waxed paper to prevent the cookies from damaging each other. Very delicate cookies such as cutouts, deep-fried rosettes, pizzelles, and krumkakes are best packed in shallow, rigid containers in single layers. Keep them in a place in the freezer where they're not likely to get bumped by heavier items.

small bowl to make a smooth icing. Drizzle the icing down the length of the hot cookies.

While the cookies are still warm, cut them at a 45° angle into 1-inch lengths. Let cool on the baking sheets. When the frosting is set, transfer to an airtight tin. Store in a cool place or freeze.

Makes about 48 cookies

Sacher Torte Cookies

Sacher torte is a classic Austrian apricot-filled chocolate cake. These cookies are miniature versions of the cake; they're little, buttery cookies filled with apricot preserves and topped with chocolate frosting.

  1 cup (2 sticks) unsalted butter, at room temperature
 ¼ cup sugar
  1 large egg
 ¼ cup dark unsweetened cocoa
  2 cups all-purpose flour

Filling
 ½ cup store-bought or homemade apricot preserves (see Note)

Frosting
 ½ cup semisweet chocolate chips
  2 tablespoons unsalted butter

Preheat the oven to 350°F. Lightly grease 2 cookie sheets or cover with parchment paper.

In a large mixing bowl, cream the butter and sugar together. Beat in the egg until the mixture is fluffy. Sift the cocoa and flour together into the creamed mixture and blend well.

Shape the dough into 1-inch balls and place 2 inches apart on the cookie sheets. Make an indentation in the center of each with your thumb.

Bake the cookies for 12 to 15 minutes, until they feel firm and are light brown. Slide the cookies on the parchment paper off the baking sheet onto the countertop to cool or remove to wire racks.

Fill the indentation with a dot of apricot preserves.

Melt the chocolate chips and butter together in a small bowl set over hot water. Stir until smooth and drizzle over the cookies to frost them. Allow to stand until set.

Makes 36 to 48 cookies

NOTE: To make apricot preserves from dried apricots, cover ½ cup dried apricots with water in a saucepan. Heat to boiling over medium-high heat and cook for 5 minutes. Add ½ cup sugar and boil for 5 minutes longer. Turn into a food processor or blender and purée. If the mixture is watery, return to the saucepan and boil, stirring until the liquid is reduced.

Scandinavian Butter Cookies—Many Ways

 With this basic dough you can shape many different cookies and even invent some new ones as the inspiration hits you.

> 1 cup (2 sticks) unsalted butter, at room temperature
> ½ cup sugar
> 1 large egg yolk
> 2½ cups all-purpose flour
> 1 tablespoon rum, amaretto, or orange liqueur (optional)

In a large bowl, cream the butter with the sugar and egg yolk. Blend in the flour to make a smooth dough. If the flour is very dry, the dough may be crumbly and will not bind. Add rum, amaretto, or orange liqueur to moisten the dough. Make some of the following variations from the dough; all call for additional ingredients and some call for chilling the dough at this stage. I prefer to cover baking sheets with parchment paper, but you may grease them if you'd rather. Preheat the oven to 350°F for all the variations given here.

Makes about 60 cookies

Almond Fingers

Additional Ingredients
> 1 large egg white, beaten
> ¼ cup finely chopped almonds
> 3 tablespoons sugar

Chill the dough for 30 minutes wrapped in plastic wrap or until firm enough to handle. Divide the dough into 8 parts. Roll each part between your palms and shape into long ropes that are ½ to ¾ inch thick. Place the ropes close together and brush with the egg white. Mix the almonds and sugar together in a shallow bowl. Cut the ropes into 1½-inch pieces and then roll each strip in the almond mixture. Place on the prepared baking sheet 2 inches apart. Bake for 15 minutes or until golden. Slide the cookies on the parchment paper onto the countertop to cool or remove to a wire rack.

Spritz

Additional Ingredient
> Chopped candied cherries (optional)

Put the unchilled cookie dough into a spritz press or a pastry bag with a ½-inch star tip. Press into long strips or fancy shapes 2 inches apart on the prepared baking sheet. Decorate with bits of candied cherries, if desired. Bake for 10 minutes or until golden. Slide the cookies on the parchment paper onto the countertop to cool or remove to a wire rack.

Butter Slices

Additional Ingredients

- 2 teaspoons vanilla
- 1 tablespoon sugar
- 1 tablespoon cocoa
- ½ cup semisweet chocolate chips

Mix the vanilla into the basic cookie dough. Divide the dough in half. Using your palms, shape each half into a long roll about 1½ inches thick. Mix the sugar and cocoa together in a jelly roll pan. Roll the dough in the sugar and cocoa mixture. Wrap each roll in plastic wrap. Chill for 30 minutes or until firm enough to handle. With a sharp knife, cut the rolls into ⅛-inch-thick slices and place 2 inches apart on the prepared baking sheet. Bake for 6 to 8 minutes, until firm but not brown. Slide the cookies on the parchment paper onto the countertop to cool or remove to a wire rack. Place the chocolate chips into a heavy-duty plastic bag with a zipper closure and fasten securely. Place into a bowl of very hot (not boiling) tap water for 3 to 5 minutes, until the chocolate is melted. Snip ⅛ inch off the corner of the bag and squeeze out the chocolate to drizzle over the cookies.

Hazelnut Cookies

Additional Ingredients

- 1 large egg white, lightly beaten
- ½ cup finely chopped hazelnuts (filberts)
- 1 tablespoon unsalted butter
- 1 ounce semisweet, milk, or white chocolate
- ½ cup confectioners' sugar

Chill the dough, covered, for 30 minutes or until firm enough to handle. Shape into ¾ inch balls. Roll the balls in the egg white and then in the nuts. Place the balls 2 inches apart on the prepared baking sheet. Indent the center of each ball with your thumb.

Bake for 10 minutes or until light brown. Slide the cookies on the parchment onto the countertop to cool or remove to a wire rack. While the cookies are baking, melt the butter and chocolate in a small bowl over hot water. Stir in the confectioners' sugar. When the cookies are still warm, place a dot of icing in the indentation of each cookie.

Swedish Jelly Cookies

The top butter cookies of this sandwich allow the jelly filling to peek out through a hole. These are especially attractive cut with scalloped cookie cutters, one large and one a bit smaller to cut out the center; you can make heart-shaped cookies with two heart-shaped cutters. I use a two-inch cookie cutter (no larger) and make the cutouts with a tiny aspic cutter.

2 cups all-purpose flour
1 cup (2 sticks) unsalted butter,
    at room temperature
½ cup plus 2 to 3 tablespoons sugar,
    divided
1 large egg, separated
⅓ cup finely chopped almonds
    About ⅓ cup red seedless jam
    or jelly

In a large mixing bowl or a food processor, combine the flour, butter, ½ cup of the sugar, and the egg yolk. Mix to make a smooth dough. (If the dough is crumbly, add 1 to 2 teaspoons water.) Wrap in plastic wrap and chill for at least 30 minutes.

Preheat the oven to 350°F. Cover 2 baking sheets with parchment paper or use ungreased baking sheets.

Working with half the dough at a time, roll the dough out to a ⅛-inch thickness on a lightly floured board. Cut out an even number of 2-inch rounds. Using a thimble, a ½-inch cookie cutter, or an aspic cutter, cut the center out of half the rounds. Brush the ring cookies with the beaten egg white and sprinkle with the almonds and the remaining sugar. Leave the full rounds plain. Place the cookies 2 inches apart on the prepared baking sheets and bake for 10 to 12 minutes or until just barely golden around the edges. Transfer the cookies to wire racks to cool or slide the parchment paper with the cookies on it directly onto a countertop. Spread each uncut cookie with about ½ teaspoon jam or jelly. Place the ring cookies on top, almond side up, to make sandwiches.

Makes about 50 cookies

Tiny Pecan Tarts

 These tender-crusted tarts are something like miniature pecan pies.

Dough

- 1 cup (2 sticks) unsalted butter, at room temperature
- 2 packages (3 ounces each) cream cheese
- 2 cups all-purpose flour

Pecan Filling

- 3 large eggs, beaten
- 1¾ cups packed brown sugar
- 3 tablespoons unsalted butter, soft or melted
- ¼ teaspoon salt
- ¾ teaspoon vanilla
- 1 cup pecans, coarsely chopped

Make the dough. In a large bowl, cream the butter and cream cheese with an electric mixer until light. Mix in the flour until well blended. Flatten the dough into a 1-inch-thick disk; wrap in plastic and refrigerate for at least 30 minutes.

Preheat the oven to 375°F. Cut off one-quarter of the dough at a time. Roll out to a ⅛-inch thickness on a lightly floured surface, and using a 2¾- to 3-inch cookie cutter, cut out rounds. Fit the rounds into the bottom and sides of 4 dozen ungreased miniature muffin cups. Repeat with the rest of the dough.

To make the filling, beat the eggs, brown sugar, butter, salt, and vanilla together in a large bowl until well mixed. Spoon 1 tablespoon of the filling into each pastry-lined muffin cup. Top evenly with the pecans.

Bake for 20 minutes, until the pastry is brown and the filling is set. Cool briefly in the pan on a wire rack, then remove from the pan and cool completely on the rack.

Makes about 48 tarts

Be sure to have children wash their hands, tie back their hair, roll up their sleeves, and put on an apron (it can be a kitchen towel).

Kids who can read: Read through recipes and check to make sure you have all the ingredients and utensils on hand. Children can help find the necessary items.

Teach caution to all young bakers. Sharp knives and electrical appliances should be handled only by adults. Teach children to turn the handles of saucepans on the stovetop toward the center of the stove so they will be out of reach of smaller children, and they will not accidentally be tipped. Teach children to use pot holders or mitts when placing pans into and taking pans out of the oven.

Teach older children to turn the mixer off before scraping the sides of the bowl or adding ingredients and to unplug the machine before removing the beaters.

Encourage older children to take turns doing things that everybody wants to do.

Talk about family traditions. If a recipe has been in the family, tell kids about its history to help them feel connected to their past.

Teach kids to measure correctly and to use appropriate measuring utensils. Dry measuring (nested) cups are for flour, sugar, and other dry ingredients. Spoon flour into a cup and level off with a straight edge. Dip the cup into sugar and level off. A liquid measuring cup is usually made of glass and is used for milk, water, and other liquids. Pour liquid into the cup and read the scale at eye level. Use measuring spoons for smaller amounts. Teach children to level off dry ingredients.

Teach children to use a timer when baking. Explain how to test for doneness in each recipe.

Teach kids the difference between baking pans and baking sheets. Show them how to butter or grease the pans.

For a first baking project, make cookies, muffins, or cupcakes. Teach kids how to shape drop cookies (cookies of the same size bake evenly). Show them how to space the cookies evenly or how to spoon equal amounts of batter into muffin cups or cupcake tins, filling them about two-thirds full (you may need to indicate an amount by demonstrating with the first cup).

Let kids taste and experiment with ingredients and teach kids to use best-quality ingredients. Explain what the ingredients do in a recipe. For example, sugar, salt, spices, vanilla, and extracts add flavor. Nuts, fruits, and chocolate add texture and flavor. Flour usually is the main ingredient, adding structure and body. Butter or shortening makes cookies tender. Baking powder (which feels fizzy in the mouth) makes baked goods rise, as does baking soda. Eggs make the cookies soft and make the other ingredients hold together. Some cookies don't have eggs, but they are usually rich with butter or shortening and sometimes have some added liquid.

Baking with Very Young Children

What You Can Do with Infants (Crawlers). Put them into a backpack while you bake so they can "supervise" without interfering.

What You Can Do with Toddlers. Sit them at a small table, in a booster chair at the kitchen table, or on a plastic cloth or mat on the floor. Give them a set of measuring cups and a piece of dough.

Young children can do things like unwrap packages, mix dry ingredients, and add pre-measured ingredients to the bowl.

FAVORITE AND CLASSIC COOKIES

Peppernuts

I like to make these spicy peppernuts in quantity so that I can serve them in baskets—like salted nuts or candy. They add a wonderful, spicy aroma to the air. This is based on a recipe I received many years ago from a Danish friend. Although the mere idea of baking hundreds of nut-size cookies sounds like an enormous amount of work, I've simplified the procedure. I just roll the dough into ½-inch-thick strips and cut them into ½-inch pieces with scissors, dropping the dough bits right on an ungreased cookie sheet. I can bake a hundred or more on one baking sheet! The flavor of the peppernuts mellows and improves after being stored in an airtight tin in a cool place for three to four days.

1 cup (2 sticks) unsalted butter, at room temperature
1 cup packed brown sugar
1 large egg
1 cup ground toasted hazelnuts (filberts) or almonds
2½ cups all-purpose flour
1 teaspoon baking powder
½ teaspoon baking soda
1 teaspoon freshly ground cardamom
½ teaspoon ground cinnamon
½ teaspoon ground cloves

 PEPPERNUTS

Peppernuts are spicy little holiday sweets about the size of a hazelnut (filbert). They can range from dark and peppery to soft and light to crisp and crunchy. The Dutch call them *pepparnotter*, the Danish call them *pebernodder*, the Latvians call them *piparkukas*, and the Germans call them *pfefernüsse*. In some families, it was traditional to pack five-gallon crocks with the dough and let it sit for a week or more so that the spices could blend smoothly and the flavor would develop. Baking days were a community affair, and peppernuts were made assemblyline style. There were those who rolled the dough into strands, those who sliced them, those who baked them. Finally, gallons of peppernuts were stored in jars to mellow until Christmas.

Round cookies can be painted to look like faces, wheels, or flowers or they can be decorated with stripes, dots, or grids. Cookies that have been cut out into animal or other shapes can be painted to resemble the real thing. Paste food colors are brighter after baking than liquid food colors.

½ teaspoon ground allspice
½ teaspoon freshly ground nutmeg

Preheat the oven to 375°F. In a large bowl using an electric mixer, cream the butter and the brown sugar together. Add the egg and nuts. In another large bowl, mix the flour with the baking powder, baking soda, cardamom, cinnamon, cloves, allspice, and nutmeg. Blend the dry ingredients into the creamed mixture until a stiff dough forms. Shape the dough into a ball. (At this point, you can wrap the dough in plastic wrap and refrigerate it to develop the flavor, for up to a week). Cut off portions of the dough and roll each between your hands and a lightly floured work surface to make slim ropes, about ½ inch thick. Dip clean scissors in water and snip off ½-inch pieces of the dough from the ropes onto an ungreased baking sheet; place the pieces about ½ inch apart.

Bake for 8 minutes or until the cookies are light brown and dry. Remove from the oven; cool on the baking sheet.

Makes about 600 peppernuts

Painted Sugar Cookies

These are a lot of fun to do, and you can get the kids to paint their own designs on the cut-out cookies before they are baked. You'll need some clean paintbrushes for these.

½ cup (1 stick) unsalted butter or margarine, at room temperature
½ cup vegetable shortening
½ cup sugar
1 large egg
1 teaspoon vanilla
½ teaspoon baking soda
½ teaspoon salt
2½ cups all-purpose flour

Corn Syrup Paint
4 teaspoons corn syrup
1 teaspoon water
Four different paste colors or liquid food color

In a large bowl using an electric mixer, cream the butter, shortening, and sugar.

Add the egg and vanilla and beat until light. In a small bowl, stir the baking soda, salt, and flour together. Stir the dry ingredients into the creamed ingredients until well mixed. Wrap in plastic wrap and chill the dough for at least 30 minutes.

Preheat the oven to 375°F. Divide the dough in half. Rewrap half the dough and return to the refrigerator until you are finished with the first half. Roll out the dough to ⅛-inch thickness on a lightly floured surface. Cut the cookies with a cookie cutter of any design and place on ungreased cookie sheets, about 2 inches apart.

Put 1 teaspoon corn syrup and ¼ teaspoon water into each of 4 different custard cups. Tint each of the four mixtures with food color. Stir each well. Paint designs on the unbaked cookies, using small paintbrushes.

Bake for 9 to 10 minutes or until cookies are light brown. Remove the cookies with a spatula and cool on a wire rack.

Makes about 60 cookies

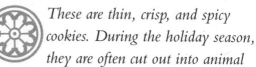

Pepparkaker

These are thin, crisp, and spicy cookies. During the holiday season, they are often cut out into animal shapes that are decorated with icing after baking. Finns often cut out pigs; the popular name for pigs is nissu-nassu, *which is comparable to our "kitty," used for cats. The Swedes cut out goats, which they call* julbukka. *I like to dip the animals' feet, heads, and tails into melted white chocolate. The chocolate tastes great with the spicy cookie.*

    ½ cup (1 stick) unsalted butter,
         at room temperature
    ½ cup packed dark brown sugar
    ¼ cup light molasses or dark corn
         syrup
    1 tablespoon ground cinnamon
    1 tablespoon ground ginger
  1½ teaspoons ground cloves
    1 teaspoon baking soda
    2 cups all-purpose flour
    2 tablespoons cream, milk, or water
         About 2 ounces melted white
         chocolate, for decoration

In a large mixing bowl, cream the butter, brown sugar, molasses, cinnamon, ginger, cloves, and baking soda together until the mixture is smooth. Blend in the flour and cream to make a stiff dough. Chill at least 30 minutes or until firm.

Preheat the oven to 375°F. Cover 2 baking sheets with parchment paper.

On a lightly floured surface, roll the dough out to ⅛-inch thickness and cut into desired shapes using cookie cutters. Place about 2 inches apart on the baking sheet.

Bake the cookies for 8 to 10 minutes, until light brown. Slide the parchment paper off the baking sheet onto the countertop to cool. Dip the cooled cookies into melted white chocolate for decorating.

Makes about 48 cookies

Chocolate Chip Lace Cookies

 Lace cookies always remind me of snowflakes because no two are exactly alike. Crisp and studded with chocolate chips and pecans, these are more like a delicious confection than a cookie. Be sure to bake them on a foil-lined baking sheet, because you can peel the foil away from the cookie more easily than the cookies can be lifted from the sheet. While still warm they will be flexible so that they can be bent into cones or tubes.

½ cup (1 stick) unsalted butter, at room temperature
½ cup sugar

1 large egg
1 teaspoon vanilla
½ cup all-purpose flour
1 cup semisweet or milk chocolate chips
⅓ cup chopped pecans

Preheat the oven to 350°F. Line 2 baking sheets with foil and coat with nonstick spray.

In a large bowl, cream together the butter and sugar. Add the egg and beat until light and fluffy. Stir in the vanilla and flour until a smooth batter forms. Stir in the chocolate chips and nuts. Drop the batter by teaspoonfuls at least 3 inches apart on the prepared pan.

Bake for 7 to 10 minutes, until the edges are golden and the centers are set. Slide the foil off the sheet onto a countertop to cool. Peel the foil away from the cookies when cooled. They will be soft when hot, but they become crispy as they cool.

Makes 24 to 30 cookies

Cranberry-Orange Cookies

Soft and chewy with a sour bite from the cranberries, these drops make a perfect simple holiday dessert.

¼ cup (½ stick) unsalted butter, at room temperature

½ cup granulated sugar

⅓ cup packed brown sugar

1 large egg

1 teaspoon grated orange zest

3 tablespoons orange juice concentrate

1½ cups all-purpose flour

¾ teaspoon baking powder

¼ teaspoon baking soda

¼ teaspoon salt

1½ cups halved fresh or 1 cup dried cranberries

½ cup chopped walnuts or pecans

Frosting

2 cups confectioners' sugar

¼ cup (½ stick) unsalted butter, at room temperature

3 tablespoons orange juice concentrate

¼ teaspoon vanilla

Preheat the oven to 375°F. Cover 2 baking sheets with parchment paper.

In a large bowl, cream together the butter and sugars. Add the egg and orange zest and concentrate and beat until light. Stir the flour, baking powder, baking soda, and salt together in another bowl and add to the creamed mixture, mixing until the dough is smooth. Stir in the cranberries and nuts. Drop by teaspoonfuls into mounds in the prepared pan, about 2 inches apart.

Bake for 12 minutes, until light brown. Slide the cookies on the parchment paper onto the countertop to cool.

To make the frosting, stir the confectioners' sugar, butter, orange juice concentrate, and vanilla together in a small bowl until smooth. Spread onto the cooled cookies.

Makes about 36 cookies

Lebkuchen

I am grateful to my friend Leonora Baumler, who still bakes lebkuchen as she did in her native Germany. This batter needs to be refrigerated overnight.

5 large eggs

1¾ cups sugar

2½ cups unblanched almonds, finely ground

1 cup all-purpose flour

½ cup finely diced candied orange peel

½ cup finely diced candied lemon peel

2 teaspoons ground cinnamon

1 teaspoon freshly ground cardamom

½ teaspoon freshly ground nutmeg

¼ teaspoon ground cloves

ABOUT LEBKUCHEN

Typical of traditional recipes, every German baker has a favorite version of lebkuchen. The size and shape of lebkuchen vary from a round drop cookie three to four inches in diameter to large squares that are cut into bars.

Leb refers to honey, and in Medieval German, *lebchen* meant "honeybee." Today *lebchen* is a term of endearment, meaning "my dear one." When I visited Germany, it was during lebkuchen season. While having afternoon tea one day in that late November visit of ours, our German friend observed that lebkuchen only tastes good to him at that time of year because it is a traditional holiday cookie. Chewy, spicy, and irresistible, lebkuchen are sold on every street corner in German villages from the beginning of Advent until Christmas. And in Germany, as in the United States, they push the season forward into the middle of November (Advent actually begins on the fourth Sunday before Christmas).

The cookies are baked on a thin, edible wafer called *oblaten*. *Oblaten* are crisp, white wheat wafers that are available in specialty food shops. If you do not have a specialty food shop that handles *oblaten*, check with a local religious supply house. Wafers that are used for communion come in various sizes, including 2¾- and 3-inch diameters, and can be used for lebkuchen.

¼ teaspoon ground allspice
¼ teaspoon ground ginger
42 to 48 round German baking
    wafers (*oblaten*) 2¾ or 3 inches
    in diameter (see Box)

Icing
1 cup confectioners' sugar
About 2 tablespoons fresh
    lemon juice

1 cup semisweet chocolate chips
Halved blanched almonds

In the bowl of an electric mixer or in a large bowl, beat or whisk the eggs and sugar together until light and fluffy. Place the bowl over a pan of simmering water over low heat and heat, whisking until the mixture is thick and very warm (about 130°F). Remove from the water bath and continue beating until the mixture is cool. Combine the almonds, flour, zests, and spices in another bowl. Stir into the egg-sugar mixture. Cover and refrigerate overnight.

Place the *oblaten* on baking sheets 2 inches apart. Spread 1 rounded tablespoonful of the cookie dough on each *oblaten*, spreading to the edges of the wafers. Let the cookies stand, uncovered, for 1 hour before baking so that the top will dry.

Preheat the oven to 350°F. Bake the cookies for 15 to 20 minutes, until the cookies are crusty on the upper surface, but still moist in the center. Remove the cookies from the baking sheet and cool on a wire rack.

In a small bowl, stir the sugar and lemon juice together to make a thin glaze. Spread over half of the cooled cookies. Place the chocolate into a glass bowl and heat in the microwave at high power for about 2 minutes, stirring every 15 seconds, until melted. Spread the melted chocolate over the remaining cookies. Decorate with the almonds.

Makes 42 to 48 cookies

Oatmeal Lace Cookies

 These are lacy, caramel cookies that can be shaped into rolls or be curved into U shapes while they are warm from the oven. The most difficult part is to catch the cookies at just the right stage of coolness so that they are firm enough to be removed from the baking sheet, yet flexible enough to curve. If they become too stiff to curl, you can return the cookies to the oven for a minute or so.

    ¼ cup (½ stick) unsalted butter
    1 cup regular or quick rolled oats
    ⅔ cup sugar
    1 large egg, beaten
    1 tablespoon all-purpose flour
    ½ teaspoon baking powder

Garnish

    About ½ cup semisweet chocolate chips

Preheat the oven to 400°F. Line a baking sheet with foil and coat with nonstick cooking spray.

In a medium saucepan, melt the butter over medium-low heat. Stir in the oats, sugar, egg, flour, and baking powder and blend well. Drop the batter by teaspoonfuls onto the baking sheet, about 3 inches apart.

Bake for 4 to 8 minutes or until the edges are light brown. Slide the foil onto a countertop and let the cookies cool until you can peel the foil away from their bottoms. Shape as desired or cool flat on a wire rack.

Place the chocolate chips into a small glass bowl and microwave on high power about 1 minute, stirring every 15 seconds until the chocolate is melted.

When the cookies are cool and firm, paint the bottoms with melted chocolate or dip the edges in the chocolate. When the chocolate is set, pack the cookies in layers in an airtight container, separating the layers with waxed paper; store in a cool place.

Makes about 48 cookies

Norwegian Krumkake

Not just at Christmas but always at Christmas, Norwegians enjoy this thin, crispy cookie that is baked in a special iron on top of the range. While hot, it is pliable and is traditionally rolled into a tube or cone shape. Although krumkakes can be filled with whipped cream (as the Italians do with cannolis), they are most often served plain on the coffee table along with other Christmas cookies.

Krumkakes can be baked early in the season, but because they are fragile, they need to be stored in a rigid container, preferably in the freezer or in a cool place for a month or longer.

They don't mail well. I make my krumkakes in an electric krumkake iron, which looks a lot like a waffle iron, but when opened up, there are two elaborately embossed rounds for baking the cookie. It heats up to the perfect temperature. Don't try making krumkakes on a griddle.

- 1 cup sugar
- 2 large eggs
- ½ cup (1 stick) unsalted butter, melted
- 1⅓ cups all-purpose flour
- ⅔ cup milk
- 1 teaspoon vanilla or lemon extract, or freshly ground cardamom

In a small bowl, beat the sugar and eggs together with an electric mixer at high speed until light and lemon colored. Beat in the butter. Blend in the flour, milk, and flavoring of your choice. Let the batter stand for 30 minutes, covered, or refrigerate overnight.

Heat the krumkake iron over medium-high heat on both sides until a drop of water sizzles when dropped on the inside of the iron. Coat with nonstick cooking spray. Place 1 rounded teaspoonful of the batter onto the center of the grid and close the iron. Cook for 1 minute on each side, or until light brown. To control the browning, cook over medium or medium-low heat at first. Increase the heat gradually as you get accustomed to the procedure. Remove the cookie using a thin spatula, and while it's still warm, shape

Cookie cutters are used in many countries. When I travel, I like to collect them. My collection includes large Swedish Dala-horse cutters, ginger-bread men and women of various sizes, Finnish piggy cutters, various kinds of animal cutters, German honeycake cutters, tiny aspic cutters, and nested hearts and stars (which contain cutters ranging in size from one to six inches). Mail-order catalogs even have cookie cutters in the shape of each state in the union!

Rosette irons, for making the delicate, deep-fried Scandinavian cookies, are available in designs ranging from snowflakes, to stars, hearts, angels, bells, and Christmas trees.

Springerle cookies, a specialty of Germany and Austria, are shaped using specially carved wooden boards, carved rolling pins, and stamps.

Tartlette tins are traditional in many European countries. In Scandinavia, the counterpart is the fluted sandbakkel tins, which are available in sizes ranging from one- to three-inch diameters.

Electric and nonelectric pizzelle irons make delicious and crisp embossed Italian cookies.

Scandinavian krumkake irons also come in electric and nonelectric models to make the wafer-thin embossed Norwegian specialty cookies that are shaped into cones or rolls.

the cookie into a cone or a tube. To shape into tubes, roll the warm, flexible cookie around a wooden stick, such as a clean broom handle. To shape into a cone easily, drop the hot cookie into a tulip sundae glass or wooden cone mold. Krumkake becomes firm very quickly. By the time the next cookie is baked, the first will have hardened.

If using an electric krumkake iron, follow the manufacturer's instructions. To stack and store, fit cone-shaped cookies inside each other. Tube-shaped cookies must be carefully stacked in a rigid, airtight container.

Makes about 50 cookies

Ladyfingers

Although ladyfingers are great served just as they are, they're also used to line all sorts of dessert molds. Being a pushover for all sorts of fancy baking molds and pans, I bought a ladyfinger baking mold which produces very nicely shaped ladyfingers. Still, I find that with a steady hand, it is much more time-efficient to press the batter through a pastry bag to make evenly shaped cookies on a baking sheet.

    4   large eggs, separated
    ⅔   cup sugar
    1   teaspoon vanilla
    ¾   cup plus 1 tablespoon
        all-purpose flour

Garnish (Optional)
    4   ounces semisweet chocolate, melted

Preheat the oven to 350°F. Lightly grease 2 baking sheets or cover with parchment paper.

In a large bowl using an electric mixer, beat the egg whites until foamy. Slowly beat in ⅓ cup of the sugar, beating until the whites are glossy and stiff.

In a medium bowl using the electric mixer and without washing the beaters, beat the egg yolks until foamy. Slowly add the remaining sugar, beating until light and lemon colored. Beat in the vanilla.

Fold the egg yolk mixture into the egg white mixture until evenly blended. Put the flour into a sieve and sift it over the mixture; fold together until evenly blended.

Put the mixture into a pastry bag with a ½-inch round tip. Press the batter out onto the baking sheets to make 4-inch strips about 2 inches apart.

Bake for 10 to 13 minutes or until light brown. Slide the parchment paper with the ladyfingers onto the countertop to cool or remove to a wire rack.

If desired, dip the ladyfingers into the melted chocolate or sandwich two ladyfingers together, flat sides facing inward, with the melted chocolate.

Makes 48 ladyfingers

Springerle Cookies

Classic "picture" cookies date back into early German history. Special carved wooden molds are used to press a design into the rolled-out dough. After the pictures are embossed on the dough, the cookies are cut apart and baked. Cookies are also formed by pressing the dough into a floured mold, which is then unmolded onto a baking sheet. German gift shops offer rolling pins, boards, and metal blocks with carved designs for embossing the dough. This is a tender, delicious cookie, firm enough to hold the picture.

1 cup (2 sticks) unsalted butter,
   at room temperature
2/3 cup packed brown sugar
1/2 teaspoon lemon extract
1 large egg
3 cups sifted cake flour

In a large bowl, cream the butter and brown sugar together until smooth. Add the lemon extract and egg; beat until light and fluffy. Stir in the flour until the dough is stiff. Cover tightly and chill overnight.

Preheat the oven to 300°F. Divide the cookie dough into 3 equal parts. On a lightly floured surface roll out 1 portion of the dough to 1/4-inch thickness with a plain rolling pin. Dust molds or a springerle rolling pin with flour and shake off the excess. Press the dough with the cookie mold or roll with the springerle rolling pin, rolling slowly and firmly to make a clear design. With a sharp knife, cut the cookies apart. Trim the outside edges and place on an ungreased baking sheet about 1 inch apart.

Bake for 25 to 30 minutes or until light brown. Cool on the baking sheet placed on a wire rack. Remove the cookies and store in an airtight tin up to 1 week. The cookies can be frozen, tightly wrapped with waxed paper between the layers, for up to 2 months.

Makes about sixty-six 1¹/₄ × 1³/₄-inch cookies

Almond Rusks

 Sweet rusks are twice-baked cookies of Scandinavia. Rusks are baked into long logs, which are then cut into diagonal slices after baking and rebaked until crisp; similar to Italian biscotti. Perfect to have on hand in the summertime, they keep well in a tightly closed jar away from direct sunlight. Sunlight speeds the breakdown of the fat in any cookie, producing a rancid taste.

1/2 cup (1 stick) unsalted butter,
   at room temperature
1/2 cup sugar
2 large eggs
1 teaspoon baking powder
1 teaspoon almond extract
1/2 cup coarsely chopped
   unblanched almonds
2 cups all-purpose flour

Preheat the oven to 375°F. Lightly grease a large baking sheet or cover with parchment paper.

In a large bowl, cream together the butter and sugar. Add the eggs and beat until light. Stir in the baking powder, almond extract, and almonds. Mix in the flour just until incorporated. Turn the dough out onto a lightly floured surface, divide into 3 parts and dust each lightly with flour. Shape each piece into a strand 12 inches long. Place on the baking sheet, evenly spaced, about 3 inches apart.

Bake for 15 to 20 minutes, until light brown. Cool for 5 minutes on the baking sheet. Cut each strand into 1-inch-wide slices on the diagonal. Turn the pieces so that one of the cut sides faces down and return to the oven. Turn the oven off and allow the rusks to dry, about 2 hours.

Makes about 36 rusks

Cardamom Toast

This is a twice-baked bar cookie that is made a little differently from the rusk, or biscotti-type, cookie. The rather soft dough is spread in a rectangular baking pan to bake like a cake. After the dough is baked, cooled, and removed from the pan, it is cut into $1/2$-inch slices, and each slice is cut into 2- or 3-inch bars. The bars are placed on a baking sheet and slow baked until dry and crisp. These cookies keep well.

1	cup (2 sticks) unsalted butter, at room temperature
2	cups sugar
1	cup sour cream
2	large eggs
2	teaspoons freshly ground cardamom
$3\frac{1}{2}$	cups all-purpose flour
2	teaspoons baking powder
$\frac{1}{2}$	teaspoon salt

Preheat the oven to 350°F. Grease a 13 × 9-inch baking pan.

In a large bowl, cream together the butter and sugar until smooth. Add the sour cream, eggs, and cardamom and beat until light. In another bowl, stir the flour, baking powder, and salt together and add to the creamed mixture. Mix until smooth and spread the dough into the prepared pan.

Bake for 40 to 50 minutes or until light brown. Lower the oven temperature to 275°F. Remove the pan from the oven and cool on a rack for 10 minutes. Invert the pan and remove the cake. Cut into $1/2$-inch slices crosswise. Lay the slices close together in a single layer with cut side up on a baking sheet. Cut each slice into 3-inch pieces and leave them in place. Bake until dry and crisp, 1 to 2 hours. Cool the cookies on the baking sheet.

Makes about 78 cookies

Pistachio Biscotti

There are many variations of this Italian cookie. These feature pistachios and are delicious dipped into sweet wine.

 1 cup (2 sticks) unsalted butter, at room temperature
2¼ cups sugar
 5 large eggs
 5 cups all-purpose flour
4½ cups shelled and salted pistachio nuts
 3 teaspoons baking powder
 2 tablespoons vanilla
 1 teaspoon salt

Preheat the oven to 325°F. In a large bowl, cream the butter and sugar together until smooth. Beat in the eggs until light and fluffy. Add all the remaining ingredients and mix until the dough is smooth. Chill, covered, for 30 minutes or until firm.

Divide the dough into 4 sections. Shape each part into a log about ½ inch thick and 12 inches long. Place the logs on an ungreased baking sheet spaced about 2 inches apart.

Bake for about 30 minutes, until golden brown. Then reduce the oven temperature to 250°F. Cool on the baking sheet for about 15 minutes.

Cut the logs diagonally into ½- to ⅓-inch slices. Arrange the slices, with one cut side down, on the baking sheet and bake until dried, 15 to 20 minutes. Let cool completely on the baking sheet. Store in an airtight container.

Makes about 48 biscotti

MACADAMIA NUT BISCOTTI: Substitute 2 (3½-ounce) jars of salted macadamia nuts, coarsely chopped, for the pistachios.

A GIFT OF BARS AND BROWNIES

Black-and-White Brownies

This is an easy saucepan-type brownie made with dark chocolate, but white chocolate chunks are folded into the batter to melt as they bake, providing color, contrast, and texture to the brownies.

1 cup all-purpose flour
¼ teaspoon baking soda
¼ teaspoon salt
¾ cup sugar
⅓ cup unsalted butter
2 tablespoons milk
2 ounces (2 squares) unsweetened chocolate
1 teaspoon vanilla
2 large eggs
1½ cups (10 ounces) chopped white chocolate or white chocolate chips

Preheat the oven to 325°F. Butter a 9-inch square baking pan.

In a small bowl, mix together the flour, baking soda, and salt.

In a small, heavy saucepan, combine the sugar, butter, and milk. Place over medium-high heat and bring to a boil, stirring until the butter has melted. Remove from the heat. Add the unsweetened chocolate and vanilla. Stir until the chocolate melts and the mixture is smooth. Place into a pan of cold water to cool the mixture to room temperature.

With an electric mixer, beat in the eggs. Gradually blend in the flour mixture until smooth. Fold in the white chocolate. Spread evenly into the prepared pan.

Bake for 25 to 30 minutes, until the center is just set and feels firm when touched. Cool on a wire rack. Cut into squares.

Makes nine 3-inch or thirty-six 1½-inch brownies

PACKING BROWNIES OR BAR COOKIES AS GIFTS OR FOR FREEZING

To pack in a gift box, place each three-inch square onto a fluted cupcake liner. Arrange in a gift box.

To freeze, pack into a plastic container with an airtight lid. Separate layers with waxed paper.

Butterscotch Brownies

Drizzled with melted chocolate, these chewy, sweet blond brownies are a pretty addition to a cookie tray or a gift box of bars and brownies.

¼ cup (½ stick) unsalted butter, melted
1 cup packed light brown sugar
1 large egg
1 cup all-purpose flour
1 teaspoon baking powder
½ teaspoon salt
1 teaspoon vanilla
¼ cup chopped walnuts
½ cup semisweet chocolate chips

Preheat the oven to 375°F. Butter a 9-inch square cake pan.

In a large bowl, beat the butter, brown sugar, and egg together until light and fluffy. Sift the flour, baking powder, and salt into the creamed mixture and stir until blended. Mix in the vanilla and nuts. Spread the batter into the prepared pan.

Bake for 20 to 25 minutes or just until the center is firm to the touch.

Meanwhile, measure the chocolate chips into a small, heavy-duty zipper-lock bag (do not use one with a pleated bottom). Be sure to close the bag tightly. Place into a bowlful of the hottest tap water. Knead occasionally until the chocolate is melted.

When the brownies are done, remove from the oven and place the pan on a wire rack. Dry the outside of the bag of chocolate carefully. Snip a small hole with scissors, cutting across the corner of the bag. Press the melted chocolate out onto the hot brownies, drizzling in a zigzag pattern across the top. Let cool until set. Cut into squares.

Makes nine 3-inch or thirty-six 1½-inch brownies

Caramel-Fudge Brownies

These chewy and fudgy brownies are topped with a creamy caramel layer, dark chocolate frosting, and crunchy nuts.

½ cup (1 stick) unsalted butter
2 ounces (2 squares) unsweetened chocolate
2 large eggs
1 cup sugar
½ cup all-purpose flour
1 teaspoon vanilla

Caramel Layer
½ cup (1 stick) unsalted butter
½ cup packed light brown sugar

Frosting and Topping
3 ounces (3 squares) semisweet chocolate
2 tablespoons dark corn syrup
1 tablespoon unsalted butter
1 teaspoon milk
1 cup coarsely chopped walnuts or pecans

Preheat the oven to 325°F. Butter and flour an 8-inch square pan.

In a small, heavy saucepan, melt the butter and chocolate together over low heat. Remove from the heat; cool. Beat the eggs in a medium bowl until light and fluffy. Add sugar, beating well. Blend in the chocolate mixture. Stir in the flour and vanilla. Spread the batter evenly in the prepared pan. Bake for 20 minutes.

Meanwhile, make the caramel. In a small saucepan, bring the butter and brown sugar to a boil over medium heat, stirring. Simmer 1 minute, stirring constantly. Carefully pour the hot caramel mixture over the brownies, covering the entire top. Bake for 10 to 15 minutes more or until the caramel is bubbling.

To make the frosting, combine the chocolate, corn syrup, and butter in a small, heavy saucepan. Stir over low heat until the chocolate is melted. Mix in the milk. Pour over the caramel layer immediately after you remove the brownies from the oven. Top by sprinkling with the walnuts or pecans. Cool in the pan on a wire rack. Cut into squares.

Makes nine 3-inch or thirty-six 1½-inch brownies

Chewy Date Bars

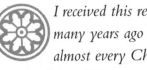 *I received this recipe from a friend many years ago and make them almost every Christmas. These dense bars, loaded with dates and nuts, stay moist and chewy when packed in an airtight container for at least one week in a cool place and up to three months in the freezer.*

- 1 cup pitted dates, finely chopped
- 2 tablespoons dark rum
- 2 large eggs
- ½ cup sugar
- ¼ cup all-purpose flour
- ½ teaspoon baking powder
- 1 cup coarsely chopped walnuts or pecans
  Confectioners' sugar, for dusting

Preheat the oven to 350°F. Butter a 9-inch square pan.

In a small bowl, mix the dates and rum; set aside.

In a large bowl, beat the eggs until frothy and gradually beat in the sugar until fluffy. In a small bowl, mix the flour and baking powder together; stir into the beaten egg mixture. Stir in the nuts and the date mixture. Spread in the prepared pan.

Bake for 25 to 30 minutes or until the center feels firm to the touch. Cool in the pan on a wire rack for 10 minutes. Cut into squares. Dust with confectioners' sugar.

Makes nine 3-inch or thirty-six 1½-inch brownies

Macadamia–Chocolate Chip Brownies

Oils pressed from toasted nuts add a delicious nutty flavor to baked goods. Look for these oils in well-stocked supermarkets or in specialty food stores. If you cannot find them, you can substitute corn oil or, preferably, melted butter for more flavor.

- ½ cup macadamia nut oil, corn oil, or unsalted butter, melted
- 4 ounces (4 squares) semisweet chocolate
- ½ cup sugar
- 2 large eggs
- 1 teaspoon vanilla
- ½ cup all-purpose flour
- ½ cup coarsely chopped macadamia nut (optional)
- 1 cup semisweet chocolate chips
- 1 cup milk chocolate chips

Preheat the oven to 350°F. Butter and lightly flour a 9-inch square pan.

Combine the oil or melted butter and chocolate in a large, heavy saucepan and stir over low heat just until the chocolate is completely melted. Remove from the heat and cool. Add the sugar and eggs and beat until light and fluffy. Stir in the vanilla. Stir in the flour until blended, then mix in the macadamia nuts, if desired, and the semisweet chocolate chips. Spread the batter evenly in the prepared pan.

Bake for 25 to 30 minutes or just until firm and a wooden skewer inserted in the center comes out clean. Remove from the oven and sprinkle the milk chocolate chips over the top. Place the pan on a wire rack. When the chocolate chips have melted, spread them over the brownies with a knife or rubber spatula. Refrigerate the brownies until the chocolate topping is set. Cut into squares.

Makes nine 3-inch or thirty-six 1½-inch brownies

Pecan-Toffee Bars

These crisp, nut-topped, chocolate-glazed cookies taste like English toffee candy. Be sure to cut them into squares before they cool or they'll crack randomly.

- 1 cup (2 sticks) unsalted butter, at room temperature
- 1 cup sugar
- 1 large egg, separated
- 2 cups all-purpose flour
- 1 teaspoon ground cinnamon
- 1 cup chopped pecans
- 1 cup semisweet chocolate chips

Preheat the oven to 275°F. Butter a 13 × 9-inch jelly roll pan.

In a large bowl, cream the butter and sugar until smooth. Add the egg yolk and beat until light. In a small bowl, stir the flour and cinnamon together and add to the creamed mixture, stirring until a dough forms. Spread in an even layer over the bottom of the prepared pan. Beat the egg white until stiff but not dry and spread over the top of the dough. Sprinkle evenly with the nuts, pressing them lightly into the egg whites.

Bake for 1 hour or until golden. Sprinkle evenly with the chocolate chips. Let stand for about 1 minute until the chocolate melts, then use a knife to swirl the chocolate over the bars. Cut into 1½-inch squares while still hot. Cool in the pan on a rack.

Makes about 60 bars

Raspberry-Oatmeal Streusel Bars

There's an earthy quality to bars made with oatmeal. Maybe it is a throwback to my childhood when I used to love to snack on a handful of rolled oats. We picked wild raspberries, too, and my mother made wonderful jam, which she used to make these Christmassy bars. When fresh raspberries are in season, I use them instead of the jam.

1½ cups all-purpose flour
 1 teaspoon baking powder
¼ teaspoon salt
½ cup granulated sugar
½ cup packed light brown sugar

¾ cup (1½ sticks) unsalted butter, chilled and cut in pieces
1½ cups uncooked quick-cooking (not instant) rolled oats
 2 cups fresh raspberries tossed with 1 cup sugar, or 1 cup red raspberry jam
½ cup sliced almonds
 Confectioners' sugar, for sprinkling

Preheat the oven to 350°F. Butter a 9-inch square baking pan.

In a large bowl, stir together the flour, baking powder, salt, and sugars until well blended. Cut in the butter until crumbly. Mix in the oatmeal. Press two-thirds of the mixture into the bottom of the baking pan. Spread the sugar-coated raspberries over the crumb layer, or spread the raspberry jam over the crumb layer. Sprinkle with the remaining crumbs. Top with the sliced almonds. Pat down firmly.

Bake for 30 to 35 minutes or until golden. Cool in the pan on a wire rack, then sprinkle with confectioners' sugar. Cut into squares.

Makes nine 3-inch or thirty-six 1½-inch brownies

Scottish Fruit Squares

This is a classic Scottish bar cookie from the city of Eyemouth.

In Scotland, it's a standard bakery item all year, although I think the buttery pastry and the colorful icing make it perfect for Christmas.

Butter Pastry

2½ cups all-purpose flour
¼ teaspoon salt
½ cup (1 stick) unsalted butter, cut into pieces
¼ cup corn oil
1 large egg, separated
2 teaspoons fresh lemon juice
2 to 3 tablespoons cold water

Filling

1 cup chopped walnuts
1 cup currants
1 cup flaked sweetened coconut
1 cup raisins
1 cup sugar
½ cup (1 stick) unsalted butter, melted
1 large egg, beaten

Icing and Topping

2 cups confectioners' sugar
4 to 5 tablespoons fresh orange juice
1 cup candied cherries, chopped

Measure the flour and salt into a large mixing bowl. Cut in the butter until the mixture resembles coarse crumbs. In a small bowl, beat together the corn oil, egg white, lemon juice, and 2 tablespoons of the water. Sprinkle the liquids over the flour mixture and toss with a fork until the pastry holds together in a ball. Add more water if necessary. Cover and chill for 30 minutes.

Preheat the oven to 375°F. Roll the pastry out to fit the bottom and sides of a 15¼ × 10¼ × ¾-inch jelly roll pan. Prick all over with a fork. Bake for 10 to 15 minutes, until light brown.

To make the filling, combine the walnuts, currants, coconut, raisins, and sugar in a large bowl. Mix in the melted butter, the egg, and the egg yolk. Spread the mixture over the bottom of the pastry. Bake for 30 minutes or until set and the edges are golden brown.

While the bars bake, make the icing. Mix the confectioners' sugar with the orange juice in a small bowl until the icing is smooth and rather soft, but not runny, and spread over the bars. Sprinkle evenly with the cherries. Cool completely before cutting into squares. The bars are easiest to cut the day after baking.

Makes twelve 3-inch or forty-eight 1½-inch bars

Chocolate-Mint Brownies

Chewy brownies topped with a mint filling and chocolate drizzle are a perfect after-dinner treat when cut into very small squares.

Brownies

- ½ cup (1 stick) unsalted butter
- 2 squares (2 ounces) unsweetened chocolate
- 2 large eggs
- 1 cup sugar
- ½ cup all-purpose flour
- 1 teaspoon vanilla

Mint Filling

- 1½ cups confectioners' sugar
- 2 to 3 tablespoons crème de menthe
- 1 tablespoon unsalted butter, melted

Chocolate Drizzle

- ½ cup semisweet chocolate chips
- 2 tablespoons unsalted butter

Preheat the oven to 350°F. Grease and flour a 9-inch square pan.

To make the brownies, place the butter and chocolate into a small, heavy saucepan over low heat and stir until melted. Remove from the heat and cool.

In a medium bowl, beat the eggs and sugar until light and fluffy. Stir in the chocolate mixture, flour, and vanilla until the batter is smooth. Spread into the prepared pan.

Bake for 30 minutes or until the brownies feel firm in the center. Cool in the pan on a wire rack.

To make the mint filling, in a small bowl, stir the confectioners' sugar and crème de menthe together until smooth. Mix in the butter. Spread the filling over the top of the cooled brownies and refrigerate until firm.

To make the chocolate drizzle, combine the chocolate chips and butter in a heavy-duty plastic bag with a zipper-lock top and close it securely. Place into a bowl of very hot tap water until the chocolate and butter are melted. Remove from the water and pat the bag dry. Knead the bag until the drizzle is evenly mixed. With scissors, snip about ⅛ inch off one corner of the bag. Drizzle the chocolate mixture over the mint layer. Refrigerate until firm. Cut into 2¼-inch squares.

Makes 16 brownies

Linzertorte Bars

It was a baker in Linz, Austria, who first created linzertorte. It is usually baked in a shallow, round tart pan and cut into wedges, then topped with whipped cream. I like to bake it like a bar cookie and serve it along with a selection of other bars, brownies, and cookies.

¾ cup (1½ sticks) unsalted butter,
   at room temperature

½ cup sugar

1 large egg

1 cup ground toasted hazelnuts
   (filberts) or almonds

1 tablespoon dark unsweetened cocoa

¼ teaspoon freshly ground nutmeg

¼ teaspoon ground cinnamon

⅛ teaspoon ground cloves

1½ cups all-purpose flour

1 cup seedless raspberry
   or apricot jam
   Confectioners' sugar, for dusting

In a large bowl, cream the butter and sugar until smooth using an electric mixer or a wooden spoon. Add the egg and beat until light and fluffy. Stir in the nuts, cocoa, spices, and flour. Cover with plastic wrap and refrigerate for 30 minutes.

Preheat the oven to 350°F. Lightly grease a 9-inch square baking pan.

Remove one-third of the dough and return it to the refrigerator. Place the remaining dough between sheets of plastic wrap and roll out to make a 10-inch square. Remove the top sheet of plastic wrap and place the dough into the prepared baking pan, plastic up. Pull off the other sheet of plastic and with your fingers, press the dough onto the bottom and ½ inch up the sides of the pan.

Spread the dough evenly with the jam. Place the reserved dough between 2 sheets of plastic and roll out to a 9½-inch square with about ¼-inch thickness. With a pastry wheel, cut into ½-inch strips. Place the strips in a crisscross fashion over the jam and press the ends onto the edges of the bottom crust.

Bake for 40 to 45 minutes or until light brown. Cool in the pan on a wire rack. Cut into 2¼-inch squares. Dust with confectioners' sugar.

Makes 16 bars

CHRISTMAS CAKES AND FRUITCAKES

Almond-Fig Cake

Studded with dried fruits and nuts this Finnish-inspired buttery pound cake keeps well stored in an airtight container in a cool place, or it can be wrapped in plastic wrap and frozen for up to three months. The optional soaking syrup adds moistness; add it before storing or freezing the cake.

1 package (8 ounces) dried mission figs, stemmed and chopped

½ cup orange liqueur, citron vodka, or orange juice

⅓ cup finely ground almonds

¾ cup (1½ sticks) unsalted butter, at room temperature

¾ cup sugar

3 large eggs, beaten

2 tablespoons grated orange zest

1½ cups all-purpose flour

1 teaspoon baking powder

½ cup sliced almonds

Soaking Syrup (Optional)

4 tablespoons orange liqueur, citron vodka, or orange juice

½ cup sugar

¼ cup fresh orange or lemon juice

In a small bowl, combine the figs and liqueur or juice and marinate for 30 minutes.

Preheat the oven to 350°F. Generously butter a 6- to 8-cup fancy tube pan. Dust the pan with the ground almonds.

In a large mixing bowl, cream the butter and sugar together until smooth. Add the eggs and beat until light and lemon colored. Mix in the orange zest. In another bowl, mix together the flour and baking powder, then add the flour mixture to the creamed mixture, mixing just until combined. Stir in the figs with their liquid and sliced almonds. Turn the batter into the prepared pan, spreading it evenly.

Bake for 40 to 45 minutes or until a skewer inserted into the middle of the cake comes out clean. Cool in the pan for 5 minutes. Invert the cake onto a wire rack and cool completely.

For the soaking syrup, combine the liqueur with the sugar and orange juice in a saucepan; heat to boiling over medium-high heat. Remove from the heat and stir until the sugar is completely dissolved. Spoon the hot syrup over the warm cake slowly so that the cake absorbs the liquid. Wrap well to store.

Makes 1 cake

Chocolate-Pistachio Yule Log

This splendid classic Christmas cake may look involved, but when you analyze the separate elements, it is really pretty simple to make. It begins with a chocolate-nut sponge cake roll that is filled with a lightly sweetened, nutty buttercream and finishes with a chocolate frosting that you can make to look like bark on the log. The ends of the roll need to be trimmed for cosmetic reasons, but if you make those cuts slightly on the diagonal, the pieces can be "glued" with frosting to the sides of the roll to resemble branch stubs on the log. Because I like to make meringue mushrooms (recipe follows) as part of my Christmas cookie baking spree, I use a few of them to garnish the log. It's a lot of fun to make this centerpiece.

> 6 large eggs, at room temperature
> 1 cup sugar
> 1 teaspoon vanilla
>   Pinch of salt
> ½ cup all-purpose flour
> ⅓ cup unsweetened cocoa
> ½ cup ground pistachios or toasted hazelnuts (filberts)

Filling

> 2 cups whipping cream
> ½ cup confectioners' sugar
> 1 teaspoon vanilla

> ½ cup ground pistachios or toasted hazelnuts (filberts)

Chocolate Glaze

> 1 cup sugar
> 1 cup whipping cream
> 6 ounces bittersweet or semisweet chocolate
> ½ cup (1 stick) unsalted butter, cut in pieces

Garnish

> Meringue Mushrooms
> (recipe follows)

Preheat the oven to 350°F. Lightly spray a 17¼ × 11½-inch jelly roll pan with non-stick spray and line the bottom with waxed paper. Lay a length of paper towels about 20 inches long on the counter and dust with confectioners' sugar.

Beat the eggs, sugar, vanilla, and salt in a large bowl with an electric mixer on high speed until thick and pale yellow, 5 to 7 minutes. Put the flour and cocoa into a sieve and sift over the egg mixture. Fold the flour in gently, using a rubber spatula, until the flour is completely blended in. Sprinkle the ground nuts over and gently fold into the batter. Spread the batter evenly into the prepared pan.

Bake in the upper third of the oven until light brown, and the edges start to pull away from the sides of the pan, 12 to 14 minutes. Loosen the edges with a knife and invert onto the sugar-sprinkled paper towels. Peel away the paper and roll the cake up from the long side. Place the roll on a wire rack to cool.

To make the filling, put the cream in a heavy saucepan or in a large glass bowl. Place the saucepan over low heat until the cream comes to a boil. Boil gently, stirring occasionally, until the cream is reduced to about 1¼ cups. Or put the glass bowl into the microwave oven and heat on high power until the cream boils, 3 to 4 minutes, and then heat on medium power for 10 to 13 minutes, until the cream is reduced to about 1¼ cups. Remove from the heat and cool. If the cream separates, don't fear, it will come together if you whisk it as it cools. Beat this "double cream" until light; then beat in the confectioners' sugar, vanilla, and ground nuts.

Carefully unroll the cake and spread with the nut filling. Reroll and wrap in plastic. Chill for 1 hour or longer.

To make the chocolate glaze, combine the sugar and cream into a heavy saucepan and bring to a boil over medium-high heat, stirring. Turn the heat to low and continue simmering for 5 minutes, until slightly thickened, stirring occasionally. Put the chocolate and butter into a bowl. Add the hot cream mixture and stir until the chocolate and butter have melted. Place the bowl over a bowl of ice water and beat with an electric mixer until the glaze is thick, cool, and glossy, about 5 minutes.

Unwrap the chilled cake roll. Frost with the chocolate glaze. Carefully trim the ends of the cake roll on the diagonal, making one end

of the slice only ½ inch wide and the other end about 2 inches thick. Place the trimmed ends onto the log with cut sides exposed so that they look like cut-off branches. Patch with more frosting. Give the log a rough, barklike texture by pulling a fork through the chocolate glaze. Chill until ready to serve. (The log can be stored 3 to 4 days, refrigerated, before serving.) Just before serving, place the Meringue Mushrooms on the log and around the edges to decorate.

Makes 1 yule log

Meringue Mushrooms

   2 large egg whites
  ½ cup sugar
  ¼ cup semisweet chocolate chips
      Unsweetened cocoa, for dusting

Preheat the oven to 275°F. Cover a baking sheet with parchment paper. Beat the egg whites and sugar together with an electric mixer until glossy in a heatproof bowl set over a pan of boiling water. Remove from the heat and beat at high speed for 3 minutes, then continue to beat at low speed until the mixture is very stiff.

Fit a pastry bag with a ½-inch plain tip. Fill the bag with the meringue. Pipe the meringue onto the sheet in 1-inch mushroom caps and 1½-inch long stems, placing them about 1 to 2 inches apart.

Bake for 40 minutes until the mushrooms are dry. Remove from the oven. Place the chocolate chips in a small glass bowl and put in the microwave oven. Heat on high power about 1 minute, stirring every 15 seconds until melted. Attach the caps to the stems with a little melted chocolate. Dust the mushrooms with unsweetened cocoa.

Dried Fruit Cake

Now a greater variety than ever of dried fruits are available, including cherries, cranberries, blueberries, and strawberries. I buy most of my dried fruits and nuts at the whole foods cooperative grocery where lots of interesting ingredients are available. This cake is stuffed with a variety of fruits and nuts. It will slice easily after it has been refrigerated for a few days.

  1 cup coarsely chopped pecans, walnuts, pistachios, or macadamia nuts
½ cup dried cranberries
½ cup dried tart red cherries
½ cup golden raisins
½ cup chopped dried papaya
½ cup chopped candied pineapple
½ cup light rum
  2 cups all-purpose flour
¾ cup sugar
½ teaspoon baking powder
½ cup (1 stick) unsalted butter, at room temperature

  1 teaspoon vanilla
  3 large eggs, beaten

For Aging
  3 tablespoons light rum

Combine the nuts, cranberries, cherries, raisins, papaya, pineapple, and rum in a medium bowl. Stir, then cover and let stand overnight.

Preheat the oven to 350°F. Butter an 8½ × 4½ × 3-inch loaf pan. Line the bottom and sides with parchment paper.

In a large bowl, combine the flour, sugar, and baking powder. Add the fruit mixture and stir to coat evenly. Blend in the butter and vanilla.

Fold the beaten eggs into the batter with a rubber spatula. Spoon the batter into the prepared pan.

Bake for 1 hour or until a wooden skewer inserted in the center comes out clean. Cool in the pan for 10 minutes, then remove from the pan and peel off the parchment paper. Let the cake cool completely on a wire rack.

Pierce holes in the cake with a wooden skewer and spoon the rum over, 1 tablespoon at a time. Wrap in cheesecloth, then wrap with plastic wrap or foil. Refrigerate at least 3 days before cutting.

Makes 1 fruitcake

Kransekake, Norwegian Almond Ring Cake

This is a showy centerpiece cake that Norwegians serve at all festive events, especially at wedding or anniversary celebrations. In Copenhagen, the Kransekage Huset, a famous Danish kondituri (a shop selling fancy baked goods), shapes logs of the kransekake mixture into fanciful designs such as bicycles and boats, for special birthdays, graduations, or confirmation celebrations. But for the classic towering cake, the batter is baked in rings that are graduated in size from about 8 inches in diameter down to 1½ inches and stacked to resemble a towering Christmas tree; it is then decorated with colorful marzipan figures, flowers, or flags. The easiest way to shape the rings is to bake them in special forms, which you can buy from shops that specialize in Scandinavian foods and equipment.

    3   cups (about 1 pound) almonds,
        blanched, unblanched, or a
        combination
    1   pound (3¾ cups) confectioners'
        sugar
    3   tablespoons all-purpose flour
    3   large egg whites, slightly beaten

Royal Icing

        1   pound (¾ cups) confectioners' sugar
    1 to 2 large egg whites
        1   teaspoon almond extract

Put the almonds into a blender or food processor and process until finely ground. In a large bowl, blend together the almonds, confectioners' sugar, and flour. Mix in the egg whites to make a smooth and pliable dough. Knead the dough well, using the dough hook of an electric mixer, if desired, or by hand on a lightly floured surface. The dough should be firm but pliable enough to handle.

Preheat the oven to 350°F.

To make the Christmas tree, coat the special kransekake rings with nonstick spray (spray works better than shortening or butter) and dust with flour. Shape the dough into ropes about the thickness of a finger and in lengths to fit the various sizes of the rings. Fit the ropes into the rings, smoothing the dough where the ends join. Place the filled rings on baking sheets (they can be placed close together and smaller rings can be placed inside larger rings to save space on the baking pan).

Bake for 10 minutes or until pale gold. Cool until firm, about 30 minutes, then remove from the molds and brush off any loose flour (see Note).

Or cut the ropes into lengths starting with a rope that is 16 inches long and shape into a perfect circle on a parchment-covered baking sheet. Cut each succeeding rope 1 inch shorter—the smallest should be about 2½ inches long—shaping them all into perfect circles on baking sheets about 2 inches apart.

Bake the rings for 10 minutes or until

golden. Cool on the baking sheet until firm, about 30 minutes.

To make the icing, mix all of the ingredients in a small bowl until the mixture is smooth and thin, but not runny. Place the icing into a pastry bag with a small, plain tip.

To assemble the cake, place the largest ring on a serving plate. Press the icing in a zigzag pattern all around the ring. Top with the next largest ring. Repeat the zigzag piping procedure, stacking the rings until they form a tall, balanced tower. If you wish, decorate the top with a fresh flower or a marzipan figure and decorate the sides of the cake with marzipan figures or flags in wooden picks.

To serve the cake, lift the top part of the tower off and break the remaining rings into 2- or 3-inch pieces.

Makes 48 servings

NOTE: If you are making the layers ahead of time, it is best to store the layers separately and assemble the cake just before serving. The layers can be frozen up to six months, or can be kept, tightly wrapped, in a cool place for up to two weeks before assembling. I usually stack the rounds in their baking rings inside an airtight tin or plastic container to protect them from breaking.

Lingonberry Spice Cake

 This is pretty when baked in a fluted loaf pan; however, shiny pans, especially fancy ones, reflect the heat and the cake may need a little extra baking time. Although this cake is usually served along with other pastries, cakes, and cookies on the coffee table, it makes a very nice dessert served on its own with the lingonberry sauce.

½ cup (1 stick) unsalted butter,
    at room temperature
1 cup sugar
2 large eggs
1½ cups flour
1 teaspoon freshly ground cardamom
½ teaspoon ground cinnamon
½ teaspoon ginger
1 teaspoon baking powder
¼ teaspoon baking soda
¼ teaspoon salt
½ cup sour cream
½ cup lingonberry jam or preserves,
    or seedless raspberry jam

Lingonberry Sauce (Optional)

1 cup lingonberry preserves or jam
3 to 4 tablespoons cranberry-
    or orange-flavored liqueur

Preheat the oven to 350°F. Grease and flour a 9 × 5-inch loaf pan.

In a large mixing bowl, cream the butter with the sugar and eggs until light and fluffy. In a separate bowl, thoroughly mix the flour, cardamom, cinnamon, ginger, baking powder, baking soda, and salt. In another small bowl, combine the sour cream and jam.

Blend the dry ingredients and the sour cream mixture into the butter mixture, mixing until smooth. Turn into the prepared pan.

Bake for 55 to 60 minutes or until a wooden skewer inserted in the center comes out clean. Let cool in the pan for 5 minutes, then turn out onto a wire rack to finish cooling.

To make the sauce, in a small bowl mix the lingonberry preserves with the liqueur to taste. To serve, cut the cake into slices and serve with the sauce on the side.

Makes 1 loaf

Mosaic Fruitcake

Almost pure confection! This fruit-cake is so packed with fruit and nuts that the cake itself is almost invisible. I bake it in a 9 × 13-inch baking pan, then cut it into five slender logs. Wrapped in clear plastic and tied with a colorful ribbon, this makes a pretty gift. This is an adaptation of a recipe from Eleana Ostman, food editor of the St. Paul Pioneer *press.*

    4 cups mixed candied cherries and
       pineapple, or other dried fruits such
       as dried papaya, cherries, cranberries,
       blueberries, and strawberries
    1 pound pitted dates, halved
    1 cup broken walnuts
    1 cup pecan halves
    1 cup shelled pistachios
    2 cups sliced almonds
    ¼ cup light rum
    1 cup all-purpose flour
    1 cup sugar
    2 teaspoons ground ginger
    2 teaspoons cinnamon
    ½ teaspoon ground cloves
    ½ teaspoon ground nutmeg
    4 large eggs, lightly beaten

Glaze
    ½ cup light corn syrup

Preheat the oven to 300°F. Butter a 13 × 9-inch baking pan and line the bottom with parchment paper.

In a very large bowl, mix the candied fruits, dates, walnuts, pecans, pistachios, and almonds. Stir in the rum. In a small bowl mix the flour, sugar, ginger, cinnamon, cloves, and nutmeg; pour over the fruits and blend well. Add the eggs and mix until the dry ingredients are moistened. Pour into the parchment-lined pan. Pack the mixture firmly and levelly into the pan. Bake for 1½ hours or until the center of the cake feels firm.

To make the glaze, in a small saucepan, bring the corn syrup to a boil over medium heat.

Brush the hot syrup evenly over the hot cake. Cool until the glaze is dry. Loosen the edges carefully and invert the cake onto a cutting board. With a sharp knife, cut crosswise to make 5 equal-size logs. Wrap individually in plastic wrap. The cake is ready to eat the next day, or it can be kept in the refrigerator for up to 3 months. To serve, cut into ½-inch-thick slices using a sharp knife dipped in water.

Makes 5 cakes, about 9 × 2½ inches

Old English Fruitcake

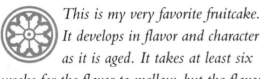 *This is my very favorite fruitcake. It develops in flavor and character as it is aged. It takes at least six weeks for the flavor to mellow, but the flavor improves steadily over the span of a year or longer. I like to serve a thin slice of fruitcake with a shaving of sharp Canadian Cheddar or Norwegian gjetost and a small glass of chilled white wine or port for a tasty holiday dessert.*

1½ pounds candied cherries
2 pounds candied pineapple
1 pound other mixed candied fruits, such as tropical fruit mix
1 pound whole pitted dates
1 cup currants
1 cup golden raisins
2 pounds (8 cups) broken pecans and/or walnuts
1 cup dark rum or brandy

½ cup double-strength espresso
1½ tablespoons grated orange zest
1 teaspoon grated lemon zest
½ cup fresh orange juice
2 tablespoons fresh lemon juice
2 cups (4 sticks) unsalted butter, at room temperature
2 cups packed brown sugar
12 large eggs, separated
4 cups all-purpose flour
2 teaspoons ground cinnamon
2 teaspoons ground mace
1 teaspoon ground cloves
1 teaspoon ground allspice
1 teaspoon freshly ground nutmeg
1 teaspoon salt
Rum or brandy, for wrapping and aging

Mix the fruits, nuts, rum or brandy, and coffee in a very large bowl and stir to combine. Cover and marinate overnight. Stir in the orange and lemon zest, and orange and lemon juices.

Preheat the oven to 250°F. Line twelve 5 × 3-inch or four 9 × 5-inch loaf pans with parchment paper.

In a large mixing bowl, cream the butter and sugar together until light. Add the egg yolks and beat until light and fluffy.

Sift the flour with the cinnamon, mace, cloves, allspice, nutmeg, and salt in another large bowl. Add 1 cup of the flour mixture to the fruits and nuts and mix well. Add the remainder of the flour to the creamed mixture

TO AGE FRUITCAKES

Cool the cakes completely and remove the parchment paper. Spoon one to two tablespoons of rum or brandy over each cake. Moisten a double layer of cheesecloth with rum or brandy and wrap that around the cake. Wrap in plastic or seal in a heavy-duty storage-type plastic bag. Store in a cool spot (50 to 60°F) or, if necessary, in the refrigerator. If stored in the refrigerator, at a temperature of about 40°F, the cakes may take up to two months to age well. Check the cakes for dryness every two weeks. Open up the bag or wrapper and brush with rum or brandy. Rewrap and return to storage.

and mix until smooth, then add this to the fruits and nuts, mix until well blended. (Use a strong wooden spoon, a large rubber spatula, or your hands.)

In another bowl, beat the egg whites until they hold soft peaks. Fold into the fruitcake batter. Spoon the batter evenly into the prepared pans.

Adjust the oven rack so that the upper rack is in the center of the oven and the lower rack is at the first level above the heating element. Place a shallow pan of water onto the lower rack. Place the cake-filled pans onto the upper rack and bake for 2½ to 3 hours for the large cakes, or 1½ to 2 hours for the small cakes, or until a wooden skewer inserted in the center of a cake comes out clean. Add water to the shallow pan as needed. Cool the cakes in the pans for 10 minutes, then remove from the pans. Peel off the paper liners. Drizzle about 4 tablespoons rum or brandy over each large cake or 2 to 3 tablespoons over the smaller cakes. Cut cheesecloth into enough large squares to wrap the cakes individually. Moisten the cheesecloth squares with the rum or brandy and wrap each cake in the cloth. Place the wrapped cakes into plastic bags or wrap individually in foil. Age in a cool place for at least 1 month, preferably for a year. Check occasionally and add more brandy or rum, then rewrap in foil.

Makes twelve 1-pound or four 3-pound fruitcakes

Walnut-Date Cake with Orange Buttercream

 It's always nice to have a dessert tucked away in the freezer, and this cake with its orange buttercream stays moist and delicious. All you need to do is remove it from the freezer an hour or so before serving so that it will have time to thaw and come to room temperature.

½ cup (1 stick) unsalted butter,
   at room temperature
1 cup sugar
4 large egg whites, lightly beaten
1½ cups all-purpose flour
1½ teaspoons baking powder
¼ cup milk
½ cup chopped pitted dates
½ cup chopped walnuts

Orange Buttercream

4 large egg yolks
¾ cup sugar
1 tablespoon grated orange zest
¼ cup fresh orange juice
1 tablespoon orange liqueur
¾ cup (1½ sticks) unsalted butter,
   at room temperature
1 cup confectioners' sugar

Preheat the oven to 350°F. Butter a 10-inch springform pan and line the bottom with parchment paper.

In a large bowl, beat the butter and sugar together with an electric mixer until smooth. Add the egg whites and beat until light and fluffy, about 2 minutes. Add the flour and baking powder and beat at medium speed until totally blended. Beat in the milk, then stir in the dates and walnuts. Spread the batter evenly into the pan.

Bake for 25 to 30 minutes, until light brown and a skewer inserted into the center comes out clean. Cool on a wire rack.

To make the buttercream, in a medium heatproof bowl, beat the egg yolks, sugar, and orange zest together until blended. Stir in the orange juice. Place over a skillet of simmering water. Cook, stirring, until the mixture thickens, about 5 minutes (the mixture should cook to a temperature between 165 and 170°F). Stir in the orange liqueur and set aside to cool.

In another bowl, beat the butter and confectioners' sugar with an electric mixer until light and fluffy. Add the orange mixture and beat for 2 to 3 minutes or until very light.

To assemble the cake, remove the cake from the pan and cut it horizontally into 2 layers. Spoon 1 cup of the buttercream onto the center of the bottom layer and spread it out evenly. Top with the second cake layer, cut side down. Spread the remaining buttercream on the top and sides. Refrigerate until the buttercream is firm. When set, wrap the cake and freeze up to 2 weeks. To defrost, remove from the freezer and refrigerate 3 to 4 hours, overnight, or at room temperature for 1 hour. Unwrap and let set at room temperature for 15 minutes before serving.

Makes one 10-inch cake

White Coconut Fruitcake

 Because this cake doesn't need to be aged, it's great for last-minute baking. My mother-in-law was famous for this cake in Warba, Minnesota, where she lived.

1 cup (2 sticks) unsalted butter, at room temperature
2 cups sugar
1 can (12 ounces) sweetened condensed milk
2 cups flaked sweetened coconut
1 cup mixed cocktail nuts without peanuts
2 cups golden raisins
1 cup diced mixed candied fruits
½ cup candied pineapple
½ cup candied red cherries
½ cup candied green cherries
1 tablespoon grated lemon zest
3½ cups all-purpose flour
2 teaspoons baking powder
½ teaspoon salt
5 large egg whites
1 tablespoon vanilla

Preheat the oven to 300°F. Grease two 8 × 4-inch loaf pans and line them with parchment paper.

In a large bowl, cream together the butter and sugar. Add the milk and beat until light and fluffy. In another bowl, combine the coconut, nuts, raisins, candied fruits, and lemon zest. Add ½ cup of the flour and mix well. In a separate bowl combine the remaining flour with the baking powder and salt. Add the fruits and the flour mixture to the creamed mixture and stir to combine thoroughly. In another bowl, beat the egg whites until stiff. Fold the whites and vanilla into the batter until well blended. Turn the batter into the prepared pans, spreading it evenly.

Bake for 2 hours 15 minutes or until a skewer inserted into the center of the cakes comes out clean. Cool in the pans for 15 minutes. Turn the cakes out of the pans and finish cooling on a wire rack. To keep, wrap in plastic and store for up to 4 weeks.

Makes 2 loaf cakes

FESTIVE CHRISTMAS DESSERTS

Christmas Cranberry Crumble

Cranberries baked in this sweet and crunchy way are a perfectly delicious and simple ending to a holiday meal.

  2 cups fresh cranberries, rinsed and drained
  ½ cup chopped walnuts
1½ cups sugar
  2 large eggs
  1 cup all-purpose flour
  ¼ teaspoon salt
  ¾ cup (1½ sticks) unsalted butter, melted
  3 tablespoons vegetable oil
     Whipped cream, for serving (optional)

Preheat the oven to 350°F. Grease a deep, round pottery or glass baking dish or 10-inch pie plate.

Sprinkle the cranberries and walnuts evenly over the bottom of the prepared pan and sprinkle them with ½ cup of the sugar.

In a medium bowl, beat the eggs with the remaining sugar until light and fluffy. Blend in the flour, salt, butter, and oil. Pour the mixture over the berries and nuts.

Bake for 45 minutes to 1 hour or until the crumble is light brown. Cool at least 10 minutes on a wire rack before cutting into wedges. Serve warm or cool with whipped cream or ice cream, if desired.

Makes 8 to 12 servings

Individual Croquembouche

Croquembouche is French for "crisp in the mouth." The classic dessert is an elaborate, tall, conical tower of tiny cream puffs wrapped in a shroud of glistening caramel that makes a spectacular centerpiece dessert, resembling a whimsical Christmas tree. Even though it is fun to assemble, it is a challenge. So now I make individual versions, which are so much easier to handle; they can also be filled and frozen ahead. I stack four tiny puffs on a dessert plate and swirl it with the caramel before serving. If I haven't the energy or time for the caramel drizzle, I drizzle each serving with melted chocolate.

When making the cream puff paste, it helps to use a food processor fitted with the steel blade to blend in the eggs.

Pâte à Choux
(Cream Puff Paste)

- 1 cup water
- ½ teaspoon salt
- 1 teaspoon sugar
- ½ cup (1 stick) unsalted butter, cut into pieces
- 1 cup all-purpose flour
- 4 large eggs, at room temperature

Filling

About 1 quart of your favorite ice cream, such as eggnog, Nesselrode, or chocolate, if you will freeze the puffs ahead or Grand Marnier Filling (recipe follows)

Caramel Drizzle

- 2 cups sugar
- ⅔ cup water
- 2 tablespoons corn syrup

In a large, heavy saucepan, combine the water, salt, sugar, and butter. Measure the flour and have it ready. Place the saucepan over medium heat and heat, stirring until the butter is melted. Increase the heat to high and stir until the mixture comes to a full rolling boil. Dump in the flour all at once. Stir vigorously with a wooden spoon until the paste forms a ball in the pan and comes away from the sides, about 1 minute. Remove from the heat.

Turn the paste into a food processor with the steel blade in place. Turn on the processor and add the eggs, one at a time, through the feed tube; process until the eggs are thoroughly blended into the mixture. Or, if working by hand, add the eggs one at a time to the paste in the saucepan and stir vigorously until the eggs are thoroughly blended in and the paste is smooth and shiny.

Set the cream puff paste aside to cool for 10 minutes. The mixture should be fairly stiff.

Preheat the oven to 425°F. Lightly grease 2 baking sheets or cover with parchment paper.

To shape the puffs you will need two spoons. With one spoon, scoop up 1 tablespoonful of dough. With the other spoon push the dough off the first spoon onto the baking sheet, placing the mounds 2 inches apart. Or use a pastry bag with a 1-inch tip to pipe out the dough.

Bake for 15 to 20 minutes or until the puffs are golden and crisp. Slash the sides while the puffs are hot to allow steam to escape and keep the shells crisp. Cool completely, then fill the puffs with tiny scoops of ice cream, or spoon the Grand Marnier Filling into a pastry bag fitted with a ½-inch tip and press the cream into each puff. Freeze the ice cream–filled puffs or refrigerate the pastry cream–filled puffs until ready to serve. Remove the puffs from the freezer just before serving.

For the caramel drizzle, combine the sugar, water, and corn syrup in a large, heavy saucepan. Bring to a boil over high heat, swirling the pan until the sugar has completely dissolved and the syrup is clear. Cover the pan to allow the steam to condense on the cover and wash down the sides of the pan about 10 minutes. Remove the cover and continue boiling until the syrup turns a golden amber. Swirl the pan slowly until it darkens to a caramel brown and reaches 310°F (the hard crack stage) on a candy thermometer. Place the syrup over a pan of simmering water over low heat to prevent hardening.

When ready to serve, dip 4 filled puffs quickly into the Caramel Drizzle and stack on individual plates placing 3 puffs in a triangle and the fourth on top. Dip a fork into the caramel and swirl it over each individual croquembouche to surround it with threads of spun caramel. Serve immediately.

Makes 12 servings

Croquembuche with Chocolate Drizzle

Place chocolate chips into a heavy-duty plastic bag with a zipper-lock top. Close firmly. Set into a bowl of hot water until the chocolate is completely melted. To serve the cream puffs, place 3 filled puffs on each serving plate and top with a fourth filled puff. Wipe the outside of the bag of melted chocolate until completely dry. Snip a $\frac{1}{8}$-inch triangle off one corner to make a small hole. Swirl the chocolate onto the puffs. Serve immediately.

Grand Marnier Filling

    2 cups light cream or milk
 $\frac{3}{4}$ cup sugar
 $\frac{1}{2}$ cup all-purpose flour
 $\frac{1}{8}$ teaspoon salt
    1 large egg, beaten
 $\frac{1}{4}$ cup ($\frac{1}{2}$ stick) unsalted butter,
      cut into pieces
    2 tablespoons Grand Marnier,
      Cointreau, or dark rum
    1 teaspoon vanilla

In a small saucepan on the range or in a glass measuring cup in the microwave oven, heat the cream or milk to boiling.

In a large, heavy saucepan, stir the sugar, flour, and salt together. Whisk in the hot cream until well blended. Whisk in the egg. Place over medium-high heat and heat, whisking constantly so it does not scorch, until the mixture comes to a boil. Whisking constantly, boil until the mixture is very thick and smooth. Remove from the heat and whisk in the butter. Place over ice water and stir until cooled to room temperature. Beat in the Grand Marnier and vanilla. Cover and chill until ready to use.

Makes about 2 cups

Irish Plum Pudding with Brandy Sauce

Plum pudding needs to be made ahead and aged three weeks to two months. A few years ago, when I was teaching a holiday baking cooking class, my friend Cristabel Grant, who is from Dublin, gave me this recipe. We've enjoyed it ever since. This recipe contains beef suet, which is the authentic fat used in plum puddings.

¾ cup dark raisins

¾ cup golden raisins

¾ cup currants

½ cup candied orange peel

½ cup chopped almonds

1 tart apple (such as Granny Smith) pared, cored, and grated

½ teaspoon freshly grated lemon zest

1 cup chopped beef suet

½ cup all-purpose flour

⅔ cup packed brown sugar

1¼ cups fresh bread crumbs

½ teaspoon allspice

¼ teaspoon salt

3 large eggs

2 tablespoons brandy

1 tablespoon fresh lemon juice

Brandy for aging and flaming

Brandy Sauce (recipe follows)

In a large bowl, combine the raisins, currants, orange peel, almonds, apple, and lemon zest. In another bowl, combine the suet with the flour; add the sugar, crumbs, allspice, and salt and mix well. Beat the eggs in a small bowl and add to the flour mixture; blend in the fruit and nut mixture, brandy, and lemon juice. Cover and let stand in a cool place (not refrigerated) overnight. Turn into a well-greased 1-quart pudding mold or bowl. Tie a piece of cheesecloth over the top.

Place a steaming rack into a large pot. Pour water into the pot just to the bottom of the rack and heat to boiling over high heat. Place the pudding on the rack and reduce the heat to medium high or just to keep the water boiling. Cover and steam for 4 hours, replacing the water as necessary.

When the pudding is done, it will feel firm to the touch and a long wooden skewer inserted through the center will come out clean. Remove from the steamer. Cool on a wire rack. Unmold and wrap the pudding in cheesecloth moistened with brandy. Wrap in foil and age in a cool place (about 50°F) for 3 weeks or longer.

To serve, remove the foil. Place the cheesecloth-wrapped pudding on a rack in a pot over boiling water and steam for ½ hour to heat through. Or warm in a microwave oven on low power for 5 minutes until heated through. Place on a serving plate.

To serve, warm the brandy in a metal ladle over a flame (a candle is fine). Carefully ignite the brandy with a long match and pour over the pudding. Cut the pudding into wedges and serve with warm Brandy Sauce.

Makes 12 servings

Brandy Sauce

- 1¼ cups water
- 3½ tablespoons cornstarch
- 4 tablespoons (½ stick) unsalted butter, at room temperature
- 3 tablespoons sugar
- ⅓ cup brandy

In a small saucepan, combine the water and cornstarch; heat to boiling, stirring, and cook, stirring, for 1 to 2 minutes, until thickened and clear. Remove from the heat and blend in the butter, sugar, and brandy. Serve warm.

Makes about 1½ cups

White Christmas Pavlova

 The recipe for pavlova, the delicate "soft-hard" meringue is one that starts arguments in New Zealand and Australia. Everybody has an opinion about how this traditional dish should be prepared. When we had it for dessert in the home of a New Zealand family, I asked for the recipe, and I received four different versions. I've worked out a method that works well for me, but I'm including all four baking methods here. It's important that the pavlova not turn the least bit brown or it will be chewy rather than delicate. Think of it as drying in the oven rather than actually baking.

Pavlova makes a spectacular Christmas dessert with green kiwifruit and fresh strawberries. Strawberries aren't in season at Christmastime here, but they are *in Australia and New Zealand. Of course, when our local berries are in season, I remember this dessert because it makes a delicious base for raspberries, blackberries, and peaches, too.*

- 4 large egg whites, at room temperature
- ¼ teaspoon salt
- 1 cup sugar
- 4 teaspoons cornstarch
- 2 teaspoons white vinegar

1 teaspoon vanilla
1 cup whipping cream
Sliced fresh fruit, such as kiwifruit, strawberries, bananas, raspberries, peaches, or any other soft fruit in season

Preheat the oven to 200°F. Line a 15½ × 11½-inch baking sheet with parchment paper or foil, grease, and sprinkle with flour. Draw a 9-inch circle in the flour.

In a large bowl, beat the egg whites and salt together with an electric mixer until soft peaks form. Stir the sugar and cornstarch together in a small bowl. Beating on high speed, add the vinegar and vanilla to the egg whites. Add the sugar mixture a heaping tablespoon at a time, and beat until the whites are very stiff and glossy.

Turn the meringue into the prepared pan onto the center of the circle, spreading it to the circumference of the circle. The meringue will be about 1½ inches deep. Run a spatula around the edges to make the sides straight; smooth the top.

Bake the pavlova for 2 hours; for alternate baking directions see below. Turn the oven off and leave the pavlova in the oven with the door closed until cold, or overnight.

Up to 2 hours before serving, place the pavlova onto a serving plate. In a bowl, whip the cream until it forms soft peaks and spread it over the top. Decorate with fresh fruit. Serve within 2 hours.

Makes 6 to 8 servings

ALTERNATIVE BAKING DIRECTIONS

1. Bake at 350°F for 5 to 10 minutes, then turn the oven down to 250°F and bake for 35 to 40 minutes longer, then turn the oven off and leave it in the oven until cold, or overnight.

2. Bake at 275°F for 1½ hours. Turn the oven off and leave it in the oven with the door closed until cold, or overnight.

3. Bake at 300°F for 45 minutes, turn the oven off, and leave it in the oven cold, or overnight.

QUICK BREADS

Apricot-Almond-Pistachio Bread

The day I found a two-pound jar of shelled pistachios at our local whole-sale market I was so excited that I came home and created this bread immediately. The pistachios, almonds, and apricots make a pretty mosaic in each slice of this light nut bread.

1 cup dried apricots, chopped
½ cup brandy
¼ cup (½ stick) unsalted butter, at room temperature
½ cup sugar
1 large egg
1¾ cups all-purpose flour
2 teaspoons baking powder
¼ teaspoon baking soda
¼ teaspoon salt
¼ cup milk
¼ cup chopped almonds
¼ cup shelled pistachios, coarsely chopped

In a small bowl, combine the apricots and brandy. Cover and let stand for 4 hours.

Preheat the oven to 350°F. Butter and flour two 5¾ × 3½-inch pans or one 8½ × 4½-inch loaf pan.

In a large mixing bowl cream together the butter and sugar. Blend in the egg and beat until light. In a small bowl, mix the flour, baking powder, baking soda, and salt. Add to the creamed mixture along with the milk, apricots, and the soaking liquid. Mix in the almonds and pistachios. Spoon into the prepared pan or pans.

Bake for 40 to 45 minutes for the small loaves, or 55 to 60 minutes for the large loaf, or until a wooden skewer inserted in the center of the loaf comes out clean. Remove the breads from the pans and cool on wire racks. Serve warm or cool. To mellow the bread, wrap the cooled loaf in clear plastic wrap and store in a cool place for 2 days. To keep longer, wrap in foil, label, and freeze.

Makes 1 large or 2 small loaves

Banana-Walnut Bread

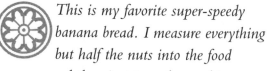

This is my favorite super-speedy banana bread. I measure everything but half the nuts into the food processor and then just turn the machine on.

1½ cups all-purpose flour
1 teaspoon baking soda
½ teaspoon salt
¾ cup sugar
½ cup (1 stick) plus 2 tablespoons unsalted butter, at room temperature

Quick breads are quick to make because they do not require kneading or rising time. They are leavened with baking powder or baking soda instead of yeast. The term *quick bread* usually includes biscuits, muffins, popovers, scones, spoonbreads, and a variety of sweet and savory loaves.

⅓ cup milk

2 large eggs

2 ripe bananas, sliced

1 tablespoon lemon juice

1 cup chopped walnuts

Preheat the oven to 350°F. Butter one 9½ × 4½-inch or three 5¾ × 3½-inch loaf pans.

In a food processor or a large bowl with an electric mixer, combine the flour, baking soda, salt, sugar, butter, milk, eggs, bananas, lemon juice, and half the nuts. Process for 30 to 45 seconds in the food processor or mix at high speed, scraping the sides of the bowl with a rubber spatula until the mixture is smooth. Pour into the prepared pan or pans. Sprinkle the remaining nuts over the top.

Bake for 1 hour 15 minutes for the large loaf, or 40 to 45 minutes for the small loaves, or until a skewer inserted in the center of the loaf comes out clean. Cool for 5 minutes in the pan, then turn out onto a wire rack to finish cooling.

Makes 1 large or 3 small loaves

Blueberry-Almond Bread

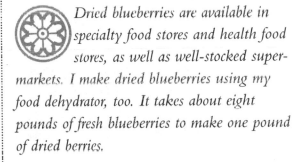
Dried blueberries are available in specialty food stores and health food stores, as well as well-stocked supermarkets. I make dried blueberries using my food dehydrator, too. It takes about eight pounds of fresh blueberries to make one pound of dried berries.

½ cup (1 stick) unsalted butter, at room temperature

½ cup sugar

1 large egg

1 teaspoon grated lemon zest

2 cups all-purpose flour

2 teaspoons baking powder

¼ teaspoon baking soda

¼ teaspoon salt

¾ cup milk

½ cup dried blueberries

¼ cup chopped almonds

1 tablespoon sugar

2 tablespoons sliced almonds

reheat the oven to 350°F. Butter and flour three 5¾ × 3½-inch or one 8½ × 4½-inch loaf pan.

In a large mixing bowl cream together the butter and ½ cup sugar. Blend in the egg and beat until light. Mix in the lemon zest. In a small bowl, mix together the flour, baking powder, baking soda, and salt. Add to the creamed mixture alternately with the milk. Fold in the blueberries and chopped almonds. Spoon into the loaf pan or pans. Sprinkle the tops of the loaves with the 1 tablespoon sugar and the sliced almonds.

Bake for 45 minutes for the small loaves, or 55 to 60 minutes for the large loaf, or until a skewer inserted in the center of the loaf comes out clean. Remove from the pan or pans and cool on a wire rack. Serve warm or cool. Wrap in clear plastic to store or wrap in foil, label, and freeze.

Makes 1 large or 3 small loaves

Zucchini-Carrot–Black Walnut Bread

 Black walnuts are a native American nut that has a strong, slightly bitter flavor. They are not always easy to find in the grocery, but you can substitute English walnuts with equally good results.

2 large eggs
½ cup vegetable oil
½ cup granulated sugar
½ cup packed brown sugar
1½ teaspoons vanilla
½ cup packed shredded zucchini
½ cup shredded carrot
2 cups all-purpose flour
½ cup wheat germ
2 teaspoons baking powder
½ teaspoon baking soda
1 teaspoon salt
½ cup chopped black walnuts

 FREEZING QUICK BREADS

ll quick breads, except for spoonbreads, freeze beautifully. As soon as possible after cooling, enclose them in a plastic freezer bag, plastic wrap, or foil and seal well. They will stay fresh for two to three months if they are not exposed to the air in the freezer. Be sure to label and date each item. When you are ready to serve them, simply remove the wrapped breads from the freezer and allow the breads to stand, still wrapped, at room temperature until thawed. Or unwrap the bread and place on a baking sheet in a 350°F oven for ten to fifteen minutes until thawed.

Quick breads make wonderful gifts. Wrap them in clear plastic wrap and tie with ribbon or twine. Sometimes I like to place them, wrapped, into a pan the same size that the bread was baked in. I attach a handwritten copy of the recipe. A wrapped quick bread placed on a small bread board or in a bread basket also makes a nice gift.

Preheat the oven to 350°F. Butter one 8½ × 4½-inch or three 5¾ × 3½-inch loaf pans.

In a large bowl using an electric mixer, beat the eggs until foamy. Add the oil, sugars, and vanilla and beat at high speed until the mixture is very thick and fluffy.

With a spoon, stir in the shredded zucchini and carrot.

Stir the flour, wheat germ, baking powder, baking soda, salt, and walnuts together in another bowl. Blend into the zucchini mixture just until the flour is no longer visible. Pour the batter into the prepared loaf pan or pans.

Bake for 1 hour for the large loaf, or 35 to 45 minutes for the smaller loaves, or until a wooden skewer inserted in the center comes out clean. Cool in the pan for 10 minutes, then turn out onto a wire rack to cool thoroughly.

Makes 1 large or 3 small loaves

Orange-Cranberry Bread

When cranberries are in season I like to buy a few extra bags and keep them in the freezer. They can be used like the fresh berries; add them frozen to the dough. The frozen berries will stiffen the dough a little and require about five minutes more baking time, but otherwise they will behave in the same way as fresh cranberries. You can also use dried cranberries in this bread.

 2 cups all-purpose flour

 1 cup sugar

1½ teaspoons baking powder

 1 teaspoon baking soda

 ½ teaspoon salt

 ¼ cup (½ stick) unsalted butter, melted

 1 large egg, beaten

 1 teaspoon grated orange zest

 ¾ cup orange juice

 1 cup halved fresh cranberries or ½ cup dried cranberries (see Note)

 1 cup chopped walnuts

Preheat the oven to 350°F. Butter and flour one 8½ × 4½-inch or three 5¾ × 3½-inch loaf pans.

Mix the flour, sugar, baking powder, baking soda, and salt together in a large mixing bowl. Stir in the butter, egg, and orange zest and juice all at once, stirring just until the mixture is evenly moist. Fold in the cranberries and nuts. Spoon the batter into the prepared pan or pans.

Bake for 1 hour 10 minutes for the large loaf, or 50 to 55 minutes for the smaller loaves, or until a wooden skewer inserted in the center comes out clean. Cool for 5 minutes in the pan and then turn out onto a wire rack to cool.

Makes 1 large or 3 small loaves

NOTE: Dried cranberries, sometimes called craisins, are available all year round and are convenient to use.

Papaya-Apple Loaf

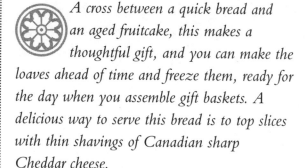 *A cross between a quick bread and an aged fruitcake, this makes a thoughtful gift, and you can make the loaves ahead of time and freeze them, ready for the day when you assemble gift baskets. A delicious way to serve this bread is to top slices with thin shavings of Canadian sharp Cheddar cheese.*

1 cup packed brown sugar
½ cup vegetable oil
2 tablespoons cream sherry
2 large eggs
1 teaspoon vanilla
1 cup raisins
1 cup coarsely chopped dried papaya
1 cup chopped walnuts or pecans
1 cup pitted chopped dates
1½ cups chopped tart cooking apples
  (such as Granny Smith)
2 cups all-purpose flour
2 teaspoons baking soda
½ teaspoon salt
½ teaspoon ground cinnamon
¼ teaspoon freshly ground nutmeg

Preheat the oven to 350°F. Grease and flour three 5¾ × 3½-inch loaf pans.

In a large mixing bowl, stir together the brown sugar, oil, sherry, eggs, vanilla, raisins, papaya, nuts, dates, and apples. In another bowl, stir the flour, baking soda, salt, cinnamon and nutmeg together and blend into the fruit mixture just until combined. Spoon into the prepared pans.

Bake for 30 to 35 minutes or until a wooden skewer inserted into the center of the loaves comes out clean. Cool for 5 minutes in the pans. Invert onto a wire rack to finish cooling.

Makes 3 small loaves

Pumpkin-Nut Bread

For breakfast or morning coffee, spread slices of this bread with pineapple- or orange-flavored cream cheese. Or make cream cheese sandwiches and brown them in a little butter in a skillet; cut the warm sandwiches into narrow fingers.

½ cup (1 stick) unsalted butter,
   at room temperature
1 cup sugar
2 large eggs, beaten
¼ cup orange juice
1 cup fresh cooked or canned
   puréed pumpkin
1⅔ cups all-purpose flour
1 teaspoon baking soda
¾ teaspoon salt
½ teaspoon baking powder
1½ teaspoons pumpkin pie spice
½ cup chopped walnuts
½ cup raisins

Preheat the oven to 350°F. Grease one 9 × 5-inch or three 5¾ × 3½-inch loaf pans.

In a large bowl using an electric mixer, cream together the butter and sugar. Add the eggs, orange juice, and pumpkin and beat until light. Combine the flour, baking soda, salt, baking powder, and pumpkin pie spice in another bowl. Stir the dry ingredients into the pumpkin mixture just until blended. Stir in the walnuts and raisins. Turn the batter into the prepared pan or pans.

Bake for 55 to 60 minutes for the large loaf, or 35 to 40 minutes for the small loaves, or until a wooden skewer inserted into the center comes out clean. Cool in the pan for 5 minutes, then turn out onto a wire rack to finish cooling.

Makes 1 large or 3 small loaves

TO TEST FOR DONENESS

When quick breads have baked to perfection, the edges and top of the loaf will be brown. For the ultimate test, insert a long wooden skewer into the center of the loaf. When pulled out of the loaf, the skewer will be clean and dry. If it is not, continue baking until the loaf tests done. If the loaf appears to be browning too quickly, place a small piece of foil over the top to prevent it from becoming too dark.

Spicy Apple-Carrot Bread

Apples and carrots add moistness and color to this spicy nut bread. Offer it with a tray of sliced cheeses and a bowlful of whipped butter seasoned with a bit of cinnamon.

½ cup shredded carrots
1 cup shredded tart apple
   (such as Granny Smith)
2 large eggs
½ cup vegetable oil
¾ cup sugar
1 teaspoon vanilla
1½ cups all-purpose flour
1 teaspoon baking soda
½ teaspoon baking powder
½ teaspoon salt
1½ teaspoons ground cinnamon
¾ teaspoon ground ginger
¼ teaspoon freshly ground nutmeg
1 cup chopped walnuts
1 cup raisins

Preheat the oven to 375°F. Butter one 8½ × 4½-inch loaf pan.

In a large mixing bowl, stir together the carrots, apple, eggs, oil, sugar, and vanilla. In another bowl, stir the flour, baking soda, baking powder, salt, cinnamon, ginger, and nutmeg together and add to the egg mixture. Stir just until blended. Stir in the walnuts and raisins. Turn the batter into the prepared pan.

Bake for 1 hour or until a skewer inserted in the center comes out clean. Cool for 5 minutes in the pan and then turn out on a wire rack to cool.

Makes 1 large loaf

Strawberry-Coconut Bread

Dried strawberries are soft and chewy, with a prunelike texture. Naturally sweet yet tart, they add a burst of flavor as well as color to this special nut bread.

½ cup (1 stick) unsalted butter, at room temperature

½ cup sugar

1 large egg

1 teaspoon grated lemon zest

2 cups all-purpose flour

2 teaspoons baking powder

¼ teaspoon baking soda

¼ teaspoon salt

¾ cup milk

½ cup dried strawberries, halved

½ cup sliced almonds

1 tablespoon sugar

2 tablespoons flaked sweetened coconut

Preheat the oven to 350°F. Butter and flour three 5¾ × 3½-inch or one 8½ × 4½-inch loaf pan.

In a large bowl cream together the butter and ½ cup sugar. Blend in the egg and beat until light. Mix in the lemon zest. In another bowl, mix the flour, baking powder, baking soda, and salt together. Add to the creamed mixture alternately with the milk. Fold in the strawberries and almonds. Spoon into the loaf pan or pans. Sprinkle the tops with the 1 tablespoon sugar and 2 tablespoons coconut.

Bake for 40 to 45 minutes for the small loaves, or 55 to 60 minutes for the large loaf, or until a skewer inserted in the center of the loaf comes out clean. Cool for 5 minutes in the pan, then turn out onto a wire rack to cool. Serve warm or cool. To mellow the breads, wrap in clear plastic wrap and store in a cool place for 2 days. To keep longer, wrap in foil, label, and freeze.

Makes 1 large or 3 small loaves

Berry-Nut Scones

Dried fruit scones make a wonderful last-minute gift, especially if you can deliver them soon after they're baked. Pack them in a pretty basket and tuck in a jar of homemade jam. The hint of cardamom brings out the flavor of the fruits.

3 cups all-purpose flour

1 tablespoon baking powder

1 teaspoon freshly ground cardamom

¾ cup sugar

½ cup dried blueberries, strawberries, cherries, or raisins

½ cup chopped almonds

1 cup (2 sticks) unsalted butter, chilled and cut into pieces

3 large eggs

½ cup lemon yogurt or buttermilk

1 tablespoon sugar

Preheat the oven to 400°F. Lightly grease a large baking sheet or cover with parchment paper.

Combine the flour, baking powder, cardamom, ¾ cup sugar, fruit, and the almonds in a food processor or a large bowl. Cut in the butter until it is in pea-size pieces. If using a food processor, turn the mixture into a large bowl.

Mix the eggs and yogurt or buttermilk in a small bowl. Add to the dry ingredients and blend quickly just until a dough forms (add a bit more yogurt if needed). With a ½-cup-size ice cream scoop or measuring cup, scoop the dough onto the prepared baking sheet, placing the mounds about 3 inches apart. Sprinkle the tops with the 1 tablespoon sugar.

Bake for 10 to 15 minutes until light brown. Slide the parchment paper onto the countertop to cool or remove to a wire rack to cool. Serve warm.

Makes 12 scones

Almond–Cardamom Scones

Aromatic with cardamom and crunchy with almonds, these scones are perfect for any holiday.

3 cups all-purpose flour
1 tablespoon baking powder
1 teaspoon freshly ground cardamom
½ cup sugar
1 cup chopped almonds
1 cup (2 sticks) unsalted butter, chilled and cut into pieces
3 large eggs
½ to ⅔ cup plain yogurt or buttermilk
1 tablespoon sugar

Preheat the oven to 400°F. Lightly grease a large cookie sheet or cover with parchment paper.

Combine the flour, baking powder, cardamom, ½ cup sugar, and the almonds in a food processor or large bowl. Add the butter and cut in until the butter is in pea-size pieces. If using a food processor, turn the mixture into a large bowl.

Mix the eggs and ½ cup of the yogurt in a small bowl. Add to the dry ingredients and blend quickly, just until a dough forms (add a bit more yogurt or buttermilk if needed). Using a ½-cup-size ice cream scoop or measuring cup, scoop the dough and place the mounds in the prepared baking sheet about 3 inches apart. Sprinkle the tops with the 1 tablespoon sugar.

Bake for 10 to 15 minutes, until light brown. Slide the parchment paper onto the countertop to cool or remove to a wire rack or directly into a serving basket. Serve warm.

Makes 12 scones

Winter Blueberry Muffins

 When fresh blueberries are out of season, dried blueberries lend their summery flavor to these muffins.

2 large eggs, beaten
1 cup lemon yogurt
1 tablespoon lemon juice
1 teaspoon freshly grated lemon zest
6 tablespoons unsalted butter, melted
1 cup dried blueberries
2 cups all-purpose flour
1 teaspoon baking powder
1 teaspoon baking soda
½ teaspoon salt
¾ cup sugar

Preheat the oven to 400°F. Lightly grease 12 muffin cups, or line with paper liners.

In a bowl, combine the eggs, yogurt, lemon juice and zest, butter, and blueberries. In another bowl, stir together the flour, baking powder, baking soda, salt, and sugar. Stir the blueberry mixture into the flour mixture just until combined. Scoop the muffin mixture into the muffin cups, filling them three-quarters full.

Bake for 15 to 20 minutes, until light brown. Remove from the pan onto a wire rack to cool slightly or directly into a serving basket. Serve warm.

Makes 12 muffins

Holiday Spoonbread

 Spoonbread is so named because you really can eat it with a spoon or a fork. I've added the nip and color of a hot pepper to this puddinglike side dish.

1 tablespoon unsalted butter
1 medium-size ancho chili, cored, seeded, and chopped
1 red bell pepper, cored, seeded, and chopped
1 teaspoon ground cumin
2 cups water
1 teaspoon salt
1 cup cornmeal
2 cups milk
4 large eggs
2 teaspoons baking powder

Preheat the oven to 425°F. Butter a 2-quart casserole.

In a large saucepan, heat the butter and add the ancho chili and red pepper; cook over medium heat for 2 to 3 minutes, until the vegetables are bright colored. Add the cumin, water, salt, and cornmeal. Cook, whisking, until thickened. Remove from the heat, then whisk in the milk, eggs, and baking powder. Turn into the casserole. Bake for 25 minutes, until puffy. Serve hot with melted butter passed on the side, if desired.

Makes 6 to 8 servings

S P E C I A L
P A S T R I E S

D u t c h   C h r i s t m a s   W r e a t h

Many favorite Dutch pastries consist of flaky pastry and almond filling. This is one that is constructed in a loglike shape and twisted into a wreath. Dutch letters are constructed in a similar way, but the pastry is twisted into an initial, usually that of the guest of honor.

Pastry
1⅓ cups all-purpose flour
¼ teaspoon salt
½ cup (1 stick) unsalted butter, chilled and cut into pieces
3 tablespoons ice water
2 tablespoons unsalted butter, at room temperature

Filling
1 cup blanched almonds, finely pulverized
½ cup sugar
1 large egg white
1 tablespoon lemon juice

Glaze
1 tablespoon whipping cream
½ cup confectioners' sugar
1 teaspoon lemon juice

Decoration
Candied fruits and nuts

To make the pastry, combine the flour and salt in the work bowl of a food processor or in a large mixing bowl. Cut the ½ cup butter into the flour until the mixture resembles coarse crumbs. If using a food processor, turn the mixture into a bowl. Add the water and toss with a fork until the pastry holds together in a ball. Knead lightly once or twice. Shape into a ball. On a floured board, roll the dough out to ⅛-inch thickness. Spread evenly with the 2 tablespoons soft butter and roll up tightly. With a rolling pin, pound, then roll the pastry into a rectangle with a thickness of about ¾ inch, measuring about 15 by 3 inches. Fold the dough into thirds, folding 5 inches of the dough from each short end 5 inches over the center to make 3 layers. Wrap the dough in plastic wrap and chill for 1 hour.

Preheat the oven to 400°F.

To make the filling, in a bowl mix the almonds with the sugar, egg white, and lemon juice until the mixture resembles a paste. Shape the mixture into a roll about 1 inch thick. Dust the roll lightly with flour; cover and set aside.

On a lightly floured surface, roll the pastry to make a rectangle about 20 by 5 inches. Lay the almond roll down the center of the rectangle and bring the pastry up over the roll to enclose the filling, overlapping the pastry slightly. Brush the pastry with water and

Frozen puff pastry sheets are available in a 17¼-ounce package, which contains two sheets. They should be kept frozen until you are ready to use them. To thaw, remove as many pastry sheets as needed from the package. Rewrap the unused pastry in plastic or foil and return to the freezer.

Thaw the pastry at room temperature about twenty minutes before gently unfolding. Keep the pastry cold to the touch; if it becomes warm and soft, chill for a few minutes. Handle as little as possible.

Thawed puff pastry sheets are about ten inches square and they can be rolled out on a lightly floured board to make a larger square or rectangle, depending on the needs of the recipe.

---

arrange seam side down on an ungreased cookie sheet in the shape of a wreath. Bake for 40 minutes or until golden brown. Remove from the pan onto a wire rack to cool.

To make the glaze, in a small bowl, stir the cream into the confectioners' sugar, then blend in the lemon juice. Spread the glaze over the baked wreath. Decorate with candied fruits and nuts. Serve in slices.

Makes 12 servings

Prune-Filled Pastry Stars

Prune-filled stars made with a flaky pastry are a holiday tradition in Finland. To make the stars, the pastry is first cut into squares, the corners are slit to the center and then formed into a pinwheel, or a four-pointed star. Many Finnish cooks like to use frozen puff pastry rather than go through the trouble of making a dough from scratch (see Note). Other Finns like to make a sour cream butter pastry. Whichever pastry you choose, these attractive pastries always turn out festively delicious.

Sour Cream Pastry (or frozen puff pastry—see Note)

2½ cups all-purpose flour

2 teaspoons baking powder

½ teaspoon salt

1 cup (2 sticks) unsalted butter, at room temperature

1 cup sour cream

Prune Filling

1 cup pitted prunes

1 cup water

½ cup sugar

1 tablespoon lemon juice

Glaze and Decoration

1 large egg beaten with
1 tablespoon milk
Pearl sugar, granulated sugar, or coarsely chopped almonds, for sprinkling

To make the pastry, in a large bowl or in the food processor, combine the flour, baking powder, and salt. Cut in the butter until the mixture resembles coarse crumbs. Transfer the mixture to a bowl if using a food processor. Stir in the sour cream to make a stiff dough. Wrap in plastic wrap and chill for 30 minutes.

To make the filling, combine the prunes, water, and sugar in a saucepan. Heat to boiling over medium-high heat, then lower the heat and simmer for 5 minutes, covered. Remove from the heat and cool. Purée in a food processor or blender and stir in the lemon juice. Cool.

Preheat the oven to 400°F. Cover 2 baking sheets with parchment paper or use ungreased baking sheets.

On a lightly floured surface, roll the chilled pastry out to make a 16-inch square, folding in the ragged edges to make straight sides. Cut into sixteen 4-inch squares. With a small, sharp knife or with a pastry wheel, make 2-inch cuts from each corner of each square toward the center. Dot the center of each square with 1 tablespoon of the prune filling.

Fold one half of each corner over the center, press the tips of the pastry together at the center to seal; brush with water to assist sealing.

Place the stars 2 inches apart on the baking sheets and brush lightly with the egg glaze; sprinkle with sugar or almonds.

Bake for 10 to 12 minutes or until golden. Slide the parchment onto a cooling rack to cool or transfer the stars onto the rack.

Makes 16 stars

NOTE: Thaw the puff pastry as directed on the package. Carefully remove one 8¾-ounce sheet, and unfold onto a lightly floured surface. Roll out to make a 16-inch square and cut into 4-inch squares. Fill and shape as directed.

Rosettes

These delicate, tender pastries can look like a star, snowflake, flower, butterfly, or any other whimsical shape, depending on the rosette iron used. They're at their very best when eaten the day they are made; however, you can freeze them successfully. There are many recipes for rosettes, but this one is simple and quick to mix. The effervescence of the beer or mineral water lightens the batter.

1 large egg
1 cup milk
½ cup beer or mineral water
½ tablespoon sugar
1 cup all-purpose flour
Vegetable oil, for frying
Confectioners' sugar, for dusting

In a large bowl, beat the egg, milk, beer, sugar, and flour to make a smooth batter. The consistency should be similar to un-whipped heavy cream. Cover and refrigerate for 1 hour.

Heat the oil in a deep fryer to 375°F. Fix the rosette iron onto its handle and place into the oil as it heats.

Stir the batter. Wipe the hot iron quickly with a paper towel and dip into the batter just to the top edge of the iron. Lower the iron into the oil and cook until the rosette is golden brown, about 1 minute. Carefully remove the rosette from the iron with the help of a fork and place it on a wire rack lined with paper towels to cool. Dust the rosettes with confectioners' sugar.

Makes about 36 rosettes

 HELPFUL HINTS FOR ROSETTES

1. If the rosettes will not come off the iron, the iron may have been dipped too deeply into the batter, allowing it to cover the top of the iron. Or they may not have been cooked long enough.

2. If the rosettes have blisters, the egg was beaten until frothy, making the batter too bubbly. Stir the batter gently until the bubbles disappear.

3. If the rosettes drop off the iron into the oil, the iron was not heated sufficiently before dipping into the batter, or the oil isn't hot enough. Or the batter-dipped iron was not lowered deep enough into the oil.

4. If the rosettes are not crisp, they may not have been cooked long enough.

5. If the rosettes brown too quickly, the oil is too hot; lower the temperature.

Christmas Bows or Fattigman

 The dough is rolled and twisted in a special way before it is deep fried, resulting in these Scandinavian Christmas pastries, which look like bow ties.

  5 large egg yolks
  ½ cup sugar
  ½ cup (1 stick) unsalted butter, melted
  2 cups all-purpose flour
  ½ teaspoon grated lemon zest
  1 tablespoon brandy
     Oil, for deep frying
     Confectioners' sugar, for dusting

In a mixing bowl, beat the egg yolks and sugar until lemon colored. Add the butter, flour, zest, and brandy and mix to make a soft dough. Cover and chill 2 hours or overnight.

Turn the dough out onto a lightly floured surface and roll out until very thin, ⅛ to ¹⁄₁₆ inch thick. With a pastry wheel or a sharp knife, cut 1 × 4-inch strips. Cut a 1-inch slit lengthwise in the exact middle of each dough strip. Pull the 2 ends of each strip through the slit to form a bow.

Heat the oil to 370°F and fry the cookies a few at a time, lowering them into the oil with a slotted spoon, until they are pale golden brown, about 1 minute. Remove with the spoon and drain on a paper towel–lined wire rack. Dust with confectioners' sugar.

Makes about 60 bows

Danish Pancakes, Æbelskiver

 Freshly make Æbelskiver and hot glögg is the traditional Danish menu for entertaining during Advent. The gathering is usually a casual Glögg Party that takes place on a Sunday afternoon, and children and adults alike are invited to make decorations for the Christmas tree—though the tree itself doesn't appear until Christmas Eve.

To make these pancakes, you need a Danish pancake or Æbelskiver pan with round indentations. They are so delicious served immediately after they're cooked that whoever is the Æbelskiver cook can hardly keep ahead of the demand, which makes them a perfect family party food, so people can take turns cooking.

Æbelskiver pans are made of cast iron and are available in specialty cookware shops and through mail-order catalogs such as Maid of Scandinavia in Minneapolis (see page 239).

  1 cup milk
  ½ cup (1 stick) unsalted butter plus butter for Æbelskiver pan
  3 large eggs, separated
  2 tablespoons sugar
  1 teaspoon freshly crushed cardamom (optional)
 1½ cups all-purpose flour

2 teaspoons baking powder
½ teaspoon salt
  Applesauce (optional)
  Confectioners' sugar

In a saucepan, heat the milk until it is warm. Cut the butter into slices, add to the milk, and stir just until the butter is melted.

In a small bowl, whisk together the egg yolks, sugar, and cardamom, if desired, then slowly add the milk and butter mixture, mixing until well blended.

In a large bowl, stir together the flour, baking powder, and salt. Whisk in the milk mixture until no lumps remain.

In a medium bowl, beat the egg whites until stiff but not dry. Fold the beaten egg whites into the batter.

Place the Æbelskiver pan over medium-high heat until a drop of water sizzles when dripped into one of the cups. Put about ½ teaspoon butter into each indentation and spread around to coat each cup evenly. Spoon about 1 tablespoon of the batter into each cup and cook for about 30 seconds. Drop 1 teaspoon of applesauce into the center, if desired, and top with 1 to 2 tablespoons batter to cover the applesauce. When the bottoms are browned, turn the cakes over (use a long wooden skewer or knitting needle). Cook until browned. Remove from the pan and place on a serving plate. Dust with confectioners' sugar and serve immediately.

Makes 20 Æbelskiver

Hanukkah

Jelly Doughnuts

This recipe is from Marge Portella, who says she makes these every year for her family at Hanukkah.

2 packages (5½ teaspoons) active dry yeast

3½ tablespoons sugar, divided

¾ cup milk, scalded and cooled to warm (105 to 115°F)

2½ cups all-purpose flour

2 large egg yolks

Pinch salt

Pinch ground cinnamon

1½ tablespoons margarine

Vegetable oil, for deep frying

Red fruit jelly, such as raspberry, strawberry, or currant

Sugar, for rolling

In a small bowl, dissolve the yeast and 2 tablespoons of the sugar in the milk. Sift the flour into a large bowl; make a well in the center. Add the yeast mixture, egg yolks, salt, cinnamon, margarine, and remaining sugar. Mix until stiff. Turn out onto a floured surface and knead until smooth and elastic, about 5 minutes. Cover and let rise for 1 hour or until doubled.

On a lightly floured surface, roll out the dough to about ½ inch thickness. With a cookie or biscuit cutter, cut into 2-inch rounds. Reroll the scraps and cut additional circles. Cover the rounds and let rise for 15 minutes.

In a deep, heavy saucepan or in a deep-fat fryer, heat the oil to 375°F. Lower the doughnuts into the oil with a slotted spoon, and cook on one side for 2 minutes; turn over and

 HANUKKAH (CHANUKAH), THE FESTIVAL OF LIGHTS

Hanukkah means "dedication." It recalls the rededication of the temple in Jerusalem more than 2,100 years ago and commemorates the victory of the Maccabees over the Syrians, who had tried to destroy the Jewish way of life. After their victory, the Maccabees noticed that the eternal light over the altar had only enough pure oil to burn for one day. By a miracle, the oil lasted for eight days until new oil could be prepared. Therefore, Hanukkah is celebrated for eight days, and for each night of the holiday, one candle is lit in the menorah (a nine-branched candelabra) with one candle holder for each night plus one for the leader. Because of the miracle of the oil, traditional foods for Hanukkah, such as jelly doughnuts and potato pancakes, are cooked in oil.

cook until brown on the second side, about 1 to 2 minutes longer. Remove and drain on several thicknesses of paper towels.

Make a small opening on the top of each doughnut and insert a small spoonful of jelly into the doughnut. Roll in sugar. These are best eaten immediately.

Makes 30 to 35 doughnuts

Rugalach

These cream cheese cookies are a tradition in many Jewish households at Hanukkah. The base is a tender cream cheese pastry that is rolled out into a round and cut into wedges that are then rolled up to enclose a cinnamon, raisin, and nut filling.

  1 cup (2 sticks) unsalted butter,
    at room temperature
  1 (8-ounce) package cream cheese,
    at room temperature
  2 cups all-purpose flour

Filling
  ⅓ cup sugar
  1 tablespoon ground cinnamon
  ½ cup raisins
  ½ cup chopped walnuts
  1 tablespoon sugar, for sprinkling

In a large bowl, cream the butter and cream cheese together. Mix in the flour until the dough is well blended and smooth. Shape into a ball. Divide into quarters. Shape each quarter into a ball. Flatten each ball into a disk, wrap in plastic wrap, and chill for 30 minutes until firm.

Preheat the oven to 375°F. Cover 2 baking sheets with parchment paper.

To make the filling, combine the sugar, cinnamon, raisins, and walnuts in a bowl. Set aside.

On a lightly floured board, flatten each ball of dough, one at a time, then roll it out to make a circle ¹⁄₁₆ inch thick and about 12 inches in diameter. Sprinkle with one-quarter of the filling. Gently press the filling into the pastry to make it adhere. Cut into 16 equal wedges. Roll each wedge up from the wide side toward the point. Place the rolls on the baking sheets, at least 2 inches apart. Brush with water and sprinkle with sugar.

Bake for 15 to 20 minutes, until light brown. Cool on a wire rack.

Makes 64 rugalach

Babka

Babka is an Eastern European holiday bread and has many different variations. All of them are rich with eggs and butter. This is an easy-to-mix batter bread. The name Babka, which means "grandmother" in Polish, seems to have been given to the bread because when baked in a brioche mold and turned out onto a serving plate, the loaf resembles a grandmother's skirt.

¾ cup golden raisins
1 package (2¾ teaspoons) active
   dry yeast
¼ cup warm (105 to 115°F) water
½ cup sugar
½ cup (1 stick) plus 2 tablespoons
   unsalted butter, at room temperature
2 large eggs, lightly beaten
1 teaspoon grated lemon zest
1 teaspoon salt
½ cup milk, scalded and cooled
   to lukewarm
3 cups bread flour
¼ cup slivered almonds
   Confectioners' sugar

Place the raisins in a small bowl. Add hot water to cover and let stand for a few minutes, until the raisins are plumped.

In another small bowl, dissolve the yeast in the warm water. Sprinkle 1 teaspoon of the sugar over the yeast mixture. Let stand for 5 minutes or until the yeast is foamy.

In a large mixing bowl, cream together the remaining sugar and butter. Add the eggs and beat until the mixture is light and fluffy. Add the lemon zest, salt, and milk; mix until well blended. Stir in the yeast mixture. Add the flour 1 cup at a time, beating until the batter is very smooth and satiny. It will be quite stiff by the time the last cup of flour is added. Drain the raisins and stir them into the dough. Cover the bowl with a towel and let the dough rise in a warm place until doubled.

Butter and flour a 10-inch brioche mold or fancy tube-type baking pan. Place the slivered almonds into the grooves of the pan to decorate.

Beat down the batter and turn it into the mold. Cover the dough and let it rise in a warm place until it has doubled in bulk, 30 to 40 minutes.

Preheat the oven to 375°F. Bake the babka for 30 to 35 minutes or until a wooden skewer inserted in the center comes out clean. Note that the baking time will vary greatly depending on the pan you are using. A tube-type pan will bake the most quickly, while a shiny brioche pan may take half again as long. Keep checking the bread with a wooden skewer, and if it begins to brown too quickly, cover the top with foil and reduce the temperature to 350°F. Check every 5 minutes until the bread is done.

Remove the loaf from the oven and cool for 5 minutes, then turn it out onto a wire rack to finish cooling. Dust with confectioners' sugar. Serve warm.

Makes one 10-inch loaf

Kichel

 These are delightfully crunchy, light and airy, eggy, nonsweet cookies that are awfully simple to make providing you have an electric mixer. I use a KitchenAid mixer with the whisk attachment to make the lengthy mixing time a breeze.

    3 large eggs, at room temperature
    3 tablespoons sugar
    ½ cup vegetable oil
    1 cup all-purpose flour
       About 1 tablespoon sugar, for
       sprinkling over tops of cookies

Preheat the oven to 350°F. Cover 2 small, or 1 large cookie sheet with parchment paper, or lightly grease.

In the bowl of an electric mixer, beat the eggs until fluffy. Add the sugar and oil and beat at high speed for 10 minutes, until the mixture is very light. With the beater at low speed, add the flour, scrape the sides of the bowl, turn the beater to high, and beat again for 5 minutes or until the mixture is very smooth and stretchy. Using small spoonfuls of the dough, drop onto a baking sheet about 1½ inches apart. Sprinkle with the sugar.

Bake for 30 minutes or until light brown. Remove the cookies with a spatula and cool on a wire rack.

Makes 36 cookies

Sugar Cookies for Hannukah

 There are so many shapes of cookie cutters available today for specific occasions. For Hannukah, find a Driedel-shaped cutter for making dough shapes you can improvise by cutting into squares or triangles and adding a top "handle." You may also find cookie cutters shaped like a menorah, the candleholder used to hold the eight candles that symbolize the oil that the Jews burned for eight days and nights after they drove out the invading Syrians.

    ½ cup (1 stick) unsalted butter, at room
       temperature
    ½ cup sugar
    1 large egg, lightly beaten
       Pinch of salt
  1½ cups all-purpose flour
    ½ teaspoon baking soda

Icing

    1 large egg white
    ⅛ teaspoon cream of tartar
       Pinch of salt
    2 cups sifted confectioners' sugar
       Food coloring, if desired

In the large bowl of an electric mixer, cream the butter and sugar until smooth. Add the egg and salt and beat until light and fluffy. Sift the flour and baking soda together and add to the creamed mixture. Mix until the dough is smooth. Wrap and chill at least 30 minutes.

Preheat the oven to 400° F. Cover 2 or 3 baking sheets with parchment paper. Roll the cookie dough out to ¹⁄₁₆ inch thickness. Cut out the cookies using cookie cutters and place them on the prepared baking sheets about 1½ inches apart. Bake the cookies for 5 to 7 minutes or until lightly browned on the edges; then remove from the cookie sheets and cool on a rack.

For the icing, in the small bowl of an electric mixer, beat the egg white with the cream of tartar and salt for 1 minute using high speed. Add the confectioners' sugar and beat slowly until blended; then beat at high speed until very stiff, 3 to 5 minutes. Divide the icing into as many bowls as icing colors you desire. Stir the food coloring into the icings until evenly blended. Using pastry bags, press the icings onto the cooled, baked cookies to decorate them.

Makes about thirty-six 2-inch cookies

Pecan Horns

"Kissing cousins" of Mexican wedding cakes and Greek koura-biedes, these crescent-shaped cookies with their dusting of confectioners' sugar just melt in your mouth.

¼ cup sifted confectioners' sugar
2 cups all-purpose flour
¼ teaspoon salt

1 cup (2 sticks) unsalted butter, firm but not hard
¾ cup finely ground pecans
Additional confectioners' sugar, for dusting the cookies

Have 2 cookie sheets ready, either covered with parchment paper or ungreased.

In a large bowl, or in the work bowl of a food processor, mix the sugar, flour, and salt. Cut in the butter until completely incorporated and no butter lumps are visible. Add the pecans and continue to process, or mix with an electric mixer, until a dough forms that is smooth and pliable.

Divide the dough into 2 parts and shape each part into a 1-inch-thick roll. With a knife, cut the dough into 1-inch pieces. In the palm of your hand, shape each piece into a strip with a point at each end, then turn the strip into a crescent shape. Place the pieces on a cookie sheet about 1 inch apart. Chill at least 30 minutes before baking.

Preheat the oven to 350°F. Bake the cookies for 10 to 15 minutes or until they are firm to the touch but not completely browned. Allow the cookies to cool right on the cookie sheet. They are very fragile while warm. Put the confectioners' sugar into a sieve and dust the cookies heavily. When the cookies are completely cooled, transfer into a large, flat container. Stored in the refrigerator, they will stay fresh up to a month.

Makes about 60 cookies

Sweet and Savory Treats for New Year's Eve

Stuffed Italian Bread

 When I think of New Year's Eve, I think of families, sleigh rides, skiing, fireworks, "ringledanz," stories, fortunes, dancing, games, prizes, and hearty appetites. I guess that's because that's what goes on at our house on December 31. I like to serve this stuffed bread, which is something like calzone, because it appeals to kids and adults alike. You can make it with frozen bread dough from the supermarket or mix up a single loaf of white bread quickly in the food processor. Use either filling, or make two breads and use both fillings. This bread can be baked and frozen, well wrapped. To reheat, place it in a 300°F oven until heated through, about 10 minutes.

Food Processor White Bread (or 1 loaf of frozen bread dough)

- 3 cups bread flour
- 1 package (2¾ teaspoons) active dry or rapid-rise yeast
- 1 tablespoon sugar
- 1 teaspoon salt
- 2 tablespoons extra-virgin olive oil
- 1 cup warm water (about 130°F)
  Italian Sausage Filling (below) or Spinach Filling (below)

 NEW YEAR'S EVE FOOD

New Year's Eve is more of a time for parties, noisemakers, and inspired madness than for traditional foods. New Year's food to many of us has come to mean snack food for a party. That's why I've included savory stuffed breads in this section.

In Greece and Eastern European countries, a special bread is traditional. It is usually a fancy bread that has a coin or some other symbolic treasure hidden in the center of the loaf. The person who receives it is the lucky one who will receive some designated fortune. This bread is usually served on New Year's Day with coffee for breakfast.

An American tradition stems from the Moravians who observe "love feasts" several times a year, one of them being on New Year's Eve. Special buns are served at a religious service, along with a hot beverage such as cocoa or coffee. These buns make a delicious accompaniment to hot cocoa after our New Year's Eve sleigh ride.

Thaw the frozen bread dough. Or to prepare food processor white bread, measure the flour, yeast, sugar, salt, and olive oil into the work bowl of the processor. Turn the motor on. Add the water through the feed tube, processing until the dough comes together in a ball and cleans the sides of the bowl. Pinch the dough; if the dough is sticky, add flour, a tablespoon at a time, processing after each addition. If the dough is stiff rather than smooth and springy, add more water a tablespoon at a time. Let the dough rise in the work bowl until doubled, covered, about 1½ hours.

Make one of the fillings.

Roll either the thawed frozen dough or risen dough out to a 20-inch square on a lightly floured surface. Spread one of the fillings over the dough to within 1 inch of the edges. Roll up tightly, jelly roll fashion, into a shape similar to a long loaf of French bread. Seal the long edge and tuck the ends under. Place on a greased baking sheet, with the seam side down. Let rise until puffy, about 15 minutes.

Preheat the oven to 400°F and bake for 35 to 45 minutes or until golden. Remove from the baking sheet onto a cutting board. Cool for 10 minutes. Cut diagonally into 1-inch-thick slices.

Makes about 16 thick slices

Italian Sausage Filling

    1 pound mild Italian sausage
    1 teaspoon dried basil leaves
    ½ teaspoon chopped fresh rosemary
    2 cups shredded provolone,
        mozzarella cheese, or a combination
    ¼ cup freshly grated Parmesan cheese

Crumble the sausage into a heavy skillet and cook over medium heat, stirring with a fork until the sausage is no longer pink, 5 to 10 minutes. Drain well and add the basil and rosemary. Mix well. Spread the sausage mixture over the dough; sprinkle with the cheeses. Roll up and bake as directed.

Spinach Filling

    6 strips bacon, cut into ½-inch pieces
    ½ cup chopped onion
    1 garlic clove, minced or pressed
    1 package or bunch (10 ounces)
        fresh spinach, washed, stemmed,
        and dried
    1 cup shredded Monterey Jack cheese

Cook the bacon in a large skillet until crisp; drain and discard the grease, and remove the bacon to a dish. Add the onion and garlic to the pan. Cook for 1 minute, add the spinach, and cook until the spinach is wilted, about 4 minutes. Cool. Spread the spinach mixture over the rolled-out dough. Sprinkle with the cheese and the bacon. Roll up and bake as directed.

Sun-Dried Tomato and Rosemary Focaccia

Focaccia is a cousin to pizza, but with a thicker crust and fewer toppings. I sometimes like to embellish it with pine nuts, cheese, or coarse pepper and salt.

2½ cups all-purpose flour

½ cup whole wheat flour

1 teaspoon salt

1 package (2¾ teaspoons) active dry yeast

¾ to 1 cup warm water (130°F)

6 tablespoons extra-virgin olive oil (include the oil from the sun-dried tomatoes), divided

6 oil-packed sun-dried tomatoes, drained (oil reserved) and coarsely chopped

2 cloves garlic, minced or pressed

4 tablespoons chopped fresh rosemary

Combine the flours, salt, and yeast in the work bowl of the food processor. Turn the motor on to mix well. Add ¾ cup of the water through the feed tube, with the motor going, and pour in 4 tablespoons of the oil. Process until dough is smooth, adding more water a tablespoon at a time if necessary. Add the sun-dried tomatoes and process just until they are mixed in. Let rise in the work bowl for 45 minutes, covered, until doubled.

Preheat the oven to 425°F, with a pizza stone or tiles covering the center of the middle oven rack, if possible.

Roll the dough out on a well-floured surface to make a circle 14 to 16 inches in diameter and at least ¼ inch thick. Transfer the dough onto a square of foil. Make dents on the surface with your fingertips. Sprinkle with garlic and rosemary and press into the dough. Brush with remaining 2 tablespoons oil. Let sit for 15 minutes or until slightly puffy. Transfer the bread (on the foil) onto the hot pizza stone or a baking sheet.

Bake for 15 to 20 minutes or until golden brown around the edges. Serve hot, warm, or at room temperature.

Makes 6 to 8 servings

 FOCACCIA

This Italian bread is shaped into a large, flat round that is liberally drizzled with olive oil and sprinkled with salt. There are many variations on the theme, one of which is included here. Focaccia is usually eaten as a snack or served with soups or salads.

Greek Honey-Glazed Cakes

Soaked in a honey syrup and coated with finely chopped nuts and cinnamon, these cakes are sweet and "juicy." They keep well stored in an airtight container in a cool place up to three weeks, or freeze up to three months.

1 cup (2 sticks) unsalted butter
  or margarine, at room temperature
¾ cup sugar
1 large egg yolk
⅓ cup fresh orange juice
2 tablespoons brandy
2 teaspoons grated orange zest
1 teaspoon baking powder
½ teaspoon baking soda
½ teaspoon salt
3½ cups all-purpose flour

Glaze

¾ cup water
¾ cup honey
¾ cup sugar

Garnish

1 cup finely chopped walnuts
  or pecans
½ teaspoon ground cinnamon

In a large mixing bowl, cream the butter and sugar together. Add the egg yolk, orange juice, brandy, orange zest, baking powder, baking soda, and salt. Mix in the flour until combined. Shape the dough into a ball. Wrap in plastic wrap and chill at least 1 hour.

Preheat the oven to 350°F. Roll the dough into logs about 3 inches long and 1 inch wide; taper each end to a point. Place on an ungreased baking sheet, 2 inches apart. Bake 17 to 18 minutes or until golden. Transfer the cakes onto a rimmed baking sheet in a single layer.

To make the glaze, heat the water, honey, and sugar in a saucepan to boiling over medium-high heat. Reduce the heat and simmer for 10 minutes. Pour three-quarters of the honey syrup over the cakes.

Mix the nuts and cinnamon in a small bowl. Sprinkle over the cakes and let cool. Place the cakes on wire racks over waxed paper and spoon the remaining syrup in the pan over the cookies. Let stand for 1 hour.

Makes 48 cakes

Greek Orange and Pine Nut New Year's Bread

This sweet, cakelike coiled loaf has a coin hidden in the center. In Greek tradition, the person who receives the coin is sure to have a happy new year. The bread is irresistible when it is hot out of the oven, which may not be practical on New Year's Eve unless it is a family or party project. The job of hiding the coin in the bread is given to one devious member of the bread-baking team.

4 cups bread flour or unbleached all-purpose flour
2 packages (5½ teaspoons) active dry yeast (do not use rapid-rise)
½ cup sugar
1 teaspoon salt
1 tablespoon grated orange zest
1 tablespoon grated lemon zest
1 cup milk
½ cup (1 stick) unsalted butter, chilled and cut into pieces
3 large eggs, beaten
1 large egg yolk beaten with 1 teaspoon water for glaze
½ cup pine nuts or blanched slivered almonds, for topping
1 to 2 tablespoons sugar, for topping

Measure the flour, yeast, sugar, salt, and orange and lemon zests into a large bowl.

Heat the milk to scalding in a small saucepan over medium heat. Remove from the heat and add the butter; stir until the butter is melted. Mix in the eggs and pour over the yeast mixture in the bowl. Beat with an electric mixer until the dough is smooth and soft. Cover with plastic wrap and refrigerate for several hours or overnight.

Butter a large baking sheet or pizza pan or cover with parchment paper. Remove the dough from the refrigerator and punch it down. Turn out onto a floured surface and roll into a rope about 48 inches long. Coil the dough onto the prepared pan, making a loaf about 10 inches in diameter. Wrap a coin in foil and place it inside the bread, from underneath so it will not be seen. Cover with a towel and let rise in a warm place until doubled, 45 to 60 minutes.

Preheat the oven to 375°F. Brush the dough with the egg yolk glaze, then stick the pine nuts or slivered almonds in the creases of the bread, following the spiral's pattern. Sprinkle with the sugar.

Bake for 30 to 35 minutes or until golden and a wooden skewer inserted in the center of the loaf comes out clean. If the loaf begins to brown too quickly, cover with foil until the loaf tests done. Serve warm, or cool on a wire rack.

Makes 1 large loaf

Moravian Love Feast Buns

These are served by Moravians for Christmas and New Year's, two of the five "love feasts" they observe during the year to commemorate the Last Supper of Christ. This version is based on an easy-to-stir-up refrigerator yeast dough. The chilled dough is not sticky and is easy to shape into smooth round buns. The buns are punched down in the center, and then the hole is filled with butter, cinnamon, and brown sugar before baking.

4 cups bread flour or unbleached all-purpose flour

2 packages (5½ teaspoons) active dry yeast (do not use rapid-rise)

½ cup sugar

1 teaspoon salt

1 cup hot water (140°F)

½ cup (1 stick) unsalted butter, cut into pieces

3 large eggs, beaten

Filling

3 tablespoons butter, cut into 24 tiny pieces

3 tablespoons packed brown sugar

1 teaspoon ground cinnamon

Measure the flour, yeast, sugar, and salt into a large bowl and stir to combine. Mix the water with the butter and stir until the butter is melted. Pour over the flour mix-ture; pour the eggs over and stir or beat with an electric mixer until the dough is smooth and soft. Cover with plastic wrap. Refrigerate for several hours or overnight.

Lightly grease 2 baking sheets or cover with parchment paper. Remove the dough from the refrigerator and turn out onto a lightly floured board. Divide into 24 pieces. Shape each piece into a round bun. Place 3 inches apart in the prepared pan. Let rise, covered with a towel, until doubled, about 1 hour.

Preheat the oven to 350°F. Poke a hole in the center of each bun. Place a piece of butter into each hole. In a small bowl, mix the brown sugar and cinnamon and spoon a little of the mixture onto each piece of butter. Bake for 35 minutes or until the buns are golden. Serve warm or cool on a wire rack.

Makes 24 buns

Honey-Walnut Potica

People who live on the "Great Iron Range" in Northern Minnesota think it isn't a holiday or a celebration without potica (pronounced po-teet-sa). New Year's Eve is no exception. This tightly spiraled honey walnut, strudellike bread requires a tender touch to stretch the dough to eggshell thinness. My friend Susan had the ingenious idea of stretching the dough on a shiny, smooth vinyl tablecloth. The dough will cling to the vinyl, but it is easy to lift up again so that you can continue stretching it.

Honey-Walnut Filling

 2 cups (8 ounces) chopped walnuts
 ½ cup sugar
 ½ cup undiluted evaporated milk, or more if needed
 ¼ cup honey
 1 teaspoon vanilla

Potica Yeast Dough

 1 package (2¾ teaspoons) active dry yeast
 2½ cups all-purpose flour
 3 tablespoons instant nonfat dry milk
 ¼ cup sugar
 ½ teaspoon salt
 ½ cup very warm water (130°F)
 ⅓ cup unsalted butter, melted
 2 large eggs, beaten

To make the filling, combine the walnuts and sugar in the bowl of the food processor and process until the walnuts are pulverized. Turn into a heavy saucepan and add the milk and honey. Heat to boiling over medium-high heat, stirring constantly, for 5 minutes, until thick. Or combine the pulverized walnut mixture, milk, and honey in a 3-quart glass bowl. Stir. Heat to boiling in the microwave oven, on high for 5 to 6 minutes. Stir again. Cook on medium power for 5 minutes more. Cover and cool, then add the vanilla.

To make the potica yeast dough, in a large bowl or the bowl of an electric mixer, mix the yeast, 2 cups of the flour, dry milk, sugar, and salt. While mixing with an electric mixer, add the water, butter, and eggs. Beat until the dough is smooth and shiny. Beat in the remaining flour. Or mix with a wooden spoon in a large bowl, beating the liquids in vigorously until the dough is smooth and shiny.

Grease another large bowl. Turn the dough into the bowl. Cover with plastic wrap and let rise until doubled, about 1 hour.

Dust the top of the dough lightly with flour. Lightly spray a smooth surface, such as a vinyl tablecloth or a smooth plastic laminate work top, with nonstick cooking spray and dust with flour.

Turn out the dough onto the center of the work surface and pat it out as flat as possible. With a rolling pin, gently roll out the dough until it is about ½ inch thick and even on the top.

With palms up, reach under the dough and gently, but evenly, stretch it, working your way all the way around until the dough is eggshell thin and is about 20 inches wide and 36 inches long.

Stir the cooled filling. If it has thickened too much on standing, stir in additional milk until it is the consistency of a spreadable frosting. Spread the filling over the pastry to within 4 inches of the edges. Trim off the thick edges.

From the two long sides of the rectangle, fold the 4 inches of unfilled edges over the filling. (This will result in a rectangle 12 inches wide and 36 inches long.) Starting from a short end, roll up the potica to enclose the filling. Place on a greased or parchment-covered baking sheet, seam side down. Cover and let rise until almost doubled, about 1 hour.

Preheat the oven to 350°F and bake for 25 to 30 minutes, until golden. Remove from the pan and cool on a wire rack. Cool completely before slicing.

Makes 1 loaf

Chocolate Beer Cake

Several years ago, in search of an antique door, I met a local artist/antiques decorator, Walter Pietrowski. Walt has totally redone a bungalow on Duluth's Park Point, incorporating everything from brass elevator doors from a bank to wood carvings from old mansions. He's a man who loves the outdoors and good food. When the winter winds blow, he told me he "hunkers in" with wonderful simmered stews, hearty homemade breads, and generous squares of his favorite chocolate beer cake. He shared his recipe with me, and it has been a favorite of ours ever since! Beer brings out the flavor of chocolate and gives the cake a deep mahogany color.

⅔ cup unsalted butter,
    at room temperature
2 cups sugar
2 large eggs, beaten
2 squares (2 ounces) unsweetened
    chocolate, melted
2¼ cups all-purpose flour
2 teaspoons baking soda
½ teaspoon salt
¾ cup buttermilk
1 cup dark beer,
    at room temperature
½ cup well drained, chopped and
    pitted maraschino cherries

Chocolate Frosting

- ½ cup whipping cream
- 1 cup sugar
- 2 squares (2 ounces) unsweetened chocolate
- 1 teaspoon vanilla

Preheat the oven to 350°F. Lightly butter a 13 × 9-inch pan.

In a large bowl, using an electric mixer, cream the butter with the sugar. Add the eggs and beat until the mixture is light and fluffy, scraping down the sides of the bowl. Beat in the melted chocolate.

In another bowl, stir together the flour, baking soda, and salt.

In a large measuring cup, mix the buttermilk and beer. Add the dry ingredients to the creamed mixture alternately with the liquid ingredients, beating until the batter is smooth and fluffy. Fold in the cherries.

Pour the batter into the prepared pan and smooth it out to the edges. Bake for 40 to 45 minutes or until a toothpick inserted in the center comes out clean. Remove from the oven and place on a wire rack to cool.

TO MAKE THE FROSTING

In a medium-sized saucepan, combine the whipping cream and sugar. Heat to boiling and boil for 1 minute, stirring constantly. Add the chocolate and stir until the chocolate is melted. Remove from the heat and cool, stirring occasionally. Mix in the vanilla.

Spread the frosting over the top of the cake. Let stand until the frosting sets.

Makes 12 to 16 servings

Savory Pickups for New Year's Day

Peppered Cheese Twists

You can make these savory, crispy twists ahead for a holiday party. They'll keep crispy and delicious at least two months in the freezer.

  1 cup all-purpose flour
  1 teaspoon coarsely ground black pepper
  ½ teaspoon baking powder
  ⅛ teaspoon salt
  ⅛ teaspon cayenne pepper
  ¼ teaspoon dry mustard
  ¾ cup freshly grated Parmesan cheese, divided
  6 tablespoons unsalted butter, at room temperature
  1 large egg, separated
  2 tablespoons water
  1 teaspoon fresh lemon juice
     Paprika, for sprinkling

Preheat the oven to 400°F. Grease 3 baking sheets or cover with parchment paper.

Stir the flour, pepper, baking powder, salt, cayenne, and dry mustard together in a large mixing bowl and stir in all but 1 tablespoon of the Parmesan cheese. Blend in the butter until the mixture resembles fine bread crumbs. In a small bowl, mix the egg yolk with the water and lemon juice. Add the liquid ingredients to the dry ingredients and mix until a dough forms.

Turn the dough out onto a lightly floured surface and roll out to make a 13 × 9-inch rectangle. Trim the edges to straighten. Brush with the beaten egg white and sprinkle with the remaining tablespoon of Parmesan cheese. Cut the rectangle in half crosswise (halves will measure 6½ × 9 inches). Cut the halves into ¼-inch strips (they will be 6½ inches long). Twist two strips together and place on the prepared baking sheet. Repeat with the rest of the strips, spacing the twists 2 inches apart.

Bake for 8 to 10 minutes or until just light brown. Remove to wire racks to cool. Sprinkle lightly with paprika.

Makes about 50 twists

Sesame Wheat Crackers

These crisp, grainy crackers taste great with cheese spread or mushroom pâté.

  2 cups whole wheat flour
  ¾ teaspoon salt
  ¾ teaspoon baking powder
  ½ cup (1 stick) unsalted butter, at room temperature
  1 large egg, beaten
  4 tablespoons milk
  1 egg white, beaten
  ¼ cup sesame seeds

Preheat the oven to 375°F. Grease 2 baking sheets or cover with parchment paper.

In a medium bowl, mix the flour, salt, and baking powder. Cut the butter into the flour mixture until the mixture resembles fine crumbs. Add the egg and 2 tablespoons of the milk. Mix to make a stiff dough, adding the remaining milk, 1 tablespoon at a time, if necessary. Gather the dough into a ball, flatten it slightly, and place on a lightly floured surface and roll the dough out to ⅛-inch thickness. Using a 2-inch round cookie cutter, cut out circles from the dough; place on the prepared baking sheets, about 2 inches apart. Reroll the trimmings and cut out more circles. Continue until the dough is used up.

Brush the crackers with the beaten egg white, then sprinkle evenly with sesame seeds.

Bake for 15 minutes or until light brown. Remove to a wire rack to cool.

Makes about 72 crackers

Mushroom Profiteroles

 These are miniature cream puffs with a filling made with fresh mushrooms, walnuts, and spices.

Pâté à Choux (Cream Puff Paste)

- 1 cup water
- ½ teaspoon salt
- 1 teaspoon sugar
- ½ cup (1 stick) unsalted butter, cut into pieces
- 1 cup all-purpose flour
- 4 large eggs, at room temperature

Mushroom-Walnut Filling

- 2 tablespoons unsalted butter
- ½ pound button mushrooms, cleaned and chopped
- ¼ cup minced shallots
- 1 (3-ounce) package cream cheese
- ½ cup freshly grated Parmesan cheese
- 1 cup toasted walnuts, finely chopped
- 1 tablespoon chopped fresh or 1 teaspoon dried basil leaves
- ½ teaspoon salt
- ¼ teaspoon cayenne pepper
- ⅛ teaspoon freshly ground nutmeg

Make the cream puff paste. In a large, heavy saucepan, combine the water, salt, sugar, and butter. Measure the flour and have it ready. Place the saucepan over medium heat and heat, stirring, until the butter is melted. Increase the heat to high and stir until the mixture comes to a full rolling boil. Add the flour all at once. Stir vigorously with a wooden spoon until the paste forms a ball in the pan and comes away from the sides, about 1 minute. Remove from the heat.

Turn the paste into a food processor fitted with the steel blade. Turn the motor on and add the eggs through the feed tube one at a time; process until the eggs are thoroughly blended into the mixture and the dough is silky and smooth. If working by hand, add the eggs one at a time to the paste in the saucepan and stir vigorously until the eggs are thoroughly blended. Set the cream puff paste aside to cool for 10 minutes.

Preheat the oven to 425°F. Lightly grease 2 baking sheets or cover with parchment paper.

To shape the puffs you will need two spoons. With one spoon, scoop up 1 tablespoonful of dough. With the other spoon push the dough off the first spoon onto the pre-pared baking sheet, placing the mounds 2 inches apart. Or put the paste into a pastry bag with a ½-inch round tip. Press the paste out into small mounds about 1 inch in diameter.

Bake for 15 to 20 minutes or until the puffs are golden and crisp. Slash the sides while the puffs are hot to allow steam to escape and keep the shells crisp. Cool completely.

To make the mushroom-walnut filling, heat the butter in a large, heavy skillet over medium-high heat. Add the mushrooms and shallots and cook, stirring constantly until the vegetables are tender and the liquids evaporate, about 8 minutes. Turn into a large mixing bowl and add the cream cheese and Parmesan cheese. Stir until well blended. Add the walnuts, basil, salt, cayenne, and nutmeg. Stir until well blended.

Spoon about 1 teaspoonful of the filling into each cream puff. Serve immediately or within 2 hours, or freeze the filled puffs (see Box).

Makes about 48 puffs

 FREEZING CREAM PUFFS

To make ahead and freeze, fill the puffs and place them on a cookie sheet in a single layer in the freezer. When frozen, package them in plastic containers, separating the layers with waxed paper. To reheat and serve, remove from the freezer and place about one inch apart on a cookie sheet. Reheat in a preheated 375°F oven for fifteen minutes or until heated through.

Spinach Pesto Puffs

These tender, crispy puffs are a flavor sensation when filled with a creamy fresh spinach pesto.

48 miniature cream puffs
   (see Mushroom Profiteroles,
   page 320)
 1 cup loosely packed fresh spinach
   leaves, washed and stemmed
 1 cup loosely packed fresh basil leaves
 ¼ cup loosely packed fresh
   parsley leaves
 3 large garlic cloves, minced
 1 teaspoon salt
 ½ cup whipping cream
 2 tablespoons toasted pine nuts,
   almonds, or walnuts
 ½ cup freshly grated Parmesan cheese

Prepare the cream puffs and cool them on a rack.

In a food processor or blender, combine the spinach, basil, parsley, garlic, and salt. Process or blend until the mixture is finely chopped. With the motor going, slowly add the cream to the mixture until well blended. Transfer the mixture to a bowl and stir in the nuts and Parmesan by hand until well mixed.

Place a teaspoonful of the filling into each cream puff. Serve immediately or within 2 hours, or freeze (see Box on page 321).

Makes 48 puffs

Rosemary and Sun-Dried Tomato Biscuits

These tiny biscuits are flecked with sun-dried tomatoes and aromatic rosemary. They're delicious served hot out of the oven.

 2 cups all-purpose flour
 1 tablespoon baking powder
 2 teaspoons fresh or dried
   rosemary leaves
 ½ teaspoon salt
 ¾ cup (1½ sticks) unsalted butter,
   chilled and cut into pieces
 6 tablespoons finely chopped, drained,
   oil-packed sun-dried tomatoes
 ½ to ⅔ cup milk

Preheat the oven to 450°F. Mix the flour, baking powder, rosemary, and salt in a large bowl. Cut in the butter until the mixture resembles coarse crumbs. Add the tomatoes and toss until they are evenly mixed into the dry ingredients. Sprinkle in ½ cup of the milk and mix with a fork until moistened (use more milk, if needed); do not overmix.

Turn out onto a floured surface; knead two or three turns, just until the dough holds together in a ball. Flatten dough slightly and roll out to about ½-inch thickness. Using a 2-inch round cutter, cut out biscuits. Place on ungreased baking sheets, about 1 inch apart.

Bake for 12 to 15 minutes or just until

golden. Remove from the baking sheet onto a wire rack or into a serving basket. Serve warm.

Makes about 36 biscuits

Spicy Cheddar Cookies

Put half of this dough into a spritz cookie press and make shaped cookies for a holiday party. Roll the remaining dough out and cut with fancy cookie cutters to get two different-looking batches of savory cookies out of one dough.

¾ cup (1½ sticks) unsalted butter, at room temperature
½ cup shredded sharp Cheddar cheese
2 large egg yolks
½ teaspoon salt
½ teaspoon sugar
¼ teaspoon dry mustard
⅛ teaspoon cayenne pepper
1¾ cups all-purpose flour
Poppy seeds or sesame seeds

In a large bowl, cream the butter and cheese together using an electric mixer or a wooden spoon. Mix in the egg yolks, salt, sugar, mustard, cayenne, and flour and beat until the dough is smooth.

Preheat the oven to 375°F. Divide the dough into 2 parts and wrap 1 part in plastic wrap and chill for 1 hour. Put the other part into a spritz cookie press. Press the cookies onto an ungreased baking sheet.

Bake for 10 to 12 minutes or until light brown. Remove from the baking sheet onto a serving plate or into a basket and serve warm or cool completely on a wire rack.

Roll the refrigerated dough out on a floured surface, to about ¼-inch thickness. With cookie cutters, cut into fancy shapes. Sprinkle the cut-out shapes with the poppy seeds and gently press so the seeds adhere. Place the cookies on ungreased baking sheets.

Bake for 10 to 12 minutes or until light brown. Remove from the baking sheet onto a serving plate or into a basket and serve warm or cool completely on a wire rack.

Pack cookies in an airtight tin and freeze to serve later. To serve, remove from the freezer and warm in a 300°F oven to bring out the flavors.

Makes about 48 cookies

Stuffed Baby Brie in a Crust

A mushroom stuffing in a baby brie is encrusted with puff pastry. Your guests will think you went through a lot more trouble than you actually did for this luscious appetizer. For speed and convenience, I use frozen puff pastry. Assemble the whole thing and freeze it up to a month ahead of the party, then let it thaw in the refrigerator for about an hour before you bake it. Allow time for the baked brie to cool a bit before serving or the brie will be runny.

2 tablespoons unsalted butter

2 garlic cloves, minced or pressed

½ pound fresh mushrooms, washed and sliced

1 wheel (about ¾ pound) baby brie, chilled

1 sheet (8¾-ounce) frozen puff pastry

1 large egg beaten with 1 tablespoon water

In a heavy skillet, heat the butter and add the garlic and mushrooms. Cook over medium heat, stirring, until the mushrooms are tender and the liquid is evaporated, about 5 minutes. Transfer to a bowl and cool.

Using a sharp knife, cut the chilled brie horizontally into two layers. Spread the mushroom filling over the cut side of the bottom layer. Place the top layer over the mushroom filling. Cover and chill about 20 minutes.

Thaw the puff pastry for 20 minutes. Preheat the oven to 375°F. Unfold and roll out on a lightly floured surface to make a 14-inch square. Place the chilled, stuffed brie onto the center of the pastry and brush the edges of the pastry with the egg mixture. Fold the pastry over the brie to enclose the cheese. Twist the corners of the pastry to fashion into a topknot and press the pastry together to seal it. (You may refrigerate the brie at this point and bake just before serving.) Place the pastry-wrapped brie on an ungreased baking sheet and brush with the egg mixture.

Bake for 25 minutes or until the pastry is puffed and golden brown. Remove from the oven and transfer onto a wire rack to cool for at least 30 minutes before serving. Serve warm.

Makes 8 to 10 servings

Sun-Dried Tomato Tarlets with Cilantro

These are miniquiches, baked in miniature muffin tins. Coriander in the pastry backs up the flavor of fresh cilantro in the filling and garnish. They'll stay delicious at least a month in the freezer.

Coriander Pastry

1½ cups all-purpose flour
1 teaspoon ground coriander
½ teaspoon salt
½ cup (1 stick) plus 1 tablespoon unsalted butter, chilled and cut into pieces
2 teaspoons fresh lemon juice
4 to 6 tablespoons ice water

Sun-Dried Tomato Filling

4 ounces crumbled feta cheese
½ cup light cream or undiluted evaporated milk
¼ cup finely chopped, oil-packed sun-dried tomatoes, well drained
¼ cup chopped fresh cilantro
Pinch of cayenne

Garnish

¼ cup sour cream
Fresh cilantro leaves

Preheat the oven to 375°F. Into a large bowl or a food processor measure the flour, coriander, and salt. Cut in the butter or process until the mixture resembles coarse crumbs.

In a small bowl, whisk the lemon juice and 3 tablespoons of the ice water. Sprinkle over the flour mixture and toss with the fork until blended. Press the dough together into a ball, adding more water if necessary. Wrap in plastic wrap and chill for at least 30 minutes.

On a lightly floured surface, roll out the pastry to ⅛ inch thickness. With a 3-inch cookie cutter, cut 24 rounds of pastry. Fit the pastry rounds into mini-muffin tins to cover the bottom and sides of the cups. Refrigerate while preparing the filling.

In a medium-sized bowl, blend the goat cheese, egg, cream, tomatoes, cilantro, and cayenne. Spoon the filling into the prepared tartlet shells, dividing it equally.

Bake for 15 to 20 minutes or until the filling is set and the pastry is light brown. Cool for about 15 minutes (see Note). Remove the tartlets from the muffin tins and place them on a serving tray. Spoon ½ teaspoon of sour cream onto the center of each tartlet and garnish with a sprig of fresh cilantro.

Makes 24 tartlets

NOTE: You can make and bake the tartlets up to a month ahead of your party. After cooling, leave the tartlets in the baking pan, then slip them, pan and all, into a heavy-duty plastic freezer bag. Thaw and reheat them in a 375°F oven for 5 to 10 minutes, until heated through. Garnish them just before serving.

Rosemary Mushroom Tartlets

Phyllo pastry sheets brushed with garlic butter make a quick and tasty crust for these savory herbed mushroom tartlets.

½ cup (1 stick) plus 2 tablespoons unsalted butter

2 garlic cloves, minced or pressed

½ pound (8 ounces) fresh mushrooms, cleaned and sliced

¾ cup regular or light sour cream

1 (3-ounce) package cream cheese, softened

¼ cup seasoned dry bread crumbs

1 teaspoon minced fresh rosemary leaves

½ teaspoon salt

1 teaspoon fresh lemon juice

8 (18 × 14-inch) frozen phyllo pastry sheets, thawed

Fresh rosemary sprigs for garnish

Preheat the oven to 550°F. In a large nonstick skillet, heat the butter and garlic over low heat for 5 minutes, until the butter is well flavored. Pour off and reverse all but 2 tablespoons of the butter. Add the mushrooms to the remaining butter in the pan and cook over medium-heat until the mushrooms are tender, about 10 minutes. Cool.

In a medium-sized bowl, combine the sour cream, cream cheese, bread crumbs, rosemary, salt, lemon juice, and mushrooms.

Brush 24 miniature muffin cups with the reserved garlic butter.

Unroll the phyllo sheets and cover with plastic wrap or a damp towel to prevent drying. Brush one phyllo sheet with the warm garlic butter. Top with the second phyllo sheet and brush with garlic butter. Repeat with the remaining phyllo sheets until all 8 sheets are stacked.

With a sharp knife, cut the phyllo into 24 rectangles. To do this, cut the 18-inch side into 6 equal pieces and the 14-inch side into 4 equal pieces. This will result in roughly 5-inch squares. Press each square of phyllo into a buttered muffin cup. Spoon about a tablespoonful of the filling into each cup. Drizzle with any remaining garlic butter. (At this point the tartlets can be covered and refrigerated for up to 4 hours before baking.) Bake for 18 to 22 minutes or until golden brown. Garnish with small pieces of fresh rosemary sprigs.

Makes 24 appetizers

Spicy Chicken Empañadas

Empañadas are part of every Spanish-influenced cuisine in the Americas. They make a perfect accompaniment for a simple meal, like a salad or soup. They can be frozen unbaked for up to two months. When you are ready to serve them, unwrap and place them frozen onto a baking sheet and allow an extra 5 minutes of baking time.

   1 tablespoon unsalted butter or corn oil
   1 garlic clove, minced or pressed
   ¾ pound ground chicken or turkey breast
   1 bunch green onions, thinly sliced
   1 teaspoon salt
   ½ cup chopped almonds (optional)
   ½ cup currants
   ¼ teaspoon ground cinnamon
   ¼ teaspoon ground cloves
   ⅛ to 1 teaspoon red pepper flakes
   ½ cup fresh tomato salsa
      Pastry for one double-crust pie (page 172)

Glaze
   1 egg
   1 tablespoon milk

Preheat the oven to 425°F. In a large, nonstick skillet, heat the butter or oil and add the garlic, chicken, and green onions. Sauté over medium to high heat, breaking up the mixture with a fork, until the meat is no longer pink. Add the salt, almonds if desired, currants, cinnamon, cloves, red pepper flakes, and salsa to taste. Turn into a large bowl and cool the mixture to room temperature.

Divide the pastry into 12 parts. Roll each part out on a lightly floured surface to make a 6-inch round. Place about ¼ cup filling on each round. Moisten the edges of the pastry and fold over so that the moistened edges meet, forming a half-round. Seal the edges together with the tines of a fork. Place on an ungreased baking sheet.

For appetizer-sized empañadas, roll out pastry to about ⅛ inch thickness. With a 3-inch cookie cutter, cut out rounds. Place a heaping tablespoonful of the filling onto the center of each. Fold pastry over to form a half-round and seal the edges.

To make the glaze, in a small bowl, whisk the egg and milk together. Brush pastries with the mixture.

Bake for 15 to 20 minutes or until light brown. Serve hot or at room temperature.

Makes 12 sandwich-sized or 24 appetizer-size empañadas

Valentine's Day

Valentine's Day is named for two early Christian martyrs whose common feast day was February 14. Medieval folk tradition maintained that the springtime mating of birds took place on St. Valentine's Day, which led to a later custom of choosing a valentine, or sweetheart, for the day by a random drawing. Messages of affection were passed between these randomly chosen "lovers," which were the precursors of the valentine card.

The heart shape, according to the *Oxford English Dictionary*, was considered "the seat of love and affection." But the symmetrical, double-lobed figure that tapers to a point at the bottom is not the shape of the heart that beats in our bodies. It has been said that the valentine heart shape is more that of stylized human buttocks, the female torso with prominent breasts and a "wasp waist," or even the lipstick mark left by a woman's kiss.

Adapted in part from Tad Tuleja, *Curious Customs* (New York: Harmony Books, 1987).

Cheesecake with Raspberry Sauce

This is a light, textured cheesecake. For Valentine's Day, I bake it in a heart-shaped pan.

Crust
8 to 10 zwiebacks, depending
    on their size
1 tablespoon sugar
2 tablespoons unsalted butter,
    at room temperature

Cheesecake Filling
6 large eggs, separated
1 teaspoon cream of tartar
1¾ cups sugar, divided
3 tablespoons all-purpose flour
½ teaspoon salt
3 (8-ounce) packages cream cheese,
    at room temperature
2 cups sour cream
1 teaspoon vanilla

Raspberry Sauce
2 cups frozen unsweetened raspberries,
    thawed
1 cup sugar

HANDLING RASPBERRIES

It is best to store raspberries in a single layer in a moisture-proof container in the refrigerator for up to two days. Because raspberries are very fragile, it's best not to rinse them at all. If it is necessary, rinse them lightly just before serving.

Preheat the oven to 375°F. Butter a 9-inch springform pan.

Grind the zwiebacks in the food processor and measure 1 cup of the crumbs. In a small bowl, mix the crumbs with the sugar and butter until well combined. Press into the bottom of the prepared pan. Bake for 10 minutes or until the crust is lightly toasted. Remove from the oven and cool the pan on a wire rack. Lower the oven temperature to 325°F.

To make the filling, beat the egg whites and cream of tartar in a medium bowl until light and frothy; gradually beat in ¼ cup of the sugar until stiff peaks form; set aside.

In a small bowl, mix the remaining sugar with the flour and salt. In a large bowl, beat the cream cheese until creamy; gradually beat in the flour mixture and the egg yolks until well blended. Beat in the sour cream and vanilla. Fold in the beaten egg whites. Turn the mixture into the pan on top of the crust.

Bake for 1¾ to 2 hours, or until the center of the cheesecake feels firm. Turn off the heat; open the oven door and let cool in the oven for 10 minutes. Remove from the oven and cool on a wire rack away from drafts.

Refrigerate at least 4 hours, overnight, or up to 3 days. Or wrap well and freeze up to 1 month.

To make the raspberry sauce, combine 1 cup of the raspberries and the sugar in a small saucepan. Heat slowly to a boil over medium heat, then reduce the heat and simmer for 5 minutes. Remove from the heat and stir in the remaining cup of berries. Cool. Serve the sauce warm or chilled with wedges of the cheesecake.

To slice the cheesecake, dip a thin-bladed sharp knife in hot water to prevent sticking.

Makes 16 servings

Chocolate-Amaretto Cheesecake

To reduce the fat in this cheesecake, I use low-fat sour cream, Neufchâtel cheese, and part-skim ricotta. To further reduce the fat, you can use egg whites in place of the whole eggs. It's a nice way to show you care.

20 chocolate wafers
1   tablespoon unsalted butter, at room temperature
1   cup low-fat sour cream
1¼ cups sugar, divided
2   tablespoons amaretto
½   teaspoon almond extract
2   (8-ounce) packages Neufchâtel cheese, cut into 1-inch chunks
6   large eggs, or 10 large egg whites
½   cup dark Dutch process unsweetened cocoa
1   cup part-skim ricotta cheese

Preheat the oven to 350°F. Grease the bottom and sides of an 8- or 9-inch springform pan.

Grind the chocolate wafers in the food processor to make fine crumbs and mix with the butter in a small bowl until well blended. Turn the crumbs into the pan and tilt and turn the pan until the bottom and sides are coated.

In a small bowl, mix the sour cream with 3 tablespoons of the sugar and the amaretto; set aside. In a large bowl with an electric mixer or in the work bowl of a food processor, mix the remaining sugar and almond extract with the Neufchâtel. Beat or mix until the cheese is completely incorporated. Add the eggs or egg whites, 2 at a time, beating until light and fluffy. Beat in the cocoa and ricotta. Pour the batter into the prepared pan and place on a baking sheet.

Bake for 70 to 90 minutes or until set. Remove the cake from the oven and spread the sour cream mixture on top. Return to the oven and bake for 10 to 15 minutes longer or until the topping is set and a knife inserted in the center of the cake comes out clean. Cool on a wire rack for 15 minutes. Remove the sides of the pan. Cool completely and chill for 4 hours or overnight before serving. The cake freezes well if carefully wrapped.

Makes 10 to 12 servings

Cinnamon-Chocolate Tart

This tart is smooth and creamy with a hint of cinnamon. When made with walnut oil, the easy press-in pastry shell has a wonderful, toasted-nut flavor.

Shortbread Pastry Shell

1 cup all-purpose flour
2 tablespoons sugar
½ teaspoon salt
5 tablespoons walnut oil or corn oil
1 tablespoon milk

Cinnamon-Chocolate Filling

1 cup light cream or half-and-half
1 cinnamon stick
8 ounces bittersweet chocolate, finely chopped
1 large egg, lightly beaten
1 tablespoon unsweetened cocoa, for sifting
1 cup whipping cream
3 tablespoons confectioners' sugar
Pinch of ground cinnamon

Preheat the oven to 375°F. In a bowl stir the flour, sugar, and salt together. Add the oil and milk and stir with a fork until the mixture is crumbly. Turn the crumbly mixture into a 9½-inch tart pan with a removable bottom. Press evenly to cover the bottom and sides of the pan. Pierce the crust all over with a fork. Bake for 10 minutes or just until the pastry is very light brown. Remove from the oven and cool on a wire rack. Leave the oven on.

In a saucepan, combine the cream and cinnamon stick. Heat to simmering over medium-low heat, and stir for 2 minutes. Remove from the heat and remove the cinnamon stick. Add the chocolate and stir until the chocolate is melted and the mixture is well blended. Set aside to cool to lukewarm.

Beat the egg into the cooled chocolate mixture until well blended. Pour the batter into the pastry shell. Place in the center of the oven. Bake for 12 to 15 minutes or until the filling is slightly firm but still a little soft in the center. Do not overbake or the tart will be dry. Remove from the oven and cool on a wire rack. Sift unsweetened cocoa over the top of the tart. In a small bowl, beat the cream until stiff. Add the sugar and cinnamon and mix well. Spoon over slices of the cooled tart.

Makes 8 servings

Lemon Hearts

These heart-shaped cookies are sandwiched together with lemon butter. Pack them in a heart-shaped basket as a gift for somebody special.

   1 cup (2 sticks) unsalted butter,
      at room temperature
   1 cup sugar
   1 large egg yolk
   2 teaspoons grated lemon zest
   2 cups all-purpose flour
  ½ teaspoon baking soda
  ½ cup ground almonds

Lemon Butter

   3 tablespoons fresh lemon juice
   1 teaspoon grated lemon zest
  ¾ cup sugar
  ¼ cup (½ stick) unsalted butter,
      at room temperature
      Confectioners' sugar, for dusting

Preheat the oven to 325°F. Cover 2 baking sheets with parchment paper.

In a large bowl using an electric mixer, cream the butter and sugar together until smooth. Add the egg yolk and lemon zest and beat until light and lemon colored. In another bowl, stir the flour, baking soda, and almonds together; add to the butter mixture. Stir until the dough is smooth.

Turn out onto a lightly floured surface and roll out to ⅛-inch thickness. With heart-shaped cookie cutters, cut out cookies and place 2 inches apart on the baking sheets.

Bake for 20 minutes or until cookies begin to brown on the edges. Remove from the oven and cool on wire racks.

To make the lemon butter, whisk the lemon juice and zest with the sugar in a saucepan. Heat to boiling over medium-high heat, whisking constantly. Remove from the heat and cool to room temperature. Whisk or beat in the butter until the mixture is light colored, smooth, and creamy.

Sandwich two heart cookies together with the lemon butter. Dust with confectioners' sugar.

Makes thirty-six 2-inch cookie sandwiches

Mocha Meringue Torte

Meringues do not spread while baking, so they're a lot of fun to shape in different ways. For Valentine's Day, it is appropriate to shape the two layers of this torte into hearts. Avoid baking meringues on a very humid day, because the meringues will not get crisp and dry. The best way to bake them is in a low oven, then leave them in the turned-off oven to become crisp and completely dry. You can make meringues ahead, but be sure to wrap them airtight.

Meringue

- ½ cup (about 4 large) egg whites, at room temperature
- ½ teaspoon cream of tartar
- 1 cup sugar
- 1 tablespoon cornstarch
- 1 teaspoon vanilla

Mocha Cream Filling

- 1 teaspoon instant coffee powder
- 4 tablespoons coffee-flavored liqueur, such as Kahlua
- 2 cups whipping cream
- 1 cup milk chocolate chips

Preheat the oven to 250°F. Cover a baking sheet with parchment paper, then coat with nonstick spray, and dust lightly with flour. Trace two 8-inch hearts on the flour-dusted surface.

In a large bowl using an electric mixer combine the egg whites and cream of tar-tar. In a small bowl, stir the sugar and cornstarch together.

Beat the egg whites at the highest speed until mixture is frothy. Continue beating while adding the sugar mixture, 1 tablespoon at a time. Scrape the bowl frequently. Add the vanilla and beat 1 minute longer until the whites hold stiff, sharp peaks. Divide the meringue between the two heart shapes. Spread to the edges of the hearts, leveling the meringue mixture evenly. Or put the meringue into a pastry bag and pipe out in even rows onto the parchment to fill in the heart outlines. Make one of the layers smooth; pipe decorative puffs and swirls onto the second layer.

Bake for 1½ hours, then turn the oven off and leave the meringues in the closed oven for 3 to 4 hours until dry.

To make the filling, blend the coffee powder with the coffee liqueur in a small bowl. In another bowl, whip the cream until stiff, then fold in the coffee mixture. Put the chocolate chips into a food processor and process until coarsely chopped. Fold into the whipped cream.

Place the smooth meringue heart on a serving dish. Spread the cream filling over the top. Place the decorated meringue, if you made one, on top of the filling. Cover and refrigerate for 8 hours or until the next day to mellow and soften the meringue so that it will cut easily.

Makes 8 to 10 servings

Sour Cream–Chocolate Layer Cake

 This old-fashioned layer cake is moist and chocolatey. To some people, nothing says love like chocolate.

1 cup sour cream
2 teaspoons baking soda
1 cup (2 sticks) unsalted butter, at room temperature
2 cups sugar
2 large eggs
2 squares (1 ounce each) unsweetened chocolate, melted
2 teaspoons vanilla
2½ cups all-purpose flour
¼ teaspoon salt
1 cup boiling water

Sour Cream Frosting

2 cups confectioners' sugar
⅓ cup dark, unsweetened Dutch process cocoa
⅛ teaspoon salt
½ cup (1 stick) unsalted butter, at room temperature
½ cup sour cream, or more if needed
1 teaspoon vanilla

Preheat the oven to 350°F. Butter and flour two 9-inch round cake pans.

In a small bowl, combine the sour cream and baking soda; set aside.

In a large bowl, cream the butter and sugar together with an electric mixer. Add the eggs, one at a time and beat at high speed until light and fluffy. Add the chocolate, vanilla, and sour cream mixture.

In another bowl, stir the flour and salt together. Add to the creamed mixture alternately with the boiling water. Pour the batter evenly into the prepared pans.

Bake for 30 to 35 minutes or until the cakes feel firm in the center and the edges begin to pull away from the sides of the pans. Remove from the oven and cool in the pans for 5 minutes, then turn out onto wire racks and cool completely.

To make the frosting, combine the sugar, cocoa, salt, butter, sour cream, and vanilla in a

---

BAKER'S TIP

To melt chocolate in the microwave, place chocolate squares into a glass custard cup. Microwave on high power for one minute. If necessary, stir and microwave thirty seconds more until the chocolate is melted; remove from the oven and cool.

medium bowl. Beat with an electric mixer until thick, creamy, and very smooth. Add a bit more sour cream if the mixture is too thick.

Line the edges of a serving plate with 4 strips of waxed paper, each about 12 inches long and 3 inches wide. Place one cooled cake layer upside down on the plate (the waxed paper strips should be just under the edges of the cake). Spread the layer with about ¾ cup of the frosting. Place the second cake layer on top, right side up. Spread the remaining frosting over the top and sides of the cake, swirling it. Gently pull out waxed paper.

Makes one 9-inch layer cake

Valentine Coffee Cake

With this easy refrigerator dough, you can mix the dough two days ahead and shape the coffee cake the night before baking. First thing in the morning on Valentine's Day, all you need to do is to bake this delicious nut and cinnamon cake and bring it to your still-sleeping sweetheart.

  ½ cup milk scalded and cooled
      to lukewarm (105 to 115°F)
  1 package (2¾ teaspoons) active
      dry yeast
  ¼ cup sugar, divided
  ½ teaspoon salt

  1 large egg, lightly beaten
2½ cups all-purpose flour
  1 cup (2 sticks) unsalted butter,
      chilled and cut into pieces

Cinnamon-Nut Filling
  ¼ cup (½ stick) unsalted butter, melted
  ½ cup sugar
  1 teaspoon ground cinnamon
  ½ cup chopped walnuts

Icing
  1 cup confectioners' sugar
2 to 3 teaspoons cream or milk
  1 teaspoon vanilla

In a small bowl, combine the milk, yeast, and 1 tablespoon of the sugar. Let stand for 5 minutes until the yeast foams. Whisk in the salt and egg. Set aside.

Measure the flour into a large mixing bowl or into the work bowl of a food processor. Cut the butter into the flour until the mixture resembles coarse crumbs.

Pour the liquid ingredients over the flour mixture. Mix lightly with a fork or use short pulses if using the food processor, until the flour is just moistened. Cover with plastic wrap and refrigerate at least 4 hours or up to 2 days.

When you're ready to shape the cake (you can shape the coffee cake, cover, refrigerate overnight, and bake it in the morning; or you can shape it, let it rise, and then bake it), remove the dough from the refrigerator.

Lightly grease a baking sheet or cover with parchment paper.

Turn the dough out onto a lightly floured surface and roll it out to make a 15-inch circle about ⅓ inch thick. To fill the cake, brush with the melted butter. Mix the sugar and cinnamon in a small bowl and sprinkle over the dough. Sprinkle with the nuts.

Roll up jelly roll fashion. Place on the prepared baking sheet. Fold the roll in half so that one half is on top of the other. Seal the open ends together. With a sharp knife, make a cut from the folded end lengthwise down the center of the roll, cutting from the top roll through to the bottom to within 2 inches of the sealed end. In so doing the folded end of the roll will separate out to form the two lobes of a heart shape. Spread out the two sides to expose the filling.

Let rise, lightly covered, until puffy, about 45 minutes, or cover and refrigerate overnight. If refrigerated, remove from the refrigerator 1 hour before baking so that the coffee cake can rise and come to room temperature.

Preheat the oven to 375°F. Bake for 20 to 25 minutes until light brown. Remove and cool on a wire rack.

In a small bowl, combine the icing ingredients. Drizzle over the warm coffee cake.

Makes 1 heart-shaped coffee cake

Swiss Meringue Cookies

 I like to have a tin of these crunchy, nutty cookies stashed away, ready to pull out when I need something special. For Valentine's Day I serve them with strawberry or raspberry sherbet.

- 4 large egg whites, at room temperature
- ¼ teaspoon salt
- 1 cup sugar
- 1 cup toasted and skinned filberts, finely ground
- ½ cup blanched almonds, finely ground
- 42 whole filberts or almonds

Preheat the oven to 300°F. Cover 2 cookie sheets with parchment paper, or grease lightly.

In a large mixing bowl, using an electric mixer, whip the egg whites and salt until stiff. Beat in the sugar a tablespoonful at a time, beating until the mixture is smooth and glossy.

Measure and reserve 1 cup of the meringue. Fold the ground filberts and almonds into the remaining meringue mixture. Drop the batter by spoonfuls onto the prepared cookie sheets to make 3½ dozen cookies. Bake for 10 minutes. Remove from the oven and dot each cookie with a scant teaspoonful of the reserved meringue. Top each cookie with a nut. Return to the oven and bake 10 minutes longer, until cookies are firm and dry.

Remove the meringues from the cookie sheet and cool on a wire rack. The meringues will keep for up to 2 months in an airtight container in a cool place.

Makes about 42 cookies

Valentine Blitz Torte

This is just perfect baked in two heart-shaped layer cake pans for Valentine's Day; otherwise, you can use plain rounds. This old-fashioned favorite is a simple-to-make buttercake topped with a baked-on meringue. Fill the center with fresh strawberries or homemade strawberry jam.

  1 cup less 2 tablespoons
     all-purpose flour
  1 teaspoon baking powder
  ¼ teaspoon salt
  ½ cup (1 stick) unsalted butter,
     at room temperature
1¼ cups sugar
  4 large eggs, at room temperature,
     separated
  ¼ cup milk
  1 teaspoon vanilla
  1 teaspoon lemon extract
  ¼ teaspoon cream of tartar
  ⅓ cup sliced almonds
  1 cup whipping cream
  1 cup sliced fresh strawberries or
     strawberry jam

Preheat the oven to 350°F. Lightly grease and dust with flour, or line with parchment paper, two 9-inch heart-shaped or round cake pans.

In a medium-sized bowl, stir together the flour, baking powder, and salt.

In a large mixing bowl with an electric mixer, cream the butter and ½ cup of the sugar until blended. Add the egg yolks and beat until light and fluffy. Add the dry ingredients alternately with the milk and mix until the batter is light. Stir in the vanilla and lemon extract.

In a large, clean, dry bowl beat the egg whites with an electric mixer until light. Add the cream of tartar and beat until blended. Gradually beat in ½ cup plus 2 tablespoons of the remaining sugar, beating the meringue until stiff peaks form.

Divide the cake batter between the 2 prepared pans and spread evenly to the edges. Top with the meringue, dividing it equally between the 2 pans. Spread to the edges of the pan. Sprinkle 1 tablespoon sugar over the top of each. Sprinkle with the almonds, dividing them equally.

Bake for 30 minutes or until the meringues are golden. Remove from the oven and place pans on a wire rack to cool for 10 minutes. Turn cakes out of the pans and cool completely. In a small bowl, whip the cream until stiff.

To assemble the torte, place one layer on a cake plate. Top with half the strawberries or strawberry jam. Spread with half the whipped cream. Top with the second layer and spread the center of the torte with remaining strawberries or strawberry jam. Top with the remaining whipped cream. Serve immediately or refrigerate until ready to serve.

Makes 8 servings

Chocolate-Nut Shortbread

 Place a circle of this buttery and chocolatey shortbread on a lacy doily and give it instead of a card to your favorite valentine.

2¼ cups all-purpose flour
¼ cup dark, unsweetened cocoa
½ cup sugar
¼ teaspoon salt
1 cup (2 sticks) unsalted butter
2 squares (2 ounces) unsweetened chocolate, melted
½ cup finely chopped walnuts or pecans
2 teaspoons sugar

Preheat the oven to 300°F. Cover a cookie sheet with parchment paper and draw two 7- to 7½-inch circles about an inch apart on the paper.

Measure the flour, cocoa, sugar, and salt into a food processor or the large bowl of an electric mixer. Mix until blended. Cut the butter into thin slices and add it to the flour mixture. Mix until the mixture resembles moist sand. Add the chocolate and nuts and continue mixing until a smooth dough forms.

Cut the dough into 2 parts. Shape each part into a smooth ball. Place one ball in the center of each circle on the parchment paper. With your fingers or a rolling pin, flatten the round to within ½ inch of the inside edge of the round. With a fork, make impressions on the top of each round, then press the edges to smooth and decorate the round. Sprinkle each with 1 teaspoon of the sugar. With a sharp knife, cut the round into 8 wedges, leaving the wedges in place.

Bake for 1 hour or until the shortbread is lightly browned. With a sharp knife, immediately cut to separate the wedges.

Makes 32 wedge-shaped cookies

Presidents'
Day

Cherry Cheesecake Roll

 This is a classic sponge cake roll with a cherry cheesecake filling made with dried cherries, which are available all year round. It's drizzled with a bittersweet chocolate glaze and topped with more chopped, dried cherries.

- 3 large eggs, at room temperature
- 1½ teaspoons fresh lemon juice
  Dash salt
- ½ cup sugar
- ¼ cup white rum
- ½ cup all-purpose flour
  Confectioners' sugar, for sprinkling

Cherry Cheesecake Filling

- 1 small (3-ounce) package cream cheese
- ½ cup confectioners' sugar
- ½ teaspoon vanilla
- 1 cup whipping cream
- 1 cup dried tart cherries

Chocolate Glaze

- 4 ounces bittersweet or semisweet chocolate

Garnish

Chopped dried cherries

Preheat the oven to 325°F. Line a 15 × 10-inch jelly roll pan with waxed paper and coat the paper with nonstick spray.

In a large bowl, beat the eggs, lemon juice, and salt with an electric mixer at high speed until thick and lemon colored. Add the sugar a tablespoon at a time, beating until light and fluffy. Fold in the rum. Put the flour into a strainer and dust over the mixture, then fold in gently. Spread the batter into the

---

 PRESIDENTS' DAY

This is a rather recently declared holiday. In the past, Lincoln's birthday (February 12) and Washington's birthday (February 22) were celebrated separately. Now the two holidays have been combined, and we celebrate them both on the Monday that falls in between the two birthdays.

History books haven't actually clarified whether George Washington really liked to eat cherries. However, the cherry tree story associates Washington's birthday, and, consequently, Presidents' Day, with the fruit.

It has been said that Abe Lincoln had a passion for molasses and that his table was always set with a container of it along with salt and pepper.

prepared pan and bake for 20 minutes, until the cake springs back when touched lightly.

Meanwhile, sprinkle confectioners' sugar on a double layer of paper towels. Invert the hot cake onto the towel and peel the waxed paper from the cake. Gently roll the cake up starting at a narrow end, rolling the towels into the cake. Place on a wire rack and cool.

Beat the cream cheese, confectioners' sugar, and vanilla in a bowl until smooth and creamy. Whip the cream and fold in along with the dried cherries.

Carefully unroll the cake and discard the towels. Spread the cake with the filling and reroll. Place on a serving plate or board. Sprinkle with confectioners' sugar.

Put the chocolate into a small heatproof bowl and place over a pan of hot water until the chocolate is melted. Or place in a glass bowl and microwave on high power, stirring every 1 minute, until the chocolate is melted. Drizzle the roll with the melted chocolate and sprinkle with chopped dried cherries. Serve immediately.

Makes 8 servings

Cherry-Oatmeal Cookies

 These cookies are perfect for grade-schoolers in need of a treat for Washington's birthday. These chewy oatmeal cookies are studded with dried tart cherries, but if you have trouble finding dried cherries you can use dried cranberries or raisins instead.

  2 cups all-purpose flour
  1 teaspoon baking soda
  ½ teaspoon salt
 1½ teaspoons ground cinnamon

 ABOUT CHERRIES

Cherries got their name from the Turkish town of Cerasus and are said to date as far back as 300 B.C. Of the edible cherries, there are basically two types: sweet and sour. Cherries are available fresh when they are in season from May through August. During this time, there are cherry festivals in cherry-growing regions. A festival in Michigan begins just after July 4 and continues for ten days. Canned, preserved, frozen, and dried cherries are available all year round and can often be used in place of fresh.

1   cup (2 sticks) unsalted butter,
      at room temperature
1   cup packed brown sugar
2   large eggs
1   teaspoon vanilla
1½ cups uncooked rolled oats,
      old-fashioned or quick
1   cup chopped walnuts or pecans
1   cup dried tart cherries,
      cranberries, or raisins

Preheat the oven to 375°F. Lightly grease a baking sheet or cover with parchment paper.

In a medium bowl, stir the flour, baking soda, salt, and cinnamon together; set aside. In a large bowl, cream the butter and brown sugar together with an electric mixer. Add the eggs and vanilla and beat until light. Blend in the flour mixture until smooth. Stir in the rolled oats, nuts, and cherries until well mixed. Drop by heaping tablespoons onto the baking sheet 3 inches apart.

Bake for 15 minutes or until the cookies are golden around the edges. Slide the cookies on the parchment paper off the baking sheet onto the countertop to cool. Or remove the cookies to a wire rack to cool.

Makes 36 cookies

Presidential Molasses Pie

Abraham Lincoln had such a craving for molasses that while he was president he had a standing order for molasses pie at William Taussig's New York Excelsior Steam Cracker Bakery in Washington. The original recipe in the old White House Cookbook *reads like this:* "Take two teacupfuls of molasses; one of sugar, three eggs, one tablespoonful of melted butter, one lemon and nutmeg; beat and bake in pastry." *I have altered this recipe to suit today's tastes. If you add the pecans, it tastes a lot like southern pecan pie.*

1   unbaked 9-inch pie shell
      (see page 176)
½   cup light molasses
½   cup dark corn syrup
½   cup packed light brown sugar
3   large eggs, lightly beaten
2   tablespoons unsalted butter, melted
1   tablespoon fresh lemon juice
½   teaspoon freshly ground nutmeg
1½ cups coarsely chopped pecans
      (optional)

Preheat the oven to 400°F. Prepare the pastry.

In a large bowl, mix the molasses, syrup, brown sugar, eggs, butter, lemon juice, and nutmeg until well blended. Sprinkle half the pecans (if using) into the pie shell. Pour in the molasses mixture. Sprinkle with the remaining pecans, if desired.

Bake for 25 to 30 minutes or until the filling is set. Remove from the oven and cool on a wire rack.

Makes one 9-inch pie

Winter Fruit Tart

This is a delicious tart made with dried fruits encased in a delicate sweet pastry. It has an intense fruit flavor and is delicious served with a little whipped cream or a scoop of ice cream.

Sweet Pastry

1½ cups all-purpose flour
  3 tablespoons sugar
½ teaspoon salt
½ cup (1 stick) unsalted butter, chilled and cut into pieces
  2 large egg yolks
  2 teaspoons fresh lemon juice
2 to 3 tablespoons ice water

Filling

  3 cups fruity white wine or white grape juice
  1 cup sugar
  1 cinnamon stick
2 to 3 whole cloves
  1 vanilla bean, split

1½ cups dried apricots, chopped
  1 cup pitted prunes, chopped
  1 cup dried black mission figs, chopped
½ cup dried tart cherries
½ cup mixed chopped dried fruit
¼ cup currants
  1 cup sugar
  1 tablespoon cornstarch
  3 tablespoons unsalted butter

For the Top

  1 large egg, lightly beaten
  2 teaspoons sugar

Preheat the oven to 400°F. Grease a 10-inch tart pan with a removable bottom.

Combine the flour, sugar, and salt in a large bowl or food processor with the metal blade in place. Cut in the butter until the mixture resembles coarse crumbs. In a small bowl, with a fork, beat the yolks, lemon juice, and 2 tablespoons of the ice water. Sprinkle the liquids over the dry ingredients and mix with a fork until the dough resembles large-curd cottage cheese (use more water if too dry). Press half the crumbs into the tart pan to cover the bottom and sides evenly.

Bake for 10 to 15 minutes, until the pastry is golden.

Gather the remaining dough together in a ball; wrap in plastic wrap and chill while preparing the filling.

Combine the wine or juice, sugar, cinnamon, cloves, and vanilla bean in a large, heavy saucepan. Place over medium-high heat and heat to simmering. Add the apricots, prunes, figs, cherries, mixed fruit, and currants. Return to a simmer and cook for 20 to 25 minutes, until the fruit is tender. Reserving the liquid, drain the fruit and return the cooking liquid and the cinnamon stick to the saucepan. Boil the liquid down until reduced to ⅓ cup. Remove and discard the cinnamon stick. Combine the 1 cup sugar and cornstarch in a small bowl. Mix the fruit with the sugar mixture, butter, and reduced cooking liquid. Spoon the fruit mixture into the cooled tart shell.

On a lightly floured surface, roll out the remaining pastry and cut it into ½-inch strips. Place the strips in a lattice pattern on top of the tart. Pinch the edges of the dough to seal the strips. Or, as an alternative, cut the rolled pastry into leaves, flowers, or other fanciful shapes and place on top of the tart. Brush lightly with the beaten egg and sprinkle with the 2 teaspoons sugar.

Bake for 25 to 35 minutes or until golden brown. Cool on a wire rack. Serve with whipped cream or ice cream, if desired.

Makes 8 to 10 servings

Index

Conversion Chart
EQUIVALENT IMPERIAL AND METRIC MEASUREMENTS

American cooks use standard containers, the 8-ounce cup and a tablespoon that takes exactly 16 level fillings to fill that cup level. Measuring by cup makes it very difficult to give weight equivalents, as a cup of densely packed butter will weigh considerably more than a cup of flour. The easiest way therefore to deal with cup measurements in recipes is to take the amount by volume rather than by weight. Thus the equation reads:

1 cup = 240 ml = 8 fl. oz.   ½ cup = 120 ml = 4 fl. oz.

It is possible to buy a set of American cup measures in major stores around the world.

In the States, butter is often measured in sticks. One stick is the equivalent of 8 tablespoons. One tablespoon of butter is therefore the equivalent to ½ ounce/15 grams.

Liquid Measures

Fluid Ounces	U.S.	Imperial	Milliliters
	1 teaspoon	1 teaspoon	5
¼	2 teaspoons	1 dessert spoon	7
½	1 tablespoon	1 tablespoon	15
1	2 tablespoons	2 tablespoons	28
2	¼ cup	4 tablespoons	56
4	½ cup or ¼ pint		110
5		¼ pint or 1 gill	140
6	¾ cup		170
8	1 cup or ½ pint		225
9			250, ¼ liter
10	1¼ cups	½ pint	280
12	1½ cups or ¾ pint		340
15		¾ pint	420
16	2 cups or 1 pint		450
18	2¼ cups		500, ½ liter
20	2½ cups	1 pint	560
24	3 cups or 1½ pints		675
25		1¼ pints	700
27	3½ cups		750
30	3¾ cups	1½ pints	840
32	4 cups or 2 pints or 1 quart		900
35		1¾ pints	980
36	4½ cups		1000, 1 liter
40	5 cups or 2½ pints	2 pints or 1 quart	1120
48	6 cups or 3 pints		1350
50		2½ pints	1400
60	7½ cups	3 pints	1680
64	8 cups or 4 pints or 2 quarts		1800
72	9 cups		2000, 2 liters

Solid Measures

U.S. and Imperial Measures		Metric Measures	
Ounces	Pounds	Grams	Kilos
1		28	
2		56	
3½		100	
4	¼	112	
5		140	
6		168	
8	½	225	
9		250	¼
12	¾	340	
16	1	450	
18		500	½
20	1¼	560	
24	1½	675	
27		750	¾
28	1¾	780	
32	2	900	
36	2¼	1000	1
40	2½	1100	
48	3	1350	
54		1500	1½
64	4	1800	
72	4½	2000	2
80	5	2250	2¼
90		2500	2½
100	6	2800	2¾

Oven Temperature Equivalents

Fahrenheit	Celsius	Gas Mark	Description
225	110	¼	Cool
250	130	½	
275	140	1	Very Slow
300	150	2	
325	170	3	Slow
350	180	4	Moderate
375	190	5	
400	200	6	Moderately Hot
425	220	7	Fairly Hot
450	230	8	Hot
475	240	9	Very Hot
500	250	10	Extremely Hot

Equivalents for Ingredients

all-purpose flour—plain flour
cheesecloth—muslin
confectioners' sugar—icing sugar
cornstarch—cornflour
granulated sugar—caster sugar

shortening—white fat
sour cherry—morello cherry
unbleached flour—strong, white flour
vanilla bean—vanilla pod
zest—rind

light cream—single cream
heavy cream—double cream
half and half—12% fat milk
buttermilk—ordinary milk